COMPENSATING NEW SALES ROLES

COMPENSATING
NEW
SALES
ROLES

How to Design Rewards That Work in Today's Selling Environment

Second Edition

Jerome A. Colletti
Mary S. Fiss

AMACOM
American Management Association
New York • Atlanta • Boston • Chicago • Kansas City • San Francisco • Washington, D.C.
Brussels • Mexico City • Tokyo • Toronto

Special discounts on bulk quantities of AMACOM books are available to corporations, professional associations, and other organizations. For details, contact Special Sales Department, AMACOM, a division of American Management Association,
1601 Broadway, New York, NY 10019.
Tel.: 212-903-8316   Fax: 212-903-8083
Web site: www.amacombooks.org

This publication is designed to provide accurate and authoritative information in regard to the subject matter covered. It is sold with the understanding that the publisher is not engaged in rendering legal, accounting, or other professional service. If legal advice or other expert assistance is required, the services of a competent professional person should be sought.

Library of Congress-Cataloging-in-Publication Data

Colletti, Jerome A.

> *Compensating new sales roles: how to design rewards that work in today's selling environment / Jerome A. Coletti, Mary S. Fiss—2nd ed.*
>
> > *p.   cm.*
> > *Includes bibliographical references and index.*
> > *ISBN 0-8144-7106-4*
> > *1. Sales personnel—Salaries, etc.   2. Incentives in industry.*
> *3. Compensation management.   I. Fiss, Mary S.   II. Title*
> *HF5439.7.C646   2001*
> *658.3/22—dc21*   *01-018865*
> *CIP*

Printing number

10   9   8   7   6   5   4   3   2

CONTENTS

ILLUSTRATIONS

FOREWORD

In July 1998, I was appearing as a panel member at a national conference on sales management. A member of the audience posed the first question: "I'd like to ask each of the three panelists which, in their opinion, is the best book on sales compensation?" The panelists, who were all leading figures in the sales performance field, looked at one another uneasily. "There's not much out there," said the first. "Um . . . I think I'll pass on this one," said the next. Then it was my turn. "A good book on sales compensation? There's no such animal," I had to admit. "Everything I've read is impractical, overcomplicated and—well—out of touch with how selling is changing." The questioner was clearly dissatisfied with our answers. "It's an important area," he protested. "There's got to be *something*." There was an awkward silence, and we moved on to the next question, leaving the panelists feeling guilty, as if they were personally responsible for the miserable poverty of the sales compensation literature.

None of us knew it at the time, but as we were speaking, Colletti and Fiss were finishing the manuscript of *Compensating New Sales Roles*. When it was published early in 1999, it was like a breath of fresh air. Up-to-date, simple, and eminently practical, it provided the blueprint that so many people had been searching for in vain. I bought fifty copies and sent them out to clients. When I heard that Colletti and Fiss were busy writing a new edition, less than two years after the original breakthrough book, I was intrigued. "I know it's a fast-moving field," I protested, "but I can't believe there's a need for a second edition yet." So they sent me the manuscript of the new edition so I could judge for myself. And, much though I admired the original, I have to admit that the new edition has important and worthwhile changes. For example:

- It has more than 100 pages of new material, most of it focusing on the practical "how to's" of designing compensation systems that really work.

- There's a chapter on telesales and teleweb—the fastest-growing area of selling and one where there is precious little compensation help available for practitioners.
- There are interesting case studies of companies that have implemented the advice offered by the first edition.
- There's a chapter on the web and its impact on sales compensation.
- There's a fascinating new chapter on compensation for very large sales. It's here that conventional compensation practices are notorious. They either turn salespeople into undeserving millionaires or, even worse, get in the way of large sales to the point of losing the deal. It's good to see some clear new thinking in this very muddy area.
- Most important for me, for years I've been preaching that the boundary between sales and support functions has crumbled. You can't compensate salespeople effectively without simultaneously compensating sales support. So I was delighted to see that there are new and helpful ideas on how to pay those in the ever more important support roles.

So, despite my initial reaction of "don't mess with success," I have to tell you that the new edition is a major advance. This time, I'll be sending out even more copies.

Neil Rackham
nrackham@ssiadvantage.com

PREFACE

Two years have passed since we wrote the first edition of this book. While that is not a very long period of time, a great many changes have taken place in business during those two years. The most notable, of course, is the impact that the Internet is having on the way in which business is done, both in the United States and around the world. Many experts believe that the Internet is changing the speed at which companies are doing business with their customers. We would certainly agree with that observation. However, we believe that the Internet's greatest impact on business is in how companies "go to market"—that is, the sales channels that they use to reach, sell to, and interact with customers. Essentially, the Internet has motivated top managers in all companies—large and small alike—to rethink their approach to doing business with customers. The Internet has become the single biggest new development in sales channels ever!

The first edition of our book was based on our observation that companies needed new sales roles to take advantage of revenue growth opportunities. We concluded that after years of frenzied cost cutting, business growth was a top priority at many companies. We predicted that the desire to grow—by creating new markets, winning new customers, and continuously improving processes to retain current customers—would motivate companies to implement new approaches to sales and customer relationship management. However, we did not expect to see the explosion in the number and type of new sales roles that is occurring today as many companies race to compete for customers through the effective use of the Internet. Far too often, the compensation plans that companies use to direct, motivate, and reward the new roles that sales success requires are out of step with business objectives. Rather than promote growth, the compensation plans actually hinder growth. Because of the explosion in the use of sales channels, spurred by the growth of the Internet, we felt compelled to update the first edition of our book at this time.

How This Book Can Help You

To overcome competitive threats, companies must continually increase the effectiveness of all employees who come in contact with customers and prospects. In particular, they must increase the effectiveness of the way the business rewards and recognizes those employees for their contributions to company success.

Companies require the ability to design—and redesign—their compensation plans quickly to meet and anticipate new business realities. This book will help you understand and use the concepts and techniques essential to compensating new sales roles effectively in changing business environments.

Virtually no company—regardless of its size, product, or method of distribution—is immune to the changes that are taking place in the way customers want to do business. This means that if you have not already been challenged by how to compensate employees for performing new sales roles, you will be. We define a sales role as a "part" an employee plays in the process of interacting with a customer. A new sales role comes into being when the company adds or subtracts sales responsibilities from a current job, or creates a completely new sales job where one did not exist before. The reexamination—and, in many cases, the deconstruction—of the sales and customer relationship management processes results in increased specialization of resources. As you will see throughout this book, that change is a major factor in creating the need for new sales roles and, in turn, new compensation plans to reward and recognize the employees in those roles.

Compensating New Sales Roles, second edition, provides a blueprint that allows you to clarify and confirm the new sales accountabilities associated with jobs in your organization, and to design and implement compensation plans that are aligned with your business objectives. Throughout the book, we present proven models and techniques that companies with evolving sales organizations have successfully employed—companies in which the sales organization is continually experimenting with new ways to reach and interact with customers. This book provides you with concrete advice and guidance on what it takes to realize tangible benefits from new sales roles as early as possible through new approaches in the sales compensation plan. We use actual cases and illustrative examples throughout so that you can benefit from the experiences of others.

This book is for business owners, company executives—general managers, sales and marketing executives, and human resources/compensation professionals—and consultants who lead or participate in the process of redesigning and implementing sales compensation plans for companies that deploy multiple customer contact resources to cover a diverse set of customers.

We have designed *Compensating New Sales Roles,* second edition, to be used in a number of different ways, depending upon the particular sales compensation challenge(s) your company faces.

1. It is a reference guide to the new sales roles that companies use to interact with current customers and to attract new customers. It also provides an explanation of how and why new sales roles originate within the context of a business growth model that companies have found useful in managing the change process.
2. It is a design guide that you can use to devise compensation plans for new sales roles in your company.
3. And, finally, it is a change management guide that you can use to provide advice to others in your company when it comes time to actually implement new compensation plans.

HOW THE BOOK IS ORGANIZED

Compensating New Sales Roles, second edition, is organized in three parts. The parts correspond to the ways in which we find most companies are affected by new requirements and, therefore, how their top managers are responding to the need for new sales roles and how to compensate employees differently in the jobs that result from those roles. We begin by helping you determine how to compare your experience with changes in how your company sells to and interacts with customers with the experiences of other companies.

Part 1, "New Market Requirements," sets the stage by discussing the conditions in the marketplace that motivate companies to implement new sales roles. Chapter 1, "Why Your Company Requires New Sales Roles," describes how to sense the need for new sales roles, provides examples of new sales roles that are emerging in companies, and lists the three areas of a sales compensation plan that are frequently affected when a company adds new sales roles to jobs. Chapter 2, "Why Sales Compensation Plans Fail—and How Yours Can Succeed," explains why traditional sales compensation plans are often inappropriate to reward and recognize the contributions of employees who are performing new sales roles. We identify and explain the five reasons why plans fail and help you determine the aspects of your company's plan that may require redesign or complete change to support the business objectives of new sales roles. Finally, in Chapter 3, "How to Adopt New Sales Roles to Win and Retain Satisfied Customers," we explain when and why new sales roles emerge and provide you with a comprehensive business case to show you how to use the concepts and tools we recommend to top managers when they are faced with the challenge to define new sales roles.

Part 2, "Designing Compensation Plans for New Sales Roles," is our answer to that proverbial question, "Where's the beef?" It provides you with the concepts, tools, and techniques you need in order to design compensation plans for new sales roles in your company. Chapter 4, "A Blueprint for Linking Compensation to New Sales Roles," provides you with a ten-step process to follow when designing a sales compensation plan for jobs that are assigned a new sales role. This process becomes the charter for the balance of the book. Chapter 5, "What to Expect and How to Measure Success in New Sales Roles," describes how to select performance measures for and assign performance goals to employees in new sales roles, and then illustrates how those measures are used in five prototypical jobs that have been assigned a new sales role. Chapter 6, "Designing Compensation Plans for New Sales Roles," describes the basic building blocks to use when designing a new compensation plan.

Chapters 7 through 9 are newly written for the book's second edition. Chapter 7, "Compensating Telechannel Jobs," reports on how to design and compensate new sales roles in the fastest-growing approach to sales and customer coverage, the telechannel, which includes both telephonic and teleweb selling applications. Chapter 8, "Compensating Sales Support Staff," describes the contribution that these positions make to sales success and how companies recognize that contribution through the sales compensation plan. In many industries, selling large deals is the key to business success. Chapter 9, "Compensating Sellers and Teams for Large Sales," describes the unique characteristics of large deal selling and provides two cases studies to illustrate how leading companies are rewarding employees involved with that type of selling. Chapter 10, "Compensating Sales Managers and Team Leaders," provides the details of how to design new compensation plans for new sales roles—sellers, sales managers, sales team members and leaders, and customer team leaders and members.

Part 3, "Implementing New Plans Successfully," takes you through the process of installing a new sales compensation plan. Chapter 11,

"Tackling Some of the More Challenging Design Issues," describes five "big picture" business issues and six sales compensation design issues that companies often face when they are making a change to a new sales compensation plan. Chapter 12, "How to Introduce Compensation Plans for New Sales Roles," identifies the three hurdles to overcome when implementing a new sales compensation plan and provides a change management model and four steps to follow to achieve implementation success. Chapter 13, "Evaluating Results under a New Sales Compensation Plan," shows you how to measure the effectiveness of the new plan so that you can determine the level of business success you are achieving with its help. And, finally, Chapter 14, "Future Challenges," also newly written for the second edition, describes the three most significant challenges we believe companies will face now and well into the future as top managers strive to increase sales effectiveness through improved use of compensation plans.

The concepts, tools, and techniques we describe in *Compensating New Sales Roles,* second edition, are intended to help you sense and respond to the need for change in the way your company pays its employees for new sales roles in their jobs. The benefit we hope you gain from this book is the confidence to act in situations where it appears that employees must be paid differently because their jobs have been altered by an added or new sales role. We believe that the processes and tools we describe throughout the book will, when competently applied, enable you to increase sales, profits, productivity, and customer satisfaction more than your less savvy competitors.

ACKNOWLEDGMENTS

The premise of this book—that companies need to compensate employees differently when those employees are assigned a new sales role—may appear to be splitting hairs when compared to other changes taking place on the business landscape. Yet we have observed firsthand many, many businesses that are underachieving—sales lower than forecast, profitability less than last year's, higher-than-industry-average customer defections—because the way they pay employees to interact with customers is out of sync with their business objectives. We said to ourselves, there's an opportunity here to tell the story of how successful companies pay employees when they assign them new sales roles. Fortunately, in Ellen Kadin at AMACOM books, we found an editor who shared our enthusiasm for telling this story.

We are grateful to Ellen not only for the opportunity she gave us to write the first edition of our book, but also for encouraging us to begin work on updating it shortly after the first edition was published in January 1999. Ellen must have been clairvoyant. Not only was the first edition well received by our readers, but also many clients and seminar participants began to immediately offer suggestions to us about other "new sales role" topics to address in the book's second edition. Thus, in response to the many, many suggestions for additional information, the second edition includes four new chapters, and, where appropriate, we updated the content in several of the original chapters.

We would have relatively little to say to illustrate the principles of this book if it were not for our clients, many of whom must remain anonymous because of the confidential nature of our work with them. There are some exceptions, and therefore with a great deal of appreciation, we want to acknowledge the following individuals: John Seybold, Director of Total Compensation and John Farrell, Principal Compensation Consultant, both with Honeywell IAC (Industrial Automation and Controls), for their invaluable help in preparing the case study in Chapter 9; and Kathryn T. Kemp, President, Incentive Solutions, Inc., for preparing the materials that resulted in the RSNA (Radio Systems of North America—a fictitious company) case study, also in Chapter 9. Also, we wish to thank our close personal and professional friends—David F. Fritz, President, Profitable Growth Solutions; Jim Triandiflou, President, Ockham Technologies, Inc.; and, Dick Ruff and Janet Spiers, Partners, Sales Momentum, Inc.—who contributed to our thinking about various topics in the second edition of this book.

We are grateful to Neil Rackham, a widely recognized authority in sales force effectiveness and the creator of SPIN Selling, for taking the time to read our book and write the foreword endorsing its value to our audience.

The staff at AMACOM books reviewed early drafts of the second edition and encouraged us throughout the process. Thank your for your help and enthusiasm.

And finally, we want to thank our families and friends for their patience and understanding during the summer months of this last year, 2000, while we worked on preparing this second edition. Thank you, Rebecca, Richard, David, and Anna for doing without us while we toiled away with clients, friends, and associates who helped us make the second edition a reality.

Jerome A. Colletti
Jerry@collettifiss.com

Mary S. Fiss
Mary@collettifiss.com
Scottsdale, AZ
September 2000

COMPENSATING
NEW
SALES
ROLES

NEW MARKET REQUIREMENTS

WHY YOUR COMPANY REQUIRES NEW SALES ROLES

Evidence that the Internet is permanently altering the way companies do business is everywhere. E-business is much more than just a techno-logical change; it is a fundamental change in the way business is done. How companies sell to and interact with customers is undergoing a total and complete revolution. Leading publications—*Business Week, Forbes, Fortune* and *The Wall Street Journal*, to mention a few—all seem to agree that the revolution in doing business with customers was set off in January/February 1999. It was then that top managers at most companies—regardless of industry—marveled at the magnitude of e-purchases made during the first Internet Christmas season. Shortly thereafter, evidence of the changes brought about by e-business was appearing on many different fronts. Consider these examples:

- In January 1999, Jack Welch, GE chairman and CEO, asked 340,000 employees to incorporate the Internet in the way the company does business. Almost immediately, all companies selling to or buying from GE learned that they were a step or two behind in e-business and needed to catch up, fast![1]
- Many companies hold their annual shareholders' meeting in the spring. By spring 2000, shareholders were focusing on their com-pany's plans for addressing the opportunities for growth through e-business. Regardless of the industry, shareholders asked the

same questions: Is e-business receiving an appropriate level of senior management attention? Is the company investing enough in e-business to succeed? How much business is the company doing on the Internet, and what is the company doing to increase its sales through the Web?[2] Anticipating that shareholders would ask these questions and want to see favorable results or actions, boards of directors at a few companies—Compaq and Borders, among others—replaced CEOs who were judged to not have an e-business strategy, to be moving too slowly in the e-business environment, or both.

- The May 2000 *Selling Power* cover story featured Cisco Systems, the undisputed leader in Internet routers. With a market cap of more than $500 billion in 2000, Cisco is viewed as one of the pioneers of e-business. In the last quarter of 1999, 85 percent of Cisco's orders—more than $45 million per day—were transacted over the Internet. Equally impressive is the fact that this sales volume was achieved by harnessing the market power of over 22,000 channel partners, many of whom only a few short years ago didn't even have Internet access.[3] The clear implication is that without Internet access, Cisco could not have achieved its current sales volume levels.
- The June 2000 issue of *Sales & Marketing Management* featured a special report, "E-Business or Bust," conducted in association with Mercer Management Consulting. The study's principal conclusion: The Internet is making sales channels—particularly the direct sales force—more productive. Adding e-business capabilities has helped companies increase new account wins and the number of accounts per salesperson, decrease sales cycle time, and boost annual direct sales.[4]

In the past, top managers had some margin for error in their decisions about how to organize and deploy sales resources. As the previous examples illustrate, the Internet is changing the speed at which companies are doing business. The first edition of this book was based on our observation that companies needed new sales roles to take advantage of revenue growth opportunities. We concluded that after years of frenzied cost cutting, business growth was a top priority at many companies. We predicted that the desire to grow—by creating new markets, winning new customers, and continuously improving processes to retain current customers—would motivate companies to implement new approaches to sales and customer relationship management. However, we did not expect to see the explosion in the number and type of new sales roles that is occurring today as many companies race to compete in the e-business space. It is this explosion in new sales roles and the redefinition of current sales roles that required a new edition of this book.

How to Create New Sales Roles and "Recharter" Existing Jobs

Shortly after the publication of the first edition, we conducted a series of seminars with general managers, top marketing/sales executives, CFOs, and top human resources officers to provide a high-level summary of new sales roles and the compensation implications for paying people in those roles. Our participants shared with us that they were having one or more of the following three experiences: First, customers were changing the way they buy, and, to be a "best practices" company, you had to change the way you sell. Second, a great deal of money was being spent on incorporating technology into the selling and customer relationship management (CRM) processes, and the results were mixed. One participant went so far as to quote a recent Insight Technology Group study that indicated that of all companies surveyed, 71 percent had not achieved their sales process reengineering expectations. And, finally, the sales success that companies hoped to achieve with the combination of new selling processes and technology seemed to be eluding them.

Based on those seminars and hundreds of hours of conversations with top managers about the new sales roles that are emerging in business today, we conclude that many companies have missed the opportunity to clarify or redefine sales roles for all employees who interact with customers. What we have learned in the two years since the publication of this book's first edition is that the need to clarify sales roles goes well beyond defining and implementing new sales jobs. In many companies, all customer contact jobs must be reexamined because they suffer from job contamination.

Job contamination is an "impurity" in a job's charter, its tasks and responsibilities, or both. Typically, contamination shows up in the form of (1) a "blended job," one that combines two or more dissimilar roles, or (2) a "corrupted job," one in which responsibilities have crept over from another position and this change was unintended. We find that job contamination in the form of a blended job is most common in direct sales jobs—both field and inside sales—because too often there is a view that new responsibilities can be loaded on the backs of the existing employees. There are over 15 million salespeople employed in the United States. In most of the industries in which these salespeople work, their frontline managers are responsible for their sales success. Frequently, it occurs to us that if we could help frontline managers recognize the need to decontaminate their current sales jobs, create new sales roles, or both, they could make their top managers aware of the tremendous opportunity to increase sales productivity through clarifying the roles and jobs that interact with customers.

When top managers understand this opportunity, they can take three actions that result in a new or changed sales role:

> *Add sales responsibilities to a current job.* In our experience, this is the most common way in which new sales roles are introduced into a company today. Throughout the book, we provide numerous examples of jobs that experienced a "rechartering" of their role as a result of the assignment of new responsibilities.
>
> *Subtract sales responsibilities from a current job to decrease its sales role.* We have observed companies that created new sales roles by taking away sales responsibilities from a current sales job. A couple of years ago, this was not a common practice. Today, top managers ask for much greater focus and specialization among sales and customer contact resources. Geographically deployed sales resources (e.g., territory sales rep, telephonic sales rep) are most often the jobs that are divided to create a new sales role.
>
> *Create a new sales job where one did not exist before.* Growth in the type and number of sales channels used to reach and to interact with customers is the primary reason why new sales jobs are created.

We have entered a time in our economy when doing business without new sales roles could mean that your company's sales organization will become obsolete. Thus, managers at all levels of a company must understand when there is a need for new sales roles and how to implement those roles successfully.

New Sales Roles: The Key to Business Success

The changes taking place in how companies interact with their customers often result in new sales roles, whether consciously and deliberately or accidentally. Given the pace at which businesses are changing as a result of mergers/acquisitions, globalization, and new technology, it is unlikely that the challenges associated with implementing new sales roles will go away any time in the foreseeable future.

We observe that most companies, regardless of size or industry, wrestle with the challenge of how to compensate employees for performance in these new sales roles. *The key to designing effective compensation plans for new sales roles is to understand the sales situations that make these new roles a requirement for business success.*

Managers ask us, "So what's new about new sales roles?" Webster's dictionary defines the word *role* as "a part played by an actor." It defines *job* as "a regular remunerative position." Based on our work with hundreds of companies, we define a new sales role as the responsibility assigned to a job (current or new) for playing a part in retaining, expanding, or acquiring a revenue stream through interaction with a customer or set of customers. At the outset of this book, we want to draw some distinctions between sales roles and sales jobs, and between new sales roles in companies where the sales organization is established and those in companies where it is relatively new to the business.

What's the difference between sales roles and sales jobs? Most companies—particularly ones with many products or services that they sell to other businesses—have a sales organization. There may be a variety of sales jobs within the sales organization: national account sales representative, territory sales representative, product sales representative, dealer sales representative, and so forth. For individuals performing these jobs, sales is their occupation.

On the other hand, over the last ten years there has been a notable movement to formalize the involvement of other, nonsales employees in the process of doing business with customers. The "Wal-Mart-ization" of business is largely responsible for this trend. It started in the late 1980s when Procter & Gamble implemented its first customer team in response to Wal-Mart's requirements for sales coverage through a single point of contact, rather than dealing with thirteen different divisional sales forces. The deployment of resources from different functions within a company was not exactly new to the business world; other companies outside the consumer products industry—AT&T, IBM, Motorola, to name a few—were doing it.

What was new, however, was the fact that individuals brought onto the team from other functions, on a dedicated basis, were playing important "roles" in the sales and customer relationship management processes. Effective performance of these new roles in these processes could result in greater sales and profit for the company and enhanced customer satisfaction and loyalty.

Regardless of the type of business, the Wal-Mart paradigm of doing business is changing customer relationship management. It does not matter that a company is not a retailer; there is an end-use customer for every product or service sold. The increasing emphasis being placed on managing the total customer experience, from end to end, means that jobs that once had no role in sales must assume a sales role. The fact that an increasing number of company jobs play a part in the sales process creates the need to understand how to motivate and reward these employees for their contributions to sales success.

SIX NEW SALES ROLES THAT IMPROVE INTERACTION WITH CUSTOMERS

Because companies want to grow sales at rates higher than in the past (or than competitors), they implement new approaches to interacting with customers. Most new forms of personal interaction with customers— interaction between a customer and a company representative—involve a "sales role" that did not previously exist in the company. Today it is virtually impossible to visit a company, regardless of industry, and not find new sales roles operating in the business. Consider these examples:

1. *End-user sales specialists.* Virtually any company that sells its products through distributors faces the challenge of creating demand among end users. Lexmark International, which manufactures computer keyboards, printers, electric typewriters, and related supplies, found it had to work with the end users rather than focus exclusively on resellers. To meet this challenge, Lexmark redefined the role of its sales force. Instead of the salespeople spending 85 percent of their time working with Lexmark's resellers and 15 percent with end users, the company reversed the time allocations. Sales representatives became end-user specialists; within the first year of this change, Lexmark's revenues grew substantially.

2. *Retention sales specialists.* Most companies realize between 80 and 90 percent of their annual revenue from current customers. Retaining customers and, more importantly, realizing the same or more revenue from year to year is critical to the business's profitable growth. To retain customers and protect revenue, some companies have implemented retention sales specialists. Browning-Ferris Industries, a large waste services company, recently redefined its sales process and the roles of its salespeople. One outcome of that work was a new sales job: Core Account Retention Specialist. People holding this job are responsible for retaining current revenue from current customers.

3. *New customer acquisition specialists.* Weatherchem, a division of Weatherhead Industries that specializes in closures for a variety of containers, was frustrated at failing to achieve its planned 15 percent sales

growth, a not unreasonable target given industry conditions. Management divided the sales organization into two teams: core business managers and new business development managers. This latter team was charged with the responsibility for winning new customers through a focus on selling Weatherchem's *capabilities* to companies that were in the early stages of a new package design. The first full quarter after implementing the new sales role, revenue was up 20 percent and top management projected 30 percent revenue growth for the following year.

4. *Win-back sales specialists.* The telecommunications industry is one that regularly experiences high customer defection levels. This is particularly true among cellular telephone companies. Many of these have created win-back sales specialists: either sales representatives who call directly on accounts, or telephone sales representatives who perform many of the same tasks over the phone. While success rates vary, companies have won back 15 to 30 percent of previously lost customers through this approach to sales specialization.

5. *Telephone account managers.* Increasingly, companies are learning that customers can be won and retained without deploying individual sales representatives. Cisco Systems, Dell Computer Corporation, and Office Depot are just three of the many companies that successfully sell millions of their products each day over the telephone. Office Depot, for example, implemented a specialized telephone account sales force that focuses on converting accounts into customers based on a list of target prospects. Not only were these accounts receptive to being contacted by phone, they also proved to be the fastest-growing revenue segment in the highly competitive small office/home office segment of the office products industry.

6. *Service consultants.* Recent surveys of several industries that we have conducted show that salespeople spend 15 to 30 percent of their time on service-related activities: finding the status of orders, answering questions about shipments, resolving billing disputes, and the like. If some or all of this service work can be assigned to others, the amount of time available for selling increases. To test this idea, some companies are experimenting with a new sales role: service consultant. A service consultant typically supports three or four field-based sales representatives and addresses and solves any customer problems that the sales representative or account manager cannot handle adequately.

The majority of the new sales roles companies are establishing today are not new to the business world. In fact, through benchmarking, many companies find that what may be a new sales role for them is actually a practice that a company in a completely different industry has used for many years quite successfully.

Often what limits a company's thinking about new ways to interact with customers is its history or its tradition of doing business. We believe this history has a large effect on a company's growth cycle and on the sales organization.

Most companies move through a four-phase growth cycle: (1) start-up, (2) volume growth, (3) market share growth, and (4) optimization (see Figure 1-1). As companies move through these phases, they must develop new competencies to sustain profitable top-line growth; unless they do so and move from one phase to the next, they shrivel and either die or are acquired. In each phase, the sales organization's role must change and its people must adapt to new circumstances. The competencies, in fact, develop sequentially over time; it is not possible to skip a phase in the growth cycle.

In the start-up phase, all business is good business. Selling anything is good; the company is selling to survive. The strategy is simple: one product sold to one market. The company does not segment markets. Management's view is that the market is made up of mass buyers, and

Fig. 1-1. Pattern of business growth.

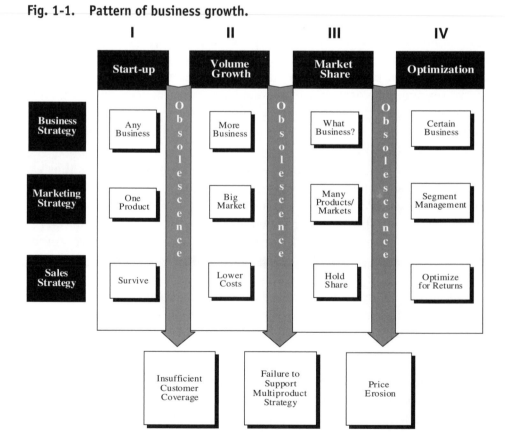

it sees virtually infinite opportunity. Customer strategies are therefore simple: The focus is on selling volume and providing service to ensure that volume levels are maintained or increased. Typically, the company uses only one marketing channel—most frequently, a direct sales force. Occasionally, however, the principal channel may be indirect; for example, agents, dealers, or distributors. The battle cry is, "Any business is good business! Let's go after it before the competitors surface!"

To successfully advance from the start-up to the volume growth phase, a company must typically overcome the challenge of insufficient customer coverage. The solution is relatively straightforward: Hire more salespeople. As a company makes the transition from start-up to volume growth, this phase becomes the period (generally lasting several years) that employees often look back on as the "golden years" of the business, because volume grows at an increasing rate. Profits grow as well because unit costs are dropping. The strategy remains relatively simple: Sell the core products to as many customers as possible. At this point in the growth cycle, managers give little attention to buyer segmentation, customer sales strategies, or additional sales channels. The battle cry is, "All business is good business! Let's own the market!" The factors limiting growth are manufacturing and sales capacities—the ability to make the product in sufficient quantities to meet demand and to hire sales representatives fast enough to retain current customers and win new ones.

As the business takes on definition and attracts competition, however, the company that created the market is challenged to hold its share. In the market share growth phase, the company's management often experiences confusion. This confusion may extend to the sales organization and to the very people, the sales representatives, who have had a lot to do with the company's success. In an attempt to hold share, the company launches new products—sometimes successfully, but more typically unsuccessfully because the sales organization has lost its ability to sell new products. Competitors enter the market with comparable products at lower prices. The pioneer often responds with price discounting, only to find its margins deteriorating as its salespeople rely on discounting to retain share. Management begins to realize that not all customers are good customers. To administer scarce resources efficiently, the company requires sales strategies for groups of customers and finds that continuing to cover customers through an expensive channel like the direct sales force may actually limit growth. The battle cry becomes, "What business is good business?" The factor limiting growth is the speed at which a company can move to prevent its own obsolescence—in particular, the obsolescence of the sales organization that up to this point in the company's history has been the source of its success.

Companies that emerge successfully from the market share growth phase (typically some of the firm's darkest days) do so with the realization that they can no longer be all things to all customers. To enter the optimization phase and achieve top-line growth at expected levels, top management—most often through a period of trial and error—comes to understand that only certain customers, or certain groups of customers, are worth the investment of direct sales coverage and superior customer service resources. It is better to carefully redeploy resources toward those customers who offer the best opportunities for sustainable growth than to attempt to reach and service all customers. The battle cry becomes, "Only certain business is good business!" Management sees that sustaining growth depends on its ability to segment and target the best customers; to develop and implement sales strategies that deliver value-added solutions to these customers; to apply multiple channels to reach customers with the right resources; and to build the processes and programs to support change in its sales organization.

TRANSACTIONS VERSUS RELATIONSHIPS: HOW TO HELP YOUR COMPANY IMPLEMENT NEW SALES ROLES

Companies introduce new sales roles because of an evolution in the number of customers served, the size of the product line, and the basis for doing business (transactions versus relationships). This evolution should occur as a company moves smoothly from one growth phase to the next. The shift often does not go smoothly, however, and we can tell that a company is struggling with the challenge of implementing and compensating new sales roles when we hear such remarks as:

> The old selling approach is out; we don't want our people to be product pushers.
> Our customers are our partners.
> We use global teams to serve our largest customers; however, the salespeople are the only ones who receive incentive pay.
> We now use many new and different types of sales channels, but we haven't changed our approach to compensation.
> The key contact at the customer level is our service manager, not the salesperson; however, the service manager is paid only salary.

Basically, what changes is the sales model that a company uses to do business with customers. In the start-up and volume growth phases of the business growth cycle, the typical sales model is a self-contained, sales representative–focused approach to doing business with customers. As Figure 1-2 illustrates, the sales representative is expected to "do it all." New jobs—for example, product sales specialist, application sales specialist, sales channel manager—may emerge during the volume growth phase. The focus of those jobs, however, continues to be the "individual" and not the end-to-end sales process.

As companies progress in the business growth cycle (volume growth to market share growth and market share growth to optimization), the self-contained, sales representative–focused sales model may limit a company's growth for at least two reasons. First, not all interactions with customers are sales interactions, and therefore other company employees can frequently provide the greatest value to customers when they need help. When customers require service or reorders or information, they do not need salespeople.

Second, as a company offers more products and services to meet customer needs, it wants to minimize the degree to which its sales model—the single point of contact—actually becomes a bottleneck to selling more to customers. To prevent this from happening, some companies implement a completely new process to define how they will interact with customers.

Figure 1-3 illustrates this process, often called the customer relationship management model. Technology and resource specialization characterize this model. Telecenters, catalog/fax purchasing, the Internet (web sites), and electronic data interchange (EDI) offer opportunities for a customer to buy from or interact with a company without going through a sales representative. The ability of a company to apply technology effectively to the sales process creates the opportunity to "deconstruct" that process, and thereby to involve other employees in meeting customer needs. Deconstructing the sales process, a necessary step for sales growth, actually creates the opportunity for new sales roles

Fig. 1-2. Traditional sales model: self-contained, sales representative–focused sales process.

Fig. 1-3. Customer relationship management model.

in companies where sales has traditionally been the sales department's exclusive domain.

THREE KEY ELEMENTS OF THE CUSTOMER RELATIONSHIP MANAGEMENT MODEL

When the customer relationship management model replaces the traditional sales model, the company has an opportunity to define and assign responsibility for the customer revenue stream throughout the organization. The model's three key elements include:

   1. *Access.* Who or what resources should be used to reach customers? In the traditional sales model, the sales representative or the sales agent (e.g., dealers, distributors) is often responsible for identifying and targeting new customers. Many companies have discovered, however, that as their "sellers" become saturated with servicing current customers, their time and ability to find and sell to new customers diminish substantially. The capability to "access" new customers on an ongoing basis through the model's customer acquisition function can be assigned elsewhere in the organization. For example, the current popularity of data mining—in which a database is sliced into dozens of narrower, smaller pools of information that the company can analyze to identify customers and prospects quickly—provides an opportunity to outsource the identification of new potential customers.

   2. *Persuade.* In many companies—perhaps most—the "job" of selling will never be replaced by technology or outsourced to a vendor. Thus, management is interested in redefining the sales representative's role in the sales process so that "sellers" actually have more time to sell (the model's customer retention and expansion elements).

3. *Fulfill.* This addresses the question "Who services the customer?" or "Who delivers on the promises made to the customer?" If the company can get its customer service department, operations department, or logistics department to follow through on delivering whatever the sales representative sold to the customer, the sales force does not have to spend time fetching and carrying.

The need to relieve the sales staff of the responsibility for customer fulfillment is one reason why more and more companies want to make it as easy as possible for customers to determine whether or not their requirements are being met. The FedEx and UPS package tracking systems are examples of this movement. Customers can service themselves. Want to know the status of your package? Just dial into the system and it will tell you.

It is true that customers do not like to be told, "The customer service department will deal with your problems." They want to talk to the sales representative who told them everything was going to be fine when they closed the sale. The only way the company will convince customers to feel differently is to make it easy for them to get an update on where they stand with the company, to say, "We have assigned an 800 number to you, and we've assigned people to you who will be familiar with your account at any time you call because they have access to your records and will be able to tell you exactly where things stand."

Customers call because something they expected to happen did not happen. They did not receive a shipment. It wasn't complete. It was the wrong item. A salesperson should be able to say, "You know, we strive for 100 percent accuracy in everything we do. But, we do know that, on occasion, something doesn't go right. And, when something doesn't go right, rather than you having to chase me, here's how you can find out how things are going—and someone who will make it right."

It turns out that customers select the fulfillment response best suited to their needs. When two major corporations appointed national account salespeople, they established call centers to support the sales representatives. They thought the call centers were going to deal with only smaller accounts. They discovered that, after the initial order, the large accounts preferred to deal with the call centers. The customers did not need the sales help once the contract had been set up.

Today, of course, it is possible to obtain utilization and usage information reports electronically. Customers can dial in to a Web site or to EDI. They don't need to chase down a sales representative who will answer questions, solve problems, or place reorders. And as the fulfillment role shifts from the salesperson to others in the company and the customer has the opportunity to interact with these people, the connection becomes another sales potential, another sales role.

Four Telltale Symptoms That a Company Needs New Sales Roles

A company needs new sales roles when the salesperson, as a central point of contact, is no longer able to retain customers and grow the business with new customers. Rather than make a change simply for change's sake, what are the symptoms that tell managers they should be considering new sales roles?

1. Excess "Churn"

A company may need new sales roles because there is too much "churn," the number of customers or amount of revenue from current accounts that must be replaced every year for the business just to stay even. "As fast as we were bringing customers in through the front door," one sales executive told us recently, "they were going out the back." This is not uncommon.

When we visit a company to discuss ways it can grow its business, we routinely investigate the customer churn. We are no longer surprised when management tells us, "Oh, we don't keep track of our accounts that way." The information is available, of course, but no one assembles it into a report a manager can study.

We ask that the company develop such a report, and when it does so, company executives are often astonished to see that the firm has been losing—and replacing—as much as 15 percent of the customer base every year. This typically means that the company has no one focused on customer retention.

The churn report will also reveal the revenue churn among customers who stay. For example, a company might find that it has retained most of its customers, but that those customers did 10 to 30 percent less business with the company this year than they did the year before.

Put another way, if top management sets a goal of a 10 percent sales increase, the sales force may actually have to obtain 25 percent or more of that revenue from new customers. "No wonder our people are burning out," said one division chief when we showed him this information.

Clearly, some churn comes with doing business. Customers change strategic direction, go out of business, or get merged into a parent with its own suppliers. But although some churn is inevitable, top managers should not use that fact as an excuse to ignore whatever is happening among customers.

2. Few New Customers

The company is not attracting new customers. This suggests that it needs someone to focus on new customer acquisition: business developers.

3. No New Markets

The company is not opening up any markets or distribution channels. When the company does open a new channel, the new role is that of channel manager, who manages that channel of distribution.

4. Customers Buying Differently

Perhaps the most basic reason a company needs new sales roles is that customers are trying to buy differently, but the company is not equipped to deal with them differently. Customers complain about how hard it is to do business with the firm. (This is the best situation; more often they don't complain, they simply go elsewhere.) They can't get information about the status of their orders. They talk to a different person every time they call—and that person doesn't know who they are, what they've done in the past, or what they're trying to do now.

If customers begin to say, "Don't send a sales rep; we don't need more reps calling on us," it should be an alarm bell to management. Customers are saying, in effect, "Putting more commissioned salespeople—or any kind of salespeople—in here is not going to help us solve our problems." One reason a company would want to institute new sales roles is to help customers solve problems with applications of its products, rather than simply pushing more products at the customer.

Today customers have many opportunities to purchase or to reorder. What management wants to do is to make it as easy as possible for them to do business with the company; so they can order through the call center, they can work with a sales representative, they can use the fax machine.

In many cases we find that these new roles are operating informally in a business, but that the company has not formalized its relationships to the customers or within the organization itself. It has a customer service center, for example, but it is only that. The center is reactive; it doesn't use any of its resources to be proactive. It takes only inbound calls and does not do any outbound business. Changing simply requires altering the mind-set to be proactive in addition to reactive. We also find companies that need new sales roles because they've packed the sales generalist jobs too full of responsibility; no one can get anything done well within the job because they are trying to be retention specialists, winback specialists, new customer acquisition specialists, and more, all at the same time.

There are probably two large-scale trends that have affected sales roles more than anything. One is the move toward increased specialization, to dealing with customers more on a one-on-one basis. The other is the technology that enables anyone in the company the customer touches to examine comprehensive information about the customer's business with the firm. These two trends have made it both necessary and possible to create new sales roles to do business with customers.

How Your Company Can Benefit from Investing in New Sales Roles

The benefits of investing in new sales roles include financial rewards, customer satisfaction, and employee satisfaction.

Financial Benefits

The company will see financial benefits in four areas: revenue growth, profit or margin contributions, productivity improvement, and probably lower absolute costs. It will obtain greater productivity from fewer direct sellers because, by adding new sales roles, the firm puts the responsibility for sales on more people than the direct resource.

Revenue should grow faster because the direct sales representatives spend more time actually selling and less answering routine questions. It should grow faster because the company has sales representatives working to acquire new customers, and other representatives working to retain existing business.

Profits or gross margins should improve because the cost of sales drops as less expensive employees take over some of the functions formerly performed by the more expensive direct sales representatives, or because customers are able to buy without even talking to a company representative, which means the sales cost is almost nothing. Recent figures indicated that the cost per sales transaction of a fax order is around a hundredth of the cost of an order taken by a salesperson.

Productivity should improve, since specialization tends to mean that employees are able to do their jobs faster and more efficiently. They have access to the information they need, they know where to find it, and they understand what to do with it when they have it.

ENHANCED CUSTOMER SATISFACTION

Why should customer satisfaction improve if a company institutes new sales roles? Providing more routes of access from the company to the customers means more routes of access back from the customers to the company. Probably what promotes customer satisfaction most (aside from product quality and value, which, for this discussion, are givens) is the ability to do business easily, simply, and on the customer's terms. The customer who is able to do business with the company twenty-four hours a day, seven days a week will be more satisfied than one who can reach the company only between 9:00 A.M. and 5:00 P.M., Eastern Standard Time, Monday through Friday. Many of the best examples of this are among companies selling to consumers: L.L. Bean, Lands' End, Mac Warehouse (indeed, a consumer catalog company that cannot take an order any time of the day or night has a serious competitive weakness). It's becoming increasingly evident that business customers want the same level of information and service.

Customers tend to be more satisfied when companies are able to respond quickly to their questions. They tend to be more satisfied when they do not have to rely on one person, when they don't have to go through the salesperson to get information about a product catalog or product capabilities, order status, or whatever. They tend to be more satisfied when they are able to get an immediate response from the company, which is possible through the technology that permits anyone the customer telephones to call up complete customer records.

IMPROVED EMPLOYEE MORALE

Companies are finally beginning to realize that anybody who touches the customer has the potential to affect the business relationship for good or for ill. In effect, companies are seeing the positive impact of enlarging employee jobs and are recognizing that those employees are, in fact, a part of the success equation. This recognition tends to result in employee satisfaction.

Aside from the potential increased motivation and improved morale that employees experience when their jobs are expanded, the fact that they have opportunities to interact with customers can be beneficial in itself. Even though this interaction may not always be comfortable, it's an opportunity to influence the customer's thinking through their actions, and perhaps take a bad situation and turn it into a good one. These days, with downsizing and questions of whether employees are loyal or not, any organization can benefit by broadening the responsibility for getting and keeping business with customers through the customer relationship management model, because management by inclusion tends to lead to employee satisfaction.

When we talk to employees, we find that they usually like to interact with customers, and often they do work with customers as part of their jobs. But just as often, their employers do not recognize them for the contributions they make. Improving employee satisfaction through more sales roles is actually a two-sided issue. One side says, in effect, that everybody has always had some responsibility for interacting with customers. The other side is that it is critical to recognize people for contributing to the revenue and profit stream that those customers generate. They're not just transactions; they are customer relationships. Employees are adding value, if for no other reason than that they are there and available for the customer to do business with. That should drive some sense of pride, and it frequently does. It should also be recognized financially, but it frequently isn't.

THREE CRITICAL COMPENSATION CHALLENGES

There are at least three compensation challenges: eligibility, "at-risk" pay, and performance tracking. To develop a successful compensation plan, management must take all three into account.

ELIGIBILITY

Eligibility means that some people who had been paid strictly on a salary are now going to be eligible to participate in variable, incentive compensation. Typically, a larger number of employees are now eligible for incentive compensation because they have a role in the sales and customer relationship management process that they may not have had before. Or, if they had the role, it was never formally recognized and compensated.

This raises several questions. The biggest challenge is to determine who is now going to be eligible for incentive pay and how quickly the company makes these employees eligible. How does the company determine which positions should become eligible and which should not? Figure 1-4, a decision tree to guide decision making, is one way to determine eligibility.

The decision tree breaks down every customer contact job, starting with whether the primary contact is internal or external. With external contacts, the employee either initiates or responds. When the employee

Fig. 1-4. Determining eligibility for incentive compensation.

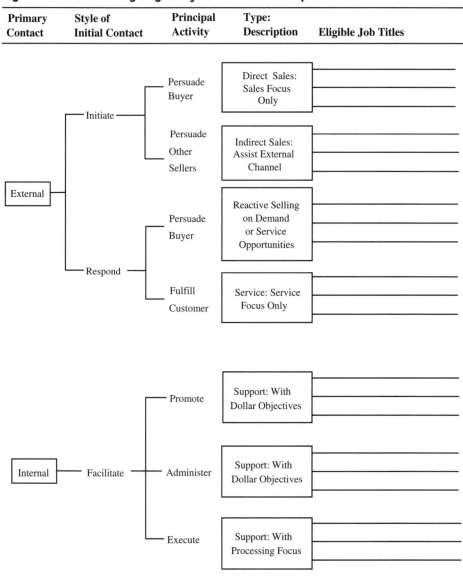

Primary Contact	Style of Initial Contact	Principal Activity	Type: Description	Eligible Job Titles
External	Initiate	Persuade Buyer	Direct Sales: Sales Focus Only	
		Persuade Other Sellers	Indirect Sales: Assist External Channel	
	Respond	Persuade Buyer	Reactive Selling on Demand or Service Opportunities	
		Fulfill Customer	Service: Service Focus Only	
Internal	Facilitate	Promote	Support: With Dollar Objectives	
		Administer	Support: With Dollar Objectives	
		Execute	Support: With Processing Focus	

initiates the contact, it is to persuade the buyer or to persuade other sellers. If the employee is responding to a customer (or prospect), it is to persuade the buyer or to fulfill a customer request.

Among the internal contacts, the principal activities are to promote, administer, and execute. While different companies will give different titles to these jobs, the functions are the same. Historically only those employees whose principal activity is to persuade buyers had incentive or at-risk pay. They were the ones who had to convince outsiders to give the company money, and they were rewarded for doing so.

Another issue is to convince employees who have been used to being paid a salary only—that's what they bought into when they joined the company—that being eligible for some sort of variable pay is an improvement.

AT-RISK PAY

This brings us to the second point, which is the concept of "at-risk" pay. It can be very difficult, depending on their level in the organization, to convince employees that it is a good idea. The employee says, "I'm not just getting a fixed compensation; part of my pay is now on the line, based on either how I do individually or how I do and my team or unit does, relative to serving customers. But when I signed on, you were just going to pay me a salary, and I got my benefits. Now you're changing the rules, and that's disconcerting. The other thing that's disconcerting is understanding how I can have any control over the results."

The concept of at-risk pay is not necessarily something that a person from customer service, or from MIS, or from the warehouse can easily grasp or accept. Aside from understanding the concept, of course, employees want to understand what they have to do to win the award: the variable pay. Employees will make a judgment about their relative ability to earn the variable pay as a function of the degree to which they think they can control the results.

If, for example, the employee is evaluated on the number of customer calls during which she has been able to up-sell—to add another case of paper, another shirt, another software program, or whatever—she has to know that she can affect the sales and will be credited for the revenue. In many cases, the company is introducing a new sales role, a part-time sales responsibility, into a current job. The job's principal focus may still be to react to or be responsive to customers vis-à-vis customer service. The new role is to contribute to a revenue stream. The issue is whether the company can trace and credit results to the employee (or the team, if the employee is now on a team).

Performance Tracking

The questions on the minds of employees when management says, "You're now going to have some pay at risk" are those of control (what can I do to affect the results?) and measurement (how will you know what I've done?). Management is saying, in effect, "You're not going to get 100 percent of your W-2 in salary; some portion is now going to be a function of performance." And therein lies the third problem, which is performance tracking. How does the company keep track of the individual's performance in the new role? What is the relative contribution of the individual as opposed to the team?

The sales manager at one company with whom we worked talked about a "universal rep." She did everything on the phone—handled problems, sold, expedited orders, everything. The problem was that it was virtually impossible to isolate and track the amount of time she spent on the specific aspects of her job. Performance results need to be sales figures. We told the manager that a universal sales rep on the phone is not the optimal way to build sales results; there was a lot of what we call job contamination. To measure the rep's contribution, the job needed to be "decontaminated." The universal rep concept does not make sense if the company really wants to drive up cross selling.

Companies institute such a job because they take a narrow view of cost. They believe it is less expensive to add roles to an existing employee than to hire another person, and in the short run it may be. Managers have a propensity to load more roles on employees. You want something done with the customer? Drop it on the customer call center. New products to sell? Throw them out to the field salespeople. (Which implies, by the way, that the employees are not already busy.) The universal rep idea was probably rooted in the single-point-of-contact, cost-efficient, we-can-load-more-stuff-on-their-backs perspective.

Another reason companies have such all-purpose reps is their inability to see the situation through the customer's eyes in terms of the specialization needed to deal with specific customer situations. Also, certain managers are uncomfortable having many points of customer contact within the organization; they prefer to have one salesperson dealing with the customer. They see the issue as one of control rather than as one of meeting customer (and company) needs. But using sales generalists makes it very difficult to measure what these reps are actually doing that contributes to the sales role that they have.

Once upon a time, of course, it made sense for the salesperson to be the customer's single contact. The salesperson knew the sales history and customer profile, and there was no efficient way (in the days of letters, memos, and telephone calls) for different people within the company to communicate with one another. Today it is possible to have every different person who interacts with the customer record the contact so that the next person who logs on to the system has a complete record.

Yet even today there are companies in which the salespeople act as gatekeepers. Indeed, we had one client not long ago tell us that the firm's salespeople were actually blocking sales. Management said, "We've got all these products at the top of the funnel and all these customers at the bottom of the funnel, and in the middle we've got this giant bottleneck called a sales rep." Because the company's sales representatives stand between the product and the customers, management is saying, "We need ways to reach those customers other than through the salespeople." This company needs new sales roles to gain access to other buyers or to acquire customers it cannot reach through the salespeople.

One way to think about the issue is in terms of customer buying needs. While there are many ways to define a customer's buying needs, we are going to consider just two variables: the importance of the buying decision and the value of the purchase. When a customer buys something relatively unimportant (the customer is familiar with the technology and how to use it) and relatively inexpensive, the decision to buy is simple. For example, a man needs cassette tapes for his dictation tape recorder; it's not a strategically important buying decision or a high-value purchase. He can pick up an office supply catalog, find the item, and order through his fax machine. But what if he were going to buy a new computer, or an in-home copier, or an in-home fax/scanner/printer/answering machine, products that are relatively important and relatively expensive? (Expense is always relative, of course; what is a major financial outlay to one customer is pocket change to another.) Because the purchase is consequential and costly, the customer wants to talk to a salesperson.

Salespeople should not spend time selling routine, repetitive, low-value, non–strategically important goods or services; but, speaking generally, salespeople spend too much time on small applications, small sales. In the case of one client, we found that 86 percent of all new orders came from small accounts. When we investigated, we found that the reason was the sales cycle time: The salespeople could close small accounts in thirty days; large orders took longer.

Interestingly, customers seldom make themselves unprofitable to do business with. It is the supplier that makes it unprofitable to do business with the customers. Suppliers do this by the way they suggest customers buy: If the company sells only through a direct sales force, that's the way customers will buy, whether or not they would buy some other way.

That was Encyclopaedia Britannica's problem—or one of them. A customer could buy the books only through a salesperson. She could not buy them over the phone or through the mail or at the demonstration desks set up at airports. In the end, the economics did not make sense.

SUMMING UP

Companies need new sales roles when revenues are not growing rapidly enough, new products are not selling well enough, new customers are not being acquired fast enough, or all three. Many companies have been informally creating new sales roles as more and more employees interact with customers.

To understand the need for new sales roles, management must understand how a company moves through the four-phase growth cycle. Even those firms in the start-up and volume growth phases—times when revenues are growing, new products are selling, and new customers are being acquired—can profitably add new sales roles, both to prepare for the next phase and to use existing resources more effectively. Even when business is booming and healthy margins mask inefficiencies, it does not make sense to have an expensive sales resource spending time on small accounts.

Companies in the market share growth and optimization phases must add new sales roles if they are to survive. Without such a shift, the sales organization grows obsolete, margins erode, revenues fall, new products fail, and customers flee to other, more efficient suppliers. With such a shift, the sales organization begins to specialize and others within the company assume sales roles. The company no longer sells the way it wants to sell (which is usually the way it began to sell), it now sells the way customers want to buy.

But often along the way, companies find that their traditional sales compensation plans have become obsolete. When and why that happens is the subject of the next chapter.

2

WHY SALES COMPENSATION PLANS FAIL—AND HOW YOURS CAN SUCCEED

Sales compensation plans fail for numerous reasons. Some pay too much relative to sales and gross profit results. Others pay for the wrong mix of business; for example, you might be paying a disproportionately high percentage of incentive compensation for selling existing products to current customers. And a few plans actually pay too little; the amount of incentive compensation salespeople can earn for exceptional performance does not make it financially worthwhile to work hard, so they hold back sales for a future period.

Often the real reason a plan fails is not poor plan design. Rather, it fails because it no longer directs, motivates, or rewards salespeople for behaving in a manner that contributes to sales success. In times of accelerating business change, the elements of sales success require redefinition. We often find, however, that during periods of rapid business change at many companies, the sales compensation plan remains the same.

Management is often slow to act because it fears the consequences of a change in sales compensation. We find the most common concerns of executives to be that the company will lose top-producing sales representatives; that the sales force will be confused over the business's direction; and that salespeople will lose motivation and productivity during the transition period, the time in which they struggle to figure out what the new plan directs them to do and rewards them for doing. As we will see later in the book, these are legitimate concerns. You can, however, address them effectively through the right plan design and attention to effective change management.

FOUR INTEGRAL PARTS OF A DYNAMIC SALES COMPENSATION PLAN

Perfect Flap Envelope Company, a $100 million division of a large, diversified paper products company, manufactures and markets standard and customized envelopes. It is a real client company, but we have changed the name, the industry, and certain identifying details. Perfect Flap sells to both direct accounts—banks, insurance companies, utilities, direct mail services—and distributors. Until 1997, the division achieved relatively steady sales growth in the range of 5 to 6 percent a year. Top management believes and marketing research supports the opinion that the division could achieve annual sales growth in the 10 to 12 percent range.

As a first step to that growth, management hired a new vice president of sales, whom we'll call Hal Jones. Jones toured the field to meet with key customers and the sales force to learn firsthand why the company was growing at only about half the rate of the estimated potential. Jones observed the following people:

Customers. The customers he visited, particularly the large accounts, said they were pleased with Perfect Flap's product quality and customer service, and with the relationship with their account executive.

Account executives. Perfect Flap has forty-five geographically deployed account executives who call on customers of widely different sizes, ranging from community banks to large direct mail marketers. The company has no national or major accounts program. The salespeople told Jones that their account planning is "informal," and Perfect Flap offers no training in how to develop complete account plans for customers, regardless of size. Overall, the account executives appear to be hardworking in the face of the competition from both national and local competitors. Perfect Flap compensates account executives with a salary and a sales commission. On average, their W-2 earnings are 50 percent salary, 50 percent commission. The company pays a commission at the rate of 3 percent of all sales over a base. The firm defines the base as the prior year's actual sales plus an upward adjustment for price increases. The average account executive earns $70,000 in total compensation,

while the annual pay among all salespeople ranges from $40,000 to
$150,000.

Customer service representatives. Fifteen customer service representatives handle accounts that account executives cannot reach on a regular basis, either because they are too busy or because there does not
appear to be enough business in the account to justify on-premises sales
calls. Typically, these accounts call the customer service representatives
to reorder, to ask about incomplete orders and billing problems, or to
inquire about new products. Some customer service representatives told
Jones that they do not have enough to do, so they are telephoning customers that their account executive has turned over to them. Perfect
Flap pays customer service representatives a salary; it does not include
them in the sales commission plan.

Field sales managers. The three field sales managers spend the majority of their time working with account executives on major sales opportunities. They spend a relatively small amount of time on sales
analysis and planning. They appear to be good trainers, motivators, and
coaches for their people. Two of the field sales managers told Jones they
believe sales results would be higher if their people specialized in certain
types of accounts: direct mail companies, for example, or utilities. The
company pays field sales managers a salary plus a 1 percent commission
(that is, an override) on the sales of their people over the sales base. The
W-2 earnings for the field sales managers averaged $125,000 last year.

When Jones returned from his field tour, he asked Perfect Flap's
product managers to meet with him. The product manager for the standard product line indicated that the current sales "run rate" was on plan
for the year, and that she was satisfied with the sales force's efforts this
year and last. The product manager for the customized product line was
not satisfied. He noted that sales results for his products were, on average, 50 percent below plan. He pointed out that Perfect Flap had made
significant investments last year in manufacturing and envelope design
capabilities to support the sale of customized products. This product
manager is concerned that the sales force is not comfortable with com-
puter-based envelope design—an essential part of the sales process—at
accounts where significant new sales have been booked. He pointed out
that in virtually every large account where Perfect Flap has won new,
customized business, he has had to play a role in the sale, particularly
in analysis of the need, design of the solution, and the business case for
the pricing.

After meeting with the product managers, Jones looked over his sales numbers for the year and the growth projections that top management had given his predecessor for next year. What he saw was discouraging. The sales force was well behind its $106 million goal for the year. Standard product sales, which represented 80 percent of the business, appeared to be on plan, but customized product sales, projected to be $21 million, were well below plan. In fact, as the product manager had pointed out, actual sales were running at about half of the year's goal. What Jones found particularly disturbing was that while customized products were projected to be 20 percent of the current year's business, next year's forecast showed they were supposed to be 30 percent of the business, and the total goal for the business was set at $118 million. This meant that the customized product sales goal would be $36 million, or slightly more than three times greater than the current sales rate.

Jones concluded that Perfect Flap had to change the way it organized and deployed the sales force. He knew, however, that he must determine how to pay the sales force early in the process. He needed to retain the productive account executives, and, equally important, he would have to hire additional salespeople. The current salary plus commission plan would not be the right plan for the new people. As we move through this chapter, we will return to the Perfect Flap Envelope Company to illustrate key points about why sales compensation plans fail, and what you can do to prevent this from happening.

How a New Sales Compensation Plan Can Help Improve Products, Service, and Cost Performance

Hal Jones's situation is fairly typical today as companies struggle to redefine how they will grow. When a company faces the problems Jones faces, we suggest three reasons a sound compensation plan for salespeople—and often for all customer contact employees—is necessary.

1. A Sound Compensation Plan Will Help Achieve Marketing Strategies and Sales Objectives

Without an effective sales compensation plan, your company will not accomplish its marketing strategies and sales objectives. Winning and keeping customers is the ultimate competitive challenge. Companies must serve customers effectively and, therefore, continually improve their value proposition. Customers demand effective products, better service and quality, and competitive prices. The sales force must deal with both the changing customer demands and the organization's developing competencies. In most industries, the sales force is the primary customer contact, and the customer often sees the sales representative as the face of the organization. The salesperson therefore occupies the position of helping customers meet their objectives by presenting the company products and services that best meet the buyers' needs.

Perfect Flap Envelope Company's products are more varied today than in the past, and they can be more complicated—customized envelopes designed to meet specialized needs—as the division endeavors to satisfy the needs of different customers in different market segments. Jones correctly concludes that a properly structured compensation plan would help to clarify the account executive role so that the account executives can spend time on the right selling activities.

2. A Sound Compensation Plan Will Attract and Retain People with the Right Skills and Competencies to Perform Effectively

Successful salespeople are always in demand. A company with a poorly designed compensation plan runs the risk that it will not be able to attract and retain the caliber of people it needs if it is to sell its products and help customers with their service requirements. By reading trade publications and general business magazines and by networking with one another at conferences and conventions, salespeople today are more familiar with compensation levels and practices than in the past. Increasingly, salespeople express certain expectations about how they should be compensated for a job well done. To be effective, a sound compensation plan must embrace the values and expectations of the people for whom it is designed.

3. A Sound Compensation Plan Will Control the Cost of Sales

Compensation is frequently the most significant cost of maintaining a sales organization. Depending on the industry, direct compensation—salary plus variable pay (commission or bonus or both)—can range from 2 to 20 percent of sales. Today, many companies are concerned with customer profitability: the mix of products customers buy and the cost of serving them. For the sales force, this frequently means that volume alone does not constitute successful performance. However, as Jones observed, if Perfect Flap does not structure the compensation plan to recognize performance requirements other than sales volume, which the salespeople are obtaining through the standard product line, it will realize a less-than-optimum return from the expenditure.

One of the most effective ways you can increase sales profitably is through the compensation plan. The plan's principal objective is to direct your salespeople to sell to and interact with customers effectively. Whether you want increased volume, a better mix of customers or product sales, or more new accounts, the right compensation plan can help you accomplish your objectives. How effective is your compensation plan in helping your company achieve its targets? You can test the effectiveness of your plan with Figure 2-1, which suggests how to interpret your results to determine the action you should take in your company.

FIVE POSITIVE OUTCOMES OF A SUCCESSFUL SALES COMPENSATION PLAN

Sales compensation is one of the most powerful tools to achieve business results available to management. The incentive component (commission or bonus) communicates the results the company needs its sales personnel to achieve. In most sales organizations, the sales force is extremely interested in the sales compensation plan. In fact, sales representatives typically judge the plan by a single criterion: "Am I making more money now than I did a year ago?"

Management, on the other hand, typically judges the sales compensation plan's success on multiple criteria. In companies where sales compensation plays a key role in shaping the effective performance of the sales force, top management looks to the plan to contribute positively to five business outcomes: growth, profits, customer satisfaction, sales talent, and sales productivity.

GROWTH

The desire to grow—by creating new markets, winning new customers, and continually improving processes to retain current customers—is a top priority at many companies. Our in-depth investigation into how companies achieve their sales objectives shows that the growth strategy they pursue is "deeper penetration of current customers." This suggests that these companies have gone back to the basic block-and-tackle approach to growth: selling more to current accounts, either new product sales to current buyers or more sales to new buyers within the same account. This sales strategy suggests a compensation plan that rewards

Fig. 2-1.   How effective is your sales compensation plan?

The principal objective of the compensation plan is to direct the sales force to sell what management wants sold. Whether it is increased volume, better product mix sales, or more new accounts, the compensation plan can help produce the right results.

Here is a short exercise to test the effectiveness of your plan:

1.   Overall, are you satisfied with how your plan rewards for sales results?

No	Somewhat	Yes
1	2	3

2.   When you launch new products, does your plan encourage and reward for these sales?

No	Somewhat	Yes
1	2	3

3.   Does your plan support market share objectives?

No	Somewhat	Yes
1	2	3

4.   Are you satisfied with the way your plan rewards for new account sales?

No	Somewhat	Yes
1	2	3

5.   Does your plan safeguard against exceeding the pay budget if you miss the sales forecast?

No	Somewhat	Yes
1	2	3

6.   Does your plan allow you to attract and retain talented salespeople?

No	Somewhat	Yes
1	2	3

7.   Are you satisfied that your plan rewards top sales achievers for high performance?

No	Somewhat	Yes
1	2	3

Scoring Your Responses

Add the numbers in the boxes you checked. The total will be somewhere between 7 and 21. The scales below show your evaluation of your sales compensation plan:

          19 – 21:   Very effective
          16 – 18:   Above average effectiveness
          13 – 15:   Average effectiveness
          10 – 12:   Limited effectiveness
            7 – 9:   Not effective

the sales organization for (1) retaining and growing sales volume in current accounts and (2) booking sales with new customers. The challenge is to motivate and reward the sales force for profitable top-line growth. Often the biggest obstacle to doing so is overcoming the inertia associated with "annuity"-oriented compensation, particularly for plans that base a disproportionately high percentage of the variable compensation (80 to 90 percent) on reaching volume objectives tied to last year's sales: Perfect Flap's problem.

Profits

Increasingly, companies want salespeople to focus on profitable business. The availability of meaningful information about purchase transactions at the account level, and the intense pressure on operating profit margins in many industries, is motivating executives in many companies to examine the mix of business sold to customers. Selling the right mix of products may produce better profits, and therefore a key question to investigate is, Is the sales force motivated to sell and rewarded for selling the right mix of products?

Marshall Industries is a billion-dollar electronics distributor, headquartered outside Los Angeles. It was founded in 1954 on the simple idea "buy low and sell high," but its world became infinitely more complicated. Marshall continued to grow, says Rob Rodin, president and CEO, "but only through staggering manipulation and brute force."[1] And the bigger the company grew, the worse the problems became. As Rodin told *Fast Company* magazine, the problem wasn't inside the system; the system *was* the problem. "It made sense for one division to hide inventory from another; they were paid to compete. It made sense for salespeople to ship orders ahead of schedule or hide customer returns; they were paid to make their monthly numbers. The system persuaded good people to make bad decisions."

Rodin's solution: Eliminate all pay for performance. In 1992, he says, "we eliminated commissions, incentives, promotions, contests, P&Ls, forecasts, budgets, the entire functional organization chart." Everyone at Marshall, including the 600 salespeople and their managers, is now paid the same way and shares in a company-wide bonus pool. This means that while a salesperson cannot win big commission checks by landing a large account, his income does not plummet when the account goes elsewhere. And there's another benefit: The new system "encourages salespeople to invest months, even years, prying companies away from other distributors and turning them into Marshall customers." As one Marshall sales rep told *Fast Company,* "I can look out for the interest of the customer. I can take the long view. I can invest time with a new customer without worrying about paying my next gas bill."

CUSTOMER SATISFACTION

In the early 1990s, we found a large number of companies embracing the idea of rewarding employees for improvements in customer satisfaction. The tremendous interest in and recognition associated with the quality movement provoked the trend. The Baldrige Award acted as a lightning rod that focused top management's attention on achieving excellence in quality and customer satisfaction. Virtually every company we met with in those days was focused on quality and customer satisfaction, and the sales organization felt the impact. Many companies took aggressive action to implement sales management practices and changed their sales compensation programs to reflect the importance they attached to customer satisfaction. Companies actually paid their salespeople as much as 25 percent of their variable compensation based on improvement in customer satisfaction scores. Figure 2-2 summarizes the results of a groundbreaking study that The Alexander Group conducted on this topic in 1991.

While companies look to the sales organization as an integral player

Fig. 2-2. Rewarding the sales force for satisfying the customers: key findings among eighty-one companies representing fourteen industries on how quality and customer satisfaction affect sales force pay.

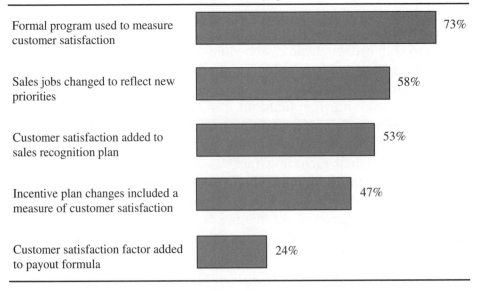

Formal program used to measure customer satisfaction	73%
Sales jobs changed to reflect new priorities	58%
Customer satisfaction added to sales recognition plan	53%
Incentive plan changes included a measure of customer satisfaction	47%
Customer satisfaction factor added to payout formula	24%

in sustaining and improving levels of customer satisfaction, a relatively recent update on the prevalence of paying sales incentive compensation based on customer satisfaction suggests that this trend may have peaked.[2] We have found (and other experts in sales compensation also report) that while the concept of paying the sales force based on customer satisfaction seemed attractive initially, the major stumbling block in doing so has been measurement. The difficulty of defining what "customer satisfaction" means and then measuring it so that it can be linked to the sales compensation process has discouraged companies from hardwiring it to the sales force's variable pay. Jim King, the director of sales at Boehringer Ingelheim, a marketer of ethical pharmaceuticals, told us he is not convinced customer satisfaction surveys are valid. He gave an example: "We can take a survey out to a managed care customer and ask, 'What do you think of Boehringer Ingelheim?' The response really depends on whether he has had any contact with Boehringer Ingelheim in his present position, and it depends on the latest contact. If we are having a lot of trouble signing a contract with them, they tend to—at least in my opinion—think that Boehringer Ingelheim are a bunch of clowns. If we give them a hard time on rebates, they think we're clowns. If we give them a lot of rebate money, and we're pretty easy to deal with, then we're great guys."

The net result is that today a smaller portion of pay—whether merit increases, special rewards, or incentive compensation—is tied to customer satisfaction because in many companies, the sales force, and in fact all customer contact personnel, have learned how to meet and exceed customer requirements.

SALES TALENT

In most companies, top management looks to the compensation plan to help attract and retain the caliber of people it needs in order to successfully sell to and interact with customers. A strong sales force is a major competitive advantage, especially in highly contentious markets—markets characterized by high product parity or markets in which all the major players offer about equally high levels of product quality and customer service. In such situations, your company's advantage is the relationship between the customer and the salesperson. As one executive told us, his company's objective in this type of competitive environment was to "shrink-wrap" the salesperson around the product offering so that a company employee became the source of differentiation. The sales compensation plan plays a pivotal role in attracting and retaining talented salespeople. Thus, a question to ask about a current plan is, Does it help the company hire and keep the right salespeople?

Sales Productivity

Today, most companies view their customers as "assets" of the business. Thus, investments in salespeople, who regularly interact with customers, are regularly reviewed for improvement. Three years ago, a sales job well done in a given industry produced $1 to $1.5 million in revenues. To justify that salesperson with today's smaller margins, two things have to happen: (1) Volume has to be higher, usually twice as much or more, and (2) the mix of business has to change, in terms of both what customers buy and which customers are addressed. If the salesperson's average productivity was $1.2 million a year, it now has to be $2.4 million to maybe $3 million with an improved product and customer mix. Otherwise you may get the volume, but not the better margins.

Moreover, the productivity issue is dynamic. Today, an entry-level person may have to produce $700,000 in sales while a senior salesperson may have to produce $2.5 million, but those numbers are not fixed. Each year they must rise by some significant factor if the company plans to continue investing in direct resources. Companies' management teams ask us what they should expect a salesperson to produce (a figure that varies by industry), and once we get the figure, they want to know if it stays set. The unhappy answer is no; it has to go up if no resources are added.

Five Reasons Why Sales Compensation Plans Fail

Experience shows that as the sales organization grows revenues and profits, the management challenges also grow. We have conducted considerable research involving many industries to identify the challenges management faces in sustaining productive, high-performing sales organizations.[3] Of particular interest to us has been the role that sales compensation plays in contributing to and sustaining sales force motivation and productivity. We find five indicators that suggest that a sales compensation plan is slipping into ineffectiveness. Let's consider these indicators relative to the situation that Hal Jones finds himself in at Perfect Flap Envelope Company.

1. The Sales Compensation Plan Does Not Support the Company's Business Objectives

In a recent study of human resources professionals, 81 percent of the respondents reported that their company had experienced some form of restructuring during the past three years.[4] They said they see improvements in leadership, productivity, customer satisfaction, and employee teamwork as a result of the restructuring efforts. Almost 91 percent of the respondents reported that their company's success was based on carefully linking its compensation programs to its business objectives. This study is the most recent of many we have seen over the years that makes a strong case for tying the achievement of business objectives to compensation. Why, then, is this the number one reason why sales compensation plans fail?

Our experience suggests that this failure results from a separation in business accountabilities. Typically, the people who write the business plan are not the people who execute the plan. The situation in which Hal Jones finds himself illustrates how this can happen. Jones's goals, as well as those of the product managers, are to grow revenue within the product categories and overall. Management tells Jones to grow the business and to deliver that growth based on a defined ratio of standard and customized product sales. Management tells each of the two product managers to realize sales growth in their respective product lines. However, the company rewards the sales force, for selling volume. The company has no explicit product mix objectives. And, equally important, the company does not reward the customer service representatives at all for their efforts when they make additional sales in the two categories. The compensation plan reflects a sales strategy prevalent in the early days of the business, when all volume was good volume and there was no customized product line. At Perfect Flap, as at many companies, while people come and go, programs and processes are slow to change. Too often we find that changes in the sales compensation plan lag behind the changes in business strategy and objectives by one to three years. The objectives change, but it takes a year or more to design and implement a new sales compensation plan that is in sync with the objectives. This appears to be the case at Perfect Flap.

2. THE SALES COMPENSATION PLAN DOES NOT REFLECT THE REALITIES OF HOW JOBS OPERATE WITHIN THE SALES AND CUSTOMER RELATIONSHIP MANAGEMENT PROCESSES

Increasingly, senior sales executives are asking their salespeople to channel their time and effort toward the high-value selling activities. To achieve this goal, it is essential to map the optimal process for selling to and interacting with customers. Such a mapping process makes it possible to clarify job roles and, therefore, identify the high-value selling activities that the compensation plan should direct, motivate, and reward.

In the Perfect Flap division, Jones has inherited a situation in which it is virtually impossible to effectively align compensation with the jobs that are interacting with the customers. For example, there is one primary sales job, the account executive position. Jones's field trip suggests that the company may need either multiple sales jobs or, at the very least, specialization within the account executive job. How Jones decides to segment, target, and assign customers—by size, by application, or by some combination of variables—will determine the types of sales jobs Perfect Flap needs and therefore the sales compensation.

Jones faces the additional challenge of integrating the customer service representative position into the sales and customer coverage processes. One alternative is to team customer service representatives with account executives. For example, he could assign three account executives to one customer service representative, and each account executive would share responsibility for customer accounts with the service rep. If the customer service representatives are responsible for retaining and expanding business with assigned customers, this arrangement offers the opportunity to recognize and reward their performance through a sales incentive compensation arrangement. However, Jones must make sure that the new "team-oriented" sales incentive compensation plan does not diminish the importance of individual effort and contribution to sales success. Our experience suggests that a major reason why sales team incentive plans fail is because the results of the team substantially outweigh individual contributions.

3. It Does Not Attract and Retain the People Required for Sales Success

A well-designed sales compensation plan is a powerful communicator of what your company values, in terms of both the types of business it goes after and the people it intends to attract and retain. Typically, a sales compensation plan fails a company when the skills required to be successful do not mesh with the company's definition of sales success. A common problem many companies face is how to find the right balance between rewarding salespeople for retaining and expanding business with current customers and motivating and rewarding the same salespeople for winning new customers. Too often, the sales compensation plan disguises the fact that the company rewards salespeople at a disproportionately high rate for retaining business with current customers and does not direct, motivate, or reward them for expanding the business by winning new customers for new business. When this happens over time, a salesperson's selling skills—particularly those needed to sell new accounts—actually atrophy; the salesperson becomes incapable of growing the business by selling to new customers. It is not clear if this is the case in Jones's situation.

4. IT DOES NOT LINK THE RIGHT MEASURES OF SALES PERFORMANCE TO INCENTIVE COMPENSATION PAYMENT

Over the years, we have conducted many studies to determine the characteristics of effective sales compensation plans. The studies consistently report that one of the most important elements of plan success is performance measurement. When we discover plan failure based on performance measurement, we find that (a) the company uses incomplete performance measures, (b) the company uses too few measures; (c) the company uses too many measures, or (d) some combination of the above.

5. IT CAUSES THE COST OF SALES TO INCREASE OVER AN EXTENDED PERIOD OF TIME

Today in most industries, top management wants sales executives to maintain or reduce the current level of selling expense. Often, management takes this stance because the firm has cut prices and, in turn, profit margins to gain competitive advantage. The company can cut selling expense in two ways. One way is to reduce head count. This is not an attractive alternative, particularly if the company views its customers as assets and its sales resources as an investment in those assets. Reduce the head count and the company risks dribbling away the assets. Another way is to carefully examine the company's buying/selling/customer service processes to determine whether there can be a more effective, cost-efficient way to engage with customers. We have found, and this book will show, that the second course is almost always possible.

CAN YOU FIX A FAILED SALES COMPENSATION PLAN?

In a word, no! Putting a fix on a current and failing plan will not, by itself, restore sales success. We find that in most cases the sales compensation plan has not caused poor sales performance. Rather, the sales compensation plan becomes the lightning rod for change because it reveals performance deficiencies.

Take a commission plan where the company pays a percentage of sales as a commission and pays it from the first dollar the salesperson brings in each year. Management comes to realize that this is not really a first-dollar commission plan. Not all the customers quit buying each year; the salespeople don't have to start fresh. In fact, the company is paying the salespeople an amount disproportionate to what they contribute. They are getting a percentage of every sales dollar, when they had to sell only perhaps 10 or 20 percent of the time. What the company really wants is to have the salespeople sell on the margin, sell to new customers or new buyers at existing customers, and sell more than the year before where selling makes a difference. So the first little tweak that companies usually make to their commission plans is to say, "Gee, we can't afford to be paying from first dollar," or "We're paying way too much in commissions and getting way too little return. We need to introduce some performance expectations."

That was the idea at Perfect Flap: The prior year's sales established the performance standard. The salespeople needed only to beat last year's gross sales figure to start earning their commission. The problem is that there is no relationship between the sales potential bonus and the territory. Perfect Flap may be beating last year's numbers but under-performing in Florida because it does not know the true sales potential. Similarly, it may be penalizing the superior sales representative in Nebraska who has a growing share of a shrinking market but is not beating last year's figures.

The next tweak we see is multiple commission rates for different types of sales. Management says, "We've got a broad product line, and some things are harder to sell than others. Let's put different rates on different products. And since that's such a good idea, we'll put different rates on different kinds of customers as well." In no time, the company has introduced serious complexity into the sales compensation plan. It becomes a menu—take one rate from column A, one from column B, one from column C—that encourages the salespeople to shop the plan. They sell whatever they feel comfortable selling, which usually is not what the company needs them to sell.

The final tweaks may be some percentage paid on profitability, and then a percentage paid for new accounts. All these little fixes lead to a more complex sales compensation plan and tend to create more problems than they solve. While it may be true that people tend to do those things for which they are rewarded, it is often a mistake to tie some pay mechanism to results the company demands.

The same thing is true with bonus plans. Usually such a plan pays a bonus for reaching a quota or some other goal the company establishes. But we find that bonus plans also run out of steam because management keeps trying to fix a business problem with an inappropriate tool. Management is trying to fix a sales problem with the compensation plan when it should deploy the sales resources differently, or establish sales specialization, or train, or do a combination of several things. The key is to make sure that the problem we're trying to fix is one that the sales compensation plan can correct and not one that we should remedy with something else, like deployment or sales specialization.

Typically we find that after a whole series of tweaks, someone from the outside or from some other part of the organization finally comes in and has the "Aha!" reaction. "Aha! We can keep tweaking this thing until we all grow old and die, but our problem is that we need to go to market differently, and tweaking the compensation plan is not the way to go to market." The company's difficulty is that it is not selling the way customers are buying, and tweaking the sales compensation will never change that.

True, it is relatively easy for top management to say, "Change the compensation plan!" Management often believes that changing the compensation plan will be faster and easier than any other approach, and that the changed plan will get more attention from employees. But we find that executives do not think the change's implications through. Modifying the compensation plan may be part of the solution to poor sales. We don't want to mislead readers; fixing the plan may be necessary. But we rarely find that repairing the sales compensation plan alone can solve a company's sales problems. Generally, a company that changes the compensation plan without making other significant changes finds management complaining a year later, "It's still not happening. We're still not getting the mix of business we want." They're not, because altering the compensation plan was an incomplete answer. Rather than tweak a plan, it is usually better to start with a new one.

Yet, like every generalization, that one has its exceptions. We occasionally find a situation where tweaking the compensation plan is the only fix necessary. A company we worked with recently had the right sales representatives in place; they were selling to the right buyers; but they were being compensated on only a single performance measure. The salespeople had the capability to influence more lines of business, but they had no incentive to do so. With a relatively small tweak to the compensation plan, the company was able to improve sales dramatically.

How to Help Your Company Make the Transition from a Failed Plan to a New Plan

Companies that make the transition from a failed plan to a new plan successfully do at least four things well.

1. Determine the Aspects of Sales Compensation That Are Not Working and Why

Before changing the sales compensation plan, management first looks for symptoms of the sales problem. Of those symptoms, management determines which ones are attributable to the compensation plan and which ones to something else. For example, one symptom may be excessive churn. Will the sales compensation plan help the company retain customers? Not if they are leaving because of poor product quality, late shipments, or inferior after-sale service. In this case, changing the compensation plan will not help retain customers.

Another symptom may be that there is no incentive to expand the business. Generally speaking, when sales compensation plans are out of whack, it's because they have only one measure—total sales volume—against which the sales representatives work, or they have inappropriate measures. Occasionally we come across a plan that has too many measures; one insurance company we worked with had seventeen sales performance measures.

The ideal is probably three correct measures for your situation. We sometimes find companies that have three measures, but two of them are wrong—for example, they relate to prior years. One of the three is invariably a volume measure. Once you set the volume, you've got two other slots to fill. One might once have been customer satisfaction, but that's no longer relevant. What is relevant today is what we call retention and penetration (R&P): retaining dollars in sales so that we don't have churn, and expanding dollars in sales with current customers. Some measure of R&P might be a very worthwhile way to break out a subset of volume, as opposed to using total volume. The third measure may be revenue dollars from new customer wins.

Specific aspects of the compensation plan that are not working are probably (1) the sales success measures, (2) the way the company determines or assigns goals or performance objectives, (3) the complexity of the plan, and (4) management's inability to manage. While setting goals is a performance management issue rather than a compensation issue, it often obstructs a plan's success. We hear managers say, "We have a very successful incentive plan on paper, but when it plays out in the organization, it doesn't seem to work because we don't know how to set goals." One manufacturer we worked with had that exact problem. On paper, the plan looked great, but management had no idea how to set goals at the salesperson level. If the plan is too complex—has too many measures, too much mechanics, too many qualifiers—neither the sales representatives nor sales management can know if they are doing what they are supposed to do.

Finally, when we find managers who do not know how to manage with the plan, it is usually because no one has ever taught them how to communicate the kind of selling behavior they expect and reward. Which brings us back to the managers' roles in how goals are set. A plan may not be working because managers have no role in it; it's all mechanical.

So the first thing you have to figure out is why the plan no longer functions properly. It may be that the plan was for a different generation, a generation that believed all business is good business and assigned generalists to geographic territories. But that's no longer the way that we must go to market.

2. Craft and Effectively Deliver an Inspirational Leadership Message Associated with the Need for Change

Too often, when a company implements a new sales compensation plan, the sales force observes that the plan being discontinued was the best the company ever had. Since it's probably the best plan we ever had, why are you changing it? Robert Digby, senior vice president of sales and marketing at Ceridian Employer Services, says that his company ran into this attitude: "We changed almost everything at the same time. We probably made more changes in two years than in the past twenty. And the toughest thing was not getting our sales reps to buy into the new program, but it was getting our middle managers—the ones they reported to, their supervisors—to buy in."

The Ceridian managers had been with the business for eight to fifteen years, and they felt comfortable and were successful with what they had been doing. Their attitude was, "We've always made quota. We're attaining our objectives each year. Why make these changes? Why change it?" Digby says, now that everyone is finally on board, that if he had to go through such a change again, "we would do a better job selling to the middle management. We actually thought we had to focus on the sales reps, and we felt that the middle management was 100 percent behind us. But some resisted to the degree they told the reps to go out and sell the old way; this was just another program corporate was push-ing. 'It's trendy,' they said. 'It'll be gone in a year. Don't worry about it.' "

Salespeople invariably assume that when you change their compen-sation plan, you do it only because you want to save money—by taking it out of their pockets. This is why management must craft and deliver an inspirational message on why change is needed. A compelling leader-ship message usually goes something like this:

> The plans we had in place in the past were the best plans for the past, but the past is not the present and it's not the future. We find that the way we have to do business with customers today is different from what we did in the past, and doing business differently with customers means that we've had to redefine the way we sell to and interact with customers. Therefore, we have to adjust how we reward to be consistent with today's business requirements.

Perhaps the company paid a modest salary and a high commission. That was a great plan when the market was fragmented, when there weren't many competitors, and when the market seemed to be unlim-ited and customers seemed price insensitive. In those days, almost all business was profitable business, and it did not make any difference where the salespeople chased buyers. Unfortunately, that no longer makes sense today.

> Today we have many more competitors, and customers have many more choices and are much more selective than in the past. We have to be much more focused; that is, we must select and target our pros-pects rather than promote and react to opportunities. If we change our sales coverage strategy from promote and react to target and select, we must also change the way we compensate for doing that well. We're trying to align rewards with success, and the definition of success has changed.

By the way, executives who don't understand the changes because they've never been in sales find it very difficult to deliver a compelling message to the sales organization. Few things can be more difficult than standing before the sales organization, having never sold to customers directly, and explaining why the company will pay them differently in the future. Such an executive lacks credibility with the salespeople. That's why the best person to deliver the message is usually a senior sales executive who came up through the sales organization in that company or some other company: someone who can relate to the sales organization and what they're experiencing.

3. Carefully Map Out the Process Used to Change the Compensation Plan and Communicate Likely Outcomes so All Potentially Affected Employees Can Prepare for the Change

This really means that the company is starting on a voyage of discovery with the changes it makes. Management may not know the definitive answer to how the company will compensate in the future. It may have some hypotheses about how the company will reach customers and prospects, but it must explore different options. To do that, it must involve the most knowledgeable people in the company so that it can predict the likely outcome.

We see this in companies when groups come together to do this planning. They say, "Here's the process we're going to use. We're going to develop some alternatives. We're going to test the feasibility of some of them. Maybe we'll do some proposed plan designs. And when we end up, we're probably not going to have a 100 percent commission plan." They tell salespeople that at the beginning. They say, "The plan we have today is probably not going to be the plan we have in the future." They start to prepare the salespeople for the change. Recently, when we started working with a company, we told the salespeople that they were going to be converted from 100 percent commission to a salary plus bonus. We had a pretty good sense of what the solution was going to be, but it took a year to ready the organization for the change—putting the systems in place, assigning the accounts, and measuring performance differently. To be successful, the company had to develop all the tools it needed and train everyone to use them before the transition. When it was time to throw the switch on the new program, it was ready and people were intellectually and psychologically prepared for the new plan.

We find psychological reorientation perhaps the single biggest issue in moving from an environment where the salespeople have a lot of pay at risk to an environment where they have less pay at risk. What defined success in the old days was a quick close and moving on to the next customer. Today, that may not be the kind of business we want our salespeople to chase after. They should be after higher-level business, and small accounts ought to be going through the telesales center.

During the transition period, individual sales representatives can compare what they're doing now with what they would be doing under the new system. That gives the company an opportunity to run parallel without pain. It is a disadvantage because the salespeople are not being rewarded for their new efforts. But it gives them a chance to begin to rethink how they're going to cover their market.

Take as an example an office products distribution company we worked with. Some 80 percent of the salespeople's business in the geographic territories came from small customers that were not profitably covered by a direct salesperson. They were much more effectively covered by telesales. We also discovered that the customers didn't want a salesperson to call; they wanted a phone number and a fax number. And we learned that these customers were not at risk. Competitors were not going after them, perhaps because they were so small. The company had to deliver a new message to the salespeople.

> Those are not the kind of customers you should be visiting. You can keep selling to them, but we're not going to give you any credit for the sales. They are not going to count toward the bonus in the new plan, so you had better start figuring out how to get into larger accounts with greater potential. We understand it will take longer to sell larger accounts, so we're going to put more compensation into the base salary to create a bigger safety net underneath you so you have the time to do that.

The reorientation is both psychological—shifting the person's mind-set—and physical—connecting the new mind-set to behavior.

Making the connection, getting comfortable with having made it, and finding the confidence to sell one or two levels higher in an account company may take a couple of months. It took about six months in one recent case for the salespeople to reorient themselves. But when they did, it was as if they started to pat themselves on the back, puff out their chests, and say, "We've got it!" They became confident and stopped calling on the small accounts, and sales began to zoom up.

4. Involve Multiple Functions in the Change Process, Typically Through the Use of Design Teams, to Gain Commitment to and Buy-in for the New Plan

When the company makes a major change, like revamping the sales compensation plan, it is important that it take time to prepare for and adjust to the new program. It must be clear that each key player contributes to the change process.

To do that, first pull all the key players together and charge them with the responsibility for aligning the business objectives with the way the firm pays sales and customer contact people. In other words, charter them to do something that's probably not being done, and point out to them that they all have a vested interest in achieving success because, without a profitable top line, everyone in the firm is at risk. This goes back to our definition of sales effectiveness: an *organization's* ability—not just the sales department's ability—to attract, retain, and expand business profitably with customers.

This means that everybody has a vested interest in making sure that all customer contact resources, and particularly the salespeople, are driving toward results that are consistent with the objectives we set for the business. The human resources people need to ensure that the company offers compensation competitive enough to attract the talent. The finance people need to ensure that what the firm sells is profitable. The marketing people need to ensure that the company's products and services are right for the market. And the sales department needs to ensure that salespeople call on only those customers they should call on, basically aligning the right resources with the best opportunities. Ideally, when we get a new plan in place, everybody should say, "Yes, that's consistent with what we're trying to do with the business."

SUMMING UP

A sales compensation plan often fails because it no longer directs, motivates, or rewards the salespeople for behaving in a manner that contributes to sales success. When the business environment changes, sales success requires redefinition; the definition, for example, is no longer simply volume. During periods of rapid business change, however, the sales compensation plan often remains the same. Management is afraid that the company will lose top-producing sales representatives, that the sales force will be confused over the business's direction, and that salespeople will lose motivation and productivity during the transition period. These are realistic concerns, but you can address them effectively through the right plan design and attention to effective change management.

Without an effective sales compensation plan, your company probably will not accomplish its marketing strategies and sales objectives.

One of the most effective ways you can increase sales profitably is through the compensation plan. Since successful salespeople are always in demand, a company with a poorly designed plan runs the risk that it will not be able to attract and retain the people it needs. A sound compensation plan must embrace the values and expectations of the people for whom it is designed.

Top management looks to the plan to contribute positively to five business outcomes: growth, profits, customer satisfaction, sales talent, and sales productivity. Plans fail because they do not support the company's business objectives; do not reflect the realities of how jobs operate within the sales and customer relationship management processes; do not attract and retain the people required for sales success; do not link the right measures of sales performance to incentive compensation payment; and cause the cost of sales to increase over time.

Tinkering with a failing sales compensation plan will not restore sales success because in most cases the plan is not responsible for poor sales performance. The tweaks that companies make tend to be a performance standard, multiple commission rates, or a percentage paid on profitability. A new bonus plan by itself will also not solve the sales problem as long as the issue is one of sales specialization, training, or account management.

To make the transition from a failed plan to a new plan, management must determine the aspects of sales compensation that were not working and why; craft and deliver an inspirational leadership message; carefully lay out the process that will be used to change the compensation plan and communicate likely outcomes so all affected employees can prepare for the change; and involve all relevant company functions in the change process, typically though design teams, to gain commitment to and buy-in for the new plan.

Once management understands the need for new sales roles and why compensation plans fail, the challenge becomes how to link compensation to new sales roles.

3

HOW TO ADOPT NEW SALES ROLES TO WIN AND RETAIN SATISFIED CUSTOMERS

Sales compensation plans do grow obsolete over time. Plan obsolescence is largely a function of the changes that take place in how customers buy or in the way they expect the purchasing process to work. This requires companies to rethink their processes for selling to and interacting with customers. This reexamination of the sales and customer relationship management processes often results in the company's defining and implementing new sales roles.

When a company wants to increase sales productivity and effectiveness, we encourage management to think first about the experience customers would like to have at the beginning of the buying process, during the sale, and after the sale through service delivery. To find out, we often ask customers, "How do you use the selling resource to help you make a purchase decision? What do you rely on the field salesperson or telesales person to do?"

If the customer says, "I would have a much better experience if I had no contact with salespeople at all," she is telling the company, "I don't need a salesperson to make a buying decision." She can use the Web site, EDI, fax, or phone.

If the customer says, "We've really come to rely on Marvin to determine replenishment and reorder points," she is saying that she likes the salesperson's presence, but she does not in fact need him. Determining reorder points may require a computer program. But company management must understand how customers make buying decisions and the role the firm's salespeople play in those decisions. If it turns out the customer does not need (or use) the salesperson, why apply selling where there's no selling to be done?

This exercise often leads to an understanding of the needs and business justification that require adopting new sales roles to win and retain satisfied customers. Consider the following sales situations, all of which resulted in companies' implementing a new sales role.

PC industry. Until Dell Computer Corporation came along, no other company had thought about selling personal computers over the telephone. In fact, at the time Dell launched its business, the PC world believed that the only way to sell this type of computer was through dealers or directly to corporate accounts. Nevertheless, telephone sales representatives, supported by an operationally excellent organization that can design, produce, and deliver a PC to a customer's specifications, have made Dell a leader in its market. Telephone sales and sales management, at the time and in this industry, were really new sales roles. Today many companies use Dell as a benchmark and imitate its successful use of those roles.

Office products and the superstores. The tremendous growth occurring in the small office/home office market has resulted in a continuous stream of new products—fax machines, copiers, telephone devices, and so forth—designed to help workers function more effectively alone or in small offices. To reach large numbers of buyers in this market, product manufacturers have elected to market their products through either the superstores (Best Buy, Circuit City) or the specialty office product retailers (Office Depot, OfficeMax, Staples). To optimize their opportunity to sell these products, many of which yield attractive profit margins, some retailers have deployed sales specialists during peak hours to help customers make the right product choice for their needs. For example, one retailer built a sales staff—professionally selected, trained, and managed—to operate as business machine sales specialists in a chain that had been founded on no-frills self-service. At the time, the sales specialist was a new role in this retail operation; the result was sales two times the rate of other retailers offering similar products.

Electronics components distribution industry. In a changing economy, the electronics components distribution industry is experiencing increased competition. Many distributors have discovered that their key customers frequently take up extensive sales staff time, for a variety of reasons: new design programs, new bids or rebids on current jobs, and so forth. The net result is that the best account executives often end up functioning by default as "account retention specialists." As such, they are not growing the business by opening new accounts. To address this problem, some companies in the industry created a new sales role, business development manager: an individual charged exclusively with opening new accounts. Once the account is up and running successfully, the business development manager passes the account to a geographic account executive, who is charged with maintaining and expanding the business. Although not a new-to-the-world sales role, when companies in this industry implemented the business development manager role, it contributed greatly to their sales growth.

Software industry. Although companies in other industries have used both direct and indirect channels for many years, the software industry is just learning how to optimize multiple channels with sales resources focused on those channels. The software industry has exploded in the last decade and become a part of nearly every "business solution"—as the language used, for the application involved, or as part of a business process. Companies in the industry have followed the traditional phases of growth, from start-up through optimization. Sales of "shrink-wrapped" software solutions have flourished in the retail setting (both bricks-and-mortar stores and teleweb). However, companies that develop applications and solutions for the business-to-business (B2B) market have found that the direct sales to the end user model is no longer sufficient. "Channel partners" such as system integrators (SIs) and independent software vendors (ISVs) directly influence the sale of software licenses through referrals and through customized or focused software solutions that use the original developer's software application. These channel partners require focused and specialized resources. As a result, software companies pursuing a strategy to increase license sales through partner channels are implementing channel manager jobs.

As these examples illustrate, changes in the sales compensation plan mechanics will not, by themselves, result in the greatest increase in sales productivity and effectiveness. Thus, it is important to understand when and why new sales roles emerge, the focus of this chapter, and how to design new compensation plans for the individuals who perform these roles, which we will cover in the next section.

Compensation Is the Caboose, Not the Engine

Because managers expect sales compensation to play an important role in linking the behavior of salespeople to the achievement of business objectives, they often expect too much from their sales compensation plan. However, as we frequently tell our clients, "the sales compensation plan is the caboose, not the engine." What we mean is this: The sales compensation plan cannot create a successful sales strategy. It can, however, be quite helpful in supporting the plan, or in reinforcing the direction of a sales strategy and communicating what that strategy is designed to accomplish.

When a company misses its sales targets, it is instructive to understand why those targets are being missed rather than jumping to the conclusion that the sales compensation plan is the culprit. Generally, changes have taken place in a business that motivated management to adopt new sales roles and that therefore require changes in sales compensation. The engine that drives the train is customer value. Our research shows that the top three things that customers value are:

- Business expertise and image
- Dedication to the customer
- Account sensitivity and guidance

Further, our research shows that in recent years, companies have changed their sales organization to improve the way it delivered value to the customer, because the sales organization is the principal way most business customers experience their relationship with a supplier. In our annual sales management survey, we ask participants to indicate why they made changes to their sales organization. The top three responses to that question are:

- To improve current customer coverage
- To expand capabilities to sell new products
- To expand into new markets

When we ask what they changed to increase their effectiveness in interacting with customers, they said they did the following:

- Added more specialized selling resources
- Introduced more value-added resources in the field (close to customers)
- Reassigned smaller customers to telesales coverage

These types of changes in interacting with customers are what create the need to redesign sales compensation plans. Our research on sales compensation practices regularly shows that change in sales compensation must logically follow changes in customer coverage. For example, not long ago, The Alexander Group conducted a survey of forty companies in the health care industry. Two-thirds of those companies had implemented sales teams to meet the needs of their strategically important customers more effectively. More and more positions, including various support functions in the business that interacted with customers on an ad hoc basis and that had not previously participated in incentive pay, became eligible for incentive pay as a result of membership on the sales team. The respondents indicated, in fact, that incentive compensation was becoming a more significant portion of both sales and service people's pay. While new members of the sales teams—that is, employees who were not previously part of the sales function—welcomed the opportunity to participate in an incentive pay plan, the hurdle management faced in this industry (and most others) was identifying the appropriate performance measures to use as the basis for earning incentive pay.

The Dartnell Corporation's *29th Sales Force Compensation Survey* provides additional insight into challenges faced by companies in getting the sales compensation plan to follow behind the engine of change. The survey included a supplemental section, to which 150 companies responded. Dartnell asked company executives, "What are the toughest sales compensation issues facing you over the next year?" Although the major response categories did not include issues related to job design and alignment of the sales compensation plan with the job, selected responses clearly indicated concerns in this area. Tough issues that the respondents identified included:

- Recruiting (attracting, enticing) qualified people
- Leveraging individual efforts with team efforts
- Ongoing reorganization

Overwhelmingly, however, responses focused on the details or mechanics of the sales compensation program, such as "striking the right balance between commission and base," rather than the alignment between the program and the job.[1]

As companies have discovered through trial and error, changing the compensation plan without giving proper consideration to how the firm should optimally deploy its resources to meet customer needs can result in both lost customers and a dissatisfied, unmotivated sales force. The fundamental objective of a sales compensation plan is to direct, motivate, and reward sales resources (field sales representatives, telephone account managers, dealer sales representatives) to sell to and interact with customers in a manner consistent with the company's business strategy. We have observed too often that the sales compensation plan is (sometimes unknowingly) the only principal business strategy statement. Consider the following comments made to us during the seminars we have conducted over the years:

Medical products company executive: "My sales reps don't seem to be calling on the CEOs/CFOs—the real buyers. How can I motivate them to do that?"

Consumer products company executive: "Our business success depends on effective category management; yet our account executives don't really understand it. How do I motivate our category managers to teach our account executives how to build effective business plans with key accounts when they aren't included in the incentive plan?"

Office products company executive: "We've built our business through a series of acquisitions; each company had its own sales commission plan when we acquired it, and we didn't change those plans. Now, with increased competition and declining margins, we find the sales force isn't selling to the right customers. While they're still making a lot of money, we're not growing as fast or as profitably as we could be."

Automotive tire company executive: "This has become an extremely competitive business; while unit sales are up, margins have declined. Our sales representatives who call on and work with our dealers are keeping their business; however, the company is not achieving its profit objective. Our compensation is not aligned with our goal to sell profitable business."

Two common threads run through these examples. First, the sales representatives treat what they are paid most for doing as synonymous with the business's objectives, whether or not they are in fact the same. In the case of the office products company, the firm's goal is clearly profitable growth. The plans for the salespeople, however, reward *volume*, which delivers the compensation the salesperson is comfortable with. The sales compensation plan does not include a measure that focuses salespeople on margin, and this measure is therefore invisible to them.

Second, in some cases the sales organization lacks the competencies or skills required for success in a new role—the selling that the business objective demands. Sales representatives in the medical products company are not comfortable calling on senior executives in customer accounts, and an incentive approach will probably not increase their comfort level. Recruiting people with the right skills and training current salespeople are keys to ensuring that the right competencies are available. The sales compensation plan cannot teach; it can only motivate and reward.

The Sales Strategy Matrix: An Essential Tool for Aligning Sales Jobs with Company Objectives

The four-phase growth model introduced in Chapter 1 provides a useful framework to help you understand the changes taking place in your market. Associated with each growth phase is a sales strategy. A sales strategy is simply a plan of action to win, retain, and expand business with customers. We have found it useful to express sales strategy in the form of a matrix, as shown in Figure 3-1.

One of the most common problems experienced by companies is the misalignment of business objectives and the selling behavior of the sales force and other company personnel who come in contact with customers. We have found the Sales Strategy Matrix a helpful tool to align the sales jobs with the company's business objectives. As Figure 3-1 illustrates, there are two variables: buyers and products. Buyers fall into two groups: prospects and customers. Products also fall into two groups: existing and new/additional in-line. This two-by-two matrix defines the types of selling opportunities facing a company in each quadrant of the matrix. The four selling opportunities are:

Retention selling. The objective of retention selling is to sell current customers current products on a reorder basis. The sales job is to successfully maintain the current revenue stream of business.

Penetration selling. Penetration selling involves maximizing the customer relationship by selling a broader range of products (new or existing) to current customers or selling more to customers within a current account.

Conversion selling. The objective of conversion selling is to get competitors' customers to switch to your company's products.

New concept selling. New concept selling is probably the most difficult; its objective is to attract new customers to the company by selling new products.

Fig. 3-1. Sales Strategy Matrix.

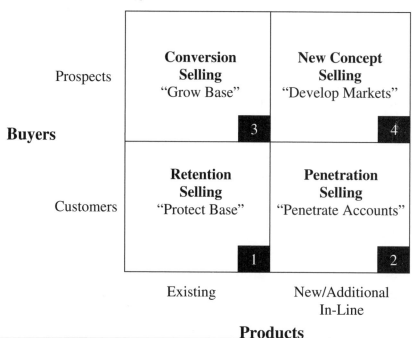

One of the principal values of the Sales Strategy Matrix is to provide a framework for understanding how much of a company's business is the result of each of the four types of selling. While every situation is individual, a company with virtually all of its business coming from retention selling—or from new concept selling, for that matter—is probably in trouble.

It is also possible to analyze how much selling resource and therefore sales expense is associated with current efforts to attract, retain, or expand the business. This understanding is important because all companies moving through the business growth cycle face a significant challenge. They must determine what type and how much of their resources to deploy in the sales organization, and the answers to these questions change over time. Different horizontal and vertical "slices" of the Sales Strategy Matrix define sales roles; and, particularly in phases 3 and 4 of the growth cycle, those roles are new to the company because of the increased need for specialization in selling to and interacting with customers.

As a company progresses through the growth cycle, its approach to sales and customer service must also evolve. That evolution offers the opportunity to implement new sales roles at each phase. Explanations of the possible strategies for each phase follow, as illustrated in Figure 3-2.

Start-up. In the start-up phase, company sales resources are typically deployed against the market opportunities defined by box 4 of the Sales Strategy Matrix: selling new products to prospects that have not bought from the company before. All companies at some point in their history are faced with the box 4 sales challenge—how to win new customers for either a product or a service that the customer has not previously

Fig. 3-2.   Horizontal and vertical "slices" of the Sales Strategy Matrix define "new" sales roles.

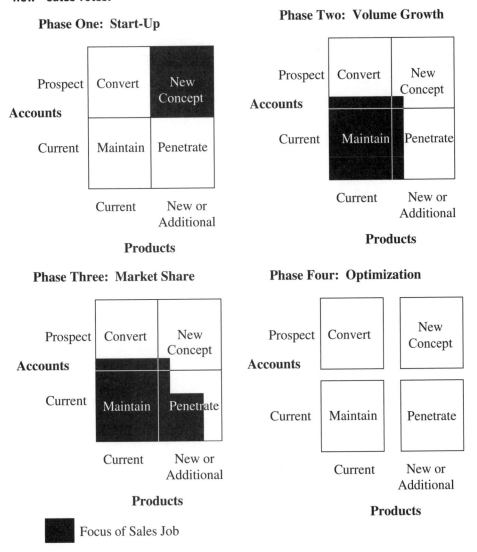

purchased from the company. Regardless of the sales resource—direct, geographically based field sales representative, dealer, telesales representative—the sales requirement is the same.

Volume growth. A company's success in the start-up phase leads to some interesting sales deployment challenges in the next phase, volume growth. New customers eventually become current customers, and along with the potential for a continuous revenue stream comes the responsibility to service these customers. Our research shows that the sales resource focus often shifts from box 4 to box 1, from "new market" to "maintain." This is obviously true when box 1 sales represent 60 to 80 percent of the business. It is typical for sales representatives to spend roughly the same percentage (60 to 80 percent) or more of their time with the existing customers. The result, assuming that only a single sales channel is being deployed, is that the company is not fully achieving sales opportunities because it is dedicating insufficient sales resources to boxes 2, 3, and 4.

Market share growth. At some point late in the volume growth phase or early in the market share growth phase, a company realizes the need for sales specialization. That specialization can take a number of different forms. It can, for example, be based on size; the firm assigns the largest customers to global or national account sales managers. Or it can be based on the application/solution associated with a product or service; the firm creates a product sales specialist or a solution sales specialist. In other cases, the specialization could be constructed around a market or industry; for example, the firm appoints a financial services industry sales representative to sell to banks and investment houses.

Optimization. In the optimization phase, management comes to realize that the only way it can address the diversity of sales opportunities available in the markets in which it competes is to organize multiple sales resources that are customer specialists. The firm defines and deploys new sales roles around the needs and complexities of doing business with these customers. During this phase, we see companies implement some very specialized resources, such as customer teams, retention specialists, new customer acquisition specialists (often referred to as business development account managers), and customer win-back specialists.

How Companies Deploy New Sales Roles

One of the most common questions we are asked by top managers is, What is the prevalence of the new sales roles defined through the use of the tools and practices described in your book? Shortly after the publication of the first edition, we initiated a study among fifty-three companies that designed 236 jobs as a result of applying the concepts, principles, and techniques described in our book. Using the Sales Strategy Matrix (see Figure 3-1) as a point of reference, we learned the following from these companies:

1. Our survey participants reported that they use four different types of selling roles, as defined by the cells in the Sales Strategy Matrix. Figure 3-3 shows the most prevalent selling role combinations and the priority companies attach to each respective role.

2. "Retention and penetration" sales specialist jobs were the most prevalent positions in our survey. We asked companies to report on their experience with various sales roles and the typical job titles used. Figure 3-4 shows the relative percentage of jobs by type of sales roles. This finding supports other research we have conducted that indicates that many companies expect to grow by retaining current customers and selling more products or services to buyers in those accounts.

3. Generally speaking, jobs that involve specialized sales roles receive higher compensation than those with a generalist role. Figure 3-5 reports compensation statistics for selling roles expressed in sales jobs. It shows that (a) using the job with C, P, and R roles as the baseline job, companies in our survey reported that two other jobs are paid more; and (b) these companies also indicated that the salary/incentive ratio varies by role/job, as does the "leverage," which was reported as significantly higher for jobs with the C & P and the C & NC roles.

Fig. 3-3. Prevalent selling role combinations.

Role*	Matrix Cells	Charter
C, P, & R	1, 2, 3	■ "Generalist" ■ #1 priority - incremental sales
R & P	1, 2	■ Retain customers ■ Achieve "add-on" sales
C & P	2, 3	■ #1 priority - gain new customers ■ Achieve "add-on" sales
C & NC	3, 4	■ #1 priority - gain new customers ■ "Missionary" selling

*Letter definitions: R = Retention selling; P = Penetration selling; C = Conversion selling; NC = New marketing selling

Fig. 3-4. Job titles.

Role	Per Cent of Jobs	Prevalent Job Title
C, P, & R	31%	■ Sales Representative
R & P	34%	■ Account Manager ■ Customer Manager
C & P	13%	■ Major Account Manager
C & NC	10%	■ New Business Developement Mgr. ■ Sales Manager
Other	12%	NA
	100%	

During conversations with our participants about their responses to the survey questions, we were told that the Sales Strategy Matrix was one of the tools they relied on to determine how to "charter" new sales jobs or redefine current jobs. Also, in multidivision companies, we were told that it provided top managers with a basis for comparing how the use of sales roles varied as a function of different sales strategies. This latter point is what motivated us to include the survey findings in this edition of the book. When you consider defining new sales roles at your company, the companies in our survey provide you with an initial basis for comparison and external practice.

THE FIVE W'S FOR CREATING NEW SALES ROLES IN YOUR COMPANY

One of the highest compliments we have received was from the president of a company, who said, "You brought order to the chaos we were

Fig. 3-5. Relative compensation practices.

Role	"Indexed" TTC (Relative to CPR Role)	Prevalent Salary /Incentive Ratio	Leverage
CPR	100%	80/20	1.5:1 to 2.0:1
R&P	90%	70/30	2:1
C&P	108%	60/40	3:1
C & CN	113%	50/50	3:1

experiencing in the coverage of our customers.'' Essentially, what we suggested for that company (and what we suggest to all companies as they progress through business growth) was that it proactively define new sales roles to match the requirements of the growth phase it was in at that time. This is important because without clear, well-defined sales roles, a company runs the risk of not attracting and retaining the people it needs in order to create and sustain differentiation in selling to and interacting with customers.

To help companies define or clarify new sales roles as they move from one phase to the next in their business growth, we developed a simple template that addresses the ''who, what, where, when, and why'' of the buying, selling, and customer service processes. Table 3-1 illustrates this template.

We find that some managers are initially skeptical about this approach to describing new sales roles. The approach is so compelling and free of the jargon too often associated with consulting processes, however, that we've discovered that they usually wind up using it. It is, after all, a quick and simple way to communicate to the organization why it needs new sales roles and what they are to do.

To clarify or define new sales roles in your company, you should start with all of the facts a journalist would include if he or she were writing up a news event. Figure 3-6 is a helpful start. Like many executives, perhaps you have concluded that the sales representative is no longer the single point of contact for doing business with customers. Everyone in your company has customer contact responsibility, and, in some cases, employees working inside the company are essential to the continued success of the business relationship with those customers. There is a need to crystallize and visualize the process of how the com-

Table 3-1. Blueprint for defining new sales roles: the five W's.

Question	Factor	Range of Answers
Who	Customer	More sophisticated Multiple levels
What	Type of offering	Product/service Commodity/solution
Where	Location of channel	Direct/indirect
When	Sales process	Sales cycle Frequency of decisions
Why	Buying criteria	Price Value

Fig. 3-6.   Spectrum of the five W's.

⬅────────────────────────────   ───────────────────────────────➡

Administrative or Individual Buyer	*Who*	Executive Decision Maker or Team
Commodity	*What*	Outsourced Solution
Telephone Orders, Retail Transactions	*Where*	On-site Business-to-Business
Frequent Small Transactions	*When*	Infrequent Large Transactions
Price	*Why*	Value

pany sells to and interacts with customers so that each employee is committed to the role that he or she plays in the process. Using the five W's can help you accomplish this. You need to describe all five elements:

1. *Who* the customer is, preferably by name and position (CFO, vice president of engineering, plant manager), not simply by account or company name
2. *What* your offering is
3. *Where* customers can purchase your products or services: the sales channel(s) used to access customers and transact business with them
4. *When* customers buy and how frequently they make purchases
5. *Why* a customer should purchase your products or services: your value proposition

Laying out the sales process in this manner should answer all of the basic questions a customer might ask about how to do business with your company. It therefore provides you with the insights to match the right sales resources—sales roles—to the needs of both the process and your customers.

USING THE FIVE W'S TO GET RESULTS: A CASE EXAMPLE

We assume that your goal in reading this book is to learn how your firm can improve its business results by better understanding how to relate compensation to new sales roles. Because companies are in different phases of the business growth cycle, it is instructive to use a case example so that we have a common information base to which to apply the five W's. For this, we are going to use Silver Arch Forms Enterprises (a fictitious name but a real company) to illustrate how both the Sales Strategy Matrix and the five W's can help you describe new sales roles in your company.

THE SALES CHALLENGE

As he looked out across the desert horizon from his Phoenix sales office, John Stevens, vice president of sales for the Southwest region of Silver Arch Forms Enterprises (SAFE), felt good about his latest results. "This has been a good year," he thought. "O'Brien will do cartwheels when she sees these 2000 sales numbers." As John closed the third quarter report, Margaret O'Brien, SAFE's national sales manager, passed John's door. "Maggie!" John shouted. "Come get a look at these numbers. With the bonus I'm delivering you this year, you'll be able to buy back the Cardinals and bring them home."

"That football team hasn't won a thing since they came to Phoenix anyway," said O'Brien as she walked into John's office. "And with the news I just got, you may want to save your sales for January."

O'Brien had just spoken with SAFE's president and CEO, Philip Plimpton, about the company's 2001 sales goal. "He gave me some of that corporate babble about stockholders and return on investment," said O'Brien, "and then he laid a $1.5 billion sales goal on me! That's up 25 percent from this year . . . and we'll do well to make this year's number!"

John joked about squeezing water from a stone, but O'Brien was in no mood to joke and was rushing out to get her flight back to St. Louis. On the way to the airport, she called John to voice her appreciation for the year he was having. "You do another $350 million, plus 50 percent next year, and I'll give you your own football team," said O'Brien, knowing that she would need John to have a great 2001 for her to reach $1.5 billion.

After O'Brien's call, John began thinking what his region's sales goal would be if SAFE had to do $1.5 billion in 2001 . . . and he didn't like the numbers he came up with. His region had been having a good year—in fact, the best year since he had been promoted to vice president of sales for the Southwest four and a half years ago. He knew that in a few weeks O'Brien was going to give him and the other four regional vice presidents their 2001 sales goals. "Now I know why they never ask us for our input," thought John. "The regional VPs would never volunteer $1.5 billion."

COMPANY BACKGROUND

Silver Arch was founded in 1948 by a sister and brother from Missouri, Phyllis and George Clemens. The company began to thrive in the mid-1950s, and built a reputation in the Midwest as a quality producer of a variety of business forms. Phyllis handled the creation and production of the forms, and George did the selling. In the early 1960s, George attended a trade show on the future of the forms business. There he met a young entrepreneur, Roberto Martinez, who sold George on an idea.

Roberto believed that American business was "fed up with you and all your forms." He told George that growth in the forms business was going to slow down once technology took off, and that new ideas would be needed if the Clemenses were going to continue to grow their business. Roberto proposed a new service for Silver Arch: document storage and record keeping. "Essentially," said Roberto, "the business will remotely store documents electronically that aren't needed regularly. When someone needs a stored document, you'll retrieve it and send it to the customer."

Roberto believed that this service would eliminate thousands of file cabinets in government offices and large companies, and would free employees to spend their time on more valuable work than moving old files and archiving unneeded documents. In return, companies would pay for each document stored and a monthly storage charge.

In 1962, Phyllis and George Clemens were persuaded by Roberto Martinez and made an agreement that changed Silver Arch Forms Enterprises forever. Roberto joined the company, and growth in Silver Arch's document storage business in the 1960s shot up faster than an Apollo rocket.

Over the next thirty years, the business grew to become a billion-dollar corporation. Silver Arch's core business became document storage and record keeping. In the mid-1980s, the U.S. Supreme Court ruled that film document reproductions were acceptable as court evidence, and this contributed to the growth of the electronic document storage business. Silver Arch divested itself of the forms business because of declining margins and slow market growth and concentrated on document storage. The company had national distribution, with an account base of over 900 customers. In 2000, revenues were expected to be $1.2 billion. SAFE had over 8,000 employees in thirty-two offices (primarily sales and local operations). Headquarters remained in St. Louis, where most functions were centralized, including finance, human resources, and marketing. Regional sales and operations offices were in New York, Atlanta, Phoenix, San Francisco, and St. Louis.

PRODUCTS AND SERVICES

In 2000, SAFE's core product was a relatively manual, paper- and electronic-based document storage service. Typical contracts (which were renewed annually) called for SAFE to provide the following:

- Document pickup
- Document indexing
- Document storage (which could include electronic media, microfilm, paper copies, or any combination thereof)
- Document retrieval on demand (i.e., companies would call an 800 number to request specific paper copies of documents)

Customers pay SAFE based on two types of fees:

- Processing fees per new document (i.e., the number of picked up, indexed, and retrieved pages)
- Storage based on the volume of documents stored and document format (paper, microfilm or both)

Annual revenues per customer range from $100,000 to $10 million, with most accounts generating between $500,000 and $1,500,000 in revenue. With some customers, up to 85 percent of SAFE's revenues are storage charges.

SAFE offers multiple "value-added services" on top of the plain vanilla offering (e.g., reporting services relative to retrieval, consultative document management services, and the like). The add-on services have been very lucrative for SAFE—they produce 10 percent of revenues and 13 percent of profits—and management is looking into ways to expand this market. In 2000, Margaret O'Brien estimated that 88 percent of SAFE's sales revenue would come from a version of the traditional business (excluding value-added services). Although 2000 was shaping up to be a good year, O'Brien knew that the market wasn't growing as quickly as it had in the late 1990s, and that it was only a matter of time before SAFE's traditional product could no longer meet the company's growth goals.

In 1997, SAFE had introduced an automated document retrieval system called SARS (Safe Automated Retrieval System) 1000. The system is computer based and offers customers on-line, real-time document retrieval. In addition to providing document pickup and storage services, SARS 1000 gives customers immediate access to all their stored documents. The system requires a significant investment in computer hardware and software for the user (up to $100,000). In 2000, SAFE introduced a more powerful version of SARS called Document Flash, which has on-line storage capability in addition to retrieving documents.

Sales for SARS 1000 have been disappointingly slow. O'Brien had forecast $50 million in sales for this product in 2000 (by converting fifteen existing buyers and selling ten new customers), but actual sales were projected to be only $20 million. Strong sales of the traditional product, and another good year in the Southwest, looked like they would get O'Brien to her goal. But O'Brien knew that her future success was tied to SARS 1000.

Business Objectives

In 1983, Silver Arch made its initial public offering (IPO), and officially changed the name of the company to SAFE, Inc. After thirty-five years as a family-held business, SAFE quickly became a hot stock on Wall Street. On the one-year anniversary of SAFE's IPO, the Supreme Court ruling sent the company's stock soaring to $40 per share, 250 percent of its initial price.

Since the company went public, SAFE has promised stockholders 20 percent earnings growth. It has met this goal every year except 1995. That was the year Phyllis Clemens retired as CEO and chairman of SAFE. Pushed by Wall Street analysts, SAFE hired an outside executive, Philip L. Plimpton, to replace Clemens. Plimpton wasted no time putting his mark on the company, reorganizing the management team and cutting costs throughout the organization. The field sales organization was reduced from eight regions to five (at that time John Stevens gained responsibility for southern California as part of the Southwest), and Margaret O'Brien was put under increased pressure to grow the business's top line.

Plimpton's objective was to grow profits 8 to 10 percent in 1999, 2000, and 2001. He knew he met his goal in 1999, based on the cost cutting completed in 1997–98 and the company's record of retaining 83 percent of its customers. In 2000 and 2001, however, Plimpton was counting on revenue growth of 25 percent each year, for $1.5 billion and $2 billion goals, respectively. Plimpton believed that the market for his traditional document storage services was mature and fully penetrated. Since he felt that growth in the traditional business was flat, he believed that SAFE needed new product sales (e.g., the SARS 1000 and the Document Flash product being introduced in 2000) and value-added services to meet his revenue goals. In addition, Plimpton was not convinced that the sales and marketing organizations had used effectively the available distribution channels, which will be necessary in order to reach these goals.

SOUTHWEST REGION

John Stevens is one of the rising stars of SAFE. First as an account executive and now as a vice president of sales in the Southwest, he has consistently exceeded the goals the company has given him. Plimpton is impressed by John's ingenuity and willingness to try new ideas.

John's organization consists of fourteen account executives and sixteen service representatives in six offices. His account executives average ten years of industry experience and are very knowledgeable on traditional document storage services and the marketplace. John feels that his account executives are very good at building relationships with midlevel managers and department heads. John and his organization have been particularly effective in retaining customers, which he believes is the key to his success. John is so committed to this strategy that he has established on-site service for his largest customers. His is also the only region that has more service representatives than account executives. John is concerned, however, that his sales organization has sold only five SARS 1000 systems.

John's market is large in comparison to other regions, by both customer numbers and sales revenue. With the addition of the Los Angeles, Orange County, and San Diego territories, John estimated sales of $350 million (versus a goal of $310 million) in 2000 on a base of 253 customers. Many of his customers are government agencies, law firms, and financial services companies. Unlike the vice presidents of the other regions, John proactively targets specific industry accounts. Of John's 253 customers, many represent a single site or department. In 2000 his region lost only 21 customers, most of whom generated less than $1 million in revenues.

As John thought about the sales target O'Brien would give him for 2001, he wondered how she would determine the final number. He figured that he would be penalized for having a great 2000 and be asked to do more than his fair share in 2001. "I've got to figure out a better way to deploy my people," John thought, "not only to increase their sales productivity but to improve the sales of the new products and services."

FIVE STEPS FOR INITIATING PRODUCTIVE NEW SALES ROLES

The situation John Stevens faces is not unusual. Successful sales executives are always being challenged to do more. Often this means finding new ways to do business more productively with current resources. What worked for John in the past may not work for him in the future, assuming that the growth opportunity that SAFE's marketing people estimate and O'Brien assigns to him is realistic. Faced with this situation, what should John do? We suggest a five-step process that will help him determine how he can organize his resources differently to achieve growth.

STEP 1: FORMALIZE THE SALES STRATEGY AND QUANTIFY THE SALES OPPORTUNITIES THAT EXIST

The breadth and depth of SAFE's product line and the size of the geographic market that John's organization must cover requires a clear sales strategy, one that defines the sales opportunities in the context of this type of business. John should start with the generic Sales Strategy Matrix (Figure 3-1) and customize it to SAFE's specific sales situation. Figure 3-7 illustrates the result of that effort, which is described below.

Customizing the axes of the Sales Strategy Matrix. As we described earlier, the x-axis of the matrix defines a company's offering (products or services), and the y-axis defines the buyers (current customers and prospects). SAFE's situation suggests a need for a Sales Strategy Matrix a bit more comprehensive than the typical two-by-two matrix because of the scope of the products and because at current accounts there are sales opportunities for both existing and prospective sites. The result is a much more complex sales and service question facing SAFE and its sales managers.

Box 1: Retention selling. Box 1 is concerned with retaining sales of all products and services in current account sites. SAFE can take two actions to sustain this business: First, it can assure a high quality of service delivery—on time, complete, and responsive—so that current customers are not motivated to cancel or reduce service because of operational deficiencies. Second, it can maintain close contact with these customers—relationship management—to understand how changes in the ways they are doing business may require either new solutions or new responses on SAFE's part.

Boxes 2 and 3: Penetration selling. For box 2, John and his managers should estimate the additional business they could get from selling additional storage and processing services and value-added services to their current accounts. However, as Figure 3-7 indicates, there are actually two types of penetration sales available to SAFE. The first (box 2) is user penetration selling, selling more storage and processing and value-added services to the current buyers at the current sites. The second (box 3) is account penetration selling, selling both core products and services to new buyers, that is, new sites in the current accounts.

Box 4: Conversion selling. Box 4 represents the sales opportunity available to SAFE as a result of selling its current products and services to prospective accounts—targeting its competitors' accounts and winning new sales to companies that are already familiar with the current products and services offered.

Boxes 5 and 6: New concept selling. Boxes 5 and 6 are concerned with new concept selling, selling something to a customer or a prospect

Fig. 3-7.   Sales Strategy Matrix customized to SAFE's sales opportunies.

that the customer or prospect has not previously bought. In SAFE's situation, there are actually two types of new concept selling opportunities. Box 5 defines the opportunity to sell SARS 1000 to customers that are using the current core or traditional SAFE storage and processing products. Box 6 is concerned with the opportunity to sell SARS 1000 and Document Flash to new sites within current accounts or to prospects (accounts that have not done business with SAFE).

Step 2: Map Out the Sales Process Associated with the Different Products/Services and the Roles of Current Sales and Service Personnel in the Process

Too often, managers assume that the sales process associated with retaining and expanding business is the same with all customers. Of course this is not the case. SAFE has at least three different sales processes that it applies to its products and services. Figures 3-8, 3-9, and 3-10 illustrate these processes.

Core products sales process (Figure 3-8). In mapping out the sales process for SAFE's core products, John Stevens and his sales staff determined that an eleven-step process was required in order to win new customers for the current core products. An account executive (AE) leads the process, and later steps (steps 10 and 11) require a service representative (SR) to be involved. Successfully delivering SAFE's services on an ongoing basis (step 11 in the process) earns the account executive the opportunity to do account penetration selling.

Value-added services sales process (Figure 3-9). John and his salespeople determined that once an account is up and running, the service representative is the SAFE employee most likely to identify opportunities to sell value-added services. Figure 3-9 shows the steps associated with that process. The steps logically follow from the work that a service representative does in step 11 of the core products sales process, and therefore the value-added services sales process could be thought of as a subset of activities related to step 11.

New product sales—SARS 1000 and Document Flash (Figure 3-10). Through careful examination of accounts where SAFE had successfully sold its new products and services, John and his staff learned that the sales process was really quite different from the process they used to sell the core products. For example, the sales process required more meetings, the involvement of both the account executive and the service representative throughout the process, and a systems trial before the customer would make a final commitment to do business with SAFE.

Fig. 3-8. SAFE's core product sales process.

Step 3: Use the Five W's to Determine If the Sales Process Requires Different Sales Roles

Using the five W's defined earlier in this chapter, John and his sales staff determined answers to each of the five questions for SAFE's three product categories. Table 3-2 summarizes the results of that exercise. For example, the basis for making a buying decision, the "why," differs for each offering. For the core products, the "why" is price and respon-

Fig. 3-9. Value-added services sales process.

Fig. 3-10.   SARS and Document Flash sales process.

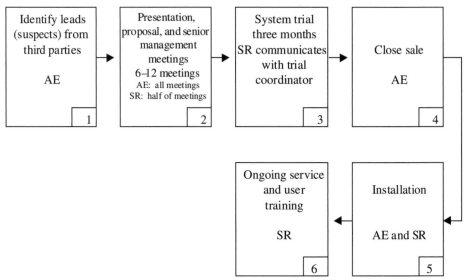

Table 3-2.   Applying the five W's to SAFE: current state.

	SAFE Product/Service Offering		
Questions	*Core Products*	*Value-Added Services*	*New Products: SARS and Document Flash*
Who (buyer/ customer)	Administrative manager (e.g., facilities manager)	Administrative manager (e.g., facilities manager)	Chief information officer or chief financial officer
What (type of offering)	Commodity	"Time-saver" service	Solutions
Where (sales or service channel used to do business with the buyer)	On-site SAFE service representative or account executive	On-site SAFE service representative or account executive	Senior sales managers
When (frequency of transactions)	Continuous (daily or weekly)	Continuous (daily or weekly)	4 to 18 months
Why (basis for making buying decisions)	Price and responsiveness	Ease of use and price	Cost savings and accessibility

siveness; for the value-added services, it is ease of use and price; and for the new products, it is cost savings and accessibility.

STEP 4: DETERMINE THE GAPS THAT EXIST BETWEEN THE CURRENT SALES PROCESS AND THE DESIRED SALES PROCESS

As a result of their analysis, John and his salespeople began to see some gaps between how they were selling and the opportunities to sell more identified in the Sales Strategy Matrix. They identified several shortcomings in their current practices:

- Service representatives were instrumental in maintaining contact with current accounts, although account executives were also involved in this type of work. John wondered if this lack of role clarity was contributing to the less-than-satisfactory performance in customer retention—85 percent retention compared to best practices in the range of 90 to 92 percent.
- Account executives may not have the skills and experience necessary to sell SARS 1000 products and services to the identified buyers, senior executives.
- Account executives may be stretched too thin across the number of selling activities and opportunities step 1 identified.

STEP 5: FORMULATE AND IMPLEMENT NEW SALES ROLES

John and his staff concluded that the current configuration of jobs—account executive and service representative—was no longer an appropriate way to address the sales opportunities they identified as available to them. To grow the business in the future, they concluded that they would have to specialize their resources. This would require new sales roles. These include:

Account executive. The account executive's job should be changed to focus on new account core product sales, with a secondary emphasis on selling SARS 1000. This will allow the account executive to spend less time on postsale service and SARS 1000.

Account manager. An account manager would focus on developing current customers. This position will allow SAFE to successfully penetrate current users (user penetration) and expand to new sites within customer accounts (account penetration).

SARS 1000 specialist. A SARS 1000 specialist position should be created to concentrate on selling this sophisticated product to new customers and penetrating large accounts with SARS 1000. The SARS 1000 specialist will both drive and support sales (for opportunities uncovered by the account executive or account manager).

SARS system support specialist. The SARS system support specialist should assist the SARS specialist with presale technical support.

Service representative. The service representative position should focus on servicing only core product customers. The service representative's new emphasis will minimize account executive involvement in servicing the core product. Additionally, the service representative may focus on expanding high penetration accounts independently and supporting the account manager on expanding low penetration accounts.

SARS installation manager. An installation manager position should be created that will allow one group of technical experts to install both SARS 1000 and the core product and to service the SARS product. This change will relieve account executives and service representatives of responsibility for SARS 1000 installation.

Once John clearly understood the sales opportunities that existed and had mapped out the sales processes necessary to sell the different products and services, it was not difficult to establish the gaps that existed between what the salespeople were doing and what they needed to do in the future. John was also able to see exactly what new sales roles were necessary if he was to accomplish his mission. He could not continue to deploy his salespeople as he had in the past, no matter how successful they had been. SAFE had changed, customers had changed; it was time for new sales roles.

NEW SALES ROLES IN AMERICA'S BEST SALES FORCES

The SAFE case illustrates the techniques and tools you could use to define new sales roles in your company. You may wonder, however, just how prevalent new sales roles are in business today. One indication of the rate at which companies are introducing new sales roles may be found in *Sales & Marketing Management* magazine's annual survey of top sales forces. In June 2000, the magazine announced its selection of the top twenty-five sales forces in America. Six of the companies profiled in the article—Dell, Cisco, Hewlett-Packard, Enron, UPS, and Wellpoint—

all known for their world-class sales organizations (or they would not have made the list in the first place), made changes in the various sales roles in their companies. And for the most part, these are new sales roles (see Table 3-3). Successful companies are continuously working to identify and implement new sales roles in their organizations in order to retain and enhance their competitive standing with customers. As the magazine suggests, even the best change.

SUMMING UP

The sales executive, like John Stevens, who faces what seems to be an unreasonably high sales quota cannot simply do more of the same. Often the sales organization is working flat-out; there is no more water to squeeze from this particular stone. What you must do is first understand the customer's buying process and the company's four selling opportunities: retention, penetration, conversion, and new market selling. These opportunities change as the business moves through the growth cycle. For a brand new business, there is no retention selling because there has been no selling at all. For a mature business, there may be little new market selling because the company has no new products (which may be another kind of red flag for top executives). Moreover, the different kinds of selling demand different sales personalities, different training, and different compensation. Without clear, well-defined sales roles, the company runs the risk that it will not attract and retain the salespeople it needs to meet management's growth objectives.

To see how the sales resources may be organized differently, we suggest a five-step process.

1. Formalize the sales strategy and quantify the sales opportunities that exist.
2. Map out the sales process required to sell different products/services and the roles of current sales and service personnel in the process.
3. Use the five W's—who, what, where, when, and why—to determine if these sales processes require different sales roles.
4. Identify any gaps that exist between the current sales process and the desired sales process.
5. Formulate and implement new sales roles to fill the gaps.

The sales executive who takes these five steps is now in a position to take advantage of the company's sales growth opportunities.

Table 3-3.   America's best sales forces as judged by *Sales & Marketing Management* **magazine.**[1]

Company	"New" Sales Roles
Cisco Systems (Co-winner with Northwestern Mutual)	Cisco leverages the internet and other technology solutions to increase the productivity of all its customer-facing resources. Sales people are an integral part of customer solutions. In order to free up the sales people from day-to-day administrative tasks, most orders are placed via the Web. The Web is also used as a learning tool for sales people, with customized home pages and e-learning paths.
Dell Computer Corporation	Dell is listed as one of the "best at e-business", and now teaches other companies how to succeed in e-commerce. Viewed as a telesales operation, 70% of Dell's business comes from corporate customers. The key to Dell's sales success is an integrated customer coverage model that uses the Web, catalogues, inside/outside sales rep teams and corporate account sales specialists
Enron Energy Services	In 1999, Enron was #1 in "America's Best Sales Forces". The company has instituted a focused and sophisticated sales process of up to 12 months. The sales job has evolved to an executive level seller focused on long term success and multi-year contracts.
United Parcel Service	With a focus on growth, the UPS sales force has achieved outstanding results. While the sales role is not "new", the use of new technology tools has enabled the sales person to spend more time with the customer. The company has also instituted a "sales leads" program that rewards drivers for bringing in leads for new business.
Wellpoint Health Networks	This health care company manages channel conflict through two sales forces: one focused on individual/small group sales, and another on large group sales. The managers of the small group sales people work with the traditional independent agents. They use the Web as an enabling tool with the agents, rather than as a replacement for agents.
Hewlett-Packard	While this company did not make the list this year, it has instituted aggressive changes to improve performance. One significant change is a move from a product-centric sales force to a customer-centric sales force. The customer will be able to deal with one HP resource, rather than the multiple sales forces and organizations it had to work with in the past.

[1] *Sales & Marketing Management,* "America's 25 Best Sales Forces", June, 2000

PART 2

DESIGNING COMPENSATION PLANS FOR NEW SALES ROLES

4

A BLUEPRINT FOR LINKING COMPENSATION TO NEW SALES ROLES

Once management recognizes the company's need for new sales roles, it must redesign current jobs or create new ones. Doing so offers the company the opportunity to link the new jobs to the sales strategy. A key challenge in making that link, however, is how to modify or formulate compensation plans for those employees who must assume new roles or new jobs. It is always difficult to modify compensation for at least two reasons.

First, management has many different compensation alternatives, particularly in the incentive pay area, from which to choose. Developing the best plan requires specialized expertise in plan design and consensus among top managers on what behavior they want to encourage and what results will count as success in the new sales environment. We often see the inability to gain consensus around these points prevent a company from implementing a new compensation plan quickly.

Second, top management is always concerned about making—indeed, is often afraid to make—a significant change in the way the company pays employees, particularly salespeople. As we noted in the last chapter, salespeople frequently tell us, "The best plan this company ever had was the plan before this one." "This one" is the current, newly implemented plan. Notwithstanding all of the hoopla about the risk-taking, roll-the-dice nature of salespeople, the fact is that they, like all other employees, do not like change. And a change in how the firm pays a salesperson affects that salesperson's basic need for survival and security. When management changes a salesperson's compensation plan, the change invariably influences the person's cash flow. This can be a frightening experience for anyone, but it can be particularly so for a salesperson who has a third to a half of his or her W-2 compensation tied to an incentive plan.

Most salespeople have developed a "mental capital investment" in their current compensation plan. They understand what they must do and how they must do it in order to be paid well under the plan. Altering the pay plan requires them not only to think differently about what they must do to be successful, but also to figure out how to do it. A new plan usually means they must write off their mental investment in the old plan.

The process we described in Chapter 3 offers a logical and proven framework to follow when you find it necessary to define new sales roles. As SAFE efficiently implements its new roles, it has the opportunity to meet its most important business objective: the profitable, compounded sales growth that is necessary to achieve the return-on-investment goal management has promised to shareholders. The pay plan for these new jobs, however, is not the same plan that SAFE used in the past.

Our experience shows that compensation plans once considered entirely effective by managers often result in behaviors that are inconsistent with current strategies and objectives. Indeed, it is the compensation plan as much as any other factor that motivates top managers to take steps to implement new sales roles in the first place. This is because in many cases sales compensation acts as a barometer, alerting managers to the need for change. Compensation levels that top managers view as either too high or too low may be the first signal that something is not right in the market. When this happens, management's first inclination is to look at the incentive formula or other related plan payout mechanics. However, the real issue may be that new customers are emerging who had not been considered in the sales forecast; or customers are consolidating, so that there are fewer accounts to call on; or sales, service, or other operational aspects of the business are overloaded, and thus deliveries are late, incomplete, or both. Also, there is always the possibility that salespeople call on the wrong accounts.

Recently, we observed one company that did an analysis of its sales, only to discover that in some parts of the country 80 percent of all new business was coming from relatively small accounts that the telesales center should have been calling on, not the field sales force. In those regions, the field sales reps regularly "prospected" through the list of new telesales center customers and then went out to the customer sites to convince the customers to do their business through the field sales reps. This was not what the company had in mind when it split small accounts from field sales and assigned them to the telesales center. Because sales reps earned over half their income from commissions and because the cycle time to close a larger account ranged from 60 to 120 days, it is no wonder that some reps continued to go after the small accounts.

Thus, it is essential that the compensation for the new sales roles align job success with both equitable pay and accomplishing the company's business objectives. Moreover (and a key point), the new compensation plan for new sales roles must be available at the time the company implements the new roles or jobs. Not having it available often results in missed business results and, perhaps worse, top management's belief that the decision to implement new sales roles was the wrong thing to do.

Consider these examples of companies that did not change the compensation plan at the same time they initiated new sales roles:

Medical instruments. This company has traditionally paid a commission on all sales from the first unit sold. The rate "ramps up" as the salesperson sells more units; however, the company has never set a quota for the sales force. With the landscape of the health care marketplace evolving dramatically, institutional customers began saying, "Don't send us your aggressive sales reps. They focus on selling units, and I don't get any additional services." To address this complaint, the company redefined the sales role from product-focused to solution-focused. The result was a salesperson who played a consultant role as much as a sales role. Management expected that with this redefinition, the sales reps would focus on meeting customer product and service needs. Nevertheless, the company continued to use a commission plan based on unit volume. Even though communications from headquarters and additional training told the salespeople they should be working differently, they largely ignored the "new job" because the way they were paid did not change.

Automotive parts. Sales representatives traditionally worked with dealers and retail outlets to ensure high-volume orders and product overflow. A quota-based plan rewarded the sales representative for meeting territory revenue objectives annually. In this very competitive marketplace, dealers were demanding help with business planning and merchandising. The company recognized that salespeople required new skills to address these needs and recast the sales job as a "business representative." The business representative was expected to assess the dealers' situations and help them formulate plans to increase their sales and profits. However, although the company assigned the new role to the salespeople, it continued to pay them based on reaching (or exceeding) territory revenue objectives. The salespeople largely ignored both dealer and company profit and inventory objectives and continued to focus on revenue volume, the only thing that really mattered to their paychecks.

Software company. This company develops and markets software that allows multiple functions and locations within a company to report, obtain, and analyze information through an integrated management information system. The sales force traditionally called on information systems or information technology executives in *Fortune* 500 companies and focused on selling the company's products (and related customization and installation services) directly to the end-using customer. The new economy momentum resulted in changing growth expectations from shareholders and senior management, and a new "go-to-market" strategy was formulated. This strategy resulted in a focus on "channels," that is, partners that could help grow the business through referrals and assisted selling activities. These channel partners, including systems integrators and independent software vendors, had to be recruited and managed, and a channel sales force was implemented to work with the partners. The same commission plan used for the direct sales force was "tweaked" for use with the channel organization. The result was a focus on "volume at any price, growth with any partner," although these salespeople were charged with developing and managing strategic, profitable long-term relationships with partners.

In all three situations, the company redefined the sales job to meet company and market requirements. In all three situations, the company aligned hiring policy, training, and organization structure with the new jobs. And in all three situations, a new sales compensation plan lagged behind launching of the new sales job. The result was salespeople whom management saw as ineffective and unsuccessful, largely because the sales compensation plan had not addressed the new job objectives. To avoid this unhappy situation, top managers should understand how to modify the sales compensation plan so that it will complement rather than frustrate the change in sales roles.

We believe that the process a company employs to identify and define new sales roles must be paralleled by a similar process to design and implement a compensation plan that motivates, directs, and rewards success in those new roles at the time the firm introduces them to the organization. That is this chapter's goal.

SALES COMPENSATION: WHAT IT IS AND WHAT IT IS NOT

Sales compensation is the pay opportunity available to employees in customer contact jobs. Typically, companies pay sales compensation to only these employees because they are the ones who interact with and persuade customers to do business with the firm. Figure 4-1 illustrates

Fig. 4-1.   Total compensation.

the components of total remuneration available to these employees and how sales compensation fits into the overall picture.

Note that total compensation has at least seven components. Sales expenses are the money the company has to pay for airline tickets, rental cars, hotel rooms, meals on the road, and all the other costs of putting a salesperson in front of a customer. Benefits address employee needs for medical care, time off, and long-term security and are generally available to all full-time employees. Salary is the fixed pay the salesperson receives. Target incentive pay is what the company pays when the salesperson reaches a sales goal. Overtarget incentive pay is just what it seems to be, money the company pays for exceeding the sales goal. Contests tend to offer short-term and limited rewards. Recognition is the intangible and (usually) noncash reward the company gives for outstanding results. The reward may be a night on the town, a week's vacation, or some other plum the employee values.

Sales compensation includes both salary and incentive pay. In companies that are defining new roles for sales jobs, these two components of cash compensation can motivate and reward the new behaviors that success requires. Salary, the fixed portion, reflects labor market levels, seniority, skills, and performance over time. Incentive pay, the variable portion, rewards the salesperson for achieving implicit or explicit goals over the short term (usually a one-year period).

The sales compensation plan cannot—and should not—do the whole job of sales force motivation and recognition. Because directing, motivating, and rewarding a high-producing sales force is a constant and difficult challenge, top managers are always looking for different and more effective ways to inspire pride, build a sense of accomplishment, and convey appreciation to the sales force. Sales contests and recognition programs can motivate and reward outstanding performance.

Increasingly we see companies use noncash programs, particularly sales and customer recognition plans, to recognize accomplishment in a new sales role. One reason why these plans are so attractive to companies undergoing a change in sales roles, in our opinion, is that they are much less likely to create "monetary envy." Even though employees are not supposed to talk about their income levels, invariably word eventually leaks out, especially in what appear to be inequitable situations, about who is making the big bucks. Using a noncash program, like a sales recognition plan that rewards with either quality merchandise or a desirable trip to a resort destination, is much less likely to create monetary envy, particularly in situations where setting realistic sales objectives is not possible. Consider this situation: A medical products distributor shifted the coverage of its customers from individual sellers (the account executives) to sales teams that included customer service representatives, equipment technicians, inventory managers, and, of course, account executives. During the transition from individuals to teams, it was not possible to measure the team's business results frequently and accurately. The company asked its customers to nominate their sales team for company reward and recognition if the customer felt that the team was doing a good job of meeting its needs. Top-ranked sales teams received noncash awards (from a three-day weekend with a significant other to a week's vacation) at the company's annual sales meeting.

Typically, a sales compensation plan design does not include intrinsic job value, benefits, perquisites, or expense reimbursement. These programs are critical in attracting and retaining talented personnel as part of the package the business offers, but they are a part that the company offers to every full-time employee. Nor does the sales compensation plan include reward and recognition programs, which generally offer noncash awards. Sales compensation programs are designed specifically to ensure that the fixed and incentive portions of the programs are aligned with the sales job.

Many companies have in the past used sales compensation as a way to define jobs and "manage" salespeople. Successful companies today find that the sales compensation program cannot (and should not) serve as a surrogate manager of the sales organization. Rather, these companies employ a design process that uses the internal skills and knowledge of the sales, marketing, finance, and human resources divisions.

IBM is an outstanding example of a company that truly reinvented its sales compensation program, which was rolled out to the worldwide sales organization in January 1996. The design process took more than a year and was motivated by widespread concerns about the lack of alignment between the pay plan and new teaming required across national boundaries. The manager of incentive strategies for IBM Canada told *Sales & Marketing Management* magazine about the reasons for change: "There was an attitude that if it's outside my territory and outside my measurements, I don't get paid for it, and I don't get involved. What's in my pay plan defines what I do."[1]

Marty Sunde, then the director of incentive strategies for IBM U.S., worked with other IBM executives and outside experts to understand what required change, the most effective way to ensure that the pay plan in each country could be aligned with the organization's requirements, and the new roles associated with the IBM vision. The program now focuses on teamwork across boundaries to meet customer needs and is directly aligned with the IBM vision and roles. As one IBM executive said in the same magazine article, "When all is said and done, people want to be paid well for treating their customers well."

How to Link Compensation to New Sales Roles

The design process that links compensation to new sales roles has ten steps, as indicated in Figure 4-2. These ten steps fall into four phases of work:

> *Phase A: Clarify sales strategy.* The first steps in the process are defining and documenting the company's business objectives and

Fig. 4-2. Optimal design process.

Phase A: Sales Strategy	Step 1: Confirm Business Objectives
	Step 2: Define Sales Strategy
	Step 3: Confirm Job Roles and Eligibility
Phase B: Financial Requirements	Step 4: Establish Compensation Levels
	Step 5: Develop a Funding Plan
Phase C: Performance Measures	Step 6: Identify Performance Measures
	Step 7: Confirm Systems Capabilities
Phase D: Program Details	Step 8: Set Goals
	Step 9: Develop Incentive Plan Mechanics
	Step 10: Develop Transition and Communication Plans

the roles required to meet those objectives. Identifying the jobs required in the sales process is the foundation for assessing eligibility for sales compensation.

Phase B: Determine financial requirements. Corporate, market, and individual financial needs are addressed in setting the total compensation levels for the new roles, and techniques are defined to ensure that funds are available at acceptable performance levels to make payments to employees in the new roles.

Phase C: Identify performance measures. Based on each job's role in the sales process, the job's ability to affect results, and the company's ability to track and credit those results, the firm defines appropriate performance measures.

Phase D: Formulate program details. The company defines the incentive formula, a goal-setting process (if applicable), and the communication strategy required to implement the program effectively.

Phases A and B set the stage for the development of a sales compensation program that is aligned with new sales roles. We'll cover these phases in more detail in the next section, but because phases C and D are the critical tactical elements of the process, we devote Chapters 5–12 to describing the key steps and outcomes of these phases.

Phase A: Clarify Sales Strategy

In Chapter 3, we described the importance of first defining the sales strategy, and then basing job definitions on the requirements for success in achieving that strategy. This process is the key to success in designing compensation programs to support the new roles as well.

Step 1: Confirm Business Objectives

The design process should begin by confirming the objectives the company has established. This includes both the "go-to-market vision" of the top executives and the financial objectives that the business must achieve for shareholders, partners, or other stakeholders. As Chapter 3 discussed, this leads to a definition of how the company will reach its objectives.

STEP 2: DEFINE SALES STRATEGY

The sales strategy is the key to unlocking the new roles required. A sales strategy is a plan of action to match the right types of resources with business opportunities. The Sales Strategy Matrix (Figure 3-1) provides a framework for defining the types of interactions required to do business with customers and determining the type and level of sales resource required to sustain or acquire a revenue stream. Once a sales strategy has been defined, more details about the sales role required can be developed. For example, you would not want to assign account executives to customer accounts to retain the revenue stream if the principal need was effective service delivery, that is, on time, complete order fulfillment. It may be more appropriate to assign service consultants or customer service representatives to these accounts. Doing so has two implications: First, it defines who should do what (you don't want account executives doing what customer service representatives can do more effectively and at lower cost). Second, it suggests the role that ought to be eligible for participation in sales compensation.

STEP 3: CONFIRM JOB ROLES AND ELIGIBILITY

This step is a critical point in developing a sales compensation program to support new roles. Once sales managers identify new roles in a sales organization, executives frequently ask, "But how different is this really?" Prior to embarking on the sales compensation design process, many companies find it useful to rate the degree of change in the job. Table 4-1 uses the five W's to estimate the degree of change in the job or jobs. Using the scale, the difference in ratings helps define the degree of change. You should complete the ratings for the old role and the new.

For example, as you look at your historical sales job, you find that the company expected sales representatives to call on administrative staff at customer companies (a score of 3; these are not executive-level customers), they were selling a commodity product (1), they go to customer sites and take phone orders (3), and they expect sales transactions weekly (3 again). Customers buy from them because they are easy to work with and the price is right (2). Add up the five W's and the score is 12.

The new job is an account executive who calls on senior executives (5) at their offices (5) to sell long-term contracts (5) for an outsourced solution (5) that is valued enough by the customer that price is not a significant issue (yet another 5). The score is 25, and clearly the new job is a significant departure from the old. A point change in the range of 1

Table 4-1. The five W's: checklist for change.

Change Factor	Scale				
	1	2	3	4	5
Who is the customer?	Clerical		Midlevel manage- ment		Executive
What are you selling?	Commod- ity product	Bundled commod- ity products	Unique product	Unique product and support	Outsourced solution
Where is the sales proc- ess taking place?	Telephone	Counter	On-site; phone ordering		Corporate on-site
When are sales oc- curring?	Many daily		Predictable periods		Long-term contract
Why are cus- tomers buying?	Price	Price and conven- ience	Sole source	Confi- dence	Value

Note: Step 1: Rate each factor and total your scores for your historical job. Step 2: Rate each factor and total your scores for changes this year. Step 3: Subtract your historical score from your new score.

to 5 generally means that the sales compensation program may require only tweaks; a change of more than five points, however, indicates that the new sales compensation program should probably start with a clean sheet of paper.

Once the job has been confirmed, you should assess eligibility for participation in the sales compensation program. Typically, positions that initiate, persuade, and fulfill in the customer coverage process are eligible to participate in the sales compensation program. Line manage- ment positions that coach, counsel, direct, and develop those involved in the customer coverage process are also generally included in a sales compensation program, rather than an executive pay program. The ex- tended decision tree in Figure 4-3 is a useful tool to help determine eligibility (it is a modification of Figure 1-4).

The primary contact is either external or internal. If it is external, the style of the initial contact is either to initiate or to respond. When it is to respond, it is either to persuade the buyer or to fulfill customer needs. When the job is simply to fulfill customer needs—when the job has a service focus only—it may or may not be eligible for incentive pay.

Corporate philosophy is also a key factor in determining eligibility for participation in a sales compensation program. For example, as com-

Fig. 4-3. Eligibility: a decision tree.

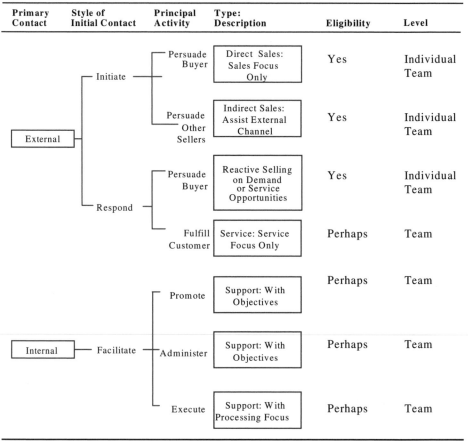

Primary Contact	Style of Initial Contact	Principal Activity	Type: Description	Eligibility	Level
External	Initiate	Persuade Buyer	Direct Sales: Sales Focus Only	Yes	Individual Team
		Persuade Other Sellers	Indirect Sales: Assist External Channel	Yes	Individual Team
	Respond	Persuade Buyer	Reactive Selling on Demand or Service Opportunities	Yes	Individual Team
		Fulfill Customer	Service: Service Focus Only	Perhaps	Team
Internal	Facilitate	Promote	Support: With Objectives	Perhaps	Team
		Administer	Support: With Objectives	Perhaps	Team
		Execute	Support: With Processing Focus	Perhaps	Team

panies develop sales teams that include members from many functions, team members may be eligible for sales compensation only so long as they are on a customer team. Consider the following situation.

A pharmaceutical company determined that to compete effectively in the new health care market, it required major account teams. The teams typically include a team leader/account manager, specialty sales representatives, and a contract administrator. During the design process, the planners concluded that all "core" positions were eligible to earn incentive pay. However, large teaching institutions have complex needs that the company can meet only by adding medical professionals to work with the team as advisors during the formulary committee decision process. These professionals would be temporary, part-time team members, but their contribution to the team's success would be critical. The planners determined that the medical professionals would be eligible for a special noncash team award for the successful conclusion of the processes to which they would contribute. In this case, the noncash awards were seminar approvals; the company paid for continuing medical education courses that the professionals wanted to take.

PHASE B: DETERMINE FINANCIAL REQUIREMENTS

The design process needs to address how much a compensation plan will cost as a percentage of sales as well as how to pay out compensation earned under the plan. Prior to detailed design, it is critical to determine the level of cash compensation that will be available for each job.

STEP 4: ESTABLISH COMPENSATION LEVELS

This task calls for a balanced approach to be sure that the pay levels are externally competitive (to attract and retain talented people) and internally equitable (to facilitate retention, career movement, and team cooperation). The cash compensation level for each job must also be large enough to motivate and to pay for performance to drive business results. You must balance mix (at-risk pay) and leverage (upside opportunity) against the position's ability to affect results. We cover these design features in detail in Chapter 6. However, prior to winding up a detailed design, completing step 4 establishes the cash compensation boundaries for each job. Figure 4-4 provides a checklist of tasks and information that the company needs in order to develop or confirm compensation levels.

STEP 5: DEVELOP A FUNDING PLAN

Many executives are finding that a new pay plan demands that they reexamine how the company funds the compensation plan. In the traditional 100 percent commission environment, "the more they make, the more we make" was acceptable; no one had to think about where the money to pay the salespeople was going to come from. Once the company begins to create roles that focus on longer-term strategies and results, it may find these roles also have a higher proportion of fixed pay. Or management may decide that an entirely new role is now eligible for incentive pay, which increases the company's costs. The design team must have an answer for the senior executive who says, "Great plan—how do we pay for it?"

Funding for a new incentive plan may come from merit increase budgets, or from other variable pay plans such as a corporate profit

Fig. 4-4. Setting compensation levels: a checklist.

1. External (Competitive) Practice

❏   What are the critical skills and experience for the job?

❏   What are the results expected from a successful job incumbent?

❏   What is this job called in the competitive marketplace? (to match in surveys)

❏   How much is the market paying for fully competent performance in this job?

    ❏   Salary range _____

    ❏   Incentive range _____

❏   Where do we historically pay within the competitive range? (What is our competitive positioning in terms of percentile?) _____

2. Internal Equity

❏   Do we have jobs in the company that have similar skill and experience requirements?

    ❏   If yes, what are we paying these jobs today? _____

    ❏   If no, can we place the sales job between two other career job families that require less and more experience and skill?

    ❏   What are the low and high ends of the scale? _____

❏   Will these jobs be expected to work as team members?

❏   If yes, will it be critical to ensure SIMILAR pay, or JOB-EQUITABLE pay?

3. Corporate Finance

❏   How much can we afford to pay as a percent of sales for success in the job?

❏   How much can we afford to pay as a percent of gross profit or margin?

❏   At what percent achievement of objectives can we afford to begin paying incentive compensation?

❏   How much revenue or profit above 100% of objectives are we willing/able to share with the sales organization?

sharing plan. A job that will be eligible to participate in the sales compensation program may not be eligible to participate in programs for other employees, like a profit or gain sharing plan. Another technique is to use the merit increase budget for the job and permit employees to "bet the merit increase." People may elect to use their merit increase as the seed for a potential incentive upside, rather than having it applied to their salary. Here's an example.

A company created a new customer service consultant (CSC) job to meet the needs of telephone customers. Former customer service representatives (CSRs) were the primary source of the new service consultants. Since the customer service consultant was now incentive-eligible, the question was, "How can we afford to give the new CSCs an incentive opportunity that's really 'at risk'?" The department merit increase budget was 5 percent for the year. During the performance evaluation process, the manager described the merit increase based on performance to each CSR, consistent with the company's practice. Each CSR who was offered a CSC position was asked to decide if (1) the merit increase should be applied to his or her base salary in the new job, or (2) the merit increase dollars should be used as the target incentive opportunity for the year. If an employee selected (1), she would not be eligible for incentive pay for the first year in the new job. If she selected (2), she could earn as much as two times a defined dollar amount if her performance against goal was well above 100 percent.

For jobs that will have a higher fixed portion of pay, companies generally use a transition or bridge plan. New approaches to sales compensation do not necessarily have to be implemented all at once (although they do have to be announced at the time the new jobs are implemented); frequently a several-stage effort helps both the company and the salesperson make the shift. Implementing the plan over a one- or two-year period provides time for the company to budget and forecast and for the salesperson to develop into the new role. If a staged implementation is the technique of choice, however, it is crucial to communicate the intent early—"no unpleasant surprises" is a useful theme.

PHASE C: IDENTIFY PERFORMANCE MEASURES

All phases and steps in the process of designing sales compensation programs revolve around one simple axiom: You get what you pay for. Defining appropriate performance measures and confirming the company's ability to track and credit results are critical success factors. Here is a summary of the two steps in this phase of the process.

STEP 6: IDENTIFY PERFORMANCE MEASURES

Chapter 5 describes in detail the process for selecting performance measures and the importance of establishing measures that are aligned with the job and with the company's requirements. Selecting and defining performance measures should include all the details management will require in order to track and measure success effectively and communicate expectations. For example, it is not enough to define "sales" as the key performance measure. The design team must also define the *level* of sales (account, territory, team, market segment, channel), the *type* of sales (by product, in aggregate), minimum expectations, and crediting procedures.

Measures must be based on job roles and the salesperson's ability to affect results. Three out of four incentive plans apply quantitative (volume, profit) measures, but emerging measures include qualitative factors such as team ratings and competency-based scores.

STEP 7: CONFIRM SYSTEMS CAPABILITIES

Assume for the moment that the design process has proceeded smoothly and you have an answer to just about every question senior management has asked. More than one design initiative has failed, however, because "we just can't measure that today." As management defines performance measures, the systems function in your company has a key role in making sure that the measures defined can be implemented and administered. Plans that require intensive manual data manipulation frequently result in infrequent reporting, questionable calculations, and uncertainty about the plan's integrity. The company may have to enhance its systems capabilities, and to do so will require a well-documented and well-thought-out rationale for selecting key measures.

PHASE D: DEVELOP PROGRAM DETAILS

At last, the up-front steps are done and you can get down to the real design of the sales compensation program for your new sales roles. Subsequent chapters discuss each step in detail; but it is important for the design team to realize that if the team has completed the first seven steps effectively, the last three steps should be slam dunks.

STEP 8: SET GOALS

Whether or not the program for your new sales roles includes a quota-based bonus, it is usually very helpful to set performance expectations. Goals may be established at an account, territory, team, or segment level and are based on the performance measure defined by the team. Chapter 5 describes various approaches to goal setting.

STEP 9: DEVELOP INCENTIVE PLAN MECHANICS

This step is frequently the first step managers take when they begin to design plans. Management says, "Let's figure out why the formula didn't work, and then we'll tweak it." When you are focusing on new programs for new roles, the same mechanics are available. However, top managers frequently think about using them in different ways. Chapter 6 describes techniques that many successful companies are using in the following areas: mix and leverage, plan period and payout frequency, and formulas.

STEP 10: DEVELOP TRANSITION AND COMMUNICATION PLANS

Even the best plan is ineffective when it is badly communicated. In fact, many executives have found that poor plans that are well implemented (communicated, trained, great reports) are likely to be perceived as successful. Chapter 12 has more detailed information about plan communication. Key topics that communication and transition plans must address include communication materials, sales management training, communication media, and timing. A plan that both managers and salespeople understand clearly will indicate the company's expectations of the new roles and motivate and reward success in the job.

HOW TO CREATE A SUCCESSFUL SALES COMPENSATION DESIGN TEAM

Traditionally, companies have charged human resources or sales administration with the task of designing and implementing the sales compensation program. As new sales roles are defined, however, companies are finding that a team approach to sales compensation design is critical to plan success. Table 4-2 includes the menu of participants in the optimal design team. As you can see from the menu, a cross-functional team is ideal for developing a plan aligned with the new sales role(s) and company objectives, one that is legal and equitable, and can be administered.

Table 4-2. The sales compensation design team.

Function	Role
Customer service	Headquarters and field management Ensure that the plan is consistent with the new role Ensure that the plan is motivational and a useful management tool
Finance	Headquarters management Assess affordability of levels
Human resources, compensation	Headquarters management and analyst Ensure that the plan is consistent with general practice, ethical, and implementable Assist with rollout and communication
Information systems	Headquarters programmer or analyst Confirm/develop systems capabilities
Marketing	Headquarters management, field marketing management (if applicable) Ensure consistency with product and/or segment plans
Sales	Headquarters and field management Gain input from field personnel Ensure that the plan is consistent with the new role Ensure that the plan is motivational and a useful management tool Lead rollout and communication
Sales administration	Headquarters manager or analyst Confirm/develop reporting and tracking capabilities

As with any team effort, it is important to start the process with a clear charter and defined objectives. Each member has a defined role that contributes to the successful completion of the design process. For many companies, employee participation on the design team that develops the sales compensation program serves multiple purposes:

- The experience is developmental; it provides team members with the opportunity to work with people across the organization and enhances the member's ability to work through a disciplined process.
- The process requires teaming between functions that may have been seen as unwilling partners in other corporate efforts.
- Widespread buy-in to the new sales compensation program, and the new sales roles, is more likely, and executives have the ability to affect the decision-making process early.

The design team generally works within a timetable, and it creates a work plan to complete the activities required to finish the design work efficiently. Based on the plan year, the process should generally begin as soon as management has defined the new sales role(s). Generally, the team is activated after the business identifies the new sales roles, and it may play a role in documenting the details of the position roles and responsibilities. Because the company has defined a new way of working with customers, it is likely that the design team will identify critical new approaches to sales compensation. The process can therefore take months to complete, as the team wrestles with the complexities of new roles, new measures, and new program details.

Periodic checkpoints should be completed with an executive steering committee charged with approving the team's key decisions. The steering committee typically has the following responsibilities:

- Confirms objectives and strategy
- Confirms new roles
- Approves compensation levels and the funding plan
- Approves the performance measures that will be used
- Approves the total estimated cost of sales and return to the company

The design team's charter typically includes details such as the process used to set goals and the mechanics associated with the program, and therefore these do not usually require executive approval. At the conclusion of the design process, however, members of the executive steering committee frequently participate in management training and program communication. Executive support for a new and potentially innovative sales compensation program is one factor that enhances the likelihood of the program's success and increases its credibility in the eyes of all participants. Executive disinterest can undermine a new plan's performance.

SUMMING UP

Sales compensation should not define the sales job, nor should companies use it to manage the salespeople. Sales compensation, however, must be linked to the company's sales roles, and when the company redefines (or creates) sales jobs, it should also change the sales compensation plan.

Linking compensation to new sales roles requires a focused, disciplined process that is completed by team members with the skills and knowledge to align the program with the new job and with marketplace and company expectations. The process that links compensation to the new sales roles has ten steps that involve four phases: clarifying the sales strategy, determining the financial requirements, identifying performance measures, and formulating the program details. We discussed how you clarify the sales strategy in Chapter 3; we will now describe the process you can use to select performance measures.

WHAT TO EXPECT AND HOW TO MEASURE SUCCESS IN NEW SALES ROLES

"If we can't measure it, it didn't happen." Frequently this is the motto of a work group charged with designing a sales compensation plan for new sales roles. While the statement may exaggerate a bit, it does clearly summarize the dilemma facing anyone charged with designing a new plan: What are the right measures of success for new sales roles? As Figure 5-1 shows, selecting performance measures is one of the critical steps in designing an effective sales compensation plan. Too often, plan designers attempt to address different—sometimes competing—views about how new sales roles are expected to operate by incorporating too many performance measures into the compensation plan. Consider the following cautionary examples.

ELECTRONICS COMPONENTS DISTRIBUTOR

After many years of achieving double-digit growth through acquisitions, a successful electronics distributor decided to pursue organic growth as its business strategy. Its top managers reorganized the business into several operating divisions, each focused on a common set of customers. Management realigned resources—sales and inside sales support per-

Fig. 5-1. Optimal design process: identify performance measures.

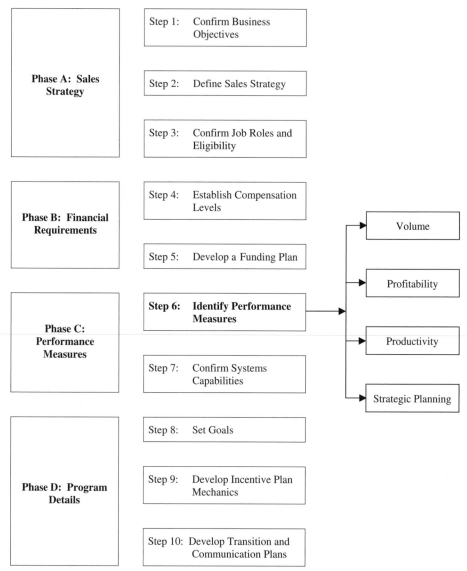

sonnel—to work exclusively with these assigned customers. The company's largest division identified one particularly attractive opportunity: the sales potential in small to medium accounts and in accounts the division had lost. Division managers decided to create a new sales role and assign it a new job, business development manager. The new job was chartered to:

1. Expand sales in small to medium accounts
2. Win back former accounts
3. Open new accounts

Further, after an account reached a certain volume level and account share, management expected the business development manager to shift the customer to a geographic territory sales representative. The distributor selected four very different performance measures to check a business development manager's success:

1. Volume growth in the assigned small and medium accounts
2. Volume realized from winning back former customers
3. Volume from new accounts
4. The number of accounts and volume shifted to geographic sales representatives

Two problems developed as a result of this approach to measurement. First, because the company used too many different and dissimilar tracking measures, it became quite difficult to establish the results and determine if this approach to the market was really paying off. For example:

1. Measuring volume growth in small and medium accounts sounds easy; the challenge was in agreeing to a definition of a small account that the company would actually assign to a business development manager, since some of these accounts were telemarket accounts. Even though this measure looked as if it should be simple, it was often difficult because the firm needed to define its terms and then understand whether its systems could actually track and measure performance relative to those terms. Often the terms were not only difficult to measure but dissimilar.
2. It may not be possible to understand who a former customer was; they just show up in the records as accounts. Also, winning back former customers may represent a different kind of volume from sales to current accounts because former customers may require price or other concessions.
3. Information may not be available to identify a new account.

Second, no one at the distributor could agree on when and how to shift accounts to geographic sales representatives, and as a result that rarely happened. Even though the whole point of having a business developer establish the account and then pass it to somebody else was to free up the business developer's time, the stumbling block was to define when a transition should actually take place. Also, among the accounts that actually were shifted from one resource to another, the company was double paying for the sale for some long period of time.

Ineffective measurement resulted in business development managers working much like the geographic sales representatives (essentially, as account managers), which was not at all what the company had hoped to accomplish. Even as we write this book, the company continues to wrestle with the right performance measures for this job.

OFFICE SUPPLIES RETAILER

A large office supplies retailer, which had thrived selling primarily to consumers, decided to pursue growth in the business market. To gain entry into that market, the company acquired a number of regional companies that already had sales forces. For the most part, these sales representatives sold to existing business customers. The service demands of these current customers and the increasing competition for their business required sales representatives to spend the majority of their time with them. Top management believed the company was missing a significant opportunity to grow the business by not opening up new accounts; so, to accomplish that, it introduced a new role—business developer—into the geographic sales organization.

The new job was titled "new accounts manager." It was chartered to open new accounts, to build sales in those accounts to a defined "run rate," and then to shift the accounts to an account manager in the geographic territory. The retailer measured performance by total sales volume and volume shifted to account managers. Shortly after the new job and its performance measures were announced to the field, debate broke out between top managers (at headquarters and in the field) and salespeople. Because the account managers' and the new accounts managers' salaries would be set in the same way—as a percentage of the prior year's sales—it was argued that new accounts managers would have no incentive to achieve the run rate required for the transition. And over time, that's exactly what happened. New accounts managers hung on to new accounts, generally well past the point they should have, and controlled their volume, so that ultimately they became more like account managers. The strategy to tap into a market growth opportunity was in large part defeated by the wrong sales measures.

MEDICAL EQUIPMENT MANUFACTURER

A successful global manufacturer of capital equipment for hospitals, clinics, and other medical institutions concluded that its line of products and services was simply too large for any one salesperson to sell effectively. Company management felt it was missing opportunities to sell more to current customers because the number of products and services required more time to sell than salespeople had available. To address this problem, the company redefined its sales process. This resulted in a new sales role and a changed sales role. The traditional sales job, account executive, was changed by taking away responsibility for closing business for a defined list of specialty products and certain on-site services. Management assigned those responsibilities to a new sales role—sales specialist. The company continued to measure account executives on, and pay commissions on, total sales volume booked and gross profit dollars realized at accounts in their territory. The firm measured sales specialists on volume and gross profit dollars for their assigned products and services—most of which represented relatively low volume and small gross margin dollars.

Because account executives were measured, in part, on total gross profit, they were reluctant to let sales specialists into their accounts. Since the company continued to use individual-level credit for sales, there was little focus on team effort in the accounts covered by the account executive and many sales specialists. The lack of a team-level measure was a serious flaw in an otherwise appropriate plan, a flaw we see in many companies that are implementing new roles that call for active teamwork. Ultimately, this measurement flaw caused flare-ups in the field and confusion at some accounts. Top management did not realize its hope for growth in account penetration, and the company had to junk the plan midyear and change its approach to measurement once again.

In each of these situations, too many measures, the wrong measures, the wrong level of measurement, measures that conflicted with the salesperson's job, or all four resulted in the corporation's not achieving the objectives it had set out as its new approach to business growth. The use of too many performance measures in the sales compensation plan reflects top managers' lack of agreement about the most important objectives of a job's new sales role. Even in the best of companies, aligning performance measures with business objectives for various sales and customer contact jobs is challenging. When a shift takes place in who the customer is, however, and a company responds by implementing new sales roles, that change creates an immediate need for a new or revised performance measurement process. When this occurs, top managers ask us, "Where do we start? What should we measure? How many measures should we use? How will we set goals for these new measures? And how do we relate these measure to compensation?'' These are the key questions we will discuss in this chapter.

How Performance Measures and Job Expectations Work

If you want a job to accomplish one thing above all else, attach a measure to it. If you want your employees to focus on that thing—regardless of organization level, from top managers to frontline personnel—pay for success relative to that measure. The assumption is that you get what you measure; more often than not, however, you get what for you pay for. This truism places significant weight on the company's ability to determine what it expects and how to measure that. This is particularly true when a business is implementing new sales roles because these roles typically require new performance behaviors. For employees taking on new sales roles, a company can speed the process of learning the new behaviors that will result in success if it can measure the outcomes of those behaviors and reward them. This process is typically called performance management.

Performance management involves selecting the right measures to gauge business results, establishing standards to define expectations, tracking actual accomplishment, and providing guidance to help employees achieve success. When a single salesperson sells a single product (or a relatively simple product line), the performance management process is relatively straightforward, because the firm can measure sales results and attribute them to the level of sales resource (the salesperson) responsible for attracting, expanding, and retaining the business. Door-to-door selling organizations—Amway, Electrolux, and Mary Kay, among others—illustrate this relatively simple selling and performance management model.

At most companies, however, the selling environment is dramatically more complex. Large corporations in particular employ multiple sales resources and offer broad lines of products and services. Also, customers and their requirements change constantly. We are not surprised, therefore, to hear top managers express frustration over performance *mis*management. Measures, standards, tracking, and supervision—all or part—are out of sync with one another, with business goals, or with both. In response to the question "Where do we start?" we believe it is helpful to determine what top managers expect to achieve with a new sales role that former approaches to doing business with customers did not achieve. When ascertaining such expectations, it is often helpful to examine the practices of others.

THREE MEASUREMENT PRACTICES THAT SUPPORT PROFITABLE TOP-LINE GROWTH

In companies that make the transition from a focus on cost reduction to a focus on investing in top-line growth, management must rethink the approach to measurement. Measurement is largely influenced by the role that top executives expect customer contact employees—salespeople, customer service reps, market managers, dealer sales managers, and others—to play in business growth. Thus, it is important that you understand your expectations of customer contact personnel at the time that you introduce new sales roles into your organization. Our research shows that when a company introduces new sales roles, the top three reasons for doing so are to (1) improve sales productivity, (2) improve sales coverage to current customers, and (3) grow sales overall profitably. We observe that, to achieve these objectives, companies have to give consideration to new or enhanced performance measures to reinforce the strategic direction the new sales roles signal. Consider the following three broad strategic objectives.

IMPROVE SALES PRODUCTIVITY

The principal way companies seek to improve their sales productivity is to realize more volume and profit from their current investment in sales resources. The alternative—reducing sales expenses, principally head count—is a short-term solution; it ultimately penalizes a company through lost market share and slower growth than competitors. To improve sales productivity, companies adopt one or more of the following measures at the time they introduce new roles:

- New customer sales volume
- New product sales volume
- Balanced product line sales
- Reduced "churn" among current customers

IMPROVE SALES COVERAGE TO CURRENT CUSTOMERS

Regardless of industry, we regularly hear that customers want flexibility, customization, faster response, and personalized service. To meet these requirements, market-leading companies continually improve the coverage of their current customers. Often this means investments in new ways to interact with customers—catalogs, 800 numbers or fax lines, telesales, the Internet. Traditional jobs require increased or different skills, which results in training needs and new hiring profiles. These investments must be offset with profitable revenue growth. When companies introduce new sales roles to help them improve sales coverage to current customers, the measures used include:

- Overall account volume
- Greater share of the account's business
- Achievement of customer objectives
- More lines of business sold
- Account profitability

Grow Sales Overall

The past few years of our research survey show that CEOs listed "grow sales overall" as their top priority. Many CEOs have shifted their focus from cost reduction to achieving increased profits and shareholder value through revenue growth. In some industries, growth through acquisitions is a major component of CEO strategy. The number and stock value of mergers and acquisitions have been high in recent years, yet acquisitions alone are often not sufficient to achieve the double-digit revenue growth that many CEOs have set as their target.

A recent survey of executive confidence in sales growth asked, "By what percentage is your company expected to grow sales this year over the prior year?" The average expected growth in sales was 15 percent. Over one-third of the ninety-six large companies that participated indicated that they expected sales to grow by more than 15 percent.

To achieve higher growth rates, executives tell us that their companies must:

Retain customers at current or higher revenue levels. When the company loses customers and when they buy less, it is much more difficult to achieve aggressive sales growth targets. Clear measures and performance objectives related to sales and customer service at all levels of the organization are critical to holding down both customer and revenue churn.

Retain sales employees. The labor market, particularly in the United States, is very tight. Losing top-producing salespeople is often a contributing factor to revenue churn. Programs designed to motivate and reward salespeople, particularly compensation and recognition plans, are essential to realizing growth objectives.

Sell new products effectively. New products fuel growth, but too often the sales plan for new products does not recognize the need for more sales capacity in the sales organization or for new salespeople to reach new buyers. Planning for the right type and level of sales staff to achieve new product sales goals increases the likelihood of sales success.

A focus by top managers on profitable top-line growth has led to "dual path" performance measures. While financial measures primarily indicate sales performance, many companies have found that nonfinancial measures are also critical to assessing the effectiveness of new sales roles. For example, because competition for talented salespeople is so intense, and roles are changing in many industries, companies must encourage the development of new skills and competencies in their salespeople. Nonfinancial measures emphasize the importance of that training.

Today customers are more sophisticated, information systems are more complicated, and competition is more complex. Thus, new roles emerge to meet market expectations. Customer retention, profitable revenue growth, and new product selling, indicators of business success, require new skills to achieve the desired results. Therefore, the dual path measurement for many companies must include both the financial measures and the nonfinancial measures shown in Figure 5-1, where the first three measures (volume, profitability, and productivity) are financial, while the last (strategic planning) includes only milestones, activities, and the like.

Since the first (and generally most important) success measure for a new sales role is sales, it is not surprising to find that an increasing number of companies measure their success in achieving top-line growth by tracking the percent of sales realized:

- From new direct customers
- From new distribution channels
- From new products

We've learned that you must have a framework for thinking about sales measurement to select performance measures successfully. Later in the chapter, we will also examine new and successful approaches to implementing nonfinancial measures as a metric in the sales compensation program.

THE CUSTOMER-CENTRIC PERFORMANCE MEASUREMENT MODEL:
THREE INDICATORS OF SUCCESS

Effective performance management centers around a planning process. We have seen different approaches to the planning process work effectively in different companies. Increasingly, we see companies redefining their planning process to focus first on customers. Many of these processes, however, particularly as applied to the sales organization, often go right to specific measures—volume, gross profit, new accounts opened, and other tactical yardsticks—thereby skipping over what we believe is a strategic framework for thinking about measurement as it applies to sales. Figure 5-2 suggests a customer-centered approach to measurement that is ultimately useful in selecting specific performance measures for new sales roles.

Years ago, when we first developed the Sales Strategy Matrix, its value was to help top managers define and prioritize the types of selling, and therefore it suggested how to construct the sales jobs the business required. Over time, we observed that one of the most common problems experienced by companies was misalignment between the business's objectives and the sales force's selling behaviors. After seminars

Fig. 5-2.   Customer-centered performance measurement model.

and workshops with hundreds of managers, the Sales Strategy Matrix evolved into a performance planning tool. We discovered that top managers used it to align the roles of the sales jobs with the achievement of company business objectives. If, for example, a company's goal was to expand its business with current customers because it had developed new products, it could reinforce that strategy through the compensation plan with a penetration measure. Regardless of the exact measure used—dollar volume, gross profit dollars, units, or other yardsticks—the value of the Sales Strategy Matrix was to help managers set performance priorities. To help companies determine exactly how well they were achieving their sales growth strategies, we developed "metrics" for the boxes in the matrix. We called these metrics CPR Analysis, for conversion, penetration, and retention.

Typically, top executives make an annual speech to their frontline employees in which they say something like "We're going to grow the business X percent over last year's sales." This message says how much growth management expects; it says nothing about how to achieve it. In such a statement, executives give no explicit direction about where management expects the growth to come from. Potentially, it leaves to chance discussions about where resources are to be concentrated to achieve the growth. The Sales Strategy Matrix and CPR Analysis give top managers a framework and a tool to shape a leadership message that is more complete, one that says not only *how much* but *how* sales growth could be achieved and will be measured.

Figure 5-3, which is based on the Sales Strategy Matrix, can help you plan for sales growth, and it can help you develop a leadership message for your sales organization after you have completed the analysis.

Step 1: Figure out where today's growth is coming from. The classical approach to calculating sales growth is to divide this year's sales by last year's. For example, if 2000's sales were $400 million and 2001's $440 million, the business grew 10 percent [($440 − $400) ÷ $400 × 100 = 10]. This calculation does not provide any insight into the source of growth. Was it the result of winning sales with new customers? Or of doing a better sales job with current customers? To learn the answers to these questions, you should make a year-over-year sales comparison to calculate boxes 1, 2, 3, and 4 of the Sales Strategy Matrix. Assume that retention revenue is $360 million, penetration revenue is $60 million, and conversion/new concept selling revenue is $20 million. This means that the company was able to retain 90 percent of 2000's revenue (360 ÷ 400 × 100); it was able to obtain 15 percent of 2001's revenue over

Fig. 5-3.   Growth planning: the Sales Strategy Matrix.

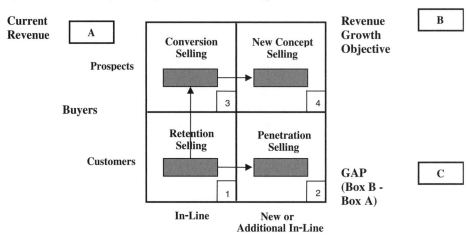

Products/Services

last year's total base sales through penetration selling, that is, current accounts with increased volume (60 ÷ 400 × 100); and it was able to obtain 5 percent of 2001's revenue over last year's total from new accounts (20 ÷ 400 × 100). The CPR calculations tell us how good a job the sales organization is doing over all three key customer-centered measures.

Step 2: Set a realistic growth objective. Typically, top management sets growth objectives based on several factors: market opportunity, new technology or product development or both, and earnings necessary to meet shareholder return on investment requirements. When helping top managers set sales growth objectives, we have found it useful to use The Alexander Group's CPR database, which contains the experiences of hundreds of companies in over fifteen industries. Table 5-1 provides an extract from that database. If, for example, our hypothetical company's growth objective is in the range of 12 to 18 percent over the prior year, Table 5-1 provides a useful reference for what level of performance management might expect relative to C, P, and R results. It ought to look for 7 to 13 percent of the revenue from conversion sales, 21 to 30 percent from penetration sales, and 85 to 92 percent from retention. If any one of these three falls dramatically below these targets, the company may reach its total target, but it will have difficulty in the future as sales grow more and more skewed.

Step 3: Monitor C, P, and R sales results. During the year, it is wise to measure C, P, and R sales results quarterly. If results are below expectations or out of line with what normative data suggest (Table 5-1), then management can zero in on the area where performance is out of line to take corrective action.

Four Performance Benchmarks for Evaluating Sales Excellence

CPR metrics are quite helpful to top managers who are charging a sales organization with a leadership message. However, as one of our clients is fond of saying, "CPR isn't granular enough to provide specific direction in the individual selling effort." Often you need another level of detail, one that specifies the exact performance measures that could be associated with C, P, and R. Performance measurement, particularly for new or changed sales roles, includes selecting the best measures to evaluate sales results, defining expectations (e.g., quotas and goals), and tracking actual accomplishment. As we saw in the company situations at the beginning of this chapter, selecting the most appropriate performance measures is critical to a new sales role's success. Unfortunately, companies sometimes select either the wrong measure(s) or too many measures. Too many or the wrong measures often reflect management's lack of agreement about the most important objective for the new or changed roles and, in turn, the actual sales jobs.

We suggest that executives have a complete understanding of the measures available to assess employee performance in new sales roles. Our benchmarking studies of the sales performance measurement practices of leading companies suggest that you should consider four key categories:

- Volume
- Profitability

Table 5-1.   Benchmark CPR data (%).

Component	Below Standard (25th Percentile)	Standard (50th Percentile)	High Performers (75th Percentile)	Best Practice (90th Percentile)
Conversion	2.0	6.9	13.2	19.9
Penetration	13.6	21.4	30.2	38.4
Retention	74.8	84.9	91.6	95.5
Total Growth	3.8	11.9	18.5	28.5

- Sales productivity
- Strategic planning

Table 5-2 defines these categories and provides illustrative measures for each category. A helpful rule of thumb suggests that three or fewer measures should be used for any sales job, but particularly for jobs that embody a new sales role. We say this because once there are more than three, it becomes very difficult and often confusing for employees to focus their behavior on the results management desires. When executives ask us about the optimum choice of measures, we say that one

Table 5-2.   Types of performance measures.

Benchmark Metrics and Definitions	When Used	Illustrative Performance Measures
Volume: Metrics to gauge "top-line" results in either absolute or relative terms	Undifferentiated sales or margins Relatively simple objectives for the sales organization Straightforward tracking and crediting	Revenue volume in dollars or units Revenue volume as percent of quota New product revenue New customer revenue
Profitability: Metrics to quantify the sale of profitable business	Complex selling situations Focus on profitable top-line growth Varied, potentially competing objectives	Gross margin dollars Gross margin percent Product mix Customer mix Price realization (i.e., actual price to list) Business mix (i.e., applications or solutions that have profit advantage)
Productivity: Metrics to measure improvement of the return on sales investment	New sales process Market expectations Financial expectations	Revenue by sales job Revenue by customer segment Revenue per first order
Strategic Planning: Metrics to confirm the degree to which planning and competency have resulted in business enhancement	Quantitative results hard to measure Long-term process New roles	Events or milestones Specifications Competency utilization Strategic sales objectives Customer objectives Customer service Account share

should be a volume measure that rewards growth. Additional criteria should complement the volume measure, communicating what type of volume is best, where the volume should come from, or how it should be achieved. Some examples are:

- More profitable volume, measured by gross margin dollars or price realization
- More balanced volume, measured by total sales and sales in each of the product lines
- More volume from key market segments, measured by volume realized from specific targeted customers

Once the categories of performance measurement and the specific measures have been determined, management has to set appropriate levels. "Level" in this context refers to the unit of aggregation: an individual's territory, a team's accounts, a district's results, and so forth. Criteria for determining the appropriate measurement level include:

- Where results are affected (individual, team, corporate)
- Where results can be accurately tracked and credited
- What behaviors are critical to success in the new role
- Why the new role was implemented in the first place—what business objectives are to be achieved

While many companies have complex, sophisticated tracking and measurement capabilities that can accurately credit sales to an individual, a zip code, or a territory, it is frequently helpful to take a step back in the process. Because a company *can* measure to this level does not necessarily mean that it *should*. For example, in the medical instruments company we described, the company *could* measure each salesperson, but it *should* have measured the account level to support the teamwork that success required.

The selection of performance measures and level of measurement is critical not only to the success of employees in new sales roles but also to the sales compensation plan design—particularly the incentive formula. To improve decisions you make about performance measures, it is useful to examine the experiences of others. What follows is a variety of currently popular new sales roles and the performance measures firms are using to gauge performance.

How to Choose the Best Performance Measures for Your Company's New Sales Roles

Selecting performance measures for a new sales role is a three-step process. First, you must decide the business objective(s) you want to achieve: growth, profitability, productivity improvement, cost reduction, customer loyalty and retention, or some combination of these five. Second, you must select the indicators or yardsticks that, in your business, reflect successful achievement of the objectives you set and have systems or processes in place for measuring them. For example, all companies want to grow and want that growth to be profitable. It may not be possible to measure profitability at the frontline sales or customer contact level because the firm does not have reliable systems to capture the required data or because assigning credit to the individual(s) who produced the result is highly judgmental (or, at best, a guesstimate).

Finally, the measures selected must be ones that employees in new sales roles can influence through reasonable effort and behavior. We often meet executives who are interested in rewarding their salespeople, both outside sales and inside sales support personnel, for selling profitable business. Unless the employees understand what constitutes profitable business and how they can influence customer buying decisions, measuring sales profitability is not worthwhile. Selecting the best performance measures almost always reflects a compromise between what salespeople influence and what the company can measure.

Pharmaceutical companies are examples of an entire industry that reexamined performance measures based on new sales roles. In the early 1990s, the industry realized that new roles were required to meet the changing needs of the health care marketplace. Managed care, sophisticated end users, and escalating competition all played a part in the need for a new customer coverage model. While new sales roles emerged, performance metrics in most companies were not tied directly to results. The activity-based measures of the past ("How many calls did you make? How many products did you promote during each call?") counted tasks rather than outcomes; DDD (drug distribution data) measured the impact of the salesperson's sales calls on the physician's prescribing habits. However, in the new marketplace, generic drugs were overtaking proprietary products. Managed care formularies could redirect purchasing decisions. Therefore, one key to success in the rapidly changing health care environment was the introduction of regional business units that could provide coverage resources directly related to the needs of a customer base that varied by geography. In this new coverage model, new roles emerged and the ability to measure profitability became especially critical, as the investment in personnel could result in decreased productivity and return on investment.

Many pharmaceutical companies began to use profitability metrics, first at a first-line sales manager level, then at the territory level. To do so required confidence in the industry data that two syndicated research firms gathered and reported, as well as the ability to establish and stick to reasonable profits and losses (P&Ls) at the appropriate level. These metrics frequently included not only sales volume, but also the relative cost of gaining that volume.

The principal of applying judgment to selecting the best performance measures clearly comes into play when the company is implementing new sales roles. With that it mind, it is always helpful to understand the action taken to create a new sales role. It is helpful to ask why the new sales role came into being. One of three actions could result in a new or changed sales role.

Sales responsibilities are added to a current job. In our experience, this is the most common way in which new sales roles are introduced into companies today. The dramatic growth in business teams is nowhere more pronounced than in the customer contact functions: sales, customer service, and market/product management. Customer teams and sales teams have resulted in a fundamental shift in support job emphasis from internal work to servicing customers. In most cases, incumbents in these jobs have gone from having no direct, meaningful responsibility for sales and customer satisfaction to playing a significant role in influencing how customers make purchasing decisions. Another area undergoing significant change in many companies is the call center operation. Traditionally, companies set up these transaction-oriented cost centers to provide customer service; now they are also operating them as revenue centers, as they have given customer service representatives added responsibility for cross selling and up-selling.

Sales responsibilities are subtracted from a current job to decrease its sales role. While this is much less common, we nonetheless observe companies that have created new sales roles as a result of taking away sales responsibilities from a current sales job. This type of change most often occurs when a company implements increased sales specialization. As the business grows, particularly in terms of the size of its product line, the need to bring focus to its selling efforts increases. Companies that once covered the market with geographic sales representatives, dealers, or both find an opportunity to increase sales by specializing resources. Examples include national or major account representatives (accountability for large customers is moved out of the geographic sales representatives' territories), telesales accounts (accountability for small customers is moved out of the geographic sales representatives' territories), and dealer sales (accountability for managing the dealers is shifted from a geographic sales representative to a channel manager).

New sales opportunities are identified that create the need for a sales job where one did not exist before. This is another dimension of sales specialization. The challenges of gaining access to new customers and the limited availability of current sales resources most often are the reasons a firm institutes a completely new sales role. We see dozens of examples in everyday life that illustrate this point. Home Depot, the successful home improvement retailer, decides there is a significant opportunity to grow its business among contractors; it creates a specialized sales force to call on contractors. Kinko's, the copy center with stores a stone's throw from most college campuses, decides that its future rests in part on winning business with corporate customers; it creates a field sales organization to call on business customers to contract for their copier needs. The electric utility industry is currently undergoing deregulation; top managements at these companies are wrestling with how to implement and effectively manage a newly significant sales function, namely, account executives or managers who will call on key customers. In these and other industries, the challenge of defining performance measurement, particularly so that companies can determine the return on investment in their sales resources, occupies a great deal of top management's time.

SIX EXAMPLES OF HOW NEW SALES ROLES AFFECT PERFORMANCE MEASUREMENT

To put into perspective how a new or changed sales role alters the use of performance measures, we have selected some representative examples:

Sales Role Change	*Illustrations*
Sales responsibilities added to a current job	#1: Team selling role added to a field sales representative's responsibility

	#2: Team selling role added to a telesales representative's responsibility
Sales responsibilities subtracted from a current job	#3: Field sales representative redirected to call on only named accounts; gives up responsibility for small accounts to telesales
	#4: Field account executive redirected to function as an account business manager, focus on total business results, and provide access to accounts for sales specialist
New sales job added where one did not exist	#5: Field sales representative introduced into the business organization for the first time
	#6: Channel representative introduced into the business organization for the first time

SALES RESPONSIBILITIES ADDED TO A CURRENT JOB

ILLUSTRATION #1: TEAM SELLING ROLE ADDED TO A FIELD SALES REPRESENTATIVE'S RESPONSIBILITY.

Position: Account executive

Current sales role: Direct sales (persuasion, close) to customers in a geographic territory

Business objectives: Grow sales volume by retaining current accounts and winning new sales at accounts targeted with new selling efforts; maintain or improve gross margins on business with current customers

New sales role (same job title): Added responsibility working as a member of an account team for a defined number of accounts in the district, thereby working outside assigned territory

Performance measures: To reflect added responsibility for winning new customers, a new customer revenue measure is included as a basis for assessing the performance of the account executives involved in this effort. Team-level measurement is critical to successful implementation of the sales role.

Current Sales Role	*New Sales Role*
Volume (sales dollars)	Volume (team sales dollars)
Gross margin dollars	Team gross margin dollars
	New customer revenue

ILLUSTRATION #2: TEAM SELLING ROLE ADDED TO A TELESALES REPRESENTATIVE'S RESPONSIBILITY.

Position: Customer service representative

Current sales role: Responds to inbound calls from customers who wish to place orders

Business objectives: Grow sales volume by focusing field sales representatives on medium-sized to large accounts and reassigning small, infrequent customers to telesales operation

New sales role (new job title): Tele-account sales representative (TAR), responsible for making outbound sales calls to specified target accounts (small) and working with assigned account executive as a team member to win incremental business at assigned major accounts

Performance measures: To reflect added responsibility for retaining and penetrating customers, a goal-based revenue measure is included in the team metrics of TARs working with account executives.

Current Sales Role	*New Sales Role*
Calls per day	Average transaction size
Team revenue goal	Growth goal in team accounts
	Revenue in TAR accounts

SALES RESPONSIBILITY SUBTRACTED FROM A CURRENT JOB

ILLUSTRATION #3: FIELD SALES REPRESENTATIVE REDIRECTED TO CALL ON ONLY NAMED ACCOUNTS; GIVES UP RESPONSIBILITY FOR SMALL ACCOUNTS TO TELESALES.

Position: Territory sales representative

Current sales role: Call on all accounts within defined geographic territory to achieve sales objectives

Business objectives: Grow profit margins by focusing skilled sales resource on larger or more strategic accounts; retain volume across accounts with a less-expensive resource focused on customer service and retention

New sales role: Account manager, responsible for developing ongoing profitable professional relationships with mid- to senior-level contacts within defined accounts to retain and grow business profitably

Performance measures: To reflect the change in responsibility to only selected accounts, the level of performance measurement was changed; the account manager received credit for specialized accounts, rather than all accounts in a geographic territory.

Current Sales Role	New Sales Role
Volume (sales dollars) in the territory	Volume in defined accounts only
	Gross margin percent

ILLUSTRATION #4: FIELD ACCOUNT EXECUTIVE REDIRECTED TO FUNCTION AS AN ACCOUNT BUSINESS MANAGER, FOCUS ON TOTAL BUSINESS RESULTS, AND PROVIDE ACCESS TO ACCOUNTS FOR SALES SPECIALISTS.

Position: Account executive

Current sales role: Direct selling (persuasion, close) to defined account portfolio

Business objectives: Retain customers against significant competitive inroads while growing business across product lines

New sales role: Account business manager, responsible for developing high-level relationships and account plans with customer contact, facilitating access across categories for company sales specialists, and growing account volume and profits through achievement of account and company objectives

Performance measures: To reflect focused responsibility for total business results, both company and customer objectives are included.

Current Sales Role	New Sales Role
Volume (sales dollars)	Account profitability (revenue minus cost)
Product mix	Achievement of account business objectives for select lines

NEW SALES RESPONSIBILITY CREATED

ILLUSTRATION #5: FIELD SALES REPRESENTATIVE INTRODUCED INTO THE BUSINESS ORGANIZATION FOR THE FIRST TIME.

Position: None

Business objectives: Increase volume and optimize inventory turns with focus on business-to-business selling to customers within the delivery radius of each retail outlet

New sales role: Account sales representative

Performance measures: To reflect the challenges associated with implementing this role, which is new to both the company and its potential customers, measures associated with both volume and account selection are implemented.

Traditional Company Measures	*New Sales Role*
Retail volume	Volume increase through retail outlets
Inventory turn	New customer revenue New customer gross margin

ILLUSTRATION #6: CHANNEL REPRESENTATIVE INTRODUCED INTO THE BUSINESS ORGANIZATION FOR THE FIRST TIME.

Position: None.

Business objectives: Increase revenue through sublicensing (resale of licenses) with independent software vendors

New sales role: Channel manager

Performance measures: To reflect the challenges associated with implementing this role, which is new to the company but familiar to sophisticated potential channel partners, measures associated with both volume and successful business planning with the partner are used.

Traditional Company Measures	*New Sales Role*
Net sales volume	MBOs: Design wins, first-year sell-in revenue, qualified leads

| Quota achievement | Partner business plan achievement |
| | Achievement of forecasted sell-through revenue |

SETTING PERFORMANCE OBJECTIVES: WHAT TO DO AND HOW TO DO IT

Selecting the right performance measures is one side of a coin. Equally important, and often the downfall of many sales organizations, is the flip side: performance objectives. Performance objectives are the goals the company assigns to salespeople. Sales goals—often called quotas—are quite helpful in planning and managing the sales effort. Many companies use sales quotas as the basis for evaluating performance and, in turn, for paying sales incentive compensation. Top managers and salespeople share a keen interest, therefore, in ensuring that quotas are realistic—neither so high that they are unreachable nor so low that the business suffers—so that they motivate salespeople to achieve or exceed their goals.

Our surveys suggest that few top executives are satisfied with how quotas are assigned to salespeople. This is because many variables—market data, sales potential, market share, salesperson selling experience, and a manager's skills in working with these variables—influence quota size. Often this makes it difficult to rely on one or two indicators to arrive at a sales quota for a particular salesperson. Generally speaking, the days are gone when all salespeople received the same sales quota increase, for example, when all territories were expected to grow 10 percent over last year. Those days are gone, if for no other reason than that most companies now have access to the data they need to set realistic quotas, at least at a regional level. The challenge, particularly in situations where new sales roles are introduced, is how to allocate the quota fairly and equitably to the individual salespeople or to sales teams.

Also, in some selling situations, particularly where the company is introducing sales roles for the first time (e.g., the utilities), it may not be possible to set quotas based solely on quantitative measures. Sales history is not readily available for customers or from the sales channel through which sales were achieved. When a company establishes a new sales role and, therefore, new sales jobs, it does so based on overall estimates of sales potential. It is not until after the sales representatives—regardless of who they are—have been operating for at least twelve to eighteen months that management can make any conclusions about sales productivity. Situations like these need qualitative measures and goals.

The most common method sales executives use to set sales quotas is historical performance. For example, a territory that contributed 2 percent of the company's national sales last year would be assigned 2 percent of the current year's sales goal. Managers do this because, in most cases, companies have good records on prior years' sales. Also, managers often favor a historical approach to quota assignment because they see it as accurate and impartial. Nonetheless, basing the assignment of sales quotas strictly on historical performance can cause problems.

A quota assignment process based on history assumes that the past is an accurate predictor of the future. Analysis shows, however, that history is not sensitive to territory sales potential. It tends to penalize top-performing salespeople while rewarding the underachiever. This is why top performers often say, "The more I sell, the higher my quota will be next year!" Our experience indicates that the most effective sales quota allocation processes share the three following characteristics.

TERRITORY SALES QUOTAS EQUAL THE BUSINESS PLAN

Sounds obvious? In 40 percent of the situations we have examined over the years, this is not the case. Such a situation is most prevalent in companies that rely primarily on commission compensation plans to pay the sales force. Frequently commission plans are not strongly linked to a sales quota (or there is no quota); the company pays from the first dollar sold. In this situation, salespeople sell what they have to sell to live, not to meet a company business plan.

A second situation occurs in organizations that do have a commission plan with a quota. The issue here is that sales managers frequently use the quota figure as a compensation delivery system rather than as a measure of the company's success. The manager will say to a salesperson, "We have a 10 percent rate above quota, and I know you can only sell $1.2 million. I'll give you as low a quota as I can so that you can kick into that 10 percent rate and get the commission I know you're worth." In theory, quotas are developed to sum to the business goal; in practice, in commissioned sales organizations, managers frequently adjust the quota to deliver compensation rather than results.

At its simplest, the principle means that the sum of all territory quotas equals the top-line (revenue) goal. There may also be a quota for gross margin, sometimes referred to as gross profit. This target is based on an informed judgment about estimates of sales by product line. Total sales and product line sales quotas assigned to salespeople communicate what managers expect overall and by mix of business.

TERRITORY SALES QUOTAS ARE CUSTOMIZED BY ASSESSING THE MARKET CONDITIONS THAT AFFECT SALES IN EACH TERRITORY

Intuitively, first-line sales managers understand the importance of doing this. In many companies, however, the process and tools to help field sales managers with this task are not formalized and readily available. The most effective quota allocation process answers three questions:

1. At what rate is the local market growing?
2. How large is the market in each territory for our company's products, services, or both?
3. What share of the market do we currently have?

You must thoroughly analyze historical data to establish an empirical relationship between market factors and company sales. Our experience shows that market factors generally relate to territory sales in the following ways, and you can therefore apply these guidelines in most sales situations:

- If market potential for products in a territory is larger than in the average territory, expect the territory to increase sales faster than the average growth rate.
- If market potential for products in a territory is growing faster than the national average, expect the territory to increase sales faster than the average rate.
- If market share in a territory is higher than the national average, expect the territory to grow more slowly than the average rate.

Evaluating market factors frequently means relying on external data resources for information about market size, share data, and trends. Increasingly, this type of data is available, in whole or part, from data services like Dun and Bradstreet or industry trade associations. Usually the data are not formatted in a way that is readily adaptable to quota allocation, and that is often the reason companies have not formalized a process or given managers the tools to use it. Our experience suggests that doing so provides you with the opportunity for a competitive advantage.

Account Plans Are Tied to the Sales Quotas

Companies that report high satisfaction with their quota allocation process tell us that one key reason for this feeling is that field sales managers insist that their salespeople develop rigorous account plans to support territory growth goals. These territory plans effectively analyze the customers and identify the 20 percent of the accounts that produce 80 percent of the business. Generally, companies formalize account plans for a territory's largest accounts. A solid account plan gauges the economic health of customers and their plans to maintain or expand their business. It forecasts how much each customer will spend on certain products, services, or both and what share of those purchases the company can expect through continuous, focused attention to quality service delivery and customer relationship management. It also provides a solid road map of ways to maintain or expand sales at the account. Finally, account plans are extremely useful as a reality check to top-down assigned quotas—the prevailing practice at most companies. Before you wrap up the year's quotas, you must reconcile any large gaps between the top-down quota and the bottom-up forecasts of sales based on account plans.

Setting Performance Expectations: What to Do and How to Do It

Software applications designed to help companies improve the process used to assign sales quotas to their salespeople are available from a limited number of CRM vendors. In fact, an article in *Customer Relationship Management* indicates that most CRM systems offer limited functionality for sales managers when it comes to decision support tools for applications like quota-assignment.[1] According to that article, there is one notable exception, and that is Ockham Technologies, a software company specializing in tools to help managers increase sales productivity.

Jim Triandiflou, Ockham Technologies' president and CEO, believes that the best way to establish quotas for a sales force is through a "top-down/bottom-up" method with strong emphasis on the "bottom-up" phase of the process. One of the problems with that approach, of course, is the time required for the process to work well. To solve that problem, and also to increase management's confidence in the quotas assigned to salespeople, Ockham Technologies developed SRQuota. This software product eliminates quota guesswork, replacing the "shot in the dark" approach with a systematic methodology that combines third-party information on market potential with best practices processes. Jim Trian-diflou tells us that if a company wants to assign its sales quotas within the first fifteen days of a new fiscal year—which fewer than 10 percent of *Fortune* 1000 companies do—then top managers must be compelled to adopt a software application to reduce cycle time and increase accuracy in the process.

For companies dedicated to continually improving their efforts to allocate ambitious, yet realistic quotas, there are three basic processes to consider, as illustrated in Figure 5-4. These three processes are major account analysis, Fair-Share assignment, and algorithm solution. Matched with these are three primary sources of information for decision making: judgment, account knowledge, and historical data.

To help you understand how to use this chart, consider the coverage model for many small accounts. Judgment and account knowledge are less useful than quantitative data, and an algorithm solution is likely to be appropriate. On the other hand, a coverage model of a few large accounts generally requires good judgment and extensive account knowledge to analyze major accounts accurately.

Fig. 5-4.   Alternative approaches to setting product quotas.

Module Type	Primary Source of Information	Type of Process

Algorithm quota allocation method. Companies with many points of purchase often use an algorithm method to make the initial assignment of quotas to salespeople in their territories. This method requires a company to build a statistical model to relate prior period territory sales for all territories to prior period market data. The objective is to develop a model that you can use to project territory sales and convert that projection into a sales quota. While companies apply many variables to increase accuracy, the two most common are market share and market growth. The method works best in situations where market data are readily available—the pharmaceutical and semiconductor industries are two in which this method is actually used—and in territories that have, on average, fifty or more accounts. Fewer accounts, we find, makes it difficult to build a model that has significant statistical accuracy and reliability.

Fair-Share sales quota method. We developed this method several years ago in response to sales situations where:

1. The product was new to the market.
2. Historical sales information was limited or did not exist.
3. The product was the only one in its category.

This method identifies a like or comparable product to determine trends in either market or product growth at the territory level. Based on this association, the company determines the previous year's percentage or share of total sales. Management then allocates an individual sales representative's goal—his "fair share" of the national goal—based on this contribution. The actual Fair-Share quota is then modified up or down based on such factors as market volatility, competitive intensity, and years of experience of the salesperson. Territories that show strong growth, overall and for the comparable product, would be assigned a proportionally higher fair share, while territories with flat or declining sales would be allocated proportionally less of the national number.

Major/key account plan–based quota method. In sales situations where you have a limited number of accounts, sufficient account profiles, and market data is outdated, inadequate, or unavailable, the best approach to assigning quotas is to use an account plan method. The account plans are the primary basis on which a company allocates quotas in this type of situation because statistical techniques applied to a few large and complex customers are not meaningful. For a limited number of accounts (five or fewer), it is much more productive to identify the strategies and tactics associated with maximizing sales at each individual account. Typically, an account plan for a large customer identifies:

1. Past sales and the share of business currently enjoyed;
2. Decision makers at the account and the basis on which they make decisions about purchases;
3. Products, services, applications, and solutions that you could sell relative to customer needs, in the short and long term;
4. The basis on which the company will differentiate itself from the competition;
5. Tactics that you will use to retain and expand current business and win new business and over what time period they will be implemented; and
6. Expected sales results.

In this type of sales environment, you can measure salespeople on the extent to which their plans meet the standards defined in the account plan and how successful they were in actually implementing the tactics the plan laid out. Some companies find it helpful to supplement the account plan approach to quota allocations with competency-based factors.

Regardless of the specific method they use, companies most pleased with their sales quota assignment practices employ a balanced approach to determining the numbers assigned to salespeople. This means that the top-down expectations must be balanced with the bottom-up estimates of sales opportunity. Because top managers see the market from the 40,000-foot level, they must rely on their frontline sales and customer service employees to center the company on the opportunities that are available at customer level, the street level of the business. Thus, before setting the quota numbers, it is prudent to listen to salespeople's responses to such questions as: "What's going on with the customers' businesses? Are those changes likely to affect the volume of business we are getting this year? Are there any emerging new customers we should focus on? Are our customers getting into new markets, and, if so, what opportunities do these represent for us?"

TWO NEW APPROACHES FOR MEASURING THE SUCCESS OF NEW SALES ROLES

Whatever financial metrics companies include in the sales compensation program, many plan designers have identified a need for less-quantifiable metrics. The rapid evolution of sales roles has resulted in rapidly expanding competency requirements for success in these roles. Longer sales processes, multiple customer interaction points, complex product/ service offerings, and disparate company coverage resources have clouded the measurement process.

The traditional "management by objective" approach is no longer popular in plans for new roles, perhaps because the planning and implementation were monitored or implemented inconsistently. Many companies have experimented successfully, however, with nontraditional measures that directly link the salesperson's success in a new role to reaching business objectives through nonquantifiable metrics. This evolution of measurement is taking place across many industries and in many new roles. The following two examples typify the most prevalent approaches being implemented for this type of measure.

CONSUMER PRODUCTS COMPANY

This company had enjoyed a long history of market dominance and profitable sales growth. The advent of category management in the retail grocery and drugstore market resulted in a significant shift in business-to-business customer expectations. The customers within the major retail chain headquarters were focused on sell-through, inventory optimization, merchandising support, and vendor value-added services that helped them achieve their objectives. Clearly, the old role of "merchandise and promote the latest deal" was no longer effective. The company implemented a new account management role and a process that required extensive business planning skills. It linked identified competencies to realizing specific business objectives. In fact, this company had concluded that many objectives could not or would not be achieved unless the sales personnel had developed the identified competencies, which include:

>   *Customer focus:* Accurate, timely, and effective identification of customer supply chain needs and objectives; ongoing collaboration with customers to build customer satisfaction while achieving business unit goals.
>   *Business skills:* Serves as a sales force resource to provide expertise in the supply chain that leads to attainment of short-term and long-term goals and customer satisfaction.
>   *Implementation/achievement orientation:* The drive to accomplish defined goals and milestones; a complete understanding of the

reasons for success. The degree to which the account executive has been successful in establishing and achieving specific geographic, account, and company objectives.

The company defined "anchors," or critical observable behaviors, for each competency (see Figure 5-5), and one of the anchors was a business objective related to that competency. The measure therefore linked observed competency to quantified outcomes. While this was not

Fig. 5-5.   Account executive: customer focus.

Customer Focus: Accurate, timely, and effective identification of customer needs and objectives; ongoing collaboration with customers to build customer satisfaction while achieving Company's business goals.

Anchors: "Effective"	Anchors: "Less Effective"
• ***Individual Objective:*** Customer satisfaction high; loyalty results in 100% retention and 20% growth in accounts	• ***Individual Objective:*** Customer satisfaction and business lower than or same as prior year
• Networks throughout customer organization for effective results	• Maintains lower-level relationships, with little focus on expanding network with account and marketplace
• Understands customer philosophies and objectives	• Focus is on Company's objectives, with little accurate understanding of customer objectives
• Maximizes Company's available tools and resources for optimal customer satisfaction	• Generally uses only traditional tools and processes; focus is on business building to the detriment of customer satisfaction
• Investigates customer/marketplace for new or incremental opportunities	• Seldom proactive in searching for new opportunities
• Ability to blend Company's strategies with customers' strategies	• Focus is primarily on either Company *or* customer plans and expectations
• Understands strengths/weaknesses with customer and works toward continuous improvement	• Focuses exclusively on Company's strengths to grow sales; customer satisfaction is static

Q2 Comments:

Q3 Comments:

Q4 Comments and Rating:

the only measure the firm used in the sales compensation program for the new role, it was the measure managers used most actively in ensuring that the sales talent available was appropriate to meet customer expectations and achieve the company's business objectives.

PHARMACEUTICAL COMPANY

This company was part of the industry evolution to region business units. As part of the reinvention, the company organized account and market segment business teams to focus on its customers' unique needs. A key success factor for each team was the ability to set and monitor progress toward achievement of account objectives together and with account contacts. This company implemented a consistent process for developing strategic sales objectives and account plans that started with management's definition of what they wanted to accomplish (volume, profit, new accounts, new product sales). Summarized, the company used this process:

Step 1: Select elements based on company business objectives.
Step 2: Formulate strategic objectives by account or by team.
Step 3: Assign relative weights for multiple objectives.
Step 4: Determine measurements of success (tools, systems, milestones).
Step 5: Establish performance-level standards (threshold, target).
Step 6: Management review/approval.
Step 7: Implement.
Step 8: Periodic management review of status and results.

Figure 5-6 provides a worksheet developed by one team to serve as the basis for management review of progress. The company found that over time, all teams were using a disciplined process to work together and with their accounts to develop appropriate objectives that supported achievement of company and account business results. At that point, the company discontinued employing this measure as a component of the sales compensation program.

THREE PERFORMANCE MANAGEMENT CHALLENGES AND HOW TO DEAL WITH THEM

Managers often tell us that performance management is one of the most, if not *the* most, challenging aspects of their jobs. Constant change makes performance management difficult—new customers, new prod-

Fig. 5-6. Strategic objective worksheet.

Strategic Objective: To attain formulary status of Product at ABC for nonrestricted use.												
Key Action Steps	**Jan.**	**Feb.**	**Mar.**	**Apr.**	**May**	**June**	**July**	**Aug.**	**Sept.**	**Oct.**	**Nov.**	**Dec.**
Determine all P&T committee members	x											
Establish relationship with each member		x										
Determine key decision makers		x										
Work with other Co. personnel: information on key decision criteria			x									
Work with medical information: information package					x							
Work with Co. personnel: other product information needed							x					
July P&T: approved for restricted use									x			
Seek additional information concerning competitor's strategy and message to the committee										x		
Provide information to P&T committee during next meeting											x	
Provide additional resources to committee as necessary to support positive decision												x
Achieve active formulary status; nonrestricted use												x

Legend

Threshold

Target

ucts, new competitors, new sales channels, new sales jobs, new processes, and more. We observe that companies that are successful in growing their business profitability do overcome these difficulties to sales performance management. They do so because they identify and resolve issues quickly. We find that the big challenges these companies face fall into three categories. Following are those challenges and what companies did to deal with them.

SELECTING THE BEST PERFORMANCE MEASURES

Managers tell us that deciding on what performance measures to use is often the most challenging task. This is particularly true when the firm introduces new sales roles, because the announcement is followed by a period of uncertainty about how the jobs should operate. We have observed many situations where companies announce new sales roles and for several months thereafter communicate minimal information about how employee performance will be measured and rewarded. Virtually all companies use a production measure of sales performance, either units or revenue, so choosing the first performance measure is usually straightforward. The challenge is to select the one or two measures that should be used in addition to volume.

How do companies deal with the challenge of selecting the best measures? First, they focus on making the new job or job role very clear. That clarity flows from the business's sales strategy: Who are the customers, what is the value proposition, and how does the sales job bring those together with the customer's requirements? Next, they define the results expected in the new sales roles or jobs by answering this question: What performance or result do we expect to get after we implement new sales roles that we were not previously getting? Finally, they look at the requirement for the interrelationship of measures up, down, and across the organization. For example, when considering new sales roles in a field sales organization, we have always found it helpful to identify the expectations for results one or two organizational levels up from the new job. If at higher levels there is an accountability for profit—gross margin, for example—then it is essential to consider in what way that measure could be applied to a new sales role. Failing to do so could result in missing an important opportunity for which a new sales job was created.

LIMITING THE NUMBER OF MEASURES TO THREE OR FEWER

As we've described above, focusing on what we expect of a new sales role is a good place to start when we study what performance measures we ought to use. The challenge of what to measure is often rivaled by the number of measures. This often comes about because companies wrestle with the trade-off between quantitative and qualitative measures. Two or three financial performance measures are selected (or have always been used), and, because of a change to a sales role, new measures are suggested. These measures may be qualitative indicators of performance, ones that top managers believe will reinforce the requirement for new behaviors in new sales roles. We find that more than three measures of performance, however, is often confusing and counterproductive. The way a company can overcome the temptation to use more than three measures is by asking top managers to rank a list of performance measures. The company can then tabulate and summarize the results, selecting the top three.

TRAINING MANAGERS IN EFFECTIVE PERFORMANCE MANAGEMENT

The single biggest obstacle to effectively implementing new sales roles, regardless of the industry or company, is the lack of managerial skill in how to determine and assign performance goals. This is actually a two-dimensional problem for companies: First, some companies lack a formal process for allocating goals to salespeople; they leave these decisions up to local managers. In good times, this is not a problem. When salespeople miss their targets—or, as occasionally happens, when some "blow out" the target, which suggests that goals were set too low—management rivets its attention on figuring out why this happened.

Second, companies often lack accurate and reliable data on new performance measures for new sales roles and, even when such data are available, frontline managers do not know how to work with them. Companies that have overcome this challenge have done so by gradually introducing new measures. This means they confirmed both the process and the tools required to manage effectively with new measures before the business used the measures to assess performance or to make decisions about sales compensation.

SUMMING UP

Too many performance measures, the wrong measures, the wrong level of measurement, or measures that conflict with the salesperson's job mean that a company may not reach a new sales plan's objectives. Too many measures reflects top management's confusion over a sales job's most important objectives. The wrong measures or measures that conflict with the salesperson's job mean that the company rewards salespeople for the wrong things.

Even among the best companies, aligning performance measures with business objectives for sales and customer contact jobs is challenging. When a shift takes place in who the customer is, however, and a company responds by implementing new sales roles, those changes create a need for a new or revised performance management process. Performance management involves selecting the right measures to gauge business results, establishing standards to define expectations, tracking actual accomplishment, and providing guidance to help employees achieve success.

The Sales Strategy Matrix and CPR Analysis give top managers a framework and a tool to shape a leadership message that is more complete, one that says not only how much but how sales growth can be achieved and will be measured. The matrix and analysis help managers see where today's sales growth is coming from, set realistic growth objectives for the future, and monitor the conversion, penetration, and retention results.

We've found that a company should use three or fewer measures for any sales job; more than three and it becomes very difficult and often confusing for employees to focus their behavior on results management desires. Selecting measures is a three-step process: Decide the business objective(s) you want to achieve; select the indicators or yardsticks that, in your business, reflect successful achievement of the objectives you set; ensure that the measures are ones that employees can influence through reasonable effort and behavior.

Companies need these measures when new sales roles come into being because the firm (1) adds sales responsibilities to a current job, (2) subtracts sales responsibilities from a current job, or (3) identifies new sales opportunities that create the need for a sales job where one did not exist before. In each case, as the sales role changes, the performance measures and performance objectives should also change. While few executives, sales managers, or salespeople are entirely satisfied with the way the company sets performance objectives (quotas), those most satisfied say that field sales managers assist their salespeople to develop rigorous account plans that support territory growth goals. It means that top-down expectations are balanced with the bottom-up estimates of sales opportunity.

DESIGNING COMPENSATION PLANS FOR NEW SALES ROLES

An effective sales compensation plan requires the company to clearly define the roles and objectives of the jobs to be paid. This is especially important when the company may be paying employees differently in the future than it has in the past, based on the new sales roles that the business has created and implemented. Often, employees who are being paid on the basis of a new sales role have never received this form of compensation before; they have earned an hourly rate or straight salary.

Increasingly, sales shares its role with other functions outside of the sales department. A study conducted by Hewitt Associates LLC of 227 corporate sales forces found that about 46 percent of these companies have organized individual sales and service or support people into sales teams. As a result, in some companies, the sales department no longer has the sole responsibility for winning and retaining customers. A shift to shared responsibility means that all company managers need a much broader understanding of how sales compensation works. In fact, managers who have traditionally managed nonsales functions such as service, customer marketing, and operations are being asked to manage employees in new sales roles and to manage with a sales compensation plan for the first time.

Of course, it is also true that as the traditional sales role evolves within a business (responsibilities added or subtracted), management can employ the sales compensation program to send a clear message to the organization about the change. It is as important to ensure that the sales compensation program is well suited to new-to-the-world (or at least new-to-the-company) sales roles as it is to reexamine the sales compensation program whenever the sales job changes significantly.

Remember that the sales compensation program is an essential management tool in directing and supporting the behaviors, skills, and results a new role requires. We find that many times, executives lose sight of this important use for sales compensation in the excitement of implementing the sales role. Often, sales (and other) managers focus on the programs that worked in the past, rather than rethinking their approach to sales compensation. Developing a sales compensation program for new roles is really a construction project, and it's important to have all the materials or building blocks in place before actual construction begins.

With that in mind, this chapter has two objectives. First, we explain the basics of sales compensation, which has a unique vocabulary to describe various plan characteristics, pay calculation, and payment terms. It helps to understand the terms and how various plan elements actually work. Second, we describe how sales compensation applies to new sales roles. We give examples to illustrate how companies that have adopted new sales roles have successfully employed the compensation concepts and techniques in this book. We present these examples within the framework of the new sales roles we described in chapter 5:

- Current sales jobs—*added* sales responsibilities
- Current sales jobs—*subtracted* sales responsibilities
- New sales roles—sales jobs *created* where none existed

Eight Key Sales Compensation Terms and Definitions

Whether you are dealing with a current sales job that has a change in responsibilities or a completely new sales job, a sales compensation plan design requires you to make decisions about a number of key elements. Managers frequently debate sales compensation plan practices because there is no common understanding of what plan terms mean or how to apply the various terms and plan mechanics to particular sales situations. We believe it is helpful for top managers to understand plan elements, their key terms and definitions. The following are the eight most important features of any plan design (see Appendix A for a more complete glossary of terms related to compensating new sales roles).

1. *Eligibility:* Determination of eligibility. The job(s) that participate in the incentive plan are determined by comparing their content to defined criteria. The two most common factors companies use to make this determination are customer contact and degree of persuasion. Typically, the job must involve both contact with customers and a persuasion role—influencing the customer to make a buying decision—to be eligible for participation in the plan. Employees in customer service jobs who have customer contact but do not persuade them to buy may therefore not be eligible for an incentive pay opportunity.
2. *Total target compensation:* The total target cash compensation (including base salary and variable incentive compensation) available for achieving expected results.
3. *Salary/incentive mix:* The ratio of base salary to incentive opportunity as percentages of the total target compensation; expressed as two portions of 100 percent.
4. *Incentive pay leverage:* The amount of upside opportunity beyond total target compensation that management expects outstanding performers to earn.
5. *Performance range:* Defined levels of achievement (most commonly termed threshold, target, and excellence) relative to objectives that the organization uses to determine the point at which payout begins and the payout rate between defined points of achievement.
6. *Incentive formula:* The mathematical ways in which the pay opportunity relates to performance, and in which one pay opportunity relates to another, in order to determine payout.
7. *Sales crediting:* Occurrence when a sale can be counted for compensation purposes for one or more employees.
8. *Performance and payment periods:* The time over which the firm measures performance and the time period for which it makes a payout.

Each of these eight design elements is really a sales compensation plan building block, and each serves a unique and distinctive role in the plan design. As Figure 6-1 illustrates, many of the building blocks for an effective plan for your new sales roles should already be in place by the time you reach the point of designing the mechanics for the incentive plan. Specifically, as illustrated in Figures 4-3 and 4-4 in Chapter 4, you should have confirmed which jobs will be eligible for sales compensa-

Fig. 6-1.   Optimal design process: develop incentive plan mechanics.

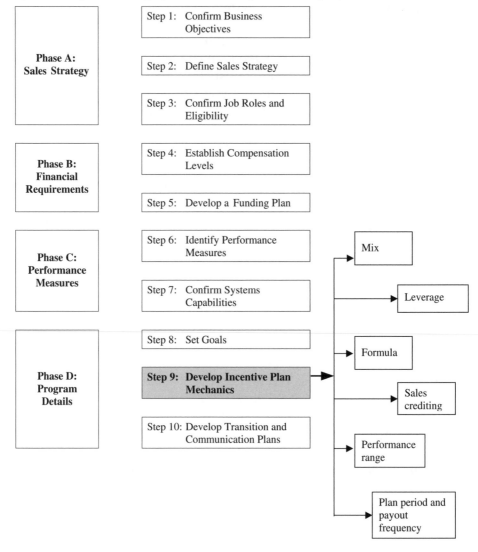

tion and have established the target compensation levels that are right for those jobs. Therefore, designing the details of the program, as shown in Figure 6-1, must include each of the six elements identified in step 9 before you can consider the plan design process complete.

How To Determine The Right Salary/Incentive Mix

The first building block that managers usually have to tackle in the detailed design process is "mix," since this establishes how much will be available for the incentive plan payout. To determine the mix appropriate to a specific new role, you must look at several criteria including:

- The role of the salesperson (or any other customer contact job) in the sales process, which must take into consideration the nature of the product or service being sold; the extent of price competition (weak or extensive); customer loyalty (to the company or to the salesperson); the degree of expertise required to be effective in the process; the types of sales objectives (strategic objectives or pure volume); and the type of selling required (consultative/ complex or transactional).
- Management style or practices the company uses in directing or working with the salesperson: Is the salesperson a team member or an individual contributor? Is the salesperson the factor or one of many variables in the sales process? Is the relationship between the salesperson and the company based on loyalty and respect or on finances (i.e., an agent relationship)?

The salary/incentive ratio defines the manner in which compensation is delivered to an employee in a current or new sales role, that is, the percent of target total compensation paid in salary versus the percent at risk through the incentive pay arrangement. The exact salary/incentive ratio for a particular sales job is based on the influence of the job in purchase decisions. Job definition, therefore, is the key to success in the plan design process. A clear definition of the job's role, responsibilities, and expected performance outcomes must be available before you design any compensation plan.

For example, the more important the salesperson is in the buying process and the shorter the timeframe to complete a sales transaction—from initial sales contact to the commitment to a sale—the more likely it is that the incentive component will be high. Industry surveys suggest that an average salary/incentive ratio is 70/30. Jobs paid with a 50/50 ratio indicate that the employee has a significant influence on the customer's buying decisions. Conversely, a job paid with a 90/10 ratio suggests that the employee is only one of many factors affecting the buying decision.

A simple way to approach determining the salary/incentive mix is to develop a rating chart like the one in Figure 6-2. Many companies customize the criteria to their own situation and complete an exercise with management to ensure that the mix for new jobs is consistent with actual job expectations and definition. You could use this as a timely check to confirm that everyone's expectations for the job are the same and that all stakeholders in the job think of the relationship of the salesperson to the company in the same way. In fact, as the design of the sales compensation plan moves forward, the designers may determine

Fig. 6-2.   Factors determining salary/incentive mix.

		Low Incentive (up to 100% Salary/ 0% Incentive)	(Check Rating)					High Incentive (up to 0% Salary/ 100% Incentive)
			5	4	3	2	1	
Role of Salesperson in the Sales Process	Nature of Product	Unique/Complex	❏	❏	❏	❏	❏	Commodity
	Price Competition	Weak	❏	❏	❏	❏	❏	Strong
	Customer Loyalty	Company	❏	❏	❏	❏	❏	Sales Rep
	Expertise	Extensive	❏	❏	❏	❏	❏	Limited
	Sales Objectives	Strategic	❏	❏	❏	❏	❏	Volume
	Type of Selling	Consultative	❏	❏	❏	❏	❏	Transactional
	Sale of	Relationships	❏	❏	❏	❏	❏	Product
	Number of Sales	Few	❏	❏	❏	❏	❏	Many
	Seasonality	Heavy	❏	❏	❏	❏	❏	None
Management & Perception of Salesperson by the Organization	View of Salesperson	Team Members	❏	❏	❏	❏	❏	"Agents"
	Impact of Salesperson	One Factor	❏	❏	❏	❏	❏	Primary Factor
	Relationship	Loyalty/Respect	❏	❏	❏	❏	❏	Economic
	Supervision	Extensive	❏	❏	❏	❏	❏	Limited
	Management Style	Value-Driven	❏	❏	❏	❏	❏	Entrepreneurial
		Totals						
		Overall Result						

Illustrative Rating Guide (customized rating tiers should be developed for each organization):

53 – 70: High salary/low incentive; complex, long-term selling process, unique product or service, team focus, high-level customer relationships

31 – 52: Median salary/incentive ratio; evolving jobs and processes, diverse products or services, both individual and team contributions

14 – 30: High incentive/low salary; transactional sales, short selling cycle, commodity products, salesperson controls the sales process

that many responsibilities or outcomes of the new role may not be paid for through incentives. This is especially true of jobs that are responsible for longer-term relationships and more complex selling situations.

A systematic approach to confirming the salary/incentive mix for each new sales role is an important first step in developing the sales compensation program. The mix decision really defines which element of pay has the highest visibility to the employee in a new sales role. Since

Table 6-1. Balancing mix and message.

Percent of Pay at Risk	Impact	Message
Less than 10%	Minimal to none	Recognize performance
10–15%	Performance reminder	Prompt
15–25%	Directional	Motivate to action
25–50%	Highly directional	Stimulate positive consistent action
Over 50%	Independent action	Act autonomously

the manager can use each element differently, it's important to be sure that the right element receives the higher weight, based on what the new job is expected to accomplish.

Salary: Salary recognizes the skills, experiences, and development that a job requires. It is the currency that provides sales managers with the opportunity to ask for behaviors, activities, and results that may not be immediately measurable or rewarded by the incentive plan. Regular performance appraisal is critical to supporting the effective use of salary as a management and development tool because through it a salary is adjusted up or down over time.

Incentive at-risk compensation: Companies use two types of variable compensation, "at-risk" and "add-on." Incentive compensation for sales roles is generally at risk, that is, some people may not receive any and some may receive more than the target amount. At-risk pay means that a person's salary is not intended to be the total cash compensation and that the person can increase the total through significant over-achievement. Another type of variable pay is an add-on incentive. Add-on incentives are *not* considered part of a target total compensation; they are added on as an additional cost to the organization, and there is no additional upside opportunity. Contests, spot awards, and recognition awards are add-on incentives, rather than at-risk pay.

The mix of fixed pay to variable (incentive) pay delivers a powerful message to the salesperson. As Table 6-1 shows, the more aggressive the mix, the more autonomously the firm expects the salespeople to act. A very low mix (10 percent or less of pay at risk) is really retrospective pay; the message is, "It looks like you did a really good job there." A median mix (20–40 percent of pay at risk) is prospective; the message is, "I really believe you can do a great job, and when you do, you'll be financially recognized for it." With a very aggressive mix (more than 50 percent of pay at risk), the message is, "Do what you gotta do; we're not going to get in your way." In fact, one manager has told us that a very high mix is really "anti–sales management," while a very low mix is "long-term and strategic."

Executives frequently ask us about mix and how to assess and use this building block. The following are some of the questions we are asked most often.

How Much Incentive Do You Need to Motivate the Salesperson?

As companies begin to design the pay plans for new sales roles, this is frequently the first question managers ask. The motivational value of pay varies by individual; however, a reasonable rule of thumb is that 10 percent of base salary is a good starting point. Employees in new roles may perceive any less as "interesting" or "a nice reward," but it does not have the motivational impact of a higher percentage of pay at risk.

Illustration: For a $60,000 sales job with a 90/10 salary/incentive ratio, the target bonus would be $6,000 or 11 percent of salary. For most people, $6,000 would be sufficient to be motivational; that is, an individual would put forth the effort required to achieve performance results associated with the target incentive pay opportunity.

Of course, it is critical for the plan designers to determine the right mix based on defined criteria, but there are no absolutes. An adjustment up or down of 5 percent may be the difference between a program that effectively supports the new role and rewards for success and one that does not.

When the Mix is Altered, Particularly from a Low-Salary/High-Incentive to a Higher-Salary/Lower-Incentive, Aren't You Actually Reducing the Motivation for Salespeople to Perform at High Levels?

The most typical examples of this type of shift in mix are from 30/70 salary/incentive to 50/50, from 40/60 to 60/40, or from 50/50 to 70/30. Typically, when managers alter the mix in a manner that reduces the incentive and increases the base, they do so because they are trying to address fundamental changes in the manner in which the buying/selling process operates, and roles involved in the process, and how success in those jobs should be addressed.

Illustration: A major cable TV company grew rapidly as a result of substantially expanding its base of advertisers to include small and mid-size businesses. The corporation accomplished this in part with a sales force that was paid 40 percent salary and 60 percent commission. Shortly after the company announced the best ad sales year in its history, top management was confronted with some serious challenges. First, sales managers reported that many of the customers the company booked when they were small were now quite large in terms of their advertising needs and in terms of the demands they were placing on the account executives' time. The account executives were spending more time acting as business advisors to their current customers. This meant that they actually had less time available to sell to new accounts because they were so busy servicing current accounts.

Second, the human resources department reported that it was becoming more and more difficult to hire talented new salespeople at the base salaries—40 percent of the total compensation opportunity—the company offered. The level of experience and talent the company sought was simply not available at the salary level the company was paying. Finally, in some metropolitan markets, the company's competitors were recruiting and hiring its people by offering higher salaries and slightly less incentive pay. For these reasons, top management shifted the salary/incentive ratio from 40/60 to 60/40. While this shift did increase fixed costs and reduce the upside earnings opportunity for the account executives, on balance, it resolved all three major challenges. Namely, it enabled account executives to spend more time with current customers because proportionately less pay was at risk; it enabled human resources to attract both more and better candidates; and it slowed turnover because the new salary levels were more in line with labor market practices.

WHEN AND WHY WOULD MIX SHIFT FROM MORE TO LESS SALARY, FROM 100/0, FOR EXAMPLE, TO 90/10, OR FROM 90/10 TO 70/30?

Typically, this happens when the company *adds* responsibility to a sales job or creates a new role in the marketing and customer relationship management processes. This kind of change generally implies that "selling" has gained a more prominent role in doing business with customers. For example, as customers have more choices, the role of personal selling can be more influential in attracting and retaining business with customers.

Illustration: The most extreme example of an increase in choices is when an industry deregulates. The breakup of AT&T in the early 1980s meant that the long distance telephone industry, once deregulated, provided both residential and business customers with the opportunity to select their phone company. Today, the electric utility industry is going through a similar change, one that will offer businesses and consumers the opportunity to select an energy provider. Before deregulation, customer service representatives (sometimes called account executives to imply a sales responsibility) in both industries essentially serviced captive demand. There was no need to persuade; the providers—AT&T or the local electric utility—had a monopoly. Deregulation changed this. Companies needed sellers to explain to customers why they would be better off staying with their current service provider rather than switching.

Another example, less extreme than deregulation, is product proliferation. Consider the cosmetics and fragrances industry. At one time, these companies usually paid the beauty consultants who worked the counters in the upscale department stores an hourly salary. Today, given the broad range of products available not only at department stores but through other outlets, counter personnel are encouraged to be much more aggressive in their selling tactics. This is achieved in no small part by the shift in compensation from predominantly salary to salary plus commission.

Generally speaking, "where there's mix, there's leverage" in the design of the sales compensation program. The next building block, leverage, is really the upside opportunity available to be paid through the incentive plan, and it is a powerful way to motivate people in new sales roles.

LEVERAGE

Leverage is the upside earnings opportunity, or the portion of compensation placed at risk, because of the nature and role of a sales job. *Upside* means the pay available to the salesperson for outstanding achievement—more than 100 percent of objectives. The rationale behind leverage is this: Management establishes target total cash compensation for a sales job based on company philosophy and labor market pay levels. The total pay level reflects the competitive rate a salesperson earns for doing a fully effective job. This assumes that the job is not new to the world and that management can assess some reasonable range of competitive pay. If the job is new to the world, management will have to determine the pay by means other than competitive rates. When a salesperson signs on for a job, however, it is almost always the case that some portion of the total pay is withheld or placed at risk on the premise that it will act as an incentive to the salesperson to deliver a certain level of results. (The mix exercise described in the first building block helps you determine this portion.)

Placing pay at risk should provide salespeople the opportunity to earn back not just the at-risk amount, but more. How much more is defined through the mechanics of leverage, which can be one to three times the at-risk pay. Generally, when discussing the leverage with salespeople, managers express the upside as a multiple of the target incentive. For example, if the incentive opportunity is $10,000 with a two times leverage, the upside incentive opportunity is $20,000 and the total incentive opportunity is $30,000. An upside opportunity (the pay above target incentive) of two times target is also referred to as *triple leverage*, since the *total* incentive opportunity is three times target (target plus two times target).

Unlike mix, which is based on the job, leverage is largely determined by (1) market opportunity and the company's assessment of the opportunity to succeed through a person's selling efforts, and (2) the profitability of additional sales and the extent to which the company can share that profitability with the employees in the new sales role. Leverage is therefore a fairly complex balancing act for plan designers—"What do we need or want to have happen?" versus "Just how profitable is that likely to be for us?" The designers do have leverage tools that they can use to help with this balancing act: the limitations tools and the rates tools.

Limitations. Using limitations tools can contain the company's financial exposure. For many traditional organizations, either the plan was capped (considered "very bad" by salespeople and "very good" by finance) or the plan was not capped and continued to pay out forever (considered "great" by salespeople and "a nightmare" by finance). The cap is really the toughest limitation tool. Above a cap, the company pays no further incentive no matter how superior the salesperson's performance. Particularly in new sales roles, where setting objectives may be difficult or impossible, companies have found an acceptable midway limiting tool, the *visor*. The visor is a technique that provides for additional payout if the employee achieves other criteria or milestones. For example, a visor may provide for payout at year end for any quarter's achievement that is truly exceptional. (Later in this chapter we will talk about how a level of performance like "truly exceptional" is defined.)

Rates tools. The *rate* is the dollar amount of the percentage of the target opportunity the company pays for each increment of achievement above and below target achievement. Rates do not necessarily have to be the same above and below target. Some rules of thumb about payout rates:

1. Increase the rate when sales are increasingly difficult, but additional sales are increasingly profitable.
2. Decrease the rate when each additional sale is easy and excessive sales are unprofitable.

For many companies, the rate tool can be used as a form of limitation. For example, the company decides to uncap the plan for a new sales role to make it more attractive to the people it will try to attract, and the firm has valid financial measurement systems in place. Management is concerned about runaway incentive costs, however, so the rate paid above a defined performance level slowly decreases. As an illustration, the company might pay $100 per percentage point of plan up to target and $50 for every percentage point above target. No cap, but earnings decelerate.

How to Establish a Performance Range

Along with implementing new sales roles, companies frequently find that traditional approaches to setting performance achievement parameters are helpful. Setting performance ranges makes it possible for the company to develop initial cost estimates and determine potential payout curves. The common terms to describe performance expectations are:

> *Threshold:* The minimum level of performance that an employee must achieve before the company pays an incentive.
> *Target:* The expected level of sales results or individual performance.
> *Excellence:* Individual sales performance that is in the ninetieth percentile (top 10 percent) of all individuals whose performance is being measured.

In a standard (bell-shaped) performance curve, you can expect 90 to 95 percent of salespeople to reach threshold level, 80 to 85 percent to perform between threshold and excellence level, and 5 to 10 percent to reach excellence level, truly exceptional performance.

You should set target goals for each salesperson at a level that they must stretch to reach. For new sales roles, management frequently expects "stretch" performances to prove to the top executives that the investment in a new type of resource has a return in value to the company. The payout for target performance is the yardstick that will determine both when the company can afford to begin paying, and how high it will pay for overachievement.

Once the company sets goals relative to target expectations (financial or nonfinancial), it can use the defined level of achievement for each objective to determine the point at which incentive payout begins. It can then calculate the payout rate between defined points of achievement. Gaining threshold is the "ticket to the game" for the person in a new sales role.

You should set excellence levels to reflect exceptional performance attained by the top 5 to 10 percent of salespeople. Excellence level achievement is psychologically valuable because it recognizes top performers while motivating others to reach this level.

Companies that are implementing new sales roles have found that establishing these key performance standards within a defined performance range requires both data analysis and assessment of the degree to which the range will motivate the behaviors required for effectiveness in the role. Data analyses generally look at historical achievement with traditional sales resources as well as at the organization's financial objectives. Once you establish a performance distribution through these analyses, you should review the threshold and excellence levels to ensure that (1) the range motivates high performance, and (2) it is possible for the company to reward that high performance financially. Once the plan designers establish the compensation mix, leverage, and performance range, they determine the optimal approach to payout.

THE THREE PARTS OF AN OPTIMAL INCENTIVE FORMULA

The development of the incentive formula building block uses three types of building materials: incentive plan type (bonus or commission), mathematical functions, and weights of performance measures.

INCENTIVE PLAN TYPE

In designing a sales compensation program, businesses most frequently apply two payout techniques: a bonus or a commission. A bonus is a percentage of base pay, or a fixed dollar amount, for accomplishing objectives. A bonus may be capped (payout is limited) or uncapped (unlimited). A commission is compensation paid as a percentage of sales measured in dollars or units.

MATHEMATICAL FUNCTIONS

There are only four mathematical functions to manipulate in any compensation program for salespeople: You can add, subtract, multiply, or divide. Addition and multiplication give a more positive message than telling salespeople their incentive pay will be subtracted or divided. The functions used to calculate payout are straightforward; it's how you use them that helps deliver the right message to salespeople about their new roles.

When companies implement new sales roles, they frequently tend to tweak the current formula in an attempt to use what's in place "one more year." To develop the optimal incentive formula, however, it's important for the plan designers to go back to the job definitions they have. One critical factor to consider is whether you are designing the incentive plan for individual contributors in a new role, or for a team of individuals who are implementing a new role with their customers. Rules of thumb to use consider both the formula (the mathematical function or functions that calculate payout for performance) and the way in which payments interact with each other.

A formula for either individual incentives or a team incentive can be "unlinked" or "linked." This concept is key for the designers, since it determines whether the firm will pay each performance measure on its own, or if there will be some interaction between measures. An unlinked formula is a series of additive payouts. An additive formula might be:

Bonus for achievement of sales + bonus for achievement of margin

One word of warning about unlinked formulas: Salespeople quickly understand virtually any incentive plan formula. An additive formula may lead eventually to "plan shopping," in which the salesperson focuses on the performance measure in the plan he or she feels offers the greatest personal payout opportunity. This may not be the measure the company feels is the most important.

A linked formula means that payout for one measure depends on attaining another. Designers frequently seek ways to communicate to the employees in a new role that focus is required in several areas simultaneously. These areas may sometimes appear to compete ("In this role, you should work with your accounts to achieve their objectives, as well as ours," or "You will need to bring up the gross margin for us while also increasing unit sales"). Therefore, linking them together in the formula ensures a clear message that the salesperson must give attention to both performance measures. Three ways to accomplish a linkage are:

1. A gate, which is the least stringent linkage mechanism, means that some level must be achieved in one measure before payout is made for another. An example of this is:

    100% of sales achieved before bonus paid on margin

2. A multiplier ("multiply" is a positive sign) modifies the payout on one measure. A multiplier might adjust payout up or down, depending on the message the design teams wants to deliver. An example is:

    Bonus for sales × modifier based on margin achievement

3. A matrix is probably the most rigorous linkage mechanism, since payouts for two measures are mutually dependent. For example, the salesperson has to obtain both sales and gross margin targets for a maximum payout.

Figure 6-3 has examples of the three linkage techniques.

PERFORMANCE WEIGHTS

The third factor to consider in the incentive formula is the weight given to each performance measure. The weight really equals how much reaching the performance measure's target is worth relative to the entire incentive opportunity. The sum of all weights must equal 100. As plan designers determine the appropriate weight to assign to a plan's performance measures, several guidelines apply:

- No measure should have less weight than 10; any less makes that measure virtually "invisible" to the plan participants relative to the other measures.
- There should be no more than three measures used in an incentive plan.
- You should give the most weight to a financial measure, one that has a system available to track, credit, and measure results.
- You should reexamine weights annually or when you add or change measures.

You can employ any or several of these techniques in the incentive formula. The way in which you use them is based on the message the orga-

Fig. 6-3.   Linkage mechanisms.

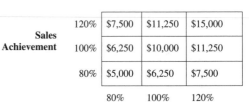

"Gate"	
Plan Elements	Sales Bonus
	Gross Margin Gate

Sales Bonus		Margin Gate
120% of Quota	$15,000	Target margin must be achieved before bonus
100% of Quota	$10,000	over $10,000 will be paid
80% of Quota	$5,000	

"Multiplier"	
Plan Elements	Sales Bonus
	Gross Margin Multiplier

Sales Bonus			Margin Multiplier	
120% of Quota	$15,000		> Target	2.0
100% of Quota	$10,000	×	Target GM	1.5
80% of Quota	$5,000		< Target	1.0

"Matrix"	
Plan Elements	Sales
	Gross Margin

Sales Achievement 120%	$7,500	$11,250	$15,000
100%	$6,250	$10,000	$11,250
80%	$5,000	$6,250	$7,500
	80%	100%	120%

Gross Margin Achievement

nization wants to send to plan participants: "You are a key individual contributor" or "You are a key member of the team." Both the ways in which the techniques are used and the importance of each are signals the plan can use to deliver its message of support to the sales strategy.

As illustrated in Figure 6-4, the prominence of performance measures (both their weight and where they are placed in the formula) and the way the measures interact can help to send either an "individual" or "team member" message. The first two examples in the figure show how a plan can be developed for individual contributor or team member roles. While you can include many measures, they would all be based on one level. For individuals, all performance measures would be for individual achievement; for a team, all measures would be based only on team achievement. In the latter case, there are several techniques for actually paying out a team-based incentive to each member. We will

Fig. 6-4. Approaches to individual and team incentive formulas.

Alternatives	Description
Individual Performance	• Incentive based on achievement of individual performance measures
Team Performance	• Based on achievement of predefined team objectives • Bonus allocated to team members based on appraisal of individual contributions
Team Performance × Individual Performance	• "Linked" plan • Initial incentive based on achievement of predefined team performance measures • Final incentive based on individual performance contribution, i.e., modifier
Team Performance + Individual Performance	• "Unlinked" plan • Separate incentive for achievement of predefined team objectives • Separate incentive based on individual performance
Individual Performance × Team Performance	• "Linked" plan • Initial incentive based on achievement of predefined individual performance measures • Final incentive based on team performance modifier
Individual Performance + Team Performance	• "Unlinked" plan • Separate bonus for achievement of individual performance • Separate bonus for achievement of predefined team objectives

explore these later in this chapter when we discuss examples of plans for new roles.

The next two examples in the figure show how you can develop an incentive formula that focuses on individual sales roles that also contribute to team success. The two approaches are linked or unlinked (multiply or add), and the most important measure or measures (those that have the greatest weight) are individual. The last two examples illustrate incentive formulas for new roles that are primarily team roles. They too can be either linked or unlinked, and the most important measures are team measures.

In summary, there are several types of building materials in the incentive formula tool kit that are helpful for designers. While a commission is frequently helpful to ensure that those in new sales roles focus on volume (dollars or units), a bonus is helpful to ensure that they also focus on reaching defined goals. The mathematical functions can be used to support a message that the new sales role is accountable for achieving results in many, perhaps competing, performance areas. And the weights of the performance measures clearly indicate the new role's highest priority.

How to Make the Right Decisions about Sales Crediting

As the company implements a new sales role and designs a new sales compensation program, one frequently asked question is, Who gets the credit when a sale is made? This is not an idle query, since the answer affects both the company's finances and the people who contributed to the sales result. Also, in recent years, companies have added sales channels and placed more emphasis on team selling. This change has increased the importance of adopting well-defined sales crediting policies. To develop policies related to sales crediting, plan designers should consider when, how much, and to whom sales should be credited. The answers to these three questions affect plan effectiveness in terms of motivating the right sales focus and achieving the company's objectives.

Figure 6-5 provides several guidelines for thinking about the "when" of sales crediting, including the events you can use to determine the point in time at which a sale can or should be credited. Determining which event or events are appropriate for sales crediting is based on several factors, including:

- The buying and selling process and the point in time at which the company considers a sale "closed";
- The point in time at which the company recognizes a return on the sale, either through an order or with receipt of revenues; and
- The event or events over which the person in the new sales role has the most significant impact.

Once you answer the "when" question, you must address the "to whom" question. For many companies, this issue presents a special challenge, since crediting more than one person for the total sale may be at odds with both the company's financial requirements and the program's motivational impact. We've found it helpful to follow a four-step process to develop the solution that is most appropriate for the company and the new sales role.

Fig. 6-5.   Sales crediting definitions and guidelines.

"When"

Credit Events	**Prior to sale:** Milestone
	Booking: When order is accepted by company
	Shipment: Order leaves the company
	Invoice: Bill is sent to the customer
	Installation: Product is installed at customer site
	Payment: Monies are received from the customer
	Combination: Two or more of the above options

"How Much and "To Whom"

"How Much" Credit Assignment Options	"To Whom" Definitions
100% Credit	Credit assigned to a single person, e.g., Territory Sales Representative, Telesales Representative
Split Credit (Totals = 100%)	Credit divided among those who contributed to the sale. Example: Territory Sales Representative ....75% National Account Representative................25% Total...100%
Multiple Credit (Totals > 100%)	Credit assigned to two or more sales resources in an amount greater than 100%. Example: Territory Sales Representative...................100% Channel Sales Representative....................100%
Partial Credit (Total < 100%)	Credit is assigned to one or more sales resources in an amount less than 100%. Example: Territory Sales Representative....................35% (on all sales made through the Partner Channel)

1. *Separate access and fulfillment from persuasion.* This first step means that you have mapped out the entire sales process and defined the role of everyone involved in the process. *Access* really means identifying and qualifying potential new customers. While this is a critical first stage in the sales process, it is frequently completed by nonsales personnel (e.g., marketing assistants, customer service reps). *Fulfillment* is delivery of products or services. *Persuasion* is, just as it sounds, convincing the customer to buy. Many new sales roles are responsible for this phase of the sales process, although buying may not be a transaction but a long-term commitment to use a company's products or services.

2. *Define individual or team participation in persuasion.* Once you have defined the new sales role's part in the process, it is then possible to determine if "one role" or "many roles" are responsible for convincing the customer to buy. For example, in a complex diagnostic instrument sale, an instrument sales specialist (traditional role) might be one participant in the process that also includes business representative and service coordinator roles to interact with key decision makers at the account.

3. *Persuasion should determine sales credit.* Once you have confirmed the role or roles responsible for persuasion, you have answered the question, "But who gets the credit?" Whether there is one role or many will determine if credit must be shared or duplicated across more than one role. In complex and emerging sales processes that require teams, this is a key issue, since doubling credit could increase each sale's cost. Therefore, we almost always see double credit in plans for new roles that are goal-based bonus plans (the payout is not a percentage of the sale). In this situation, the company can manage its costs. Split credit is the answer if the company has determined that it will apply a commission (a percentage of the sale) as the incentive technique. Each sale is split rather than doubled (figuratively speaking, of course), and the commission plan pays a percentage of the new split value, rather than of the total sale. Since the company is literally sharing the sale with the new sales role, distributing multiple pieces of each sale could result in no return to the company.

4. *Access and fulfillment should determine achievement of other measures.* While new roles responsible for either end of the sales process may receive some incentive based on sales, it is more useful to consider quantitative measures that directly reflect the role's responsibility. For example, an access role might have a portion of the incentive based on number of leads converted to active accounts, while a "fulfillment" role might have uptime (for equipment) as a key component.

There is no single, universal answer to the question, What's the best approach to sales credit? To answer this question, top managers should consider at least the following factors:

- The number and type of sales channels the company uses to gain access to customers
- The importance of team selling, particularly when a customer experiences multiple points of sales and service contacts
- The motivational "message" the company wants to send to the direct sales force about its role in team selling, cooperating with other customer contact resources, or both

- Selling expense
- Administrative capability to track and assign credit

Based on the experience of a wide variety of companies, our associate, David Fritz, President, Profitable Growth Solutions (fritz@growth solutionsinc.com), has identified the characteristics of sales situations in which different sales credit allocations are made.

Split crediting is used when:

- Sales success requires channel resources to occasionally work as a team, the team resources have defined roles when working together, and the "teaming" of these resources is necessary to secure a profitable sale.
- Management wishes to hold each sales channel accountable for its contribution to the sales result.
- It is relatively easy to objectively determine the relative contribution of each selling resource to each order.
- The amount of teaming cannot be accurately forecasted in advance, and distribution costs must be tightly managed.

An example of the proper use of split crediting is when one sales channel accesses the customer and closes the deal, but another resource is used for order fulfillment. In this case, the selling process is specified and a predefined credit amount is assigned for each process step—for example, 30 percent for customer access/relationship management, 40 percent for persuasion, i.e., "closing the business," and 30 percent for fulfillment/implementation.

Multiple crediting is used when:

- Sales success requires the selling resources to always work as a team, play flexible roles as needed, and do whatever it takes to secure profitable orders. One example of this type of situation is a multifunctional customer team that is deployed to cover an account or accounts.
- Management wishes to promote a "win-win" culture within or across the company's sales channels.
- It is difficult to distinguish the relative contribution of the selling resources for each sale.
- The aggregate amount of multiple crediting can be reasonably predicted and built into sales objectives for the various channels, thereby providing for proper selling expense management.

Multiple crediting is frequently used when two or more sales resources are involved in winning business in a sell-in/sell-through sales process. Two examples come to mind: First, in the beverage industry, a key account manager receives full credit for winning the sales contract that defines the terms and conditions of doing business with regional outlets, and the field sales representatives that "pull through" the orders at the various outlets also receive full credit. Another example can be found in the software industry: A channel sales representative receives full credit for software licenses "sold in" to an ISV (independent software developer), and the territory sales representative also receives full sales credit when those licenses are "sold through" to end users in the sales rep's accounts.

Partial crediting is used when:

- Sales success is partially determined by other resource(s), e.g., corporate management or channel partner involvement in the sales process.
- Individual or sales team roles and accountabilities are clearly defined and understood.
- It is clear and well documented that sales resources did not contribute to the sale in a manner that was "typical."
- Providing full credit would result in undesirable sales behavior, an unacceptably high level of selling expense, or both.

Partial sales credit is used in selling situations in which one or more sales resources benefit from the work of other resources that are involved in the sales process. Again, the software industry is one example where such situations occur. For example, a systems integrator (SI), perhaps one of the Big 5 accounting firms, could be involved in the process. The SI recommends to its client the use of a particular software product, naming the company that provides that product as the preferred vendor. In this case, often referred to as an "influence sale," the software company sales representative who books the sale receives less than 100 percent credit because the "access" and "persuasion" steps in the sales process were executed by the systems integrator.

REVIEW PERFORMANCE AND PAYMENT PERIODS FOR MAXIMUM EFFICIENCY

While the plan period may seem obvious, we find that plan designers frequently overlook it. Many assume that the plan period for the traditional jobs "worked fine; why change it?" In fact, it is critical to ensure that the plan period (which is really the period of time over which the plan is in effect and performance is measured) is consistent with company financial periods. With new sales roles, the company is looking for results that are measurable and have validity for both the job and the organization. A quarterly plan, for example, may not support the behaviors the company needs in a new role and may not achieve the results it is looking for, since a quarterly plan is in effect only for one quarter. Everything begins on the first day of the quarter and ends on the last day of the quarter—whatever you earn, you get paid, and you move on. This is a sure path to short-term focus, which might not be the company's objective for the sales role it has implemented.

A need for alignment with the company's accounting system has to be balanced with the human need to be recognized for a job well done. Particularly for new sales roles, it is critical to ensure that you design the plan to have maximum impact as close to "victory" as possible, since both the company and the employee will use the incentive plan as a barometer for the new job's success.

How to Compensate New Sales Roles That Affect Existing Jobs

In Chapter 5 we described various new sales roles that were created as a result of adding to or subtracting from the responsibilities of a current role and sales roles that were new to the company. We identified the measures of success for each role, but we did not spell out the incentive formula. The next several pages will give you the materials you need to build your own designs to support these jobs.

Compensating for Added Job Responsibilities

In this situation, the traditional consumer service job has expanded, adding team selling responsibilities. The new job is a tele-account sales representative (TAR) responsible for making outbound sales calls to specified target accounts (small) and working with an assigned account executive as a team member to win incremental business at designated major accounts.

To reflect added responsibility for retaining and penetrating customers, a goal-based revenue measure is included in the team metrics of TARs working with account executives. The performance measures related to success are:

- Team revenue goal
- Growth goal in team accounts
- Revenue in TAR accounts

The job will be eligible for incentive pay, and the building blocks you could use to develop a plan for this new role include:

Target total compensation: With added responsibilities, it's important to revisit the value the role will bring to the company and the competitive practices for similar jobs. In this case, additional cash compensation might be appropriate.

Mix: The addition can be used to fund a more significant incentive opportunity for the job, since it is clearly a sales role rather than telephone customer service. In fact, it may be appropriate to think about adding to the "incentive bucket" both the cash compensation that comes with the new job and any merit increase for which employees in the former role might have been eligible.

Leverage: The increase in at-risk pay may take place over time, and this new role will take some time to get up to speed. An upside opportunity of one times target could motivate the stretch needed for the employee to be effective in the new role.

Performance range: With very little history for designated TAR accounts, it would be difficult to set accurate goals. The team accounts would probably have a great deal of history, however, and you could develop goals for them. The performance range for the team account goals would therefore be fairly "tight" (e.g., from 85 to 115 percent), while the performance range for the TAR accounts would be fairly "loose."

Incentive formula: Figure 6-6 shows a formula for this type of job. As you can see, the designers have selected two different techniques: bonus for the team element, and commission for the TAR accounts. The formula is primarily additive, but they establish a linkage mechanism to be sure that the TAR focuses on both team and individual objectives. The team goals are additive, and one serves as a gate (a linkage) to the individual goals.

Sales crediting: Since the TAR is the only coverage resource for small accounts, they will receive 100 percent of the credit for those accounts (and the commission will be based on this). They are also part of a team, and sales are credited to the total team (double credit—actual credit to all team members). Since the team is paid on sales through a bonus

Fig. 6-6. Tele-account representative plan.

Plan Elements	Team Revenue Plan			Growth Goal			TAR Accounts (Tiered Commission)
	% to Plan	Payout		Actual Growth	Payout		
	>140%	2% of Team Target Bonus for Each % of Plan	**+**	>25%	1% of Growth Target Bonus for Each %	**+**	2% of Sales after Team Achieves Revenue Plan
	140%	200% of Team Target Bonus		>20% - 25%	200% of Growth Target Bonus		
	100%	**100% of Team Target Bonus**		**20% (Target Growth)**	**100% of Growth Target Bonus**		**1% of Sales until Team Achieves Revenue Plan**
	60%	50% of Team Target Bonus		15% - 19%	50% of Growth Target Bonus		
	<60%	-0-		<15%	-0-		
Payout Frequency	Quarterly against annual plan			Quarterly against annual plan			Monthly
Element Weight	40%			30%			30%

technique based on achievement of a sales goal, the company can manage the cost of multiple resources sharing in the success of their coverage strategy.

Performance and payout periods: The team has annual plans (goals) for both revenues and account growth. The performance period is annual; however, the company pays a portion of the incentive each quarter, based on year-to-date achievement. On the other hand, the TAR accounts do not have a sales goal. The performance period is monthly, and so is the payout period. This is useful for accounts and sales roles that have no history and for which there is really no way to estimate potential. It is likely that these accounts will establish a track record over time, as will the new sales role. At that point, the accounts will probably have a sales goal attached to them, and the performance period will be aligned with the company's financial period.

COMPENSATING FOR SUBTRACTED JOB RESPONSIBILITIES

Field sales representatives are now account managers in this new role and are responsible for developing ongoing profitable professional relationships with mid- to senior-level contacts within designated accounts in order to retain and grow business profitably. They will no longer be calling on small accounts, which may have composed a large portion of their business. To support this potentially difficult change (the field sales representatives are likely to grumble, "But you're taking away all my business!"), the company changed the level of performance measurement, rather than the measures themselves. The measures of success for this new role are:

- Volume in defined accounts only and
- Aggregate gross margin percent of assigned accounts.

While this type of new role generally has a very positive impact on the company's results, the incentive plan can be more difficult to design and implement than one for roles with added responsibilities or for brand new roles. Salespeople may see the change as the company's attempt to cut costs rather than grow sales. The incentive plan building blocks must therefore result in a plan that both supports the new sales strategy and ensures that the firm attracts and retains the right people for the job.

Target total compensation: A significant challenge in developing plans for roles that result from subtracting sales responsibilities is the employee concern about "compensation control" (as in "they're trying to control my compensation"). It is important for you to address this as soon as the role has been redefined to manage concern in a time of change and to ensure that the right target compensation is available based on the job that needs to be done. Generally, target total compensation does not go down with this kind of sales role modification. Although the company has subtracted responsibilities, the new job— calling on senior-level contacts in specific accounts—is actually more complex and sophisticated than the old one.

Mix: Mix is more likely to change than total compensation. The traditional salesperson had a fairly high percentage of pay at risk. The new role calls for long-term planning and the ability to sell solutions that are consistent with the account's needs. In fact, a design team that goes through the mix exercise is generally not surprised that this kind of new role should have a relatively higher percent of fixed pay in order to ensure that the sales representatives focus on long-term strategic relationships that are profitable for the company.

Leverage: While the leverage may not change, many times the incentive opportunity for these types of roles is limited—either capped (never a popular decision) or limited with a decelerator. Because of the long sales cycle and the strong possibility of windfall gains (the account makes a decision that has a positive impact on sales, but it's not necessarily due to sales intervention) or shortfall losses (same thing in reverse), a very significant upside is not consistent with the message the new job has been designed to deliver.

Performance range: Since accounts are large and well defined, the performance range can be fairly narrow. However, the company should reserve the right to adjust goals based on windfall gain or shortfall loss, for the same reason it manages leverage; things outside of the account manager's control should not impact her pay.

Incentive formula: Figure 6-7 provides an illustrative plan for this type of job. This plan uses the two performance measures in a linked plan design—a matrix, the most rigorous link. Each measure is based on reaching a defined sales goal or plan, so the selected technique is a bonus for the new role. The performance measures are of equal importance, so they receive equal weight in the incentive formula. You cannot earn 100 percent of your target bonus if you have not achieved your

Fig. 6-7. Account manager plan.

Sales Percent to Plan				
	120%	75% of Target	150% of Target	200% of Target
	100%	50% of Target	**100% of Target**	150% of Target
	80%	25% of Target	50% of Target	75% of Target
		80%	**100%**	120%

Gross Margin Percent to Plan

NOTE: Values are interpolated for each percent achievement— each percent achievement from 80% up in the matrix receives increasing payout

Payout Frequency   Quarterly; cumulative reconciliation

Element Weights
- Sales to Plan: 50%
- Gross Margin to Plan: 50%

target gross margin and your sales plan. At the same time, you must have reached the threshold on each measure to begin payout.

Sales crediting: Sales crediting is straightforward: The account manager is the only role that will cover selected accounts and receives full credit.

Performance and payout periods: The sales and gross margin goals are based on an annual plan, and the incentive plan is annual. However, quarterly payments are reconciled year-to-date each quarter. If the salesperson has not done well in the beginning of the year, her incentive pay is not lost—she can still earn it if she does increasingly well toward the end of the year.

The plan described above might be a first-generation plan for a role that is the next development in an organization's traditional sales job. As new sales roles emerge from those that existed in the past, however, incentive plan designers frequently begin to talk about the ways in which the plan can motivate and reward the new skills and behaviors the job requires. One performance measure we described in Chapter 5 is a key building block to a plan that can do this. You can use competency-based incentive pay effectively if you link it with financial measures to support a new sales role's development requirements.

Figure 6-8 illustrates one example of this kind of plan. The consumer products company we discussed in Chapter 5 had identified the need for new competencies in the account manager's role. To institutionalize the need for the competencies, the company decided to add a component to the sales incentive plan that enhanced the performance's primary financial measure.

The incentive formula became additive, and the new component used the competencies identified. Here is how this new measure of success worked:

1. Managers defined competencies related to the job. (In the figure, customer focus, business planning, and implementation.)
2. They defined key anchors, or indicators of successful acquisition of the skills and knowledge related to the competency.
3. For each competency, the account manager worked with his supervisor to develop an objective that had a quantifiable achievement measure.
4. To successfully achieve the objective, the account manager would need to acquire and use new skills.

Fig. 6-8. Financial measures linked to competencies.

Division Performance

Weighted Avg. % to Goal		Payout
Excellence	110%	200% of Division Target
Target	100%	100% of Division Target
Threshold	90%	50% of Division Target
< Threshold	<90%	-0-

Product	Weight	Achieved
Product 1	40%	
Product 2	25%	
Product 3	20%	
Product 4	15%	

Weighted Average _____

Payout Frequency: Quarterly

Weight: 75%

+

Individual Contribution

Rating	Payout
3.0	150% of Ind. Contr. Target
1.5 – 2.9	100% of Ind. Contr. Target
<1.5	-0-

Competency	Rating
1: Customer Focus	
2: Business Planning	
3: Implementation	

Simple Average _____

Payout Frequency: Semiannually

Weight: 25%

5. If the account manager attained the objective, he had, by implication, successfully acquired and put the new skills and knowledge to use.

Since the objectives linked to the competencies were quantifiable, reaching those objectives could be used as a component of the incentive plan. The primary component of the incentive plan continued to be division performance, that is, reaching the sales objectives for key products. This component used a weighted average achievement of the sales plan for each of four key product lines. Since the plan used a weighted average, it was possible for some products to sell below target and still have the division make its plan. On the other hand, key products needed to succeed for the weighted average to equal at least 100 percent of the division's plan, and at 100 percent of plan, the account manager receives 75 percent of her target incentive.

The new component was worth 25 percent of the target incentive. Since management defined three competencies for the account manager, the company designed a simple three-point scoring method. Attaining each objective was included in the scoring for each competency; so, for example, if the salesperson reached her objective and displayed the skills and behaviors related to the competency, she received a 3 for that competency. The company took a simple average of the scores to calculate this component's payout.

Here are two examples of the new component in action:

1. *Customer focus.* Accurate, timely, and effective in identifying customer supply chain needs and objectives; engages in ongoing collaboration with customers to build customer satisfaction while achieving business unit goals.

The *individual objective* is to achieve 5 percent growth in company product category overall.

- Networks within accounts to understand category requirements and business environment for company's products; understands company's strengths/weaknesses with the accounts
- Uses available tools/resources appropriately to work with customers to achieve business plan and improve customer satisfaction
- Understands objectives behind account's decision practices, as well as their business problems, merchandising philosophy, and opportunities; recognized by accounts as the expert
- Displays consistent skill in identifying and addressing issues and opportunities
- Formulates objectives for planning activities from needs expressed by customer contacts throughout each account

2. *Implementation/achievement orientation.* Has the drive to accomplish defined goals and milestones and a complete understanding of the reasons for success. Judged on the degree to which the account executive has been successful in establishing and achieving specific geographic, account, and company objectives.

The *individual objective* is to improve forecast accuracy from 30 percent error to 28 percent.

- Demonstrates ability to develop action plans with customers and determine realistic objectives
- Develops accurate forecasts and realistic, timely plans for achieving objectives
- Develops methods of testing proposed programs appropriately to reduce risk and enhance returns
- Understands retail broker capabilities and uses them effectively to achieve business results
- Achieves desired results through careful monitoring of plan implementation and promptly develops and implements plan changes to deal with problems
- Exercises good judgment in continuing successful initiatives or discontinuing failing initiatives
- Formulates and documents business plan for entire base of business, based on company and customer objectives

COMPENSATING NEWLY CREATED SALES JOBS

In Chapter 5 we described an office supply products company that introduced an account sales representative role into the organization for the first time with a focus on acquiring and retaining business-to-business customers. In the past, the company had worked successfully through retail outlets, but it had determined that a new job was required to attract business customers—those who would buy directly from the company rather than through retail transactions. Business customers would order through a customer service department located in the retail outlet, which would save the company the enormous cost of developing a new distribution system. At the same time, the retail store would now need to stock to meet the needs of these new customers. For the sales role to succeed, products would have to flow efficiently and quickly at greater volumes through the retail outlets' warehouses, and the firm would have to attract the best (frequent, high-volume order) customers.

To overcome the challenges associated with carrying out this role, which was new to the company and its customer prospects, management implemented measures associated with both volume and account selection. As Chapter 5 indicated, the new measures were:

- Volume increase through the retail outlets
- New customer revenue
- New customer gross margin

Once plan designers defined the job and the success measures, they turned their attention to the sales compensation plan for this new role.

Target total compensation: The company obtained survey data to help them "price" this job, and found that account sales representatives in like industries were significantly more highly compensated than retail counter personnel. The company decided to target pay at the seventy-fifth percentile of the market in order to attract the best from like industries.

Mix: The mix for this type of job in other companies was fairly aggressive—as high as 60 percent base salary and 40 percent incentive pay. However, the company decided to implement a moderate mix of 70 percent base and 30 percent incentive to balance the experience of the individuals they wanted to attract with the somewhat immature tracking and measurement system it had in place.

Leverage: Leverage was consistent with typical practice for the job, and the company decided, for the first year, to use a visor for the plan. The long-term objective was to uncap payout opportunity, once managers were more confident in their ability to set targets for the new role.

Performance range: The performance range was broad, again due to the immature tracking, measuring, and goal-setting systems and processes that would be in place when the company inaugurated the new role.

Incentive formula: The incentive formula was straightforward. As illustrated in figure 6-9, the designers determined that goals could and should be established for product volume moving through the retail outlets. Achieving this goal would help to ensure that the new role would pay for itself within eighteen months of implementation, so they used a bonus technique for retail volume. Because during the first year the firm would be determining the best accounts, however, they decided to use a commission technique for the new customer measures. The commission rate was tiered, which effectively linked the volume from new customers to their profitability. The salesperson's goal was not just to sell, but to sell at a profit. As the illustration shows, the company paid a commission for each order, based on the order's volume and gross profit. For a salesperson to receive the commission, the account had to be new, that is, it had no previous credit, charge, or transaction history with the company through its retail outlets. The target commission rate in the illustration is tier 2, that is, the rate the company pays when the order is at the target gross profit percentage for new customers. The

Fig. 6-9. Account sales representative illustration.

Retail Outlet Volume Bonus

Percent to Plan		Payout
Excellence	110%	150% of Target for Retail Volume
Target	100%	100% of Target for Retail Volume
Threshold	80%	50% of Target for Retail Volume
< Threshold	<80%	-0-

+

New Customer Commission

Tiered Commission on Order Volume	Gross Profit Qualifier
3: 3% of All Sales Orders When . . .	GP % for Order Is > Target GP
2: 1.5% of All Sales Orders When . . .	GP % for Order Is at Target GP
1: 1% of All Sales Orders When . . .	GP % for Order Is < Target GP

Payout Frequency:	Quarterly	Monthly
Weight:	50%	50%

rate is determined through the weight of the component and the dollars available to pay for this performance measure.

Sales crediting: Sales credit for all business from new accounts was given exclusively to the account sales representative. Credit for retail volume was shared or double credited between the account sales representative and the manager of the retail outlet to which the account sales representative was attached.

Performance and payout periods: While the bonus was semiannual, the company paid it quarterly on a year-to-date basis. It paid commissions monthly. The company advised all candidates that it intended to establish goals for new customer business in the second year and would then pay a bonus for this business each quarter.

The designs we've been describing all used common building blocks to develop plans specifically structured for new sales roles. While each plan design is illustrative rather than proscriptive, they all exhibit the traits of effective sales compensation plans: mix and leverage determined through a rational selection and decision-making process, performance measures directly aligned with the job, performance periods that support the company's objectives, and payout frequency that will motivate plan participants.

While many of the roles discussed in this chapter and in Chapter 5 have been team members, we have been treating them in the context of "new sales role" rather than as "team member in a new coverage strategy." While compensating customer teams is a complex subject, we thought it would be useful to provide some information on approaches to compensating the team as a unit.

NEW APPROACHES TO COMPENSATING NONSELLING TEAM MEMBERS

The sales teams and customer teams that many industries organize work with customers in a variety of situations. While the members of a sales team are, as the name implies, personnel in various types of sales jobs—sales product specialists, service sales specialists, account managers—the members of customer teams are frequently nonsales personnel. Research we conducted in 1996 among members of the American Compensation Association (private-sector member companies with revenues of $100 million or greater) showed that teams ranged in size from three to seventy members and included employees from sales, marketing, customer service, and technical support. Table 6-2 shows, for various industries, the members of a sales or customer team and confirms that membership does include a cross section of employees and not solely sales or sales and customer service personnel.

A customer team is multifunctional and is designed to meet the needs of complex customers or market segments. A particular challenge that designers of sales compensation programs face is how to compensate nonsales team members; these are people the team requires but who do not actually persuade customers to buy. Many companies decide that these types of jobs will be eligible for some type of reward

Table 6-2. Team membership by industry supersegment.

	Finance, Insurance, & Real Estate	Manufacturing	Services	Transportation, Communications, & Utility Services	Wholesale & Retail Trade
Customer Service	19.2	17.8	12.5		25.0
Distribution	3.8	8.9		25.0	
Finance	11.5	8.9	12.5		
Information systems	11.5	6.7		25.0	
Marketing	11.5	12.2	25.0	25.0	
Sales	19.2	20.0	25.0		37.5
Technical support	11.5	15.6	12.5	25.0	25.0
Other	11.5	10.0	12.5		12.5
Total	100	100	100	100	100

Note: Percentages represent proportion of the team from each function.

and recognition program (e.g., Team of the Year, Customer Recognition Award), but not for incentive or at-risk pay. The decision is based not only on actual job content but also on the likely life cycle of the team and the status of members (full- or part-time, temporary or permanent).

Among the challenges associated with developing and implementing incentive plans for teams, particularly multifunctional customer teams, are the following:

Team member familiarity with incentive pay. In many cases, employees on customer teams come from functions other than sales. They have little or no experience with the incentive pay element of sales compensation. The motivational aspect of the incentive program may be lost if team members do not value, or actually fear, the concept of at-risk pay. On the other hand, well-designed, well-implemented incentive plans for which all members are eligible can effectively pull together disparate resources to focus on reaching the team's objectives. Training and communication are the keys to success if management has decided to make nonsales roles incentive eligible. This is as important for the selling members as for the nonsales team members; many times, salespeople on teams fear that others' eligibility for incentive pay will decrease their incentive opportunity. This should never be true, even if a salesperson's percent of pay at risk changes as a result of being on a team. In fact, to our knowledge no company has ever successfully exercised the "rob Peter to pay Paul" premise of funding widespread team incentives for sales or customer teams.

Appropriate approach to payout. There are basically three ways to approach payout determination, and the designers of plans for teams frequently wrestle with the subtleties associated with the approaches. In order to determine the payout for each team member, a company can (1) empower the team as a whole or the team leader to rate or rank members for the purpose of prorating payout for each member; (2) fund a team pool that all team members share equally upon reaching defined objectives; or (3) design a plan that is objective and as formula-driven as possible and that provides payout opportunities that are commensurate with the level of contribution to success that each role can actually make. This last approach means that some team members may be eligible to receive more than others, but the basis for determination is objective, even if it includes team ratings or other nonfinancial measures of success.

Ensuring that the sales compensation design supports team objectives. The plan design for teams must support not only the company's business objectives but also team objectives. While this may sound simple, it is an area plan designers often overlook. A team's objectives may include objectives in addition to those that were the team charter upon implementation. For example, if "working together effectively to implement the best solution for our customer" is a team objective, it would be helpful to acknowledge and reward its achievement through the sales compensation program.

SUMMING UP

The company must clearly define the roles and objectives of the jobs to be paid to design an effective sales compensation plan. Since sales increasingly shares its role with other departments, all company managers need a much broader understanding of how sales compensation works. Also, as the traditional sales role evolves within a business (responsibilities added or subtracted), management can employ the sales compensation program to send a clear message to the organization about the change.

Whether a current sales job has changes in responsibilities or the company creates a completely new sales job, the sales compensation plan design requires decisions about a number of key elements. These include eligibility, total target compensation, salary/incentive mix, incentive pay leverage, performance range, incentive formula, sales crediting, and performance and payment periods. Each element serves a unique and distinctive role in the plan design.

Questions about salary/incentive mix include: How much incentive is required to be motivation? (At least 10 percent of base salary.) When the mix is altered, particularly from a low salary/high incentive to a higher salary/lower incentive, aren't you actually reducing the motivation? (Perhaps, but usually there has been a fundamental change in the buying/selling process making the new mix necessary.) When and why would mix shift from more to less salary, from 100/0, for example, to 90/10? (When the company adds responsibilities to a sales job.)

Leverage is the salesperson's upside earnings opportunity and is determined by market opportunity, the profitability of additional sales, and the extent to which the company can share that profitability with the employees in the new sales role.

Setting performance ranges makes it possible for the company to develop initial cost estimates and determine potential payout curves. They include threshold, the minimum performance an employee must meet to earn an incentive; target, the expected level of sales results or individual performance; and excellence, sales performance in the ninetieth percentile.

The incentive formula involves the incentive plan type (bonus or commission), mathematical functions, and weights of performance measures.

Sales crediting recognizes both when and to whom the sale should be credited, and both factors impact plan effectiveness in terms of motivating the right focus and achieving the company's objectives.

Performance and payment periods should be consistent with company financial periods. At the same time, a quarterly plan may not encourage the results the company wants, since it is in effect only for one quarter and promotes a short-term focus.

In the next chapter, we will examine the special challenges associated with compensating telechannel jobs, as they are being more widely implemented in the new millennium.

7

COMPENSATING TELECHANNEL JOBS

In Chapter 6 we described the elements of an effective sales compensation plan for new sales roles. We illustrated how to apply the design elements to sales jobs with added or subtracted sales responsibilities and to sales jobs created where none had previously existed. Now we turn our attention to an in-depth discussion of compensating new or changed roles in various functions that are involved with sales (Chapters 7 and 8) and in particular selling situations, specifically large sales (Chapter 9).

In this chapter, we discuss the role of the telechannel in the sales and customer relationship management (CRM) processes and provide examples and principles of how to compensate the different types of telejobs. We believe this is the logical place to begin because in many companies the telechannel is a critical component of marketing, sales, and customer service. Increasingly, customers are demanding the telechannel as an option through which to purchase a product or receive service.

The implementation and effective use of the telechannel also offer a company the opportunity to improve its sales productivity. For example, the telechannel makes it possible for a field sales representative to be more productive. There are two reasons why this is true:

1. Teleprofessionals are often assigned the responsibility for accounts that are too costly to sell to and service with the field sales

force. As a result, sales representatives can focus their attention on customers that offer significantly larger sales potential and therefore achieve an improvement in their sales results.

2. Teleprofessionals are often assigned lower-value activities such as reorders, after-sales "add-on" purchases, or customer support tasks. When teleprofessionals are assigned these roles, the sales representatives have more time to spend selling. This is likely to increase the average sales per sales representative. IBM, for example, increased its average sales per representative from $5 million to over $15 million over a three-year period by integrating the efforts of its field sales force and the telechannel.[1]

Another reason to begin an in-depth discussion of new sales roles with the telechannel is that it is the fastest-growing source of new sales roles in companies. The value of telephone sales is projected to grow to $667 billion by 2002 from a base of $425 billion in 1998. Also by 2002, tele-employment is projected to be approximately 11 million people. This represents a 38 percent increase over the 1998 employment base of 8 million people.[2]

The telechannel is also growing in importance relative to other sources of sales and customer contact. Figure 7-1 provides data from a research study conducted in thirty-eight *Fortune* 500 companies representing ten industries. It shows that in those companies, the telechannel ranks first in providing service to customers and second in generating sales relative to other sources of customer contact. There is no reason to believe that its importance will diminish in the future. In fact, it is more likely that the role of the telechannel will grow larger and thus accelerate the pressure top managers feel to define and compensate these roles clearly.

Fig. 7-1. How the telechannel generates sales and service transactions.

Channel	Percent of Sales Achieved	Percent of Service Provided
■ Field Sales	42%	37%
■ Telechannel	18%	39%
■ Business Partners	18%	10%
■ Retail	16%	10%
■ Direct Mail	6%	1%
■ Electronic	2%	3%

Source: Michael Kelleher, Scott Gillman, Bashar Mardem-Bey, and Matt Coleman, *The Role of the Telechannel in Go-to-Market Strategy*, Bethesda, MD, Oxford Associates, Inc., 1998, p. 14.

FIVE TELECHANNEL APPLICATIONS THAT ARE CRITICAL TO SALES AND SERVICE

Most people think that the telechannel is synonymous with telemarketing, which involves getting those unwanted evening sales calls—often during the dinner hour! However, the telechannel is really much more than telemarketing. For the purposes of this book, we define the telechannel to include call centers and the Internet, that is, those telephonic and electronic channels that companies use to sell to and interact with customers.

In Chapter 1, we reported that companies are deconstructing the sales process in an effort to not only provide greater value to customers but also do so at a lower cost. The redefinition of the sales and customer relationship management process into three key elements—access, persuasion, and fulfillment—provides a useful framework for describing the five principal applications of the telechannel and therefore the roles that are created. These applications are identified in Figure 7-2.

Before top managers decide to use one or more of these telechannel applications to achieve their business objectives, it is important that they understand how each application can contribute to sales, customer service, or both.

Fig. 7-2.   Integration of customer relationship management (CRM) and telechannel applications.

Sales/CRM Phase	Access	Persuasion		Fulfillment	
	Who or what resources are used to identify and qualify customers?	Who is responsible for persuading the prospect or customer to do business with the company?		Who services the customer or who delivers on the promises made to the customer?	
Five Telechannel Applications*	Lead Generation (Telemarketing)	Telesales	Telecoverage	Customer Service	Technical Service
Description	High volume, low cost demand creation to produce qualified leads to support sales channels	Direct sales coverage of end-use customers; typically mid-market or lower; less complex products or add-on sales to installed base of accounts	Retention and expansion of business in assigned accounts	Respond to customer inquires for nontechnical assistance	Respond to customer inquires for technical support in product or service use

*Terms adapted from Michael Kelleher, Scott Gillman, Bashar Mardem-Bey, and Matt Coleman, *The Role of the Telechannel in Go-to-Market Strategy*, Bethesda, MD, Oxford Associates, Inc., 1998, p. 15.

1. *Lead generation.* In most selling situations, the single biggest obstacle to growing sales at a more rapid rate is the lack of a sufficient number of qualified leads. Who or what resources should be used to identify prospective new customers? In the traditional sales model, the sales representative or the sales agent (e.g., dealer or distributor) is often responsible for identifying and qualifying potential customers. However, because these resources have many other responsibilities related to selling to and servicing current customers, the quality and quantity of leads are often far below the levels required to achieve business growth. The application of the telechannel to lead generation, correctly referred to as telemarketing, will generate more qualified sales leads and cost up to 50 percent less than traditional methods (namely, relying on sellers to do lead generation). When telemarketing supports field-based sellers with qualified lead generation programs, the quality and quantity of leads increase. The efforts of telemarketing professionals reduce or eliminate cold calling by the sales force and thus create the opportunity to increase sales force productivity.

2. *Telesales.* The use of the telechannel to sell products, services, or both to customers is the fastest growing of the five applications. It was not that long ago that companies resisted the notion of selling their products or services to an end user over the telephone. This was particularly true in the business-to-business marketing environment. When telesales first came on the scene, some top sales managers thought it might replace or diminish the role of the field sales force. Instead, it did just the opposite. Telesales made it possible for field sales representatives to focus their efforts on the top and middle-market customers and prospects. Telesales professionals could focus on the smaller or infrequent customers or on a limited part of the product line, for example, products that are repurchased with high frequency or regularity but yield a low transaction value. Thus, it is important with telechannels overall, and telesales in particular, to leverage them in tandem with other channels (e.g., field sales) instead of merely allowing the channels to coexist independent of one another.

3. *Telecoverage.* Essentially, telecoverage is telephonic account management. Like their field-based counterparts, telephonic account managers are assigned responsibility for a defined set of customers, on whom they call to retain current business and, in many cases, to expand sales by offering additional products or services. Increasingly, we observe that companies are deploying tele-account managers to maintain

and enhance the relationship established through either field sales or telesales. Off-loading "relationship management" from sales to a tele-account management function frees up valuable time for selling on the part of both field and telesales representatives. In other situations—for example, the one described in Chapter 6 (see Figure 6-6)—the tele-account manager is assigned to work as a member of a sales team. Regardless of the role a company chooses for its tele-account managers, our experience suggests that this position is a cost-effective way to stay in touch with customers and, in many cases, increase business substantially.

4. *Customer service.* The use of teleresources, in the form of customer service representatives, to respond to customer questions and requests has been around in some companies for over sixty years. However, in the continual quest for growth, many companies are asking their customer service representatives to not only respond to customers' inquiries but also actively ask the customer if there is more that the company can provide to him or her. We refer to this affectionately as the classic question "Would you like fries with that?"—something that every McDonald's counterperson is trained to ask when a customer does not ask for fries when placing an order. Increasingly, we observe that companies are asking their customer service personnel to take on a role—albeit a relatively small one—in selling to a customer. This role could range from asking permission to have a sales resource call on the customer to up-selling or cross selling products or services.

5. *Technical support.* In addition to deploying customer service representatives to respond to customer questions about order status, billing statement details, and numerous other aspects of order fulfillment, companies also use teleresources to provide technical support for their products and services. If you purchase a PC from Dell, Gateway, or almost any other manufacturer, you will have access to the company's technical staff through an 800 number. This type of teleresource is available not only to buyers of consumer products but also to buyers of industrial and commercial products. For example, many companies that manufacture and market highly technical products—from blood analyzers used in hospitals to complex switches used in telecommunications applications—maintain a technical staff twenty-four hours a day, seven days a week to respond to customer inquiries about applications or usage problems. Rarely do these positions have any direct sales responsibility. However, their approach to responding to and working with customers frequently not only affects a customer's satisfaction with a company but also may influence future purchases.

Three Major Challenges When Implementing Telechannel Jobs

There are three major challenges a company must address at the time it implements telechannels and the jobs associated with those channels: (1) how to define the job or jobs (i.e., distinguishing between telemarketing and telesales) that are needed and the role the employees play in the process of getting and keeping customers, (2) how to break down any unfavorable stereotypes associated with the job so that the company can attract people with the required skills and experience, and (3) what types of rewards to use to not only attract but retain talented people in the jobs.

1. Distinguishing Between Telemarketing and Telesales Jobs

We find that many companies have a difficult time correctly defining and titling their telejobs, particularly telesales positions. This is often true in companies that have a history of using the telechannel for inbound customer service, outbound telemarketing (e.g., lead generation and qualification), or both. Many of the telemarketing jobs we have examined are actually contaminated positions. And, while this phenomenon is also present among direct or field-based sales positions, in our experience, it appears to be more prevalent in the telechannel. Perhaps the reason is that for many companies, the telechannel is a new function that top managers are still figuring out how to implement.

Job contamination is an "impurity" in a job's charter, its tasks and responsibilities, or both. Typically, contamination shows up in the form of (1) a "blended job," one that combines two or more dissimilar roles, or (2) a "corrupted job," one in which responsibilities have crept over from another position and this change was unintended. We find that job contamination in the form of a blended job is most common in telemarketing positions. This is because telemarketing positions increasingly have responsibility for both inbound and outbound customer contact, where the responsibilities include not only qualification of buyer interest but also asking for the sale. Essentially, we have a very simple rule of thumb when initially testing for the role of a teleposition (marketing versus sales): Does the employee ask the prospect for his or her credit card? If the answer is yes, then it is likely that the position is correctly identified as a telesales position and therefore should be eligible for sales incentive compensation. This does not mean that telemarketing positions are not eligible for incentive compensation. Rather, it suggests that the basis for the incentive payment for these positions is tied to a nonsales (revenue) measure or measures.

2. Breaking Down the Stereotypes Associated with Telejobs

Most top managers understand that the future of selling includes the use of telechannels, particularly the telesales function. Some companies, however, are struggling with the effective implementation of telejobs because of the stereotypes that are associated with these jobs, the people who work in these jobs, or both. Consider this example. The CEO of a components supplier to the telecommunications industry believed that his company (which had $1 billion in sales) could achieve significant sales growth in small to midsize accounts through its telefunctions—inside sales, customer service, and technical support. He communicated his expectations to the director of inside sales and service, who was responsible for those functions. However, while this individual understood the CEO's direction, he did not know how to translate that direction into action. All of his experience had involved hiring and supervising customer service representatives, who performed clerical functions and were paid a base wage in the range of $22,000 to $30,000 per year. Essentially, the stereotype of the job in that company was that of a job that involved menial, routine tasks and was paid a relatively low rate of compensation. Ultimately, the director's inability to alter his view of the function and the people required for its success led to his departure from the company. He simply didn't get it!

Companies that have a history of viewing their customer service department as a low-level activity, and its employees as second-class citizens, run the risk of losing their customers. Also, this view of telejobs substantially detracts from a company's ability to attract and retain the talented people needed to work in the function. The increased use of telephonic and Internet communications is making telefunctions more important than ever before. The changes in the way in which a company communicates with its prospects and customers and the way in which a customer expects to communicate with its suppliers have had a dramatic impact on the substance of telejobs. Those jobs are difficult and require the highest caliber of talent that companies can attract. Today, more and more companies view their telejobs as being on the same organizational level as jobs in the direct channel. That means that employees in telejobs are offered larger compensation opportunities and extended participation in annual recognition programs (e.g., President's Club). These employees are also viewed as a source of talent for advancement to management positions in sales or other corporate functions involved with customers or channel partners.

Successful companies—Dell Computers, IBM, and Marriott Vacation Club International, to mention a few—view their telepositions as strategically important to the achievement of business objectives. In these companies and others, the role of telepositions is to retain and expand business with customers and to convey to the customer a positive brand image. We find that the most effective ways to ensure that unfavorable stereotypes are not a black cloud over the telefunctions are to (1) confirm that the current telefunction leadership is not only operationally knowledgeable but also contemporary in the people management aspects of the function, (2) select and appoint frontline managers who have a solid background in telesales, customer service, or both, (3) provide career opportunities to those employees in the telefunction who demonstrate the interest and potential to move into other functions within the company, and (4) continually monitor "best practices" in companies selling to and providing service to customers in similar or comparable marketplaces.

3. DECIDING HOW TO REWARD EMPLOYEES IN TELEJOBS

In many companies, the telefunction is "hot"! It is the fasting-growing segment of the customer contact workforce because the Internet is reinforcing high expectations about response times. Customers—both consumers and businesses—are demanding and getting "fast response" to orders placed and to customer service inquiries that they make. To meet and exceed customer expectations, companies must deploy talented people in their telefunctions. In many labor markets, the demand for experienced telefunction personnel far exceeds the supply. While it is important to determine how to effectively compensate telemarketing, telesales, and technical service representatives—which is the focus of this chapter—we find that compensation alone is not enough to build a winning telefunction operation.

In some companies, contests are used to motivate and reward telemarketers. We find that "contest calendars" have been a successful management tool in call centers for quite some time. Telesales, on the other hand, because it is perceived as a commissioned role, may be rewarded with $5.00 per call or 10 percent of every order. While these approaches work well for traditional telejobs in traditional environments, the emerging requirements for more sophisticated customer interaction via telephone or the web have resulted in more sophisticated approaches to rewarding employees in this workforce. It is our view that successful companies use a three-tier approach to effectively rewarding their telefunction employees. The tiers are:

- *Tier 1*: Reward the individual for desired behavior and perform-ance.
- *Tier 2*: Reward the team or unit in which individuals work.
- *Tier 3*: Reward the entire group, e.g., the telesales department or the telemarketing department.

The rewards at each tier may involve a combination of both cash and noncash. We find that the right balance of cash and noncash re-wards must reflect the demographics of the workforce and, in particular, the types of rewards that the workforce values. One example of how a company might determine what its employees value is found in Appen-dix E, "Reward and Recognition Questionnaire."

How to Clarify What Type of Telejob Your Company Needs

We believe that the starting point in initiatives to improve the effective-ness of employees in new or changed roles is the nature of the task(s) that they are asked to perform. To illustrate the importance of task clar-ity, we often encourage managers to apply a relatively simple test to their business situation. Figure 7-3 lists six questions that we find useful to describe the relative degree of clarity that may or may not exist in a company's telepositions. Scores of ten or less suggest that telepositions may not be valued by the company, that job definitions lack clarity, or that the jobs lack accountability. Any of these scenarios requires proac-tive attention in order to increase the effectiveness of these jobs and achieve the results the company expects.

To help companies define or clarify new roles, we suggest the use of the five W's, which was described in Chapter 3 (see Table 3-1 and Figure 3-6). Figure 7-4 illustrates how this tool can help you describe or clarify telepositions. In this example, the five W's are tailored to reflect the cus-tomer relationship management process and provide a scale to answer the following questions:

- *Who* is the customer (for this role)?
- *What* is the role providing?
- *Where* is the process taking place?

Fig. 7-3. Questionnaire for clarifying telejobs in your company.

Question	Answer and Score		
	Yes (3)	Don't Know (2)	No (1)
Are jobs "mapped" to a documented sales and/or CRM process?			
Have jobs changed to keep pace with customer requirements?			
Have clear accountabilities been confirmed for each job?			
Are systems and tools in place to support each job in the telefunction?			
Are you satisfied with the process for modifying other jobs when new jobs are added to the telefunction?			
Is a career development ladder in place to, through, and from telejobs?			

Scoring

15–18 Your telepositions are well defined, are supported in the organization, and have a demonstrable impact on results.

11–14 Your telepositions may not be as clearly defined and accountable as in the optimal organization.

6–10 The telepositions lack clarity or accountability, and may not be valued by the organization overall.

- *When* (how often) is the employee interacting with the customer?
- *Why* are customers interacting with the employee?

The five W's tool can be used to compare one role with another. When doing so, there is no need to rate each job; rather, the relevant answer to each of the five W questions can be circled. The result of answering each question is a clear and visible differentiation between the jobs that are being compared. In Figure 7-4, a telesales job has been examined relative to each of the five W's. Taking these results for the telesales job as a benchmark, you could then use the tool to clarify the role of a customer service job. In doing so, you may find that:

- Inventory management rather than purchasing is the "customer" for customer service.

Fig. 7-4.   The 5 W's and telejobs.

Factor	JOB: Telesales				
	Simple ⟵				⟶ Complex
Who is the customer	Clerical/ Inventory	Purchasing	Mid-mgmt.	Senior Technical	Executive
What are you providing	Tracking	Ordering	Product	Product Support	Solution or Technical Expertise
Where is the process taking place	Telephone	Internet	Counter	On-Site; Phone Ordering	Corporate On-site
When are you interacting with each customer	Often		Once		As Needed
Why are customers interacting with you	Convenience	Delivery Issues	Product Issues	Confidence	Value

- The customer service representative is providing order assistance.
- The process takes place over the phone.
- The customer service representative is interacting with each customer often.
- Customers work with the customer service representative to resolve delivery issues.

With the results of this exercise in hand and the information provided in Chapter 6, the next section gives you the materials you need to build your own compensation plans for various types of telepositions.

DESIGNING COMPENSATION PLANS FOR TELECHANNEL JOBS: THREE HIGH-LEVEL CONSIDERATIONS

Because telejobs are growing in number and importance, there are many different types of compensation plans used to pay teleprofessionals. Examples of various types of compensation plans are readily available through published compensation surveys, Internet job sites, or both. Yet some companies experience difficulty rewarding and recognizing their employees commensurate with their contributions to the business because they have implemented a plan used at another company rather than tailoring a plan to their specific needs. In order to develop an appropriate approach to compensating telechannel jobs, your company must give consideration at a high level to three strategic topics: (1) your company's philosophy of pay (i.e., the company's core compensation principles), (2) how your company will classify its telejobs (the question of Fair Labor Standards Act (FLSA) status), and (3) the role of each job in the customer relationship management process and how each role interacts with other jobs within your company. This section of the chapter addresses each of those topics.

To attract and retain the caliber of talent essential to success in today's demanding telepositions, we believe the following questions must be addressed:

- Which jobs should be classified as exempt? Which should be classified as nonexempt?
- Should these jobs be paid in a way that is similar to customer service? To field sales?
- What are the most appropriate measures of success for each job?
- What type of variable pay program is most likely to support the behavior and results that the company needs?
- How can the right linkages across functions—marketing, sales, and customer service—be created through measurement and compensation?

CORE COMPENSATION PRINCIPLES

One tool that is frequently used to make decisions about pay for these jobs is a set of compensation guidelines or principles established by the company. Often this "compensation philosophy" is developed by the corporate human resources department and used throughout the organization as a standard against which pay decisions are measured. The following guidelines are fundamental principles used by many companies to support consistent and effective compensation design decisions for their telechannel jobs.

1. Compensation must actively reinforce the company's strategy and vision for achieving its objectives. Incentive compensation plans should communicate a company's strategy and direct individuals to execute their role in achieving that strategy.

2. Compensation programs must meet legal and regulatory requirements.

3. Compensation should be internally equitable and consistent with the financial requirements, human resources policies, and administrative capabilities of the company.

4. Compensation program details must be consistent with external requirements in order to attract, retain, and motivate talented employees and be based on clearly defined jobs and their role in the buying and selling process.

5. The compensation mix (fixed versus variable pay) must be based on defined factors and must reflect the ability of each employee to affect the results upon which variable pay will be based.

Figure 7-5 illustrates one company's use of these guidelines to develop a framework for compensating two telechannel jobs, inside sales (telesales) and customer service.

JOB CLASSIFICATION

The Fair Labor Standards Act of 1938 established guidelines for minimum pay and overtime pay obligations. Since then, the minimum hourly wage has been increased periodically, and several changes or enhancements have been made in the FLSA guidelines. The guidelines for "exempt" versus "nonexempt" positions have a significant effect on both an employee's perception of the value of the job and the elements of pay for each job.

As the skill and background requirements for telepositions evolve, the need to test jobs against FLSA requirements becomes more important. Jobs that once were clearly nonexempt (i.e., jobs for which the employer was required to pay overtime) may have changed substantially in content and therefore require reclassification to exempt status. In some companies, there is a perception that nonexempt status indicates a blue-collar job, while exempt status indicates a white-collar job. Unfortunately, we find that this interpretation by employees too often leads to conversations about the "nonprofessional" versus "professional" status of jobs and employees in those jobs. We find that this interpretation has a negative impact on the value and contribution of the telejobs to business results.

The Federal Wage and Hour Laws by R. Brian Dixon provides valuable information to help companies classify telejobs appropriately.[3] A critical element of that classification is how it will affect the ability of the

Fig. 7-5. Using core compensation principles.

Principle	Application to Inside Sales	Application to Customer Service
1: Reflects Strategy	Role in sales strategy is proactive outbound selling to small accounts	Role in sales strategy is customer retention through effective order entry and fulfillment
2: Meets Legal Requirements	Based on job description and application of FLSA test, job is exempt	Based on job description and application of FLSA test, job is non-exempt
3: Meets Internal Requirements and 4: Consistent with Job	■ Pay targeted at fiftieth percentile of labor market for inside sales/entry sales positions ■ Market positions typically eligible for incentive pay ■ Company systems in place to track, credit and report highly detailed sales activity	■ Pay targeted at ninetieth percentile of **local labor market** to attract qualified personnel and be consistent with local hiring practices ■ Local practice generally does not include incentive pay for positions at salaries less than $30,000 annually ■ Company cannot credit "ongoing" sales to any one employee other than the account sales person
5: Mix Based on Factors	■ Critical role in customer persuasions ■ Impact on sales results is high ■ Ability to directly credit results is high ■ Mix is more consistent with outside sales jobs	■ Critical role in customer retention and loyalty ■ Impact is high, but ability to measure direct impact on retention and growth is low ■ Primary metrics appear to be fulfillment accuracy and customer loyalty

company to develop the right compensation plan for each teleposition. Since variable compensation such as commissions is included in the calculation of the overtime pay due to an employee, companies frequently reach one of two conclusions:

- Ignore the FLSA requirements when it comes to designing an incentive compensation plan for these jobs.
- Provide no incentive pay at all, since considering FLSA requirements is interpreted as making a plan "too hard to design."

In fact, neither of these two conclusions is appropriate, the first for legal reasons and the second for motivation and management reasons. The determination of exempt or nonexempt status should affect only the *way* in which incentive pay is calculated, not *if* it should be provided.

As explained earlier in this chapter, the key criteria for incentive eligibility for telejobs are (1) the role of each job in the customer relationship management process and (2) the impact of having some portion of pay "at risk" for jobs with a relatively low level of compensation. We have found that most companies have an informal cutoff for eligibility for at-risk pay based on salary or hourly rates. Based on today's cost of living, jobs with an annualized wage of less than $30,000 (total cash compensation) are usually not eligible for at-risk incentive pay. However, as we discuss later in this chapter, many of these jobs *are* eligible for periodic contests or other types of "add-on" rewards.

ROLE OF EACH JOB IN THE CUSTOMER RELATIONSHIP MANAGEMENT PROCESS

When multiple employees interact with customers, the challenge of determining eligibility for incentive pay and selecting the right performance measures to use in awarding that pay is quite difficult. In Chapter 4, we discussed eligibility for incentive pay and the tools that managers can use to determine if a job should be eligible to participate in such a plan. Figure 4-3 illustrates that when jobs involve "customer persuasion," the employees in those jobs are typically eligible for incentive pay. Employees in jobs that involve "customer fulfillment" are frequently also eligible. In fact, for some years now, eligibility for incentive pay has been increasing as companies focus on using "pay for performance" models for customer contact functions. Telejobs are just one job family that is being affected by this trend. The eligibility decision tree in Figure 4-3 is a useful tool to use in determining if and how a telejob should participate in an incentive plan.

Chapter 5 explained that performance management involves selecting the right measures to gauge business results, establishing standards to define expectations, tracking actual accomplishments, and providing guidance to help employees achieve success. We find that dissecting the sales process is the key to identifying and selecting the right measures of performance to use for gauging the success of various employees who play a role in selling to or interacting with customers.

Figure 7-6 shows that telemarketing jobs are responsible for accessing the customer (lead generation, promotions, prospect calls). Both telesales and tele-account management jobs are held accountable for customer persuasion; for the telesales job, this is persuading the customer to buy, whereas the tele-account management job is charged with keeping the customer and persuading the customer to buy more (if appropriate). Customer fulfillment is frequently described as "everyone's

Fig. 7-6.   Role in the customer relationship management (CRM) process.

job," but in fact it should be the defined responsibility of specific jobs, for example, the customer service representative and the technical service representative. The manager of the call center or teleresources should always be able to clearly define the roles that he or she holds accountable for success in each phase of the CRM process. This clarity will provide the focus needed to determine the right performance measures, level of measurement, and type of incentive plan that is most appropriate for each job.

COMPENSATING TELEMARKETING JOBS

Compensation plans for telemarketing jobs fall into three categories:

- Hourly wage only
- Hourly wage plus a performance bonus
- Hourly wage plus commission pay

We have found that the most common type of plan for telemarketers is an hourly wage plus a performance bonus. Thus, we have selected a position compensated in that manner to describe the building blocks that you could use to develop a customized plan for your telemarketing job.

Role description. In many companies, the process of defining jobs is a lost art. The telemarketing job is frequently defined incorrectly as "telephone selling" or "customer service." Telemarketing may involve any one (or more) of three responsibilities: (1) lead generation, (2) appointment setting for a salesperson (a field sales rep or a telesales rep), or (3) market development survey calls to estimate the sales opportunity for a particular product or service. Regardless of telemarketing's charter, our experience suggests that starting with a clear definition of job responsibilities—that is, a description of those tasks that result in job success when performed effectively—is essential to building an effective compensation plan.

For the purpose of this example, we have selected a job from the vacation time-share industry. To start with, it's important to understand the role description for a telemarketing vacation counselor. Figure 7-7 is a description of management's expectation of employees assigned to this position. Additionally, this figure provides you with a concise format to follow when writing role descriptions for your positions.

Target total compensation. The telemarketing vacation counselor position has existed in this company for several years. Recently, top managers learned that employee productivity was below the prior year's experience. A combination of performing below expectations and higher than industry average turnover among counselors with varying levels of tenure motivated top managers to ask for a reexamination of the makeup of the position. An objective review of the work performed by the counselors showed that the job was a blended job—it included both traditional telemarketing duties (e.g., lead generation) and telesales responsibilities (i.e., selling vacation packages to prospects). The top managers had to decide what they wanted counselors to do. The blending of two dissimilar roles was resulting in lost productivity and higher than typical recruiting costs. Ultimately, the top managers decided to focus the job on the telemarketing duties described in Figure 7-7.

Once that decision was made, management had to address one other question before setting a competitive target compensation for the jobs. That question was this: Should the position be a part-time or a full-

Fig. 7-7.   Illustration of telemarketing job description.

Role Summary

This is a telephonic job responsible for developing and qualifying leads from purchased lists, from marketing programs, and from lists generated from telesales, telecoverage, and site sales. This position will have telephonic and e-mail contact with prospects, and will provide qualified leads or tour appointments to sales functions.

Specific Duties

- Follow up and qualify leads over the telephone, leads from print ads, web and direct mail leads, owner referrals, and on-site prospects.
- Build the prospect database through cold calls to purchased or company list contacts.
- Complete an appropriate number of calls daily to develop optimal bookings volume.

Key Accountabilities

- Attain assigned call volume objectives by responding to caller inquiries and by identifying, qualifying, and sending preview packages to new buyers.
- Identify and provide short-term sales opportunities to telesales.

Requirements

- Proficient in telephonic communication
- Competent in using computer applications
- Competent in understanding core products information
- Competent in assessing customer needs relative to company's products
- Able to utilize organization and time management skills
- Able to work independently with little supervision as a member of the company's tele-business team

---

time job? There is a high level of stress associated with telemarketing jobs. Employees that work in these jobs experience a lot of "no" responses, rude responses, and hang-ups. To minimize stress, more and more companies are hiring part-time employees. Companies that do so find that deploying part-time telemarketing employees results in not only more effective employees but also greater productivity.

In the case of the company in our example, the telemarketing vacation counselor was a part-time position, but its responsibilities included both lead generation/qualification and selling preview packages. To clarify its role—i.e., eliminate blended responsibilities—the company created an outbound telemarketer position. The new outbound telemarketer replaced the vacation counselor position. The decontaminated job of outbound telemarketer more accurately reflected the role these employees play in customer acquisition, and more appropriately established performance expectations for generating qualified leads that sales reps could sell to. The position remains part time, but with less turnover, the company is also realizing the higher level of results from telemarketing that it needs if its overall sales effort is to be successful.

Compensation levels for telemarketing jobs vary significantly across the country. Thus, it is difficult to set a national compensation level for the position. However, the company in our example operated call centers in cities with very similar labor markets for telemarketing positions. Generally speaking, you will not find this to be the case if your company operates several call centers and they are located in cities with widely different costs of living. For the new outbound telemarketer position, the company in our example set a target compensation of $15,000 annually, based on a workweek of sixteen hours (four evenings each week).

Mix. In our example, the compensation opportunity for the former vacation counselor position was a 50/50 plan (50 percent of the $15,000 was paid in an hourly wage, and the other 50 percent was at-risk incentive pay). Because the new outbound telemarketing job no longer has specific sales goals or responsibilities, the salary/incentive ratio was changed. The new job is eligible for $5,000 in performance bonuses, based on call volume, list accuracy, lead quality, and other criteria established with call center management, marketing, and sales. The annualized base pay was increased to $10,000 (or $12.50 an hour) to reflect the fact that the employee has to invest more time in nonselling activities. Periodic "focus" contests were also offered to incumbents in the new job; however, those contests are not included in the compensation mix. They are considered "outboarded" from the incentive compensation plan.

Leverage. Because the incentive opportunity for the new outbound telemarketing job is based on MBO bonuses, there is no upside associated with the bonuses. This means that each bonus opportunity established is an "off/on" bonus, i.e., the telemarketer can earn one or all of the bonuses, but there is no overachievement available for any one bonus.

Performance range. The performance range for each bonus is based on predefined criteria. For example, each telemarketer is expected to complete thirty calls per shift, or 120 calls per workweek. A bonus of $100 a month is paid to those telemarketers who reach this goal. However, in order to ensure that calls are of appropriate quality, there is no "over goal" bonus available. Why? Because management determined early on that completing more than thirty calls per shift generally resulted in inaccurate information and less professional interaction on the phone with the prospect.

Incentive formula. The nature of MBO bonuses for the outbound telemarketing job is fairly simple: Payout for each bonus is additive, and there is no linkage to other measures. In the future, the company is considering adding a linkage to overall business unit achievement, since the quality of leads generated has a visible impact on the ability of sales resources to close business.

Performance crediting. Crediting for this particular job has become possible only because of the installation of a high-quality system that provides modules to track and time calls and to link information gained through telemarketing to the CRM and sales data in the company system.

Performance and payout periods. Bonuses for this job are currently paid monthly. However, if a measure based on the business unit achievement of sales quota is added, the company is likely to extend the payout period for the linked opportunity to a quarterly payout.

As companies review their telemarketing strategy and structure, it is critical to assess the labor market realities for the type of person needed in the job defined by the company. The example cited above is a traditional approach to compensating the telemarketing role. However, in many complex and sophisticated markets (for example, in the high technology and information media markets), telemarketing roles have a higher target total compensation that includes a higher base pay and more significant incentive opportunity based on the number and quality of leads generated. A telemarketer in Silicon Valley, for example, might have a compensation package that includes a base of $30,000 to $40,000 with an incentive opportunity of up to 50 percent of base pay. These jobs are generally full time, and employees play a vital role in the new customer identification and acquisition process.

COMPENSATING TELESALES JOBS

Telesales positions have changed substantially in recent years. Traditionally, telesellers have been associated with "quick hit" selling (those calls you get at 6 P.M. during dinner that "pitch" a new phone service, a vacation package, or any number of other "opportunities"). The explosion in e-commerce has forever changed the role of telesales. Customer expectations about being able to do business twenty-four hours a day, seven days a week, have created the need for several types of telesales roles. There are now at least three types of telesales jobs to consider when preparing a compensation plan for this role:

- Telesales, i.e., traditional positions with responsibility for direct sales
- Teleweb, i.e., positions with responsibility for sales through the Internet or e-commerce channel
- Tele-account management, i.e., positions that team with field sales to meet the needs of assigned accounts and gain incremental business

In Chapter 6, we provided an example of a tele-account representative (TAR) role with added responsibilities for making outbound sales calls to specified target accounts (small) and working with an assigned account executive as a team member to win incremental business at designated major accounts. This "teamed" role requires active management of account responsibility, and essentially "double pays" both the TAR and the field salesperson for successful selling into defined accounts.

For roles that are individual contributors, a critical issue in today's telephone/Internet/field selling model is how to address potential channel conflict between the field seller and any other channel that may be involved in interactions with the customer. Many companies have implemented a named account strategy that assigns specific accounts to the field and others to the teleweb channel. For example, field personnel may be responsible for only the large and strategically important tier one accounts, while the teleweb resources cover tier two and tier three accounts. A large copier equipment company has implemented a telesales job that is responsible for covering the tier two segment, defined as companies with fewer than 100 employees, with one location, and using less than a defined number of copies per month. This job specificity is becoming more and more common in both business-to-business (B2B) and business-to-consumer (B2C) selling.

Teleweb jobs have emerged in catalog sales ("shop our catalog online and let our personal assistants help you with your selection"), as well as more complex selling situations. One example is time-shares: log onto the site and take a "virtual tour." A teleweb sales representative will help with the tour, answer your questions, and help you purchase your choice.

Telesales jobs are frequently full-time, exempt jobs that may be either career positions (the employee expects to stay in this job for the balance of her career with the company) or one step on a sales career ladder that begins with telemarketing. Companies are finding that it is becoming even more important to provide career opportunities and more challenges in order to attract and retain the talent they need in this kind of job. This may result in either senior positions or advancement to other jobs. For example, the next step from telesales may be to an entry-level field position.

Role description. Telesales may focus on inbound calls, outbound calls, or a combination of both. The telesales job may be an integral part of the call center or of the sales team. Focusing on only one type of job can limit your thought processes when considering how best to compensate any particular job. With that in mind, in this section and the remaining ones related to telejobs, we provide guidelines that you can refer to when designing a plan for a particular job.

Like that for other sales positions, compensation for a telesales job is based on the degree to which employees in the role are expected to persuade customers (new or current) to buy the company's products or services. Ultimately, we believe you will find that the compensation package for a telesales position more closely resembles field sales compensation within the company than compensation for customer service or telemarketing.

Target total compensation. Telesales jobs typically are at the top of the teleresource career ladder and therefore have a higher target total compensation than other call center jobs such as telemarketing or customer service jobs. The compensation package reflects the increased accountability for financial results associated with this job. In tight labor markets, or in companies with technically complex products or sophisticated services, the pay may be roughly equivalent to that of an entry-level field sales resource. For example, in one software company, the entry-level field sales job has a target total compensation package of approximately $100,000, and the teleweb sales job has a target total compensation package of approximately $95,000.

Mix. The teleweb sales job in this software company is an individual contributor job with a key role in the sales process of a sophisticated and technically complex product. Applying the concepts and tools provided in Chapter 6 to help determine the mix for this job, it is clear that the job should have a relatively high proportion of total pay at risk. In this case, the mix is approximately 40/60, which results in a target base of about $38,000 and a target incentive of about $57,000.

Leverage. "Where there's mix, there's leverage." In the case of teleweb or telesales jobs, the leverage is generally quite significant, i.e., two or more times the target incentive. The teleweb job for the software company cited previously has the same proportion of upside opportunity as field sales jobs in the company—the plan is uncapped, and the upside at "excellence" is two times target, or $114,000.

Performance range. Telesales jobs generally are "quota-carrying" jobs in more sophisticated selling environments. The traditional focus of a commission on each transaction continues in some companies, with the incentive plan paying out from the first transaction. For those jobs that have a quota, New Economy companies may pay from the first percent achievement, while more traditional companies may have a threshold of results required prior to payout. The teleweb job we have discussed is paid from the first percent achievement.

Incentive formula. Commissions are a common type of plan for teleseller jobs. As illustrated in Figure 7-8, the teleweb seller for software products and services is paid a commission, with accelerators based on achievement of quota. The position is also eligible for a team bonus based on the overall achievement of the region, to ensure that there is less "poaching" of accounts and more willingness to provide the coverage that the account requires.

Fig. 7-8.   Telesales incentive plan illustration.

Job Charter: Telephone and Web-based selling to defined accounts	
Primary Role	Seller
Employment Status	Exempt
Compensation Opportunity	$95,000
Incentive Opportunity	$55,000
Salary/Incentive Ratio	40/60 (approximately)

Individual Sales Commission			**Region Achievement of Goal**	
Sales	**Rate**		**Percent**	**Rate/Percent/Month**
$1- $1,000,000	0.4%		0% - 49.9%	0
$1,000,001- $1,600,000	0.75%	+	50% - 104.9%	$12.00
$1,600,001- $2,000,000	1.25%		105% - 124.9%	$12.00
> $2,000,000	1.50%		≥ 125%	$15.00

Performance crediting. One challenge associated with this kind of incentive plan is performance crediting. We have found that named account or defined territory coverage helps to avoid that issue and results in an incentive formula that considers all sales associated with the teleseller's named accounts, defined market, or specified geography that can be tracked to the representative via the crediting system.

Performance and payout periods. Because of the high proportion of pay at risk, payouts are monthly. The quota is annual, and progress payments are made against achievement.

Compensating Customer Service Jobs

Customer service representative compensation plans fall into three categories:

- Hourly wage only
- Wages plus an individual performance bonus
- Wages plus a team performance bonus

Two factors influence a company's decision about which compensation approach to take for its customer service jobs: (1) the role of the job in the customer relationship management process and (2) the compensation philosophy of the company. This type of job has traditionally been considered an hourly nonexempt job that is not eligible for incentive pay. However, the introduction of advanced information systems, new customer requirements, and changes in job accountabilities all contribute to the use of new approaches to pay for this job.

Role description. The customer service representative (CSR) is usually accountable for "solving problems" and "providing answers to the customer." Tasks include order entry, order processing and tracking, determining product availability, handling returns, and ensuring that other company resources have handled customer issues as needed. More senior positions may be implemented to assume responsibility for specific strategic accounts as part of the account team, and in fact may be located "on site" at the customer's location. However, the CSR job is more typically located in a call center or co-located with other customer contact resources in field sales offices.

Target total compensation. One example of this job is the CSR job with an industrial tooling company. The job is an integral part of successful customer relationship management and is located in the field offices. The job is a full-time nonexempt job, and the pay is "slotted" in the career ladder at about the same annual salary level as the telesales job. Employees might start in an administrative position to learn the company and its products, and then be promoted to telemarketing or customer service. The next step in this career ladder is either telesales (with more pay at risk and therefore a higher target total compensation) or a specialized inside customer contact job such as pricing, with an increase in base pay.

Mix. Because of the nature of the job, the CSR is generally not eligible for a significant incentive or at-risk pay opportunity. In many companies, in fact, the CSR is not incentive-eligible at all. However, the industrial tooling company has taken a proactive approach to teaming, and this job is considered critical in keeping and growing customers. Both the CSR and the senior CSR positions are eligible for incentive pay, although the base wage for the entry-level CSR job is very close to the informal cutoff of $30,000 annually. However, the mix is less aggressive than that for a sales job; about 10 percent of pay is at risk.

Leverage. The upside for these kinds of jobs is frequently modest. For our illustrative CSR job, though, the leverage in the plan is consistent with the team component in the incentive plan for field sales. This approach is another indication of the value of these jobs within the company and to the sales team.

Performance range and performance crediting. Team sales success is the performance measure for the plan. This measure was selected for CSRs because the company believes that the success of CSR efforts leads to loyal customers. Customer retention and growth is a key to success, and the CSRs ensure that this is possible, even though they are not directly charged with "selling." The team focus results in a plan that is consistent with the team component in the plan for the field salespeople: defined threshold (in this case, 70 percent of target) and excellence level (110 percent of target). The level of measurement is the region sales team, and therefore credit is shared between the salespeople and the CSRs in the region (double crediting for the purpose of incentive pay).

Incentive formula. The formula is very simple: For each percent achievement above threshold up to target, the payout is $x, and the payout above target is $x "plus" (in this case, an additional dollar per percentage point per month). The plan is illustrated in Figure 7-9.

Performance and payout periods. The CSR jobs have an incentive opportunity of about $250 per month, based on team achievement of the annual region sales goal.

Fig. 7-9. Customer service incentive plan illustration.

Job Charter: Order entry, customer problem solving	
Primary Role	Problem solving
Employment Status	Non-Exempt
Compensation Opportunity	$40,000
Incentive Opportunity	$3,000 annually
Salary/Incentive Ratio	90/10 (approximately)

Region Achievement	Payout/Percent/Month	
0% - 69%	0	
70% - 104.9%	$2.50	
110% and greater	$7.50	+ Previous earnings

COMPENSATING TECHNICAL SERVICE JOBS

There is a growing interest among companies in exploring how to direct, motivate, and reward technical service employees for their contributions to business success with customers. However, the task of linking technical service employees to business success through their compensation is easier said than done. As one client told us, "Those technical people are a whole other kettle of fish." Generally speaking, determining the appropriate approach to pay for telechannel technical service jobs is based on the role of the job in the CRM process and how the job interacts with other company resources.

Role description. The technical service representative job is frequently located with other teleresources in a call center or sales office. The key responsibility is not selling-related at all. This job is charged with resolving customer questions and issues related to services or product installation, use, and quality. The job may be used to educate customers, answer basic technical questions, or provide systems component information. While the job generally does not require the same degree of technical skill and knowledge as field-based jobs such as application engineers, it is nonetheless critical to efficient and appropriate customer relationship management, particularly in technical selling environments. The employee may be the person you reach through an 800 number or a web-site "help desk."

Target total compensation. Classification of this job really varies by role definition. In some companies, it may be considered a high-level nonexempt job, while in others, it is an entry-level technical exempt job. In one company that manufactures and markets telecommunications equipment, the job is a nonexempt job, and the key pool for new employees is the customer service function. The target total compensation is more significant and provides an incentive to advance through the call center rather than rotate to other functions either at headquarters or in the field. In the industrial tooling company, however, the job is exempt and is classified on a par with entry-level sales. Interestingly, both jobs have about the same target total compensation—it's just calculated differently (incentive opportunity adjusted for expected overtime plus base wage annualized for one, and incentive opportunity plus salary for the other).

Incentive plan design. "If I wanted to be a salesperson, I'd be a salesperson. I'm on a technical path." How often has management heard this from field engineers, application developers, and other technical resources? The same sentiment is generally expressed by inside technical support as well. We rarely see inside technical service jobs with a significant portion of pay at risk; they are typically compensated more like a customer service job than like a sales job. In both the exempt job at the tooling company and the nonexempt job at the equipment company, the inside technical service job is eligible for an incentive plan that is essentially identical to the plan for customer service personnel at their respective companies.

Compensating Field Sales and Teleteams

"We put in a new telesales and tele-account coverage model, and all we got is more channel conflict." This seems to happen frequently when roles, accountabilities, and territory or account boundaries have not been clearly identified and well documented prior to implementation of new teleresources or teleresources with a new charter. It is therefore critical to be clear about expectations. Are teleresources individual contributors? Are employees in any of the jobs teamed with the field? If so, how and why? Answers to these questions establish the foundation for determining how (or indeed if) these roles should be compensated as teams.

Practically speaking, field and teleresources team for one of the following reasons:

1. To support a specific customer or group of customers
2. To cover a geography efficiently and effectively
3. To establish and develop a market for new or existing products or services

Whatever the reason, the key concepts associated with team rewards are useful to consider in this environment. Companies develop team rewards for several reasons, but the most immediate impact is seen in creating a common purpose and direction through the reward structure.[4]

In this chapter, we have described several jobs that are expected to work effectively together; in Chapter 6, we described the TAR role as a member of an account team with field sales. This latter model is becoming increasingly popular as companies wrestle with the cost of coverage versus the return to the company. Teaming field sales and technical resources with teleresources such as customer service ensures that customers receive the "care and feeding" (as one client described it) they need. Challenges associated with this kind of teaming may result from individually focused incentive pay (the "it's my account, not yours, when it comes time to calculate the commission" syndrome), lack of clarity in territory or account responsibility (the "I can't handle everyone's questions all the time—what's the field guy doing, anyway?" syndrome), or lack of management support and communication (the "the sales guy rules here, and management only looks at us when it wants results" syndrome).

As we described in Chapter 6, selection of the performance measure and incentive formula to deliver pay provides ways to signal to the organization what management wants done and the behaviors needed for success. However, while incentive pay properly designed can help to modify behaviors and dampen concerns, management vision and communication are the tools that really make field/teleresource teams succeed.

USING CONTESTS AND RECOGNITION

As companies implement increasingly more sophisticated telechannel resources, the basics of management and motivation should be used as building blocks for an effective compensation program. While incentive compensation is a visible motivational tool, many companies have traditionally used periodic contests and formal recognition programs very successfully to motivate and reward teleresources. These programs may be used in addition to or instead of formal incentive compensation plans for teleresources; most frequently they are an additional program that is used to focus efforts and motivate individual contributions to team success. Contests and informal recognition (a thank-you note from your boss, a "lunch is on me" from a grateful customer, a "thanks, I couldn't have done it without you" from a peer) help to meet the need for feeling successful in a job that is valued.

Bob Nelson's book *1001 Ways to Reward Employees* provides a whole menu of approaches to these types of programs, in addition to suggestions about option plans and other approaches to motivation and reward.[5] *Telephone Sales Management and Motivation Made Easy* provides ideas that are specific to teleresources.[6] These and other books embrace one common theme: The recognition of an employee's managers and peers is as important to feeling successful as the monetary reward.

SUMMING UP

Because companies want to meet and exceed customers' expectations about how they do business, the role of telechannel jobs is growing in importance. More and more companies are using telechannel jobs to prospect for and sell to new customers, to sell current and new products to current customers, and to meet the wide variety of service requirements essential to serving customers effectively after a sale is made. Also, top managers' interest in improving sales and service productivity, increasing opportunities for customer loyalty, and controlling the costs related to these activities at a reasonable level contributes to general interest in how to deploy telechannel jobs.

In response to these new or changed expectations about the telechannel, top managers must become even more comfortable with defining the responsibilities of telejobs within the customer relationship management process and determining the most appropriate measures of success for these jobs. These tools are fundamental in developing a reward program that truly supports the behaviors required to get the business results the company needs.

In this chapter, we've used the building blocks described in Chapter 6 to provide principles and examples of incentive plans for telejobs. As these jobs evolve from the stereotypical "$5 a call, five calls an hour" telemarketer, companies are developing a variety of creative and successful reward programs, including at-risk incentive plans for individual contributors and team members, "outboarded" bonus plans that provide additional pay opportunities for success in the job, and noncash reward programs that are vehicles to acknowledge the contribution of these employees to successful customer relationship management.

Telechannel jobs are a key area of change and opportunity for implementing new sales roles. In the next chapter, we discuss sales support staff, traditional jobs that are increasingly involved in the customer relationship management process.

COMPENSATING SALES SUPPORT STAFF

The telepositions discussed in Chapter 7 are one type of "sales support" job. In many companies, there are other jobs that interact with customers at various points during the sales process, the customer relationship management process, or both, such as systems engineer, logistics manager, project manager, and service consultant. How a company deploys its people in these jobs largely determines their impact on getting and keeping customers. More and more, we hear in our interviews with the customers of companies with which we work that the sales support staff is a major reason for continuing to do business with a given company. While sales support staffs are frequently not chartered to proactively sell, very often they can help retain the business that a company currently has. Therefore, sales compensation plan designers are often challenged with the following questions: Should the company include sales support jobs in the sales incentive plan? Or should these jobs have their own unique incentive plan? Should they, in fact, be eligible for incentive pay at all? In this chapter, we discuss the definition and roles of sales support jobs, provide tools for determining incentive eligibility, and illustrate how these jobs are paid.

HOW SALES SUPPORT JOBS ARE CRITICAL TO EFFECTIVE CUSTOMER INTERACTION

Employees in sales support jobs participate in the sales or customer relationship management process but are not directly accountable for closing sales. As we have described previously (see Figures 1-3 and 7-6), the customer relationship management process is an end-to-end process that begins with identifying and accessing a potential customer, then proceeds to persuading the customer to buy. The customer fulfillment phase of the process is the beginning of an opportunity to demonstrate to a customer the company's commitment to service quality. For example, if the customer is pleased with the product or service purchased and has additional needs, the current supplier will be considered as the provider of choice for additional purchases. Thus, more and more companies are realizing that sales support jobs are critical in all phases of the customer's interactions with the company and therefore looking for ways to reward employees in these jobs for their success. Consider these examples.

Software company. Selling software in the B2B environment is one situation in which sales support jobs are critical to sales success. The systems engineer (SE) is a key player in the early phases of the sales process (i.e., "presale" steps). The SE helps an account executive determine the solution or configuration needed by a customer, demonstrates the product's functionality and performance, and participates in presentations as a technical expert. Generally speaking, a prospective customer views the SE as the "go-to" tech person in this phase of the sales process. Once the sale is closed by an account executive, sales support is again critical to business success with a customer. At this point in the relationship, a project manager or application specialist takes over from the SE to manage the installation of the solution. In football, while the quarterback calls the plays, he can't win the game if his teammates do not execute the plays flawlessly. The same is true in this example. While the account executive is the sales process leader, he cannot close the sale and create a satisfied customer without the pre- and postsale support staffs executing their roles flawlessly.

Laboratory equipment company. A manufacturer and marketer of diagnostic equipment has charted the sales process its sales reps are expected to use to close sales worth millions of dollars. The process includes significant "postsale" support roles. The needed roles include logistics (timing of equipment availability, coordination of all aspects of the order from multiple manufacturing facilities), architectural design (how the space required for the equipment will be configured), project management (how all resources will work together, timing of the project, business management), and engineering (installation, testing). All of these roles are considered "sales support"; however, they are essentially an "insurance policy" against the cancellation of a sale as a result of a customer's not being satisfied with the purchase. Customer records show that when the company's sales support staff met or exceeded the contractual terms of a sale, the medical facility was more likely to consider the company for future purchases.

Industrial tooling. Distributors are the most common sales channel used to reach industrial buyers of machine tools. Typically, the distributor carries many lines and types of tooling products. However, to gain visibility at a plant site and actively meet the tooling needs of end users, many manufacturers deploy a field applications engineer (FAE). It is the job of the FAE to work with end-user manufacturing engineers or plant supervisors. This job has no responsibility for selling products; its main focus is to understand the plant site's ongoing needs, work directly with site technical resources to understand their lines, and help to resolve problems through tooling solutions. Of course, those solutions would ideally include the company's own line of industrial tooling products. Customers consider the FAE a technical resource from the company, and, as such, those individuals play a key role in supporting the sales efforts of both the company and the distributors of its products.

More and more, top managers tell us that they expect all employees to contribute to sales success. In companies that foster an "everyone sells" philosophy, we have observed that another category of sales support jobs has emerged. We refer to this category as "sales assist" jobs. Employees in sales assist jobs contribute to sales results, but do not directly participate in the customer relationship management process. Examples include industry market managers, channel relationship managers, and application developers. These jobs are frequently one step removed from the customer, yet the assistance that they provide to salespeople is valuable because it allows sellers to dedicate their time to sales tasks. For example, in a company that provides safety management services to manufacturers, the industry market manager position is asked to identify specific industry needs for the company's products or services and catalog those findings in an on-line database that the company's business development manager can use in sales presentations. Industry market managers are also expected to identify opportunities— trade shows, industry meetings, and so forth—for sellers to meet and network with industry executives.

In the software industry, it is not uncommon for software developers to deploy people in a position titled channel relationship manager. An individual in this position works with intermediaries (organizations between the company and the customer), and may consider the channel her "customer." The channel relationship manager's goal is to identify business opportunities for both her company and the partner to pursue; however, individuals in this position do not have any direct sales responsibility.

Application developers, as the title suggests, are asked to design new applications or products and may, on rare occasions, interact directly with a customer during the sales process. This position is prevalent in the hardware and software sectors of the high technology industry. Employees in this position are critical to ensuring that a particular solution actually works in the customer's business.

Sales support jobs all have one common characteristic: Without their assistance, the ability of the sales organization to increase sales, honor commitments made during the sales process, or both is diminished. While the roles may or may not be active participants in the sales process, their assistance in key activities increases the likelihood of sales success.

Retaining Customers: The New Goal for Sales Support

Sales support jobs are not new. Companies have used nonselling roles for years to develop products, understand their market and customer needs, perform technical reviews, install products, and coordinate delivery. However, top managers are increasingly asking their sales and support staffs to spend more time on activities tied to retaining business with current customers. Virtually all companies that we come in contact with have specific customer retention goals. Thus, because sales support jobs are an important point of contact with customers, one of the things that is new is the role employees in these jobs are asked to play in retaining business with customers.

Consider this question: In years past, how often has your company considered adding more technical or service employees to improve the support provided to current customers? The goal, of course, is to reduce the likelihood that customers will defect to another supplier. The deciding point in this situation is frequently knowing how to answer the following question: Does the sales benefit outweigh the added cost of these jobs? As customers have become more sophisticated in their buying decisions, companies need to reach deeper into their nonsales functions to ask sales support staff employees to participate in the customer buying process.

Using the five W's tool described in Chapter 4 (see Table 4-1), you can define a new role for your sales support staff positions in the customer buying process. An example is illustrated in Figure 8-1.

This example illustrates the sale of a complex software solution. Many participants from the customer's company are involved in the purchase decision. As you can see, a successful sales process will require support to engage midlevel information technology (IT) management, finance, and the senior technology officer. As we discuss in Chapter 9, nowhere is this complexity more evident than in large deal sales, where the customer's decision to make the purchase is based on the input of many functions. The organization selling to the customer must therefore match its own resources—engineering, consulting, finance, and legal resources—to the customer buying team in order to address all the criteria the customer uses to make the decision to buy.

WHEN TO INCLUDE SUPPORT JOBS IN THE SALES COMPENSATION PLAN

We are often asked to help companies decide whether or not to include sales support jobs in the sales compensation plan. Often, at the outset

Fig. 8-1.   The 5 W's and sales support jobs.

Factor	Type of Sale: Software Solution				
	Simple ⟵				⟶ Complex
Who is the customer	Clerical	Purchasing	IT Director.	Finance	Chief Information Office
What are you providing	Tracking	Ordering	Product	Product Support	Solution or Technical Expertise
Where is the process taking place	Telephone	Internet	Counter	On-Site; Phone Ordering	Corporate On-site
When are you interacting with each customer	Often		Once		As Needed
Why are customers interacting with you	Convenience	Delivery Issues	Product Issues	Confidence	Value

of a conversation with sales managers, human resources professionals, or both, we are told that they have concluded that their sales support staff jobs should participate in the plan. However, either the business general manager or the corporate human resources executives will say, "But these jobs aren't sales jobs, so why should we approve their participation in the sales compensation plan?" And so the debate begins about whether or not to provide an incentive pay opportunity for sales support jobs.

In Chapter 4, we provided a decision tree that can help companies determine if a job should be eligible for sales compensation. As that figure illustrates, internal jobs that are responsible for facilitating the initial contact, for various aspects of administering the customer relationship activities, or for promotion or contract execution activities may be eligible for sales compensation on a team level. External jobs (i.e., jobs in the field) that are responsible for customer fulfillment (think of the project manager or logistics manager described previously in this chapter) may also be eligible for sales compensation at a team level.

The decision about eligibility for sales incentive pay rests on the job's impact on sales success. Thus, let's revisit the customer relationship management process first introduced in Chapter 1 (see Figure 1-3). The three phases of the process require sales support or sales assist positions in many cases, as illustrated in Figure 8-2. If the CRM process tool and the five W's tool are used together, it quickly becomes apparent that both sales support and sales assist jobs are frequently considered eligible for some type of sales compensation, based on their contribution to sales success.

Sales support jobs are generally not active participants in closing sales, but their technical or functional expertise may be needed in order to persuade the customer, to retain the customer, and to expand business with the customer. Because both sales assist and sales support jobs are nonclosers but valuable contributors, the balance of the chapter will explore various types of support jobs and provide examples of incentive plans for these jobs.

COMPENSATING PRESALES JOBS

For years, many companies have included presales jobs in the sales compensation plan. This is especially true in companies that are engaged in business-to-business selling of complex or technically sophisticated products, services, or solutions. For some of these companies, providing an incentive pay opportunity to the sales support jobs has

Fig. 8-2.   Support roles in the customer relationship management (CRM) process.

given them both a competitive advantage in the labor market and the successful market message of customer-centered sales processes. Consider these two examples.

Medical diagnostic equipment manufacturer. This company sells test kits and analyzers to hospitals and free-standing laboratories. The sales process focuses on long-term, repeat business with named accounts, and focused selling activities with emerging, strategically important accounts. The account manager is the lead salesperson and is assisted in large accounts and in every sale involving equipment by an application engineer. The engineer's role is to ensure optimal uptime of all installed equipment from that manufacturer and to proactively identify potential areas for increased efficiency using that equipment. The engineer also engages with laboratory supervisors in presale activities for new accounts in order to understand current volume, issues with the installed equipment, potential opportunities for enhanced efficiencies (and thus a better revenue stream for the lab), and the workload that will be required with new equipment. The company instituted a sales compensation plan for these technical presale resources almost fifteen years ago; the program has been revised to reflect new business strategies and market realities, but one thing has remained constant: The AE is considered a crucial member of the presale team (both for new sales and for new opportunities with current accounts) and is rewarded for contributions to business success. This company believes that it has been successful in attracting and retaining very talented engineers and in gaining market share in a competitive environment through this proactive compensation support for team success.

Software company. Software companies are experiencing increasing difficulty in attracting and retaining systems engineers with the skills to address technical issues in order to develop an appropriate customer offer, and to communicate effectively with customer personnel and other company resources during presale activities. This blend of potentially disparate skills has led many companies to implement a team sales compensation component of the compensation plan for SEs. In one company, service management successfully laid out a business case for significant at-risk pay for these jobs (the salary/incentive mix is 70/30, rather than the more typical 90/10 or 80/20 in other companies), with performance measures based on success of the geography or major account team and personal contribution to that success. The plan has resulted in lower-than-industry turnover of this very valuable resource.

When presale jobs are eligible for sales incentive pay, you can use the building blocks we described in Chapter 6 to develop a plan for this sales role:

Target total compensation. The target total compensation for the application engineer in the medical diagnostic equipment manufacturer includes both salary and target incentive pay. The company researches competitive pay levels annually through an industry compensation survey, and pay levels are designed to be at the sixtieth percentile of the industry (that is, the company pays higher than 60 percent of other survey participants). Generally speaking, these types of technical jobs are included in a technical pay scale, and the addition of an at-risk incentive opportunity to the sixtieth percentile base pay results in a highly competitive pay package for application engineers.

Mix. Because these jobs are part of a team effort and do not directly persuade customers to buy, the mix is set at 80/20. The company determined that a less aggressive mix (e.g., 90/10) would not have sufficient monetary visibility to motivate the kinds of teaming behaviors needed for success, nor would it attract the talented individuals needed.

Leverage. There is an upside of 1.5 times target for outstanding performance. Because the job does not directly close deals, a more aggressive upside would have been financially unacceptable to the company; however, given the job's contributions, the organization believes that monetary recognition should be available for truly outstanding contributions to the success of the business.

Performance measures. The application engineer is a very real team player in the early stages of the sales process and has a great deal of influence on whether or not a current customer continues to do business with the company (new equipment), or whether a new customer trusts the company's technology and servicing capabilities. While such measures as overall uptime (i.e., the hours equipment in designated accounts is up and running, versus down because of technical problems) or customer satisfaction (based on a survey that is informal at best) were considered, they were eliminated as not truly reflective of the contributions of the job for the purposes of incentives. However, successful presale activity greatly increases the probability of closing the deal, and salespeople gravitate to the AEs that have the best track record in supporting sales efforts. Therefore, two measures were selected: region revenue versus plan (because the better the AEs do their job, the more likely it is that the region will reach or exceed its revenue plan) and number of sales reps reaching quota (because the company wants to strongly encourage proactive use of AEs in presale activities and reward AEs for helping all reps, not just a select few, to reach their quota).

Incentive formula. The company uses a very simple unlinked formula for the plan, as shown in Figure 8-3. The first component (region revenue versus plan) duplicates the approach used for the salespeople, with a threshold and excellence level of performance. Each percent achievement from threshold through excellence has a defined value, and the plan is capped at excellence. The second component has three steps, with target paid when at least two-thirds of the reps in the region (twenty of the thirty in the example) make quota.

Sales crediting. Because this is a team plan, sales crediting is not an issue—all sales in the region are credited against the quota for the purposes of percent achievement, and debookings and cancellations are subtracted. The AEs are paid based on the same region revenue quota that is used to calculate the region business manager's bonus.

Fig. 8-3. Illustrative plan for systems engineers.

Plan Elements	Region Revenue vs. Plan		Number of Reps Making Quota	
	% to Plan	**Payout**	**Number of Reps**	**Payout**
	150%	150% of Target Region Revenue Bonus	>25 of 30	150% of Target Rep Quota Bonus
	100%	**100% of Target Region Revenue Bonus**	**20 – 25 of 30**	**100% of Target Rep Quota Bonus**
	70%	50% of Target Region Revenue Bonus	15 – 19 of 30	50% of Target Rep Quota Bonus
	<60%	-0-	<15	-0-
Payout Frequency	Quarterly against annual plan		Quarterly	
Element Weight	50%		50%	

Performance and payout periods. The performance period for the revenue versus plan component is quarterly against the annual plan. This is consistent with the corporate measurement and financial periods and the way in which region management is measured for one of its plan components. Because the salespeople are paid based on achievement of their quarterly quota, the AE bonus that is paid for rep achievement is paid out quarterly. Thus, the performance periods for the AE are consistent with those for both management and team member compensation plans.

COMPENSATING POSTSALES JOBS

Postsales jobs are responsible for executing the promises about performance and service that were made to customers at the time of purchase. After the sale is made, how a product or service is implemented is an important factor in a customer's willingness to do business with the company again in the future. In fact, postsale jobs may have a direct impact on the customer's willingness to make the final payment for what was purchased. In the customer's mind, the deal may not be fully complete until the product is installed and functioning to expectations or a combination of other factors that indicate that "what I bought is what I needed and what I got." Increasingly complex B2B transactions or relationships require the proactive participation of functional experts to make sure that the company delivers, and is paid for, the products or services purchased. Consider the following examples.

In a software company, just as the systems engineer is critical in the presale efforts, the consultant position plays a key role in ensuring that the software solution is installed and functioning. Although titles for this job vary, the key accountability is the same—marshal the required resources to get the solution customized, installed, tested, and delivering the results that the customer needs. In enterprise systems selling, this may mean the difference between complete payment and a negotiated settlement, between doing business with the customer on a long-term basis or never again being considered as a key vendor. One such company used the compensation building blocks described in Chapter 6 to develop the plan described below.

Target total compensation. The target total compensation for the consultant position in the software industry is a challenge to set and maintain. Professional services firms, software companies, and technology functions in general business all compete for workers with the skills needed to ensure effective, efficient, and fully operational installation of custom software. One company has determined that it needs to set the pay level for this job at the seventy-fifth percentile of the market, rather than the fiftieth percentile (which is used for all its other jobs) because of the scarcity of talented resources. This company has, in fact, established a pay scale for this job family that falls between the scale for the systems engineering jobs and that for the sales jobs in the company. The jobs are either generalist (can project-manage less complex solutions implementations) or specialist (focused on one product area). Both types of jobs are paid essentially the same way.

Mix. The company that pays its consultants in the seventy-fifth percentile has determined that it cannot do so with a significant proportion of pay at risk. As is typical with these kinds of jobs, the mix is 80/20, with a relatively high base salary.

Leverage. The upside available for this job is based on the same principles as other "nonsales" jobs: The job contributes to, but does not close, sales. The consultant role is a team role, and, like the SE job, should participate in the success of the designated team. Therefore, the illustrative job that is paid at the seventy-fifth percentile has an upside of 1.5 times target, and the incentive plan for this job is capped.

Performance measures. Very few companies have the ability to measure, or interest in measuring, individual contributions for these jobs. Measures such as billing hours, installations complete, or customer satisfaction do not always directly reflect a consultant's performance and may not be aligned with the company's business strategy. For our illustrative job, billing hours is not, in fact, a good measure, since the key to the company's success is software sales, not services. However, specialist consultants can and do affect both their product line's success on a corporate level and the success of the geography in which they work. The plan, therefore, may have one or two measures for this job, depending on whether the job is generalist or specialist. The generalist is paid based on the region's performance, and the specialist is paid on both the region's performance and corporate achievement of the assigned product line's business plan.

Incentive formula. The incentive plan formula is a simple bonus formula and includes either one component or two additive components weighted at 50 percent each. Each bonus is based on achievement of goal at an aggregate level, and pays out after a defined threshold has been achieved. The bonus for both roles is capped.

Performance and payout periods. Although the company would prefer to provide a quarterly payout for these jobs, the revenue recognition policy and business plans of the company make this difficult. Therefore, the performance period is semiannual against an annual plan, and payouts are available semiannually as well.

How to Answer Four Tough Questions about Sales Support Compensation Plans

When top managers agree to extend participation in the sales compensation plan to sales support staff positions, they should anticipate that these newly eligible employees will have questions about how they will be paid in the future. We can identify four common questions that plan designers should anticipate and, therefore, prepare responses for front-line managers to use when those questions are raised.

Is a Portion of My Compensation at Risk? If So, How Was That Decision Made?

These questions are quite common among employees who have not been paid under a sales compensation plan. If an employee's total cash compensation is salary or salary plus a year-end bonus, where the bonus is add-on pay, then the concept of at-risk pay is really quite foreign to that individual. And if participation in the plan actually results in a decrease in salary to alter the salary/incentive ratio for the position, communicating the rationale for the change will be many times more challenging. In subsequent chapters of the book, we will provide you with tools and techniques to help you implement a sales compensation plan that will support new or changed sales roles. For now, you should anticipate that you will have to develop information to explain two things to the employees: (1) the process that was used to determine the at-risk pay for the particular job, and how that reflects the job's new responsibilities and the realities of the competitive market, and (2) why the particular salary/incentive ratio was selected for the job.

IS THIS COMPENSATION PLAN A GOOD OPPORTUNITY FOR ME?

The answer to this question requires a company to explain to the employees the difference in the compensation opportunity between the new job and the former job. Take the example of an employee who has worked in a sales support job that paid salary only. If that job changed, and total cash compensation was paid in the form of 80 percent salary and 20 percent incentive, it is the 20 percent incentive opportunity that would be attractive to the employee. This is because, as we explained in Chapter 6, it is the incentive opportunity that has an upside compensation potential. With double leverage on the incentive opportunity, a sales support employee in an 80 percent salary/20 percent incentive position could earn 20 percent more in total cash compensation than an individual in the same position who was paid salary only. Here's how that would work: Assume that the job is a $50,000 a year job. For the 80/20 position, there is a base salary of $40,000 and an incentive opportunity of $10,000. If an individual overachieves, she could earn as much as $20,000 in incentive pay. Therefore, $40,000 + $20,000 equals $60,000, which is $50,000 + 20 percent. In summary, it is the upside on the incentive opportunity that provides the compelling reason for the attractiveness of the new plan.

WHAT WILL I BE EXPECTED TO DO DIFFERENTLY, IF ANYTHING, TO EARN THE COMPENSATION OPPORTUNITY DESCRIBED IN THE NEW PLAN?

A company's answer to this question is critical to the employee's success with the new compensation plan. Typically, when a sales support job first becomes eligible for participation in a company's sales compensation plan, it is because the job's role in the sales process has been altered. Thus, top managers do have expectations about either new or changed behavior in the position. It is important that the immediate supervisor of the newly eligible sales support positions is equipped to not only explain the new behavior expectations but also indicate how this behavior can lead to performance that will enable the employee to "win" under the incentive plan.

WHEN AND HOW FREQUENTLY WILL I BE PAID AS A RESULT OF MY PARTICIPATION IN THE NEW SALES COMPENSATION PLAN?

When a sales support employee is new to participation in the sales compensation plan, it is necessary to explain when the company measures performance results—for example, quarterly, semiannually, annually—and, therefore, when the employee can expect a payout from the plan if he meets the assigned goals. It is typical for sales support staff employees to be paid either quarterly or annually, while sales representative might be paid more frequently—for example, monthly. This is because the incentive opportunity for sales support positions is generally less than the opportunity in sales jobs. Regardless of the payout timing, frontline managers should be equipped with information to explain to the sales staff participants when they are paid and why their incentive is calculated on a particular performance cycle.

SUMMING UP

More and more companies are changing the ways they do business with customers. Increasingly, those changes include a broader role for the sales support employee when he or she is interacting with customers. This is particularly true in companies where sales support staff positions are assigned responsibilities for customer retention duties.

Generally speaking, top managers, sales executives, and human resources professionals do not agree when it comes to including sales support positions in the sales compensation plan. Our experience suggests that the reasons for not including these positions in the plan are often rooted in old ways of doing business, outdated perceived notions about the role these jobs play in contributing to sales success, or both. However, we must stop short of making a blanket suggestion that all sales support staff positions should be included in the sales compensation plan. Company culture, management philosophies, and compensation policies that pertain to these roles and jobs still vary widely across industries and even among businesses within the same industry. The best advice we can offer is that you should regularly examine the role of your sales support staff positions using the tools we have provided to determine if a change to include them in sales compensation plan participation is called for.

Including sales support staff positions in the sales compensation plan is not without challenge. There are a number of tough issues that compensation plan designers may have to deal with. These challenges are largely centered on explaining to employees how they will be affected by plan participation and why participation in the plan is a good opportunity for them. Ultimately, however, when sales support positions are included in the sales compensation plan for the right reasons and employees are enthusiastic about their participation in it, everybody wins—customers, the company, and, of course, the employees.

CHAPTER

9

COMPENSATING SELLERS AND TEAMS FOR LARGE SALES

The notion that selling is selling regardless of what is being sold is no longer a widely held belief among top managers. This is particularly true in the "large deal" sales arena. Recently, a general manager in the chemicals industry told us about his desire to substantially increase the average size of a "deal." "There was a time," he said, "when we had as many as 5,000 customers and our typical sales representative sold fifteen to twenty deals a year with an average sale of $500,000. Today, we deploy business development managers who sell two or three deals a year that fall in the range of $20 to $40 million. We had to make this change quickly to enhance our competitive position with our customers; however, we made the leap to large deal selling before we were ready. And the one aspect of this change that plagued us throughout the first year of the transition was pay treatment—not only how much to pay our people, but also what performance measures to use to gauge sales success."

When a company changes its business model from transaction selling to solution selling, it potentially enters the world of large deal sales—a world that brings with it a new set of sales management challenges. Defining the sales roles, selecting the right people for those roles, and ultimately determining the best compensation plan for large deal selling is tough work. This work is exponentially more difficult when top managers do not have prior experience in how to approach large deal selling and sales management. Oftentimes, a totally new sales culture must be built to support selling large deals. This is because many sales-people spend the majority of their time harvesting sales in accounts that they either "won" in prior years or were assigned to after someone else made the sale. We refer to this type of sales force as account servicers.

A sales force that spends the majority of its time harvesting business loses its edge in new account selling over time. We have observed companies where selling to new accounts is not a top priority because of the demands on salespeople to retain current customers. What once may have been an organization of new business developers atrophies into an organization of account servicers. When this situation occurs, a transition from account servicing to large deal selling becomes very problematic for a company.

Also, it wasn't that long ago that the typical business-to-business sales representative booked annual sales in the range of $1 to $4 million, depending, of course on the industry and the size of the average sales transaction. While a "large sale" is a relative term, we have observed that a growing number of companies—both product and service businesses—are challenging their sellers to substantially increase the average deal size. The size of the deal, the length of the sales process, and the number of people (on both the buyer's and the seller's sides) represent some rather unique challenges for top managers to examine when designing a new compensation plan for large sales. Consider these examples:

- *EDS.* In June 2000, EDS was one of five companies chosen to compete for business under a $1.5 billion, ten-year contract with the U.S. Government's General Services Administration to provide smart access identification cards to federal agencies. EDS's regional director for business development and its vice president for the Government Global Industry Group reported that implementing this government contract would represent the first significant use of smart card technology at the federal level. Smart cards use silicon chips embedded with information that will enhance security and physical assets at both military and civilian facilities around the world.[1] Without doubt, winning the right to do business with the federal government through this contract, given its size and complexity, involved a long sales cycle and probably a variety of resources. Essentially, EDS won the "sell-in" phase of the deal—it is an approved supplier for the contract. The exact amount of business EDS wins over the next ten years will be the result of both continued selling efforts and effective service delivery. Thus, the compensation plan has to recognize the local "sell-through" efforts and results of its salespeople at each approved customer site.

• *Enron Energy Services (EES)*. Enron's salespeople sell long-term, outsourced energy solutions. Enron's sales team convinces its prospects—typically, senior executives in major companies—to turn all of their energy management needs over to Enron. A typical deal is, for example, the one that Enron closed with the Houston Astros baseball franchise. For the next thirty years, at a price of $200 million to the Astros, Enron will provide the ballpark with energy and facilities management services. What is even more interesting about EES is that as recently as 1996, it sold next to nothing (because customers were slow to change their energy buying habits). In 1997, its sales team closed 170 deals worth approximately $1.2 billion; in 1998, the number jumped to $3.8 billion; and by 1999, that number approached $9 billion.[2] With each customer deal ranging in size from $50 million to over $1 billion, there is little doubt that EES is engaged in selling large deals, which makes it an attractive candidate to examine when studying sales compensation best practices.

• *Honeywell*. Honeywell is another company that is capitalizing on the trend in business outsourcing. In 1998, its IAC division won a $250 million, ten-year contract with Chevron Products Company. Under the agreement, Honeywell will install and maintain all automation solutions at Chevron's refinery in Richmond, California. This contract win reflected Honeywell's implementation of a new business model called Automation Management Program (AMP).[3] Prior to this deal, it would not have been usual for customers like Chevron to purchase their automation control products and/or services in the range of $1 to $5 million annually from Honeywell or any other single supplier. Clearly, the sale of AMP reflected at least one refining company's willingness to enter into a "big" sales transaction. However, a sale of this magnitude represented a significant compensation challenge for Honeywell because it was not accustomed to selling deals of this size. Later in this chapter we will describe the approach that Honeywell took to implementing a compensation plan in this division that rewarded its people for large deal sales.

In each of these situations, the customer did not take the decision to enter into a large, long-term business commitment lightly. It is reasonable to conclude that in all three of these situations, the sellers and supporting sales staff engaged their respective customers in a series of meetings and conversations about how they could help the customer's top managers achieve their business objectives while providing the products and services the companies offered. As Enron found, completing just one deal can take anywhere from nine to fifteen months. The nature of these big deals—essentially, a partnership or alliance between two organizations to achieve a common goal—the size of the contracts, and the level of resources required to win the sale suggest that this is a unique type of selling.

Compensating sellers and sales support teams for large deals is a complex issue, and therefore one that we find is of keen interest to top managers and compensation plan designers. The balance of this chapter describes the important features of large deal selling and the new or changed sales roles that come into being when large deals emerge as a new business model. We also provide you with examples of how to compensate sellers and sales support team members involved with this type of sale.

The Challenge of Selling Effectively at the "C" Level

One fundamental premise of direct selling is that sellers have to create value if they are to be successful in motivating a buyer to do business with their company. The opportunity to add value through the sales process varies from relatively little (the customer already knows how to make the purchase decision) to high value creation (the customer is making a strategic decision and is not familiar with all the options, is concerned about reducing risk related to making a bad decision, or both). To approach prospects and customers with an appropriate value proposition to do business, more and more companies are requiring their salespeople to use a sales model. The sales model mandates the type of selling in which a seller should engage in order to successfully meet the needs of the buyer. Generally speaking, leading companies deploy one or more of three prevalent types of sales model in their selling relationships with customers. These three prevalent selling models are:

- *Transaction selling.* This approach to selling is used when the customer is concerned with efficient buying. For example, the buyer trusts the product, is familiar with its use, and is focused on the "convenience" of the purchase transaction.
- *Consultative selling.* This type of selling is used when the customer engages in competitive buying. The buyer may or may not be familiar with the product or technology, and therefore the focus is on making the best "value choice." To do so, the customer's value judgment is frequently based on the role of the sales-

person (and other sales support resources) in helping those involved in the buying process make their decision.

- *Solution selling.* This approach to selling is used when the customer is not familiar with the product or technology, views the business situation requiring attention as complex, and therefore believes that the purchase will have a significant impact on business results. The focus of buying is on making the most secure purchase decision (minimizing the risk of failure), and therefore the buyer is concerned with the vendor's competence, resources, and credibility as an enterprise. The salesperson has the opportunity to add significant value to the purchasing process as the sales process leader, bringing together resources from both sides—company and customer—to make a "win/win" purchase decision.

In our experience, the solution selling model is most frequently used for large deal sales. The reason this model is the most prevalent is because large deal selling often begins at the "C" level of an organization—namely, with the chief executive officer, chief operating officer, chief financial officer, chief information officer, and so on. However, rarely does a C-level prospect make a purchase decision alone. Studies conducted by Atlanta-based OnTarget Research show that C-level buyers get involved in the purchasing decision during the beginning and end of the buying process.[4] At the beginning of the sales process, they want to understand the current business issues, establish objectives, and set expectations for what must be accomplished through the particular purchase of products, services, or both. At the end of the sales process, they are interested in understanding how what will be bought will be implemented and how that implementation will achieve the results they laid out at the beginning of the process.

What makes selling at the C level challenging is not presenting to and communicating with these executive buyers; rather, it is all of the activities that go on in the middle of the process and in the middle of the buying organization. In most companies, it is the people in the middle of the organization that determine the degree to which a change initiative will be successful. Sales success at the C level requires that top sales managers support their sellers and sales teams with three things:

- A well-thought-out, proven value proposition that can be attested to by "reference accounts"

- An explicit and clear sales process that defines the roles and accountabilities of all participants in the process
- Executive-level participation in the sales process by the selling company

In summary, there are two major differences between selling large deals and selling "average"-size transactions. The first difference is the level of the organization where selling is done, and the second difference is the type of sales process used to win the business.

TIPS ON DEFINING A LARGE SALE

Although the expected financial returns from a "large sale" vary from company to company, and from business to business within a company, a "large sale" generally includes these characteristics:

- The sale is a multiyear contract.
- The sales process is lengthy, frequently twelve months or longer.
- Multiple resources are required from both the buyer's and the seller's organizations to conceptualize and close the deal.
- The sale is multidimensional and includes products, services, installation, and/or consulting.
- The deal provides an enterprise or facility solution.
- The dollar value of the total deal significantly exceeds that of the typical sale or contract with the company's customers.

Not all customers will be interested in entering into large, multiyear deals with a supplier or business partner. In fact, our research shows that only between 5 and 10 percent of a company's current customers will have an immediate interest in switching from a current buying relationship to what could be characterized as a large deal. This is because most companies are not immediately equipped to buy in the manner in which a supplier sells a large deal. For example, if a company has previously purchased on a transaction basis—regardless of the product or service—and the supplier suggests a contract purchase with incentives to buy for multiple years, the buying organization often does not have the tools in place to evaluate the benefits of this type of purchase.

Readiness to buy has as much to do with the buyer's capability to assess the "newness" of the offer as it does with the pain associated with the business problem the buyer is trying to solve. This is one of the reasons why Enron Energy Services places so much emphasis on targeting the right customer opportunities. EES found, for example, that its most desirable prospects—in terms of "winnable" business—were characterized as follows:

- They had previous outsourcing experience.
- They had a centralized decision-making process for large purchases.
- Energy was not their core business.
- Enron already had contacts within the company.

What Enron and others have learned is that a large sale cannot be defined exclusively in terms of current business volume. A process is required to determine the potential sales opportunity, and, frequently, the size of that opportunity is very much a function of benefits (e.g., cost savings, efficiencies, and headache-free operation) that the seller can provide to the buyer.

How to Organize Company Resources for Global Account Teams

More and more companies are using teams to enhance productivity and improve business results. Within the sales function, companies deploy teams to increase focus and improve responsiveness to customers. Nowhere is this statement more true than in large deal selling. Typically, a salesperson may be the sales process leader in pursuing a large deal with an account. However, rarely is it possible to close the business without meaningful and significant involvement of others who are members of the sales team. This is because the prospective customer often has many of her people—counterparts to the team members in the selling organization—involved in assessing the business opportunity.

Our experience shows that when companies first consider implementing a large deal sales strategy, there is a keen interest in knowing how to organize their resources. Intuitively, top managers understand that multifunctional resources will be required. Chapter 10, "Compensating Sales Managers and Team Leaders," describes in detail the alternative team structures that top managers should consider. The roles of the team leader and team members vary by account (prospective or current). However, in order to effectively sell large deals, some rules of thumb are applicable, as follows:

- A designated "business developer" or "new account seller" (e.g., a business development manager or customer acquisition executive job) must be available with the skills to gain access at the C level and effectively manage the sales process from initial access through the close of the deal.
- Business analysis and financial skills are required to develop the deal framework and details.
- Credible and experienced technical personnel (engineering, logistics, consulting, or any other specific area of solution-specific expertise needed in solution implementation) are needed to assist in the sales process

The challenge in setting up teams for large deal selling in any company is to determine what types of skills and experience are required to effectively sell to and close deals with strategically important accounts. The company must determine if new individuals must be recruited or, if current resources are used, when people with those competences should be pulled away from their other responsibilities so that they can devote their time to a sales team assignment.

Many companies operate a segment of their business with global account teams to sell to and work with large, strategically important accounts. Typically, these teams work with a company's largest customers or are implemented specifically to target and sell to a strategically important account that is not currently doing business with the company. Some of these accounts may be the focus of large deal sales. While an initial "executive-level new account seller" is frequently needed as the sales process leader for new accounts, large deal sales generally affect many facilities or businesses within a company, and a team of resources is required throughout the process. Thus, it could be helpful to you to describe how some companies structure the resources of their global account teams.

Companies that sell to and manage customer relationships on a global basis typically create a global account manager position. Individuals assigned to this position are responsible for serving as the sales process leader for new opportunities in the assigned account and as the business manager for the company's relationship with its very largest customers. While the global account manager's job is a dedicated position serving one or two major customers, other resources assigned to work with those customers are determined based on the customer's buying preferences and decision-making process, the company's sales process, and the company's confidence in its ability to reassign internal resources. Three alternative approaches that companies use to cover global accounts are:

Borrowed Resources

When this approach is used, local resources are assigned to the global account team but continue to report to the region or country manager. Financial responsibility for the account is retained at the local manager's level. Salespeople who are not fully dedicated to a global account may allocate a portion of their time to serving the global account and spend the rest of their time on local selling activities. Under this approach, the global account manager and any dedicated "business development manager" typically report to the sales executive in the host country.

The borrowed resources approach is the most common among companies that are new to large deal selling. This is because without committed revenues, a top manager is reluctant to dedicate resources to an account. As you might expect, there are several challenges associated with this approach that a company must overcome. Although many companies try to sell to and serve their customers "globally," they can encounter difficulties with product design, manufacturing, logistics, pricing, and a host of other operational issues that could justify the attention of dedicated resources. Borrowed resources frequently do not have the time or the incentive to champion the changes in an offering that may be required to meet the needs of a particular customer. Too often, the internal organization works against that type of customization.

Additionally, there frequently is little incentive for local management to provide support outside of its geographic boundaries. To be successful with a borrowed resources approach to global account coverage, a company must appoint individuals who not only are knowledgeable businesspeople but also have strong personalities when it comes to resolving cross-functional disputes within the company about what it will and will not do for its major customers.

Borrowed Resources with a Dedicated Account Development Budget

Under this approach, sales personnel also report to the region or country manager. Local management continues to have revenue and expense responsibility for its geography. However, "out of geography" activities associated with the global account management initiative are covered by a separate global account budget, e.g., a separate fund for travel and other related business development expenses that does not affect the local manager's expense budget. This approach is often used as a transition to a centralized resource structure.

CENTRALIZED RESOURCES

With this approach, the global account teams report to a separate line of business organization. A vice president of global accounts who has worldwide responsibility, including a revenue and expense plan, may head this organization. In countries where the customer opportunity does not justify a full-time salesperson, resources are shared with the local organization. Performance measurement for the global account manager and team members is based on customer results. For many companies, this is the preferred approach to pursuing large deal sales and covering major customers. However, because many companies approach this type of coverage on a "pay as you go" basis, centralized or dedicated coverage is often implemented well after the global account program has been established.

A global customer presents a company with some interesting challenges to its current organization and deployment of resources. While not all global customers are the result of an initial large sale, as both Enron and Honeywell have experienced, many of them are won on the basis of expectations for unique services and benefits. It is not uncommon to find that those customers, whether they are categorized as global, major, strategic, or some other designation, expect specialized coverage through dedicated resources. This is true when they are selecting the company with which they will do business and after the business is closed. When a company acts on those expectations, new roles are created, either formally or informally, in the company. This action is another event that should trigger top managers to reconsider a company's compensation practices.

FIVE BENEFITS OF A CONSISTENT SALES PROCESS
FOR LARGE DEAL SELLING

Generally speaking, a sales process is a method or procedure consisting of a series of steps directed toward achieving a particular business objective related to contact with customers. In most businesses, the sales process fits within the broader context of a company's go-to-market strategy. That broader context includes business strategy, marketing, sales, customer relationship management, and customer service. However, in most business situations, the sales process is the most visible part of a company's go-to-market strategy. That is because the sales process holds the potential for linking the customer to the company in a very defined manner.

The principal benefit of a well-defined and uniformly used sales process is that it minimizes the potential for uncontrollable elements to cause either selling efforts or sales opportunities to go off track. Companies that use a defined sales process swear by it as a major contributor to sales success. Enron Energy Services, chosen as the best sales force in 1999 by *Sales & Marketing Management* magazine and winner of that magazine's award for best in class in Sales Process in the year 2000, implemented a well-defined sales process in its business two years ago. Its sales grew to nearly $9 billion in 1999 from $3.8 billion in 1998, and Enron's management attributes that success to the effective use of its well-defined sales process by its salespeople.

We have studied many different sales processes. Figure 9-1 illustrates one of the sales processes that we have seen used effectively by companies involved in large deal selling. Our conclusion, however, is that there is no one "right" sales process. In fact, many of the processes in use today are variations of the same theme. What is important is that a company adopts a formal process, educates its salespeople in that process, and uses it uniformly to manage the business. Our experience suggests that doing so results in the following five benefits to the company and its salespeople:

- It closes the gap between customer expectations and company performance.
- It establishes a road map to promote consistency of sales effort.
- It helps in identifying customer needs and sales/service resource requirements.
- It fosters improved teamwork and collaboration across marketing, sales, and service.
- It provides a framework for continuous improvement.

Fig. 9-1. Illustration of "large deal" sales process.

Phase 1:	Phase 2:	Phase 3:	Phase 4:	Phase 5:
Lead Generation and Qualifying	Opportunity Processing and Relationship Building	Opportunity Relationship Management	Business Relationship Management	Service Delivery

How to Develop Compensation Plans for Large Sales: Two Case Examples

You can improve your company's practices by benefiting from the experience of other successful companies. With that thought in mind, we draw upon the experiences of two companies—Honeywell IAC and RSNA (a fictitious company)—to provide you with examples of how the concepts, principles, and tools described in this book were used to develop compensation plans for large deal sales.

Honeywell International, Inc., Case Study

Honeywell International, Inc., is a diversified manufacturing company that was formed following the 1999 merger of AlliedSignal, Inc., and Honeywell, Inc. Honeywell Industrial Automation and Control (IAC) is a $1.5 billion business unit within Honeywell's Industrial Control business segment; in 1999 it accounted for approximately 30 percent of that business segment's revenues.

Honeywell IAC focuses on four markets in the process control industry: distributed control systems, professional and support services, field instrumentation, and application software. Customers are divided between vertical market (industry) accounts and geographic accounts. Vertical markets include oil and gas, hydrocarbon processing industries, petrochemicals, pulp and paper, power generation, and food and drug processing.

To meet its customer needs, IAC offers a full range of hardware and software products. Services include project management, engineering and installation, network management and installation, and equipment maintenance and repair. IAC's early business model was product-centered (i.e., offering the product solutions that it believed would meet the needs of the customer plants) rather than customer-centered (i.e., developing and implementing full solutions to meet the needs of the client). However, IAC's business model has evolved into a solution orientation; the mission of the business today is "to improve our customers' business results by providing best value solutions and by exhibiting a passion for excellent performance."[5] That evolution has been enhanced and supported by the development and introduction of offerings that integrate products and services in solutions to meet customer needs. For example, TotalPlant Solutions delivers open hardware and software solutions through an industrial automation system "designed to unify business and control information throughout a plant or mill."[6]

IAC deploys a full complement of sales, service, and operations personnel to develop new business opportunities with facilities in their target industries and to manage the requirements of these accounts. Roles include corporate account manager, field consultant, and project manager. A typical contract can range from $1 to $20 million and include products, services, software, or any combination of the three, or a completely integrated system solution. Compensation opportunity and proportion of pay at risk vary by job. The performance measures used to determine incentive payout for these field jobs are primarily financial, for example, orders booked and margin (a key business objective for IAC is margin contribution). While incentive pay may be $15,000, $50,000, or even more, the IAC culture is not one of developing "overnight millionaires" through high commission rates and multiple new multimillion dollar deals in each territory.

Total Plant Management (TPM)

In 1998, IAC embarked on a new approach to providing a full solution to process industries, with an initial focus on gas and oil refining. This offering expands the core business process automation product into a full-service outsourcing of plant modernization and automation. The "typical" value of a contract would no longer be based on products and relatively short-term maintenance, installation, or service agreements. Rather, a preferred approach to doing business with these customers would be through a strategic outsourcing relationship. A longer-term strategic outsourcing relationship could be valued in the hundreds of millions of dollars for plants that must use contemporary methods and systems in order to remain competitive.

In 1999, IAC completed negotiations for the first sale of this type of business model and signed a $250 million, ten-year contract with a major oil company to provide an integrated solution. Under this business model, called Total Plant Management (TPM), IAC will install and maintain all the automation solutions at one of the customer company's plants. Using a process similar to the process we described in Chapter 3 to determine the need for new roles, IAC determined that the new offering clearly required a different sales process and new roles. In this business model, both the buyer and the integrated solution were dramatically different from those associated with IAC's traditional offerings. The traditional sales/service model could not provide the extensive financial expertise, contracting knowledge, and executive selling skills needed to develop, negotiate, close, and manage the business as IAC envisioned it through a TPM deal.

The process used to identify and close the contract with the customer company served as the basis for other deals, and can be summarized as follows:

- *Phase 1:* Conduct engineering study.
- *Phase 2:* Develop the offer.
- *Phase 3:* Close the deal.

Phase 3 concludes the front-end sales process and leads to phase 4, during which the contract is implemented.

In order to effectively complete the process, the company developed a conceptual model that identified a "Team A" responsible for phases 1 through 3 and a "Team B" for "pursuit support" roles and accountable for Phase 4. That process is illustrated in Figure 9-2. The first phases of the process require the expert contribution of two members of Team A. In this case, one member provided the financial skills needed to develop an offer that was both financially attractive to Honeywell IAC and financially feasible for the customer. The other member provided the executive-level selling and negotiation skills needed to demonstrate the value of the proposed solution, overcome objections, and close the contract with the support of staff resources.

Deployment of members of Team B varies by customer opportunity, but generally include specific sales, service, consulting, operations, and

Fig. 9-2. Honeywell IAC sales process summary.

Complete Engineering Study	→	Develop the Offer	→	Deal Close	→	Delivery

Feasibility study/ assessment to determine the benefits of plant automation and modernization	Develop program plan (product, equipment, service fees, timeline) based on analysis of customer needs and company's ability to meet those needs. Initiate and complete process to persuade customer to act or to realize benefits of proposal.	Negotiate final terms and conditions of the contract Contract/offer acceptance by customer	Post sale implementation and service delivery

other resources required to implement and maintain the plant modernization and automation. In order to ensure effective contract execution, there is some overlap in accountabilities for the appropriate completion of the final phases. As with any complex business relationship, effective transition is important. Therefore, members of Team A may periodically schedule and participate in status meetings with the client and IAC personnel; conversely, members of Team B are generally involved in the early phases as the solution is being developed.

COMPENSATION FRAMEWORK FOR TEAM MEMBERS

As a result of implementing new roles, IAC determined that the traditional approach to sales incentive compensation was unlikely to be appropriate for these "big deal" teams. In fact, in an informal study completed with other companies known for outsourced solutions, IAC found that successful "big deal" sellers were an integral part of the entire sales process (frequently twelve months or more long) and that they earned in the high six figures for *each deal* they closed. This was a concept that was foreign to Honeywell. The company's compensation practices did not include a provision for sales of the IAC TPM type compensated by six-figure incentive payouts. The challenge for the IAC human resources and sales management team, therefore, was twofold:

1. Determine the most appropriate approach to compensating key team members.
2. Obtain executive approval for the optimal approach.

FIVE KEY PRINCIPLES FOR COMPENSATING IAC TPM DEALS

The successful implementation of the TPM sales model requires unique sales and customer relationship management skills. Because these skills are in limited supply, the additional challenge of how to retain key TPM team members needed to be addressed through the compensation plan. A multifunctional compensation design team was formed to develop a compensation framework that would support both the business and human resources objectives of the company and the individual expectations of highly successful team members. The initial conclusions that were reached about "must have's" for this compensation program included the following:

- The program must be based on profitability of the deal for IAC.
- Key contributors must be rewarded based on successful completion of the process, but interim rewards would be needed.

- Because members of both Team A and Team B are contributors to success, they should all be rewarded for the long-term success of each deal.
- Team A members are the crucial differentiating factor in attracting initial deals and developing profitable terms with prospective customers, and therefore should share proportionately more in the rewards available.

These conclusions led to several key principles that top management agreed would serve as the road map for designing all future incentive plans for "big deal" teams.

- *Principle #1: Document the Contract Process and Outcomes to Create an Incentive Compensation Plan for Each Deal.* Because each customer plant or industry may require different processes and outcomes, the incentive plan for each deal may vary. For example, eligible participants may be on one team only, the sales process may not include an engineering study for which IAC will be paid, or the contracting process may not require the type of three-way negotiation (IAC, customer, and financial institutions) that the initial deal required.

- *Principle #2: Set Fund Based on P&L for the Deal.* Profitability is the key measure of success at Honeywell, and IAC must deliver an acceptable margin on each deal. Therefore, the incentive compensation available for payout throughout the sales and delivery process must be estimated at the beginning of the process in order to determine both the profitability of the deal and the dollars that can be paid at target achievement for each team member.

- *Principle #3: Allocate Incentive Compensation and Tie Awards to Deal Progress.* Because of the length of the sales process, "back-end-loaded" rewards, especially for members of team A, were considered both demotivational and not consistent with competitive practice. In fact, since IAC realizes some revenue from phase 1 work (the engineering study), actually paying incentive compensation early in the process is both practical and desirable in terms of rewarding the types of behavior critical to the success of a future deal.

- *Principle #4: Share Earned Awards between Major Teams (Sales and Support).* While Team A is primarily focused on developing and closing these opportunities, the degree to which the team members are supported throughout the process by technical, consulting, and service personnel is critical to success. In this highly technical sale, delivery of results by Team B is also critical—a ten-year contract is most profitable in the early years, but the ability to sell these deals in the future rests on the successful execution of the initial deals throughout the life of the contract.

• *Principle #5: Award Variable Compensation for Sellers and Support Personnel Based on Delivery Results.* Essentially, target variable pay for sales team participants would be funded based on actual contract results compared to previously determined goals. This "funding mechanism" also provides for some upside based on key outcomes agreed to with the client.

Figure 9-3 provides an illustration of how these principles were put to work. As shown, 60 percent of the reward fund would be available for payouts at the end of each of the first three phases of the process, with 40 percent reserved for payout (particularly to Team B members) in the early years of phase 4.

EXECUTIVE APPROVAL

Once the key principles were defined and illustrated based on the initial TMP deal, it was possible to develop a business case to present to executive management covering the new roles, the implications for compensation, and the results that would be delivered back to the company. Without this business case, approval would have been unlikely; however, very attractive margins could clearly be negotiated and maintained for each deal, even in the face of higher-than-traditional incentive costs per employee, based on the level and type of resources needed to get and close the deal.

Fig. 9-3. Illustration of fund allocation.

Process Overview

Engineering Study → The Offer → Close → Delivery

Illustrative Incentive Allocation

10% of Funded Reward Dollars | 20% of Funded Reward Dollars | 30% of Funded Reward Dollars | 40% of Funded Reward Dollars

Tools and Administration

Human resources and other team members developed spreadsheet tools to track team membership, member contribution, and eligibility for participation in the incentive plan for each deal. Since each deal stands on its own relative to funding and team members, this kind of tool is needed for each deal, and the administration is the responsibility of human resources professionals who are knowledgeable about both the key principles and corporate and legal requirements.

Outcomes

The process for compensating sellers of very large and profitable multi-year contracts for an outsourced solution resulted in positive outcomes, and identified key issues that are being resolved with the teams with human resources assistance.

The most positive benefit to the company has been the ability to attract and retain very talented team members who can provide leadership to others in the process of identifying, negotiating, and closing these kinds of opportunities. However, the offsetting issues are related to those in traditional sales roles: (1) a reluctance on the part of account managers to identify outsourcing opportunities or work with teams in "their" plants, as the business will now be part of a large multiyear contract and thus not considered in the account manager's commission calculation ("They're taking my business away from me"), and (2) a potential for too many applications for the Team A roles (a perception that "I can do that job," even if the skills and experience are not there).

Radio Systems North America Case Study

Radio Systems North America Group (RSNA) is a division of a multibillion-dollar manufacturer of communications and electronics equipment. RSNA provides communications and information systems for businesses and government agencies in the United States and Canada. While RSNA solutions can apply to any organization with a need for instant, effective, and private communication, the division focuses on serving four industry markets: manufacturing, public safety, utilities, and government (including federal, state, and local entities).

RSNA offers a variety of communications solutions tailored to the needs of its customers. Offerings include radio network solutions, radios, wireless data services, fixed data systems, accessories, site management, and software. RSNA's multibillion-dollar revenues come from three types of business, as described below:

- *Megaprojects.* Typically, a megaproject involves complex solutions that include systems, software, and integration. The average "deal" size exceeds $15 million. The sales process for a megaproject typically extends over several years and involves the coordination of many resources, including external players, such as lobbyists to handle FCC requirements and consultants to prepare specifications.
- *Large projects.* As with the megaprojects, a sale includes systems, software, and integration services. The sales process is also long (extending over several years) and involves many resources, both internal and external. However, average revenue per project for large projects is considerably smaller than that for megaprojects. The typical revenue is between $1 and $10 million.
- *"Baseline" projects.* Historically, this has been RSNA's largest revenue component and accounts for one-half of total sales. This business consists of small projects and radio sales. The sales process for baseline projects is considerably faster and less complex than that for large projects or megaprojects, with the focus being on the number of transactions rather than the size of individual transactions. Unlike large projects or megaprojects, the baseline side of the business has a run-rate aspect to it; that is, replacement orders as units wear out are a key driver of revenue.

Management expects double-digit growth from RSNA. The outlook for growth in large project and megaproject sales will meet management's expectations; however, the "bread and butter" baseline business has been growing at half the expected rate, and there is no reason to believe that this situation will change in the near future. RSNA management has concluded that sales success must come from an increase in the number of deals closed in the large projects and megaprojects arena, where the available growth opportunities are greater. While megaprojects are attractive because of the amount of revenue available from one deal, management knows that it cannot count on any more than one or two megaprojects per year. This is because the available market for such business, in terms of number of customers, is relatively small. To achieve its aggressive growth plan, RSNA management determined that it would have to redirect its organization's resources to increase the number of large projects sold. Ultimately, RSNA's ability to make that change will, in large measure, determine its future success.

DEFINING LARGE PROJECTS

As important as large projects have been to RSNA's business success, it has been somewhat difficult to clearly differentiate between large projects and megaprojects. However, the company is clearly able to differentiate the large deal or large project from the baseline deals that have contributed the greatest proportion of revenue in the past. A primary differentiator is the length of the sales cycle. This ability to differentiate has enabled RSNA to develop a process for providing the right resource at the right time to the account to close the business.

DEPLOYING RSNA'S SALES RESOURCES

RSNA divides its sales force into two groups:

- *Short-cycle sales team.* Account managers assigned to this sales team are responsible for geographic territories of 50 to 100 accounts. Short-cycle account managers take care of the day-to-day management of their assigned accounts, ensuring that baseline sales opportunities are well covered. About 90 percent of the RSNA sales force is assigned to the short cycle sales team at any given time.
- *Long-cycle sales team.* When a lead for a large project (or a megaproject) is uncovered within a short-cycle account manager's account assignment, this sales opportunity/account is immediately reassigned to the long-cycle team. At the same time, the short-cycle account manager who has historically covered the account moves into a long-cycle account manager role for the duration of the sales process. The long-cycle account manager is responsible only for this large project sales opportunity and is no longer responsible for calling on his other short cycle accounts. (They are reassigned to other short-cycle account managers.)

This dynamic approach to the deployment of account managers is a benefit to a customer who engages RSNA in a large project because it maintains the continuity of the relationship between the account manager and the buyer. However, this unique approach to deployment represents a challenge for RSNA management because shifting account assignments from short-cycle opportunities to long-cycle projects could cause the lower end of the market, which is the source of leads for large projects, to be insufficiently covered.

The shift in responsibilities from the short-cycle to the long-cycle role not only alters an employee's responsibilities, but also has consequences for how the individual is compensated. Thus, RSNA management became quite interested in designing an approach to incentive compensation that was appropriate for the long-cycle sales environment.

ILLUSTRATION OF CHANGING SALES ROLES

The best way to illustrate the challenge management faced as a result of shifting sales resources from one team to another is to provide an example. Sue Smith, a hypothetical employee, is a short-cycle account manager. Sue is assigned a geographic territory made up of fifty state and local municipalities (e.g., fire and police departments, etc.) in the southeast region of the United States. During the normal course of interacting with her customer contacts at one of her city government accounts, Sue learns that a consulting firm has been hired to draw up specifications for a new communication system. The new communication system is to be a trade-out for an existing system. This particular type of transaction will have political implications for the city, and therefore a lobbyist will be needed to manage the budget approval process. If the budget were approved, the project would involve a large engineering initiative. Sue estimates that this project offers a revenue opportunity for RSNA in the area of $6 million.

Sue contacts her manager to inform him of the situation. With the approval of her manager and the long-cycle sales management team, Sue is transferred to the long-cycle team with sole responsibility for the city project under consideration. Over the next twenty-two months, Sue manages the sales process, including customer needs assessment, FCC spectrum plan blueprint development, FCC filing, response to specification (including matrix pricing), proposal creation, price negotiations, contract management, resolution of legal issues, and system design.

When Sue made the transition from the short-cycle to the long-cycle team, she gave up her short-cycle accounts and, therefore, the ongoing revenue stream credited to her sales goal as the basis for her incentive compensation plan. The question management faced upon Sue's reassignment was, "How should Sue be rewarded for her performance in this new role so that her assignment to the long-cycle team will be viewed as financially worthwhile?"

THE COMPENSATION PLAN FOR THE SHORT-CYCLE TEAM

As a short-cycle account manager, Sue was assigned a sales goal at the beginning of the year. Her sales goal was based on the historical performance of her assigned accounts and an estimate of available market opportunity. At the end of each quarter, Sue's year-to-date performance relative to her year-to-date goal was calculated, and, based on a scale starting at 75 percent achievement of goal, Sue's incentive was calculated and paid. At 100 percent of goal, Sue could earn her target incentive pay, equal to 30 percent of her base salary. She also had the opportunity to earn several times that amount for significant overachievement of goal.

THE NEED FOR A NEW PLAN FOR THE LONG-CYCLE TEAM

At the time Sue was reassigned to the long-cycle team, her sales manager reflected on several questions related to how Sue should be paid: "Could the current incentive plan work for Sue in her new role as part of the long-cycle team? Given the unpredictability of the business, how would her goal be set? Since the revenue from her sales efforts is unlikely to be realized within the current sales year, how would her performance be measured?"

It was clear to management that Sue (and other long-cycle account managers in her same situation) needed a unique incentive compensation plan. That plan would have to be suitable to the sales process and sales challenges associated with large projects. A plan design committee was formed to discuss the objectives and requirements of such an incentive framework. It was agreed that the long-cycle incentive plan must:

- Offer some incentive cash flow on a quarterly basis.
- Reward specific behaviors associated with sales process management (customized to the unique nature of each large project).
- Provide a major reward for the "release" of a large project (when the contract is signed and the order is placed).
- Support a sense of teamwork throughout the entire division— including short-cycle and long-cycle teams (to minimize competition for opportunities/resources between the two teams).

The following potential issues were also identified:

- The inability to set a goal for the first year of the project, since the size of the deal is extremely volatile during this stage and the likelihood of any recording of a release is minimal.

- The unfairness of setting a goal for the second or third year of the project. At this time, the revenue potential is very certain, and setting a goal at the projected level almost guarantees the account manager 100 percent achievement of goal and an inability to greatly overachieve the goal (and earn top incentive dollars).

CONCLUSION

A plan was created to meet the criteria of the committee as follows:

- *Base salary.* Given the dynamic nature of short-cycle and long-cycle account managers, it was agreed that no change was appropriate, and the base salary range would remain the same as that for short-cycle team members.
- *Base salary/ incentive mix at target.* Given the dynamic nature of short- and long-cycle account managers, a consistent mix is required to avoid disruption associated with mix adjustments. Therefore, the target incentive opportunity would remain 30 percent of base salary (the same as that for short-cycle team members).
- *Incentive components.* The incentive plan should reflect the role that account managers are asked to play and include the following components:
  —Sales process management milestones: 80 percent, paid quarterly based on achievement of milestones.
  —RSNA team bonus (based on shipments): 20 percent, paid quarterly based on achievement of goal.
  —Releases: Not weighted in the plan, as releases are not expected until the end of a several-year sales process. A commission mechanic is used for releases, given the inability to set goals for large projects.

The milestones and team bonuses provide the ability to earn the target incentive on a quarterly basis, providing incentive cash flow. The upside in the plan is reserved for when the release is secured, paying a commission on the order to provide adequate above-target incentive across multiple years.

OUTCOMES

The plan as designed and built has several benefits, primarily related to attracting and retaining talented people in both the short-cycle and long-cycle sales roles. Since the program addresses the flexibility of deployment and pays for the results the company needs from large projects, it is consistent with both business needs and the requirements of the long-cycle account manager. Since there is no negative impact on earnings potential, and the possibility of moving to other interesting and challenging assignments exists, the short-cycle account manager sees benefits as well.

FIVE KEY LESSONS FOR SUCCESSFULLY SELLING LARGE DEALS

The Honeywell and RSNA cases illustrate the different approaches these two companies took to compensating the new sales roles involved in their large deal sales. As with many companies, there were unique aspects of each business that contributed to the conclusions Honeywell's and RSNA's top managers reached about the actions that were required if the company was to be successful with large deal sales. However, we believe that five lessons can be learned from these two cases and that those lessons could be applied to your business. The five lessons are:

1. Successfully selling large deals is the result of a change in sales strategy. At the heart of this change is a belief that a company's growth can be significantly improved by increasing the average size of sales deals. In both these cases, as well as in other companies we have studied, top managers believed that the opportunity to grow the business at a faster rate was tied to selling a value proposition that would motivate the customer to make long-term, financially sizable commitments, resulting in a "large sale." Thus, before it is possible to actually sell large deals, top managers need to have a clear idea about the needs of their customers and how the deal the company has to offer will materially and significantly benefit those customers.

2. To win large sales, top managers must be willing to allocate the resources required to develop and close the business. In both the cases described above, as well as in other situations we have observed, the key to winning substantially larger sales (assuming that the right prospects are qualified and selected) is focusing on and dedicating the right resources to the sales opportunity. Once top managers make a commitment to a sales strategy that involves large deal selling, the very next step in implementing that strategy is to identify and describe the new or changed sales roles. Using the process and tools described in Chapter 3 is a helpful place to begin that process.

3. The ability to leverage and scale revenue growth through large deal sales is materially improved by a company's readiness to formalize the sales process and reassign its customer contact employees to the new roles in that process. We have observed that almost all companies, like Honeywell and RSNA, launch into large deal selling by experimenting with this sales approach to prove is wide-scale viability. In the process of engaging in this initial experiment, some companies miss the opportunity to plan for the leverage and scalability of that sales approach. Enron, for example, assumed that it would be successful in selling large deals. Thus, right from the very beginning, its top managers committed to building a formal sales process. Having that process in place from the beginning gave Enron the opportunity to leverage the "learnings" from one deal to the next. The sales process and well-defined roles within the process also enabled Enron to quickly scale the business—that is, add more resources—to take advantage of growing sales demand for its offering in the marketplace.

4. Aligning compensation with new roles, new jobs, or both created to support large deal sales significantly increases the probability that a company will achieve its growth expectations. The fundamental premise of this book is that new roles must be reinforced by the compensation plan; therefore, this lesson in itself is not surprising. However, an important "learning" from these two cases, as well as from the experiences of other companies that we have seen, is that top managers must be prepared to lay out the new compensation plan as close to the beginning of the change as possible. To the greatest extent possible, top managers must be willing to indicate the time horizon that the plan will cover. For example, one of the things Honeywell learned was that keeping team members focused on closing the business and retaining them in the division at a time when some of them were being heavily recruited was a direct result of putting in place a long-term compensation plan.

5. For the rest of the sales organization and other customer contact employees who are not involved in large deal selling, it is important to clearly communicate how their compensation plan operates and what opportunities they may have to be considered for new roles or positions in large deal selling. Although this is not explicit in the cases, Honeywell, for example, suggested to us that this was indeed an important lesson for companies to learn. When a new initiative focusing on large deal selling is announced, one of the challenges a company faces is to how to prevent others from developing the feeling that they have become "second-class citizens" because they are not associated with that initia-

tive. Our observation is that RSNA's approach of transferring the account manager to a large deal selling unit along with the customer opportunity is one way to address that challenge. However, not all companies can take that approach. Thus, opportunities for continued recognition in the sales work they are doing for those working outside of the large deal sales arena require careful attention and communication.

To supplement these five lessons, we have prepared a checklist of the key principles that we believe are associated with best practices in compensating for large sales. Those principles are summarized as follows:

Program Must Be Consistent:

- ☑ With legal and regulatory requirements.
- ☑ With the business and financial requirements of the company.
- ☑ With the administrative capabilities of the company.
- ☑ With both internal equity needs, and esternal requirements to attract, retain, and motivate talented employees.
- ☑ With the company's philosophy of pay.

Sales Roles and Measures of Success Must Be Clearly Defined:

- ☑ Compensation program details (eligibility, levels, approaches) are based on clearly defined jobs, and their role within the buying and selling process.
- ☑ Measures of success are based on each role.
- ☑ Performance measures are consistent with the company's overall objectives.
- ☑ Performance measures are consistent with the eligible employee's ability to influence results.

Communication Must Be Clear and Complete:

- ☑ Business objectives for enterprise solutions, and for new company offerings are defined and communicated.
- ☑ Compensation programs are aligned with and communicate a company's strategy and direct individuals to execute their role in achieving that strategy.

SUMMING UP

Today, more and more companies are interested in increasing the average size of a sale made to a customer. One approach to accomplishing that goal is through selling large deals. For a sales strategy that involves selling large deals to succeed, both the customer and the company must be able to extract more value from that deal than would be possible through a series of separate sales transactions. To accomplish that goal, a company must rethink its value proposition, its sales process, and the level of resources required to be successful in the large deal sales environment.

Large deal selling is fundamentally different from the other types of selling a company is doing. The organization level at which the buying/ selling takes place, the participants involved and therefore the process used, and the expectations about value and results make large deal selling difficult to implement without a clear plan of action. That plan of action must include the definition of new roles and the implementation of a compensation plan for those roles.

10

COMPENSATING SALES MANAGERS AND TEAM LEADERS

For the purposes of this book, we define sales managers and team leaders as the individuals assigned the responsibility for supervising front-line resources—the sales staff and other customer contact resources. In Chapter 5 we suggested that one way to think about new sales roles is to consider what responsibilities the company adds to or subtracts from a current job. Applying this same thinking to a sales manager job, we find few situations where a firm subtracts responsibilities from the job. In fact, more often than not, the scope and complexity of sales manager jobs are increasing dramatically.

This is happening for at least two reasons. First, the focus of the sales manager's work is much more strategic today than it was in the past. Not that long ago, the primary requirement for success as a sales manager was to recruit and hire talented salespeople and then teach them first-rate selling skills. Today companies expect their sales managers to be "sales strategists" in addition to effectively managing salespeople. This means knowing how to identify new sales opportunities and how to redirect sales resources to win new customers while simultaneously managing today's business effectively. The ability to plan, organize, manage, and control the sales effort, something that companies always expected sales managers to do, has taken on an expanded meaning in many businesses.

Second, in many sales situations today the manager's job has changed from directing only salespeople to managing a variety of resources—sales support staff, "business partners," and technical service representatives, to name a few—to satisfy the complete, end-to-end requirements of a successful business relationship with customers. The growing use of customer teams, with their own team leaders (sometimes called customer directors or customer relationship managers), creates a new management complication for companies, one that was unusual as recently as the early 1990s.

Change in the sales manager's role and the addition of sales or customer team leaders can largely be explained by the shift in the way companies now do business with customers. Three forces are reshaping the way companies expect sales managers and team leaders to perform today and why you therefore need new compensation approaches to support those new requirements. This chapter explains how the jobs are changing and illustrates the compensation techniques that successful companies use to pay employees in these jobs. Also, because the sales manager and team leader jobs are themselves quite different, we describe their jobs and the compensation approaches in separate sections.

THREE GROUPS AFFECTING THE SALES MANAGER'S ROLE

Today the expectations of individuals in sales manager jobs are different from what they were in the past. Three groups of people are the cause of these new expectations of sales managers: top management, customers, and the resources the sales managers supervise.

TOP MANAGEMENT'S EXPECTATIONS

Today, almost everyone thinks about business growth. Everyone from government leaders to shareholders, from senior executives to frontline employees is concerned about how companies are going to grow top-line revenue. Downsizing, cost cutting, failed mergers or acquisitions, and industry deregulation are examples of factors that contributed to the uncertainty about future business growth in the early 1990s. Given this uncertainty, top executives in most industries have concluded that they have to teach their people how to grow the business again. Our research shows that the number one concern of top executives in companies coming out of a no-growth/slow growth business phase is how to build the confidence of their people so that they will make the decisions necessary to grow the business.

CEOs have told us that to achieve and sustain profitable business growth, it is essential to operate with a top-performing sales organization. One way CEOs measure the sales organization's success is to ask the following questions:

- Do we sell new product successfully?
- Do we sell to new customers?
- Do we increase our share of business with current customers?
- Do we outsell our competitors with value-added services as well as price?

To address these questions effectively, companies often find that they must retrain their sales managers. We find that the skill most lacking in frontline sales managers is the ability to accurately analyze sales potential at the market level. To overcome this deficiency, we suggest to companies that they equip their frontline managers with the training and tools they need to gauge sales opportunities in their markets.

One company that has done a particularly good job at this is Sea-Land Service, Inc., an ocean cargo carrier based in Charlotte, North Carolina. Sea-Land's innovative approach to identifying and targeting customers clearly sets it apart from its competitors. Sea-Land has taught its managers how to target customers that offer the greatest opportunity for revenue growth by using a customized "customer segmentation" process. The concept and processes that Sea-Land uses are generally available to all companies. What distinguishes Sea-Land from other companies is the passion with which its managers execute the customer segmentation process uniformly throughout the world.

The customer segmentation process that Sea-Land taught its managers involved three steps:[1]

1. *Narrow customer focus.* In 1994, Sea-Land had 164,000 customers, the vast majority of which were small, occasional shippers. The company's sales force called on them all and operated as if each customer were equally important to business growth. Sea-Land had no way to know whether its people were investing the right amount of sales time with the right customers, so management decided that its managers had to use a uniform system to determine which customers offered significant revenue growth opportunities.

2. *Identify valuable customers.* The company adopted a customer segmentation model that showed its managers how to categorize customers in terms of five variables: (1) the amount of revenue from the customer; (2) the average and total profit realized from the customer; (3) the potential for growth, both revenue and container loads; (4) the

amount of business the customer is willing to award to one carrier; and (5) the predictability, consistency, or both of the customer's shipping needs.

3. *Match sales and customer service resources to customer segments.* Based on the five segmentation variables, Sea-Land's managers around the world can determine the most appropriate sales and service resources to use to work with buyers in each customer segment. Sea-Land now uses a variety of different sales channels to access customers, maintain account relationships, and service customer needs. Matching the right level of resource to the needs of the customer, with account profitability and quality service in mind, benefits both Sea-Land and its customers.

To judge the progress a company is making toward adapting to the requirement for enduring, profitable top-line growth, we prepared a short self-test, shown in Figure 10-1, that we encourage top managers to fill out. You may find it helpful to distribute the form to all executives and sales managers in your company. The test's objective is to take a reading on the likelihood that your current sales leaders and managers, particularly your frontline sales managers, have a predisposition to move the sales organization in the direction required for future growth. Companies that are successful in inspiring confidence in their sales managers to grow the business profitably have easily met the challenges of the "from/to" characteristics Figure 10-2 describes.

CUSTOMER EXPECTATIONS

Another factor reshaping the sales manager's role is customer expectations—particularly the leadership these managers show in the business relationship. Leadership is a key ingredient in business success. It is particularly important in companies that achieve continuous, profitable top-line growth. This is because customer expectations, technology, and competition in most industries are changing rapidly, and therefore precious little time can be lost in doing business with customers at the point of sale. Thus, we observe that field sales managers in companies that outperform the market, their competitors, or both do three things well:

- They look to their customers to understand what is required to gain and sustain a competitive advantage.
- They actively participate in the processes through which their company sells and provides service to the customer.
- They match the right type and level of resources to the customer's

Fig. 10-1.   Managers' commitment to top-line growth: your company's experience.

FROM								TO
1. Internal focus	1	2	3	4	5	6	7	Customer focus
2. Managing what is in place	1	2	3	4	5	6	7	What it will take to be the best
3. Focus on functions	1	2	3	4	5	6	7	Continuous design of best processes
4. Accept current performance	1	2	3	4	5	6	7	Create and implement new vision
5. Do the same thing everywhere	1	2	3	4	5	6	7	Design and implement new organizations
6. Fear change	1	2	3	4	5	6	7	Lead change

SCORE

39 – 42   You are designing and implementing innovative processes and programs that are consistent with customer-focused, high-performance sales organizations. If these processes and programs are consistent with your company's business strategy, you should have a competitive advantage with your customers.

32 – 38   You are designing and implementing processes and programs consistent with a customer-focused, high-performance sales organization. However, you will need to sustain the momentum you have established to effectively compete in your target markets.

25 – 31   You may have processes and programs in the development stage. However, significant change is required to implement and achieve a customer-focused, high-performance sales organization.

24 or less   You have not yet begun to consider the implication of serving a more sophisticated and diverse set of customers. In today's marketplace, this means that your company may be at a significant disadvantage with your customers, and therefore you are not positioned to grow.

requirements and thereby enable their company to work productively with its customers.

Being truly customer-focused is easier to talk about than to implement. To grow profitably, a company must decide which customers are the right customers to invest in. It is those customers—and accounts that operate like those customers in terms of their growth projections, buying process, and sales and service requirements—that offer the best

Fig. 10-2. Characteristics of top-line growth culture.

From	To
• Internal focus	• Customer focus, i.e., spending time with strategically important accounts
• Managing what's in place	• Challenging existing processes, practices, programs, i.e., what will it take to be the best?
• Focusing on functions	• Designing and managing the "best" processes, e.g., sales processes related to current customers; new account acquisition processes related to attracting new customers
• Accepting current productivity and cost performance	• Creating a vision around how to increase sales productivity and improve return on sales investments, e.g., clever ways to segment customers; alternative distribution strategies and tactics
• Doing the same thing everywhere	• Encouraging the design and implementation of new forms of customer contact organizations, e.g., customer teams; managing market opportunity in terms of segments, i.e., the intersect of customers, products, and channels
• Fearing change	• Leading change, i.e., introducing new technologies, products, coverage strategies ahead of the competition

sales growth opportunities. Most companies, however, treat all customers as equals, which means that some resources are wasted on the wrong customers, customers who actually reduce the opportunity for profitable business growth. Sales managers, particularly first-level managers, are in a unique position to see how customers actually operate and, as a consequence, to judge whom to invest in and whom not to. This requires sales managers to acquire and master the skills of sales strategists and business planners. To do so, they must learn how to:

- Use the results of customer segmentation analysis to determine the type and number of accounts to target for direct selling and the accounts the company could effectively serve by other sales resources (telesales, business partners, catalog/fax service).
- Determine the number of geographic units and the number and caliber of salespeople for districts, areas, or some other aggregation to sell to and interact with customers at a defined selling-expense level.
- Assign customer and prospective accounts to the sales staff for sales coverage to achieve the sales plan.

Generally speaking, it is this type of work that, when done well, enables sales managers to achieve the expected business results in the market assigned to them and to be recognized by top management as sales strategists.

SALES PERSONNEL EXPECTATIONS OF SALES MANAGERS

During the past thirty years, the American sales force has hardly aged at all. The average age of today's sales representative, according to Dartnell's study, is thirty-five years. This is not materially different from the average age of 1969's sales representative. What is materially different is what salespeople expect of their immediate supervisor, their sales manager or team leader. The sales manager's role has always been to add value to the sales process, the customer relationship management process, or both. Today, however, salespeople demand much more of their managers than their older brothers and sisters demanded. This is particularly true for entry-level employees who are well versed in the use of computers and in various analytical applications made possible by the power of PCs, and who have been schooled in the principles of partnering with customers. In previous decades, sales representatives understood that their immediate supervisor recruited, hired, trained, assigned accounts or territories, and coached or assisted in closing big sales. Today's salespeople expect much more from their sales managers and often ask them how to locate more prospects and how to determine the market's sales potential. This is another reason that the advanced skills we described earlier are essential to a manager's success.

THREE PIVOTAL SALES MANAGER ROLES

Today's sales manager job is changing to meet top managers', customers', and salespeople's expectations. We have noticed that, in response to these new or changing expectations, sales managers take on one of three different roles. The exact one depends on the growth phase and business objectives of the company at a particular point in time. While the sales manager's duties, tasks, and responsibilities are similar across the three roles, we have observed that the emphasis placed on these elements is quite different. Those differences in how managers play the role have significant implications for the way the company compensates them.

Conventional wisdom suggests that sales managers are paid based on the performance of the salespeople they supervise. There was a period of time when "override"—a percentage of commission or bonus earned by salespeople—was the most popular sales manager pay plan. That is no longer the case. An override pay plan for sales managers is, at best, appropriate when individuals in the job are expected to act as "seller/managers," in which they have assigned accounts, play the lead role in selling with a sales representative, or both. (This job is described in greater detail later in this chapter.) While estimates are often dangerous, our experience suggests that fewer than 25 percent of today's sales manager jobs actually operate as seller/managers. Yet, in eight of every ten sales manager compensation plans we examine, the number one type of incentive formula used to pay frontline managers is an override. Clearly, there is a gap between the role and the pay practices companies use to reward sales managers.

The three managerial roles that have emerged to meet the changing expectations of top managers, customers, and sales employees are:

Coaching sales manager. Sales managers in this role focus on modeling sales behavior for salespeople. The manager builds representatives' sales skills by spending time with them making calls, analyzing what took place during the call, and pointing out opportunities for improvement in future calls. The coaching sales manager's top priority is to develop the people in the sales jobs reporting to her because:

1. Most of the sales representatives are relatively new to their jobs, new to the company, or both because the company is experiencing rapid growth, and introducing these employees to the company's sales culture is a top priority.
2. The selling process is varied and complex, and so the sales manager serves as the sales rep's "consultant," helping him or her navigate the selling course to reach a successful result for the company and its customers.
3. On-the-job training has an immediate favorable impact on sales results—a position we have researched and, later in this chapter, will support with data.

Superseller sales manager. Managers who perform in this role do so to help with difficult or big accounts that their sales reps are working with. Also, a superseller sales manager is most likely to have sales responsibility for a limited number of accounts that he or she calls on directly and that are not assigned to a sales representative. The superseller sales manager's top priority is to optimize the opportunity to grow sales volume, typically in an environment where many sales transactions take place in a short period of time. Door-to-door selling, securities selling, and insurance sales are a few examples that come to mind. This is the priority because:

1. More volume equals (potentially) more profit.
2. Market share is small and the opportunity exists to grow at a high rate.
3. All sales are "good"; undifferentiated volume is acceptable because the gross margin is roughly the same regardless of the size or mix of business that makes up the sales transaction.

Strategist/business planner sales manager. Sales managers who perform as strategist/business planners do so by bringing a market-oriented focus to the business processes of sales and customer relationship management. They develop strategies and techniques to identify opportunities for sales growth and then redirect resources to call on and service customers in these opportunity segments. The strategist/business planner sales manager's top priority is to maximize market opportunities by producing profitable sales because:

1. Profit flexibility exists; prices can be negotiated and business mix, either by customers, products, or both, will materially influence gross margin contribution.
2. Field sales costs are high; the total value of products and related services is at competitive parity; profit contribution is a critical measure of business success and, therefore, must reflect customer situations where buyers value and pay for sales solutions and relationships.

HOW SALES MANAGERS SPEND THEIR TIME

Regardless of the role in which they find themselves operating, our research shows that sales managers are working harder—certainly more hours—than they ever worked in past years. Since the late 1980s, we have tracked how sales managers spend their time during the day and on weekends using a structured questionnaire. The questionnaire has four major categories: (1) management time; (2) time spent with sales representatives; (3) selling time—time spent with customers; and (4) other, including travel, "downtime," and miscellaneous time. In the late 1980s, we found that a typical sales manager worked approximately fifty to fifty-five hours a week. Our 1998 surveys find that the typical sales manager works an average of sixty-two hours per week. The increase in the typical workweek is largely explained by the expanded scope of the job: new requirements, fewer managers due to downsizing (with the result that these managers have more salespeople to supervise), or both. See Table 10-1 for a comparison of the typical 1998 sales manager's day (which averages approximately twelve hours) and that of her 1980s counterpart.

Our most recent studies indicate that 99 percent of sales managers spend some time working on weekends, on average about three hours.

How sales managers use their time varies by the role they play in managing sales resources. Table 10-2 shows how time allocations vary across the sales manager roles described above. The most interesting finding, although not surprising, is the differences in time these managers allocate to the category "time spent with sales representatives." Generally speaking, coaching sales managers and superseller sales managers spend about twice as much time with their sales representatives as do strategist/business planner sales managers.

Table 10-1. How sales managers spend their time: 1980s vs. 1998.

Time Category	1980s (hours)	1998 (hours)	Percent Change
Time spent on management activities	5.3	6.0	13.2
Time with sales representatives	1.8	2.1	16.6
Sales time	0.4	0.5	25.0
Other time	3.0	3.2	6.7
Total	10.5	11.8	12.4

Table 10-2. Percent time allocation by sales manager's role.

Time Category	Sales Manager's Role		
	Coaching	Superseller	Strategist/Business Planner
Time spent on management activities	43	32	51
Time spent with sales representatives	32	40	18
Sales time (person)	7	17	4
Other time	18	11	27
Total	100	100	100

We mentioned earlier in this chapter that sales managers who work with sales representatives get better results than managers who do not work with their reps on a concentrated and consistent basis. The most interesting finding in our research about how sales managers spend their time is this fact: Spending more time with sales representatives translates into high performance for the sales manager's business unit, whether it be a district, branch, or sales division. Figure 10-3 provides an example from one of many studies we have done. Essentially, the results show that when a manager spends more time with sales representatives doing quality things such as coaching, role-playing, or training, sales representatives are likely to achieve a higher percent of their sales quota.

In the study illustrated by Figure 10-3, we found that sales managers who spent on average fourteen hours or more a week with their sales representatives had representatives who achieved on average 122 percent of quota. In the same study, sales managers who spent nine hours a week or less with their sales representatives had reps who achieved only 89 percent of quota on average. Our research supports the view that if a sales manager has to choose between spending time on "management activities" or "with sales representatives," the latter offers a much greater return to the business on the time invested in the short run.

As companies implement new sales roles, they frequently find that

Fig. 10-3. Relationship between sales manager's time and sales representative quota attainment.

the sales management model they have been using is out of sync with their new expectations. To ensure that the management role is aligned with its new sales roles, companies generally tweak or adjust the traditional sales management job. Because obsolete expectations for the management role often result in personnel "working around the system" and do not show the results required for new sales roles to prove their effectiveness, however, it is useful to take a more formal approach to determining the role that fits top management's new expectations.

You can use a simple sliding scale diagnostic to benchmark role requirements and to provide information about the need for role redefinition for frontline management. Figure 10-4 is a simple tool that lists factors to be considered in this type of change. As the figure indicates, the criteria (company growth phase, market, products or services, resources, etc.) are scaled from left to right. Scores further to the right generally indicate the need for a seller/manager, while scores to the left generally indicate requirements for a more complex strategist/business

Fig. 10-4. Tool for sales management role determination.

	Complex Management	(Check)				**Selling Focused**
Company Stage	Phase 4: "Only some business is good business"	❏ ❏	❏	❏	❏	Phase 1: "All business is good business"
	Profitable volume is critical	❏ ❏	❏	❏	❏	Volume is critical
	Many complex markets	❏ ❏	❏	❏	❏	One market
	Business planning is critical	❏ ❏	❏	❏	❏	Selling skills are critical
Resources	Many types	❏ ❏	❏	❏	❏	Sales generalist
	Strategic partnerships/many channels	❏ ❏	❏	❏	❏	One channel
	Team members	❏ ❏	❏	❏	❏	"Agents"
	Decentralized support available	❏ ❏	❏	❏	❏	Centralized support for resources only
Customers/ Buying Process	Business partnership/ outsourcing	❏ ❏	❏	❏	❏	Transactional
	Long, complex buying and selling processes	❏ ❏	❏	❏	❏	Short process
Overall Result	"Strategist/Business Planner"					"Selling" Manager

planner type of manager. This tool is most helpful in a more traditional sales and sales management structure, that is, frontline management of customer coverage resources. We discuss implications for sales and customer team leaders later in this chapter.

How to Match Sales Manager Jobs with the Right Compensation Plans

Sales manager jobs are situational. The type of selling resource (field-based sales representatives, dealers, telesales representatives) and top management's expectations of sales managers in the sales process largely determine how a company defines and, in turn, staffs a sales manager's job. To attract and retain qualified individuals for the sales manager's job, the compensation plan must be consistent with the job's role. We visit many companies where the sales manager's role is changing or has changed while the compensation plan has remained the same.

To illustrate the need for different sales manager compensation plans, it is helpful to use the three sales manager roles we presented earlier in this chapter. We find that these three cover approximately 90 percent of all of today's sales manager jobs. With that in mind, illustrative compensation plans for each of the sales manager roles follow.

Coaching Sales Manager Compensation Plan

Our experience shows that this type of sales manager job is the most prevalent of the three jobs. It is also the job most likely to change as the roles of the employees being supervised change. And, when these managers do experience a change in role, it is typically because top management has new expectations of them, because they are now supervising employees in new sales roles—either completely new sales jobs or sales jobs that have added responsibilities.

In the past, companies took many, diverse approaches to compensating the coaching sales manager. Many coaching sales managers were very successful salespeople (and indeed were recruited on the assumption that very successful salespeople were best equipped to coach and counsel new sales personnel). Therefore, the compensation plans were remarkably similar to the plans for salespeople. Companies in some industries, however, considered the job more closely aligned with corporate management positions, and their compensation programs resembled senior management bonus plans.

But just as changed expectations for salespeople in new sales roles resulted in new approaches to compensating them, the incentive plans for coaching managers also must change. More sophisticated selling and complex customer requirements have increased expectations for sales managers. New skills and the ability to coach through complex processes have expanded the job. Moreover, many companies have increased the job's scope (the number of salespeople managed), while still expecting managers to develop their salespeople. This frequently means that the coaching sales manager must work with senior salespeople and with support staff to ensure that appropriate training, development, and skill enhancement are provided.

One company that implemented new sales roles quickly identified new expectations for the frontline sales manager job. In the past, the district manager had been responsible primarily for "getting rookies up to speed" and coaching salespeople on an ongoing basis, particularly with strategically important or potentially difficult customers. The company's sales role, however, changed from a field sales representative (full-line, general rep) to an account manager working with executive-level contacts in large accounts. District managers had to increase their own skills so that they could provide the level of expertise and knowledge required to develop and coach their account managers. Customers also expected that the district manager would be sophisticated and able to work in senior-level relationships and with complex requirements. The company's portfolio included products suited for both consumer and commercial markets, and the district manager was responsible for reaching a quota (through his salespeople) for both lines. To be successful, district managers would have to work together to cross-train and to ensure the appropriate support levels for the account managers at all times.

In this company, the incentive compensation plan for the old district manager role was as follows:

Mix: A significant portion of pay was at risk, and there was a significant upside opportunity (leverage).

Performance range: The performance range was consistent with the range in the plan of the salespeople they managed; the threshold to excellence range for salespeople was an 80 percent threshold to a 120 percent excellence, and the same was true for their sales manager.

Incentive formula: The incentive formula was based on total volume at the district level.

Performance and payout periods: While the performance period was aligned with the company's financial periods, payouts were made monthly.

Because the firm had redefined the sales role, it could no longer determine success solely in terms of total district volume. In fact, the company recognized the direct and positive impact that the district manager could have on product mix and profitable business through coaching the account managers to identify and work with large, strategically important accounts. The new approach to compensation evolved into a program that is now fairly typical for this type of role. As Figure 10-5 illustrates, the job's success measures are:

• District commercial product quota achievement
• District consumer product quota achievement
• Region P&L

Here is a summary of the new program:

Mix: The proportion of at-risk pay was reduced and the base salary was raised to be consistent with the longer-term expectations and the job's higher skill level requirements.

Performance range: The district manager is expected to optimize the productivity of the account managers and work with them through complex selling situations. The district manager is responsible for

Fig. 10-5. Coaching sales manager incentive plan.

Plan Elements		District Consumer Products		District Commercial Products		Region P&L*
	Excellence	200% of consumer target bonus		200% of commercial target bonus		200% of P&L target bonus
	Target	100% of consumer target bonus	+	100% of commercial target bonus	+	100% of P&L target bonus
	Threshold	50% of consumer target bonus		50% of commercial target bonus		50% of P&L target bonus
Payout Frequency		Quarterly		Quarterly		Semiannually
Element Weights		40%		30%		30%

*Year-end region performance one full point above excellence pays an additional kicker to each manager in the region of 20% of their target.

achieving multiple business objectives. The district manager's perform-ance range is more closely related to 100 percent; that is, it is narrower than the range for account managers.

Incentive formula: Figure 10-5 illustrates a formula for this type of job. The plan designers established a flexible formula that included bo-nuses for three key business objectives: product mix and volume (com-mercial and consumer products), and profitability (P&L). The company can vary the weights for these measures annually.

Performance and payout periods: The district has annual plans (goals) for both product lines. The region as a whole works to a P&L. The performance period is annual. District managers are paid a portion of their incentive each quarter, based on year-to-date results. The com-pany has discontinued monthly progress payments, and district manag-ers are more focused on developing skills and coaching their salespeople for the long term.

SUPERSELLER SALES MANAGER COMPENSATION PLAN

This type of sales manager role is actually declining in sales organiza-tions because companies have found it difficult to recruit, hire, and re-tain individuals who can perform effectively in this role. The role is complicated because it combines two quite different skills—selling and managing—that the manager must perform at different cadences. None-theless, the role is likely to be around for a while because many com-panies are still recovering from downsizing initiatives, and some businesses are establishing a sales force where none existed before. Be-cause companies in both situations are likely to employ this sales role, it is helpful to illustrate how the job can best be paid.

In contrast to the coaching sales manager, compensation practices for the selling sales manager closely resemble the plan for sales repre-sentatives and are most likely to involve the use of an "override" incen-tive formula. The characteristics of a plan for this type of role in a new sales force include:

Mix: Mix is aggressive (60/40 or 50/50), and there is a significant upside opportunity.

Performance range: Measures are volume-focused, although there is generally a group measure of volume achievement (for example, district or zone).

Incentive formula: The incentive formula is frequently a commission override or some technique that parallels the compensation approach for the company's salespeople.

Performance and payout periods: Payout is generally frequent because of the aggressive mix and the implications for cash flow; a lower base means less fixed income to pay the bills.

For companies that are recovering from significant downsizing, this role may itself be new. At one company we visited, the frontline sales manager had traditionally been a coaching manager, but the dramatic changes that had resulted from a "right-sizing" effort mandated customer attention at a senior level. The company could not approve any additional head count, so the frontline sales manager was asked to assume responsibilities for calling on large customers at a headquarters level (in addition to managing the territory sales representatives). No other resource in the company was covering these senior accounts, although penetration was critical to reach the company's goals. Figure 10-6 illustrates how this "new" job was paid:

Mix: While the mix did not change, the leverage, or upside, was significant—more than two times the target incentive—and the plan was uncapped (no limit was placed on incentive earnings). The manager

Fig. 10-6. Selling manager incentive plan.

Plan Elements	District Sales Bonus				Penetration of Strategic Accounts Multiplier	
	Achievement	%	Award		%	Multiplier
	>Excellence	>120%	1% district target bonus/%			
	Excellence	120%	200% of district target bonus		120%	2.000
	Target	100%	100% of district target bonus	X	100%	1.667
					80%	1.000
	Threshold	80%	50% of district target bonus		<80%	0.667
	<Threshold	<80%	-0-			

Payout Frequency	Quarterly; annual reconciliation	
Weight	60%	40%

could earn an additional 1 percent of his or her target incentive for every percent of the district sales quota over 120 percent.

Performance and payout periods: Payout was quarterly, based on quota achievement for the district and penetration of the strategic accounts assigned to the manager.

Incentive formula: The incentive formula was a linked calculation. The primary element was district performance measured against quota, and the opportunity was unlimited (the plan is uncapped). However, the added measure for success was the second element, which was worth 40 percent of the manager's incentive at target. That element is penetration of strategic accounts (those accounts assigned to the manager); the company measures penetration on new or incremental sales, and the manager has a quota for these accounts.

As you can see, the plan is really a hybrid plan that seeks to motivate and support two dissimilar sets of expectations: managing people and selling successfully to large accounts. The measures and formula (linked) clearly support the selling sales manager role.

STRATEGIST/BUSINESS PLANNER SALES MANAGER COMPENSATION PLAN

In the newest of the three sales manager roles we have described, while the job of supervising salespeople may or may not have changed, top executive expectations of the sales manager have changed. They believe the company has missed opportunities to grow because the sales managers are not operating as business managers. In the highly centralized management structures and decision-making processes of the past, a central staff planned and disseminated sales strategy, deployment, and business planning to all managers. They, in turn, were generally expected to execute these plans rather than choose and customize them in response to their own market demands. As the market has changed, and as customer demands have become more sophisticated, many companies have come to realize that the frontline sales manager may be in the best position to bring a market focus to sales and customer relationship management.

Companies frequently measure these frontline business planner managers on bottom-line rather than top-line results to recognize the impact they are expected to have on profitability. Many of these managers' responsibilities may be long-term projects or programs as well; an element of their pay plan may be used to motivate and recognize superior planning and results orientation. Figure 10-7 shows an example of the pay plan for this type of manager.

Fig. 10-7.   Strategist/business planner incentive plan.

Plan Elements	District Contribution Bonus		Strategic Objectives Bonus	
	P&L vs. Budget			

% to Plan	Bonus Payout		Achieved	Payout
>110%	1% of district target bonus for each %			
110%	200% of district target bonus		**Achieved**	**Payout**
100%	**100% of district target bonus**	+	**Three**	**100% of target for str. obj.**
90%	50% of district target bonus		Two	40% of target for str. obj.
<90%	–0–		One	20% of target for str. obj.

Payout Frequency	Quarterly	Semiannually
Weight	75%	25%

Mix: The mix for this type of job is generally less aggressive than that for the selling sales manager, but it is significant enough to ensure the motivational value of the incentive portion. To recognize the job's significant scope and the skills required for effective execution, the base is generally higher than the base for other types of frontline sales managers.

Incentive formula: The incentive formula generally includes a profitability measurement to the level where it will be the most accurate. In Figure 10-7, this company assigned a P&L to the district level, and held managers accountable for that P&L. Note, however, that this district P&L did not include allocated headquarters' overhead costs and contained only those costs and results that the district manager could directly control and influence. The formula also includes a strategic objectives bonus that the company used to motivate and reward managers who achieved specific long-term projects. The categories for these objectives were well defined and uniform for all managers; and achievement was specified before the plan year started.

Clearly, this type of sales manager job is evolving based on market and organization needs. The pay that comes with doing this job well is generally significant, since success means that the company is realizing more profitable sales based on optimal deployment of resources against a realistic estimate of the local market's potential.

FOUR TOUGH ISSUES THAT COME WITH SALES MANAGER COMPENSATION PLANS

Regardless of the sales manager's role in your company, we believe you should be aware of the following four thorny plan design issues when you are changing the basis on which sales managers are paid.

PAY DIFFERENTIALS

While most companies have developed a base salary or total compensation program that provides increased earnings opportunities through career advancement, there is a broad range of practices related to pay differentials between the positions managed and the manager. For example, many companies' base salary programs have a 15 to 20 percent difference between the midpoints of successive salary ranges. An example of this might be:

Salary range A: $35,000 minimum / $50,000 midpoint / $65,000 maximum

Salary range B: $45,000 minimum / $60,000 midpoint / $75,000 maximum

The differential between midpoints is 20 percent. Nevertheless, a salesperson at the high end of salary range A, with a high incentive pay opportunity, could be paid more than a manager at the low end of salary range B. Companies strive to maintain an appropriate differential between the pay of managers and that of the people they supervise. However, that is sometimes not the case in practice because of the tenure of the people involved, whether it be a relatively new manager, a sales representative with long service, or the number one sales rep who simply outearns his manager because he had an outstanding year.

The goal is to ensure that *at target performance or plan* sales managers are recognized for the contributions they make to company success. In many cases, compensation programs provide a significant over-achievement opportunity to salespeople, and top management's motto is, "I hope all our salespeople make more than the VP of sales," since high pay for the salespeople should equal great results. At the same time, the sales management job should not be considered a demotion for a talented candidate, and total compensation (cash, benefits, perquisites) should be visibly more significant at target than the salesperson's pay at target. Indeed, we find that the pay differential for sales managers is frequently most evident in the base salary, benefits, and total compensation at target performance.

MIX AND LEVERAGE

Mix and leverage for sales managers cannot be easily categorized, since there are many variations in roles and responsibilities. Decisions about the appropriate mix for sales management jobs generally fall at one end or the other of a spectrum. Top executives may desire significant "frontline management skin in the game," and therefore develop a plan for sales managers with a high proportion of at-risk pay. However, most companies maintain either an equivalent portion of at-risk pay for sales managers and their salespeople, or somewhat less at-risk pay for managers, who are once removed from direct customer contact. A rule of thumb for the appropriate proportion of pay at risk for these jobs is generally that the more empowered the job is and the more the successful execution of the role influences the results being measured, the more pay can be at risk. If impact is diverse because many people or functions have a direct impact on results, generally less pay is at risk. The upside for these jobs is usually quite significant, since a good job well done will have a dramatic, positive effect on company performance.

PERFORMANCE MEASURES

As with new sales roles, selecting performance measures for sales manager roles varies by job. Measures should include the financial elements over which the manager has the greatest influence. Many companies also have used performance measures in the incentive plan to tie managers together. We described one example in the coaching sales manager program in which the company used regional-level measures to ensure that district managers worked together across geographic boundaries.

Some companies also use company or division-level performance as a "visible funding mechanism" that clearly shows that the company or division must do well for a payout to occur. Here's how this might work using the plan in Figure 10-7 for the strategist/business planner sales manager. To maximize earnings, a sales manager must do well relative to the district P&L and achieve all strategic objectives. A corporate multiplier could be used at year-end; if the company achieved its business plan, it would use the multiplier to adjust the manager's earnings upward. Of course, if a company uses this visible funding mechanism to relate how much the manager is paid to how well the company does, it sometimes also uses it to adjust the year-end pay downward if the company does not achieve its objectives.

TIMING

Almost without exception, incentive compensation payout for managers is based on the business's financial periods. While some companies may need to evolve from the biweekly or monthly draws that managers have received in the past, frontline management is generally responsible for reaching both long-term and shorter-term objectives. Accurate measurement of achievement is therefore generally no more frequent than quarterly or semiannually.

HOW TEAM LEADER AND SALES MANAGER JOBS DIFFER

At our seminars, executives sometimes say to us that a sales or customer team leader is really no different from a frontline sales manager—a district or branch sales manager. We do not find this to be the case. We find that the sales and customer team leader jobs are really quite different from the frontline sales manager job. Before we go further, therefore, we want to describe some trends and practices that lead us to this conclusion.

Our research shows that 80 to 90 percent of all companies with one hundred employees or more employ teams in their business. More specifically, among *Fortune* 500 companies, we find that 25 to 40 percent of the divisions that make up these large corporations employ teams to cover customers. The increased use of teams reflects an overall trend in how customers, particularly business customers, expect to do business with their suppliers. In many cases, the salesperson is no longer solely responsible for acquiring and keeping business. It is the other functions or departments in the company—logistics, transportation, supply chain management, credit services, customer service, telesales/call center—that customers come to rely on for doing business on a consistent and regular basis.

Figure 10-8 shows the different approaches a company can use to interact with customers. We see a migration taking place in businesses today from customer coverage models 1 and 2 to models 3 and 4. Referring back to our business growth model in Chapter 1 (Figure 1-1), we find that companies use models 1 and 2 almost exclusively in phases 1 and 2 of their growth. As they progress to phases 3 and 4 of the business growth model, they introduce new approaches to sales and customer management. They add models 3 and 4, and sometimes these become the predominant way in which the company interacts with customers. This is because companies in phases 3 and 4 of the business growth model are more likely to invest in the effort to segment and prioritize customers to optimize sales coverage.

Figure 10-9 is an illustration of how one company—ABC Industrial Controls (disguised name, real corporation)—chose to segment its customers and align its sales resources to interact with those customers. We use this company's practices to define the roles of two types of team

Fig. 10-8.   Alternative customer coverage models.

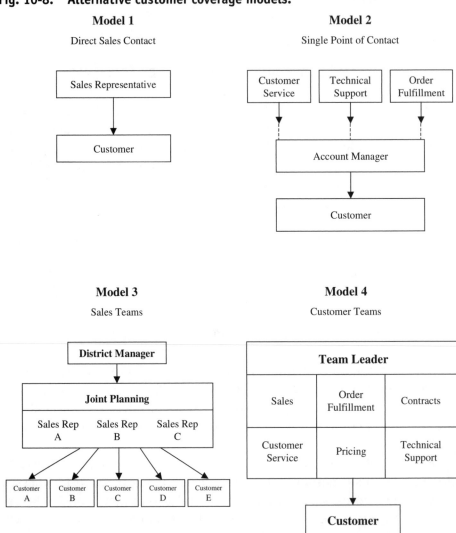

leaders—sales teams and customer teams—and to explain why and how these two types of roles come into existence at a company. Thus, if you are either using these teams or plan to do so, this can be a helpful reference.

SALES TEAM

The most typical definition of a sales team is a formal, permanent group of sales employees assigned responsibility for covering specific customer accounts. This team includes sellers representing different business units or product lines. Figure 10-9 shows that ABC Industrial

Fig. 10-9.   Illustrative customer segmentation and coverage resources.

Type of Account	Sales and Customer Coverage Approach
Strategic	Customer Team: • Willingness to partner • Large share of business • Extensive service needs
Major	Sales Team: • Significant volume • Specialized applications • Less service intensive
Core	Sales Reps: • Significant volume • Specialized applications • Less service intensive
Transactional	Telesales Rep: • Small revenue • Relatively small opportunity for growth

(Pyramid diagram, from top to bottom: Strategic Customers, Major Customers, Core Customers, Transactional Accounts)

Controls assigned sales teams to its major customers. It did so because there was an opportunity to sell multiple product lines to these customers and those opportunities required application-oriented sales specialists.

A sales team usually has a leader rather than a manager or operates as a self-directed team. ABC Industrial Controls appointed a sales team leader to provide business planning direction and support to the salespeople assigned to each team. In this company, the sales team leaders reported to the region managers, one level down from the top sales executive for the North American business group.

The leader, typically referred to as sales team leader, may also be titled team manager, and we have seen the job called "district manager" or "branch manager" even though that title is misleading. The team leader probably has a background in sales, although this does not mean that only individuals from sales populate the job. We know of companies that draw their sales team leaders from several business functions, including product marketing, market or industry management, technical/customer service, and, in one case, even divisional finance. ABC Industrial Controls selected about half of the sales team leaders from the sales manager ranks; it chose the other half from product marketing, customer service, and field operations (technical support and installation functions).

CUSTOMER TEAM

The most typical definition of a customer team is a formal, permanent group of multifunctional employees assigned the responsibility for covering a specific customer or set of customers. This team often includes sales, product marketing, customer service, sales support, and finance employees. A customer team typically has a formal leader, and companies apply a number of different titles to the job; the most prevalent are customer team leader, customer team manager, or customer director. Since top management often thinks of a customer team as a "minidivision," branch, or region of the company because of the sales and profit volume the customer represents, people in the team leader position often have quite diverse managerial backgrounds. It is not unusual to find individuals serving in customer team leader positions who have been general managers of the business or are being groomed for such a position in the future.

At ABC Industrial Controls, top management identified a relatively small number of its strategically important customers—accounts that represented substantial sales volume and profit—and approached those customers with the proposal to dedicate a multifunction team to them. Generally speaking, these accounts met the criteria listed in Figure 10-9 (willing to partner, represented a large share of the business, and had extensive service needs). Equally important, the majority of these customers—five of the six that ABC approached—were receptive to this type of coverage. The sixth customer's management felt the company could not meet the requirement to share information because of systems limitations and resolved to continue with its current field-based account executive coverage.

At ABC Industrial Controls, team leader jobs were new roles. While the company used teams in other parts of the business, such as manufacturing and product development, it had not used teams to interact with its customers. It is unusual that a company would implement both sales team and customer team leader roles at the same time because there is an element of incremental selling expense—particularly for customer teams—that comes with this change. ABC Industrial Controls learned at the time of implementation that it needed a new approach to compensating their team leaders. Using the sales manager's compensation plan or compensation plans used in other parts of the company to reward midlevel managers did not make sense because the team leader job had quite different responsibilities.

Two Incentive Plans for Compensating Team Leaders

As we described in Chapter 6, you can use the incentive plan design formula to support team initiatives. At the same time, appropriate compensation plans for the team leader positions may be dramatically different from the traditional salary/incentive compensation programs for other management and leadership positions. The same building blocks used to develop plans for new sales roles and new sales management roles may lead to quite different results when applied to team leader roles.

The first critical decision relative to compensation for these roles is whether there should be an element of at-risk pay for the job or if an add-on recognition bonus is more consistent with executive expectations of the team leader role. If the team leader is a "manager of managers," particularly across functional or political boundaries, many companies recognize skills and experience through a significant amount of base pay and benefits with no at-risk pay. Rather, a bonus for reaching team objectives may be available for the team leader and team members. If the manager plays an integral role in the customer relationship management process, some pay is generally at risk, although it's usually a smaller proportion of the total compensation than for nonteam front-line manager jobs.

Once you have decided whether any pay should be at risk, the next critical decision is performance measurement and level of measurement. If the sales team or customer team has been implemented to work with only one large account or market segment, measurement is generally done at the account or segment level, and includes financial measures of success. Team leadership, however, frequently includes responsibilities that may have no immediate financial return to the company. In this case, it is important to identify the critical success factors and include them in a structured way in the compensation program. Figures 10-10 and 10-11 illustrate two approaches to compensating team leader positions.

Compensating Customer Team Leaders

Figure 10-10 illustrates an incentive plan for a customer team leader. The team was actually multifunctional, designed to identify and access decision makers in a key market segment, persuade decision makers to form long-term contractual buying relationships with the company, and fill orders and meet customers' expectations. Team members included

Fig. 10-10. Segment team manager (customer team/multifunctional).

	Market Segment Business Objectives*				Individual Contribution (Add-on for other team members)		
Plan Elements	Ach.	Rating	Payout		Ach.	Rating	Payout
	Excellence	4.5	200% of segment target bonus		Excellence	4.5	200% of ind. contrib. target bonus
	Target	3.0	100% of segment target bonus	+	**Target**	3.0	100% of ind. contrib. target bonus
	Threshold	2.0	75% of segment target bonus		Threshold	2.0	40% of ind. contrib. target bonus
	< Threshold	< 2	-0-		< Threshold	<2	-0-

Payout Frequency:	Quarterly	Semiannually
Weight:	75%	25%

* Based on three measures of performance—volume, gross margin, share of segment

employees from sales and customer service, market planning, contract administration, finance, and operations. Many team members were in jobs outside of sales and customer service that the company did not consider "bonus eligible." (Note that several of these jobs were in new selling roles.) The compensation plan for the team leader had the following characteristics:

Mix and leverage: Mix and leverage for the job were low; that is, there was relatively little pay at risk and relatively low upside potential. Top management considered the 85/15 mix sufficiently motivational and also equitable for this job.

Performance range: The performance measures included both market segment and individual contribution objectives. In the case of this team, the individual contribution component was developed as a team, and each member had objectives based on his or her functional role. For example, the contracts administration objective was contract turnaround in five working days or less. The operations objective was on-time delivery. It was possible to measure all individual contribution objectives. The company also used this component to determine a small add-on bonus that was available semiannually for each team member.

Incentive formula: The incentive formula for the team leader was additive, and the primary measure was reaching segment objectives, all of which were financial. This financial measure worked like a "balanced scorecard" and included volume, profitability, and share of segment as the measures of team success.

COMPENSATING SALES TEAM LEADERS

Figure 10-11 provides an example of an incentive plan for the leader of a sales team (that is, all team resources are sales resources). In fact, a company used a version of this plan for all members of this sales team. The plan included two performance measures, both of which were critical to team success:

- Achievement of customer financial (profit) objectives
- Achievement of account (team) sales quota

These two measures were linked, and the company expected the team to work effectively with the account to develop the business plan that would help them both achieve their objectives. In this case, the team leader's skill at working with the team and with the customer through complex buying and selling processes would be critical to company achievement as well.

Developing sales compensation plans that are appropriate for team leader positions depends to a large extent on the company's flexibility and readiness to change. Traditional approaches to compensating front-line managers are generally not consistent with the expectations for a team leader role, although the building blocks can still be used for these plans.

Fig. 10-11. Sales team leader incentive plan.

Quarterly Bonus Matrix
(Percent of Quarterly Target Bonus)

		Threshold		Target		Excellence
	Excellence	**50.0**	87.5	125.0	162.5	**200.0**
		37.5	75.0	112.5	137.5	162.5
Customer Profit Objectives	**Target**	25.0	62.5	**100.0**	112.5	125.0
		12.5	37.5	62.5	75.0	87.5
	Threshold	0.0	12.5	25.0	37.5	**50.0**

Team: Percent Sales Quota Attained

Payout Frequency: Quarterly

Weights: 50% Customer Profit, 50% Sales

SUMMING UP

Sales managers and team leaders have the responsibility for supervising frontline resources. As such, the scope and complexities of their jobs generally increase as a company grows and changes. Today more and more companies expect their sales managers to be sales strategists in addition to effectively managing salespeople. They have to deal with top management's expectations, customer expectations, and the resources—salespeople and others—they supervise.

In response to these new or changed expectations, sales managers take on one of three different roles: the coach, the superseller, or the strategist/business planner. The exact role depends upon the company growth phase and business objectives at a particular point in time. While the sales manager's duties, tasks, and responsibilities are similar across all three roles, the emphasis on the elements is different. The coaching sales manager's top priority is to develop his salespeople. The superseller sales manager's top priority is to optimize the opportunity to grow sales volume. The strategist/business planner sales manager's top priority is to maximize her company's market opportunities.

Because the roles are different, with different priorities, goals, and challenges, the compensations plans for each of these three sales managers should be different. If they are not, the company is likely to reward the wrong thing or ignore the key element of the job. At the same time, compensation plan designers must be conscious of the issues surrounding pay differentials, mix and leverage, performance measures, and timing.

A sales or customer team leader is not the same as a sales manager; the job is different, and the compensation should likewise be different. The building blocks may be the same—salary/incentive mix, incentive pay leverage, performance range, incentive formula, sales crediting, and performance and pay periods—but the emphasis is different. For example, team leadership frequently includes responsibility that may have no immediate financial return to the company, in which case compensation plan designers must identify the critical success factors and include them in a structured way in the compensation program.

PART 3

IMPLEMENTING NEW PLANS SUCCESSFULLY

TACKLING SOME OF THE MORE CHALLENGING DESIGN ISSUES

Chapters 6 through 10 described how to design a sales compensation plan for new sales roles—new jobs, teams, and managers. To follow an orderly, logical flow in the plan design process, we intentionally stayed away from some of the more challenging design issues. We also did this because some of these questions straddle both design and implementation. Before moving on to how you should implement the new sales compensation plan, we will consider those thorny issues. Thus, the purpose of this chapter is to identify some of the most challenging problems associated with new plans and provide suggestions about how to deal with them in your company.

CHALLENGING ISSUES: AN OVERVIEW

Throughout this book, we point out that companies are changing the way they do business with customers. In many cases, they have redesigned sales and services processes to respond more quickly to customer requirements. Our premise is that nowhere are these changes more pronounced than in the sales function, where, in the main, the job of the individual seller is undergoing continuous change. Virtually no industry is immune from this change, and therefore new sales roles are emerging everywhere, in some industries more rapidly than others.

Consider this example: When Wal-Mart needed to find a way to distribute the multitude of manufacturer displays used in its stores, management talked with its shelving supplier, Famous Fixtures. The sales resource in this case was actually a team of employees from several functions who worked together to come up with the solution for Wal-Mart. "Sales" was a team in this case. Increasingly, as sales shares its role with other functions, the sales department is no longer the sole source of efforts to win and retain customers. As we have explained throughout the book, this shift to shared responsibility for sales is actually one—if not the major—driving force behind the creation and implementation of new sales roles.

Equally interesting is the change in thinking that is occurring about sales compensation and the way companies use it to support and complement the role of sales. In recent years, principally at our seminars, we have come in contact with over 2,000 top managers from over twenty different industries—consumer brands, industrial and commercial products, financial services, retail, and utilities, to mention a few. Virtually everyone we talked with had serious concerns about their company's sales compensation plan. A common thread running through their comments and questions was a concern over the use of incentive pay arrangements, specifically, how to balance rewards between sales personnel and the other customer contact personnel—many of whom were new to sales roles—for achieving success with customers.

We can divide the concerns of this broad cross section of top managers into two categories: big picture issues and specific compensation plan design issues. With that in mind, we will first list and comment on the big picture issues top managers raise and next list and describe the more specific design issues that companies wrestle with.

FIVE "BIG PICTURE" QUESTIONS TOP MANAGERS ASK ABOUT SALES COMPENSATION

When top managers think about changing their company's approach to sales compensation, a number of big picture issues come to mind. We can distill these big picture issues into five questions—the questions top managers most frequently raise with us.

1. WHY DON'T SALES COMPENSATION PLANS SEEM TO WORK WELL ANYMORE?

There was a time in American industry when companies rarely changed their sales compensation plan. In fact, sales compensation plans often remained basically the same for three, five, ten years or more. We know of two companies in the Midwest that had plans in place for thirty-five and sixty-two years, respectively, before changing them in 1997. Today, this is not the case. Our research shows that the average life of an American sales compensation plan is twelve to twenty-four months. Many companies change their plans substantially every year. Essentially, the reasons for the decline in the average life of a sales compensation plan come down to three phrases, none of which start with the word "compensation":

Customer access. Companies are focused on top-line business growth. This means implementing processes to attract new customers and to retain current customers. In doing so, companies often find that customers want to do business with other company employees in addition to sales representatives. This causes the need for new sales roles and therefore the need to figure out how to include the new or changed jobs and their incumbents in the sales compensation plan.

Buyer segmentation. In many industries, there are no more mass markets, only niche markets. Focusing on the right customers with the right mix of resources is important to business success. In some cases, the result is less need for geographic coverage by individual sellers but a much greater need for industry sales specialists, application specialists, technical specialists, and so forth—all new sales roles requiring different forms of compensation.

Sales channels. The competitive battle for more customers has extended to distribution channels. Increasingly, companies are implementing new channels to access, qualify, and reach the customers they target for business. Staffing and managing these new channels requires not only a different cadre of people but also widely different compensation arrangements to attract and retain them.

Thus, it is not that sales compensation plans do not serve a useful purpose in helping top managers lead their businesses; rather, plans are no longer useful when they fall out of step with the changing needs of the business. As we suggested in chapters 4 and 6, management must thoroughly review sales compensation plans regularly—at a minimum, annually—to confirm that the plan still supports a company's business priorities and goals.

2. Is the Use of Sales Compensation Plans on the Decline?

We often find that the real question on the mind of the top executive is something like, "If sales compensation plans don't appear to be working all that well, are companies relying on them less?" This is not the case in our experience, so the answer to this question is no. In fact, our research and consulting experience suggests just the opposite; companies are looking for the right way to include more employees, particularly those in new sales roles, in the sales compensation plan.

No one would dispute the fact that sales compensation plans sometimes get off track. Plans can sometimes be anticustomer—rewarding salespeople for selling things accounts shouldn't buy. They can be anti-company—taking orders or doing things that are not in the company's best interest. And they can be antiemployee—not fairly rewarding the right personnel for success with customers. However, sales compensation is a powerful tool, and rarely have top managers found an effective, lasting replacement for its motivational and directional value.

For example, two large, successful chemical companies merged and formed a new powerhouse in the marketplace. Prior to the merger, both companies used sales compensation plans, although of quite different design, to pay sales employees, sales team members, and inside sales staff. Six months after the merger, the merged company eliminated the sales incentive plans for all sales and sales team personnel. The reason: The merger integration team, which was dominated by nonmarketing and nonsales personnel, believed that the sales incentive plans had many of the "anti" characteristics described above. One year later, the merged companies had not achieved the results that top managers had expected—or, we might add, the results they had promised the investor community. Why? One reason appears to be that sales and customer contact employees lost the sense of direction that the sales compensation plan provided and reinforced. Although not always ideal, sales compensation plans *do* communicate what's important and therefore what employees should strive to accomplish. A carefully crafted sales compensation plan gives the company another edge in competitive battle. Taking that edge away does appear to contribute to reduced sales effectiveness.

We believe that the use of sales compensation plan principles and techniques is on the rise. We believe this because more companies are paying more employees, not just sales representatives, for achieving results with customers through sales teams or customer teams. Design for these types of plans draws heavily upon the principles and formulas used in sales compensation plans, even when the plans are called by other names such as variable pay or performance rewards.

3. What Types of Incentives Are Used for Sales or Customer Teams?

With more companies rewarding more nonsales employees for success with customers, it is not surprising that the companies using this practice are interested in knowing what others are doing. There are actually two different, though complementary, approaches companies use to reward teams: incentive pay and recognition programs.

We tell top managers that incentive pay plans for sales or customer teams fall into one of three categories, based on how the formula is constructed:

Sole determinant. Team performance as a whole is the sole determinant of the incentive pay award. Each team member receives the exact same incentive dollar award or the same percent of salary award. The rationale for this approach is that all team members contribute equal value to results and therefore all members share equally in the aggregate award earned by the team so there is no cause for monetary envy. We observe that companies mostly use this approach to team pay in "self-directed" teams, where such teams are prevalent throughout the company.

Primary determinant. Team performance is the primary determinant of the incentive pay award. This means that 60 percent or more of the incentive paid is based on the results of team performance, and the balance of the award is based on individual performance. The rationale for this approach is that while the company is promoting team performance as the value system desired in its people, individual performance does make a difference and should be recognized in incentive pay. This approach to incentive pay is typical in companies that traditionally have a strong culture of collaboration and teamwork across business functions. One example of a company that has used team performance as the primary determinant is a capital equipment manufacturer and marketer in the test and measurement industry. While most companies in this industry have traditionally focused on the salesperson's individual achievement, this company realized that the service technicians and in-house customer service representatives played a critical role in ensuring customer retention and penetration. The team members also identified new decision makers in their accounts and provided sometimes significant competitive information based on their contacts in the account. This company therefore used team revenue as the primary determinant of pay for all three positions: sales, technical service, and customer service. In addition, each functional task within the teams had individual performance metrics that were elements of the incentive plan. Of the three categories listed, our experience shows that this second approach to team incentive formula is the most prevalent.

Minor determinant. Team performance is a relatively minor determinant in the incentive pay award, for example, 25 percent or less of the total award. We often find this approach to award determination in companies with a strong sales culture where individual sellers are the driving force in a company's success. Often this is a company at the beginning of a transition from individual-based incentives to individual-plus-team incentives. The goal is to introduce a team component to incentive pay gradually, ultimately arriving at a plan where it may be the primary determinant as described above. We have worked with many companies that ease into team-based pay through this approach. The team component is generally additive, and employees consider it a bonus ("You did a good job") rather than an incentive ("I know you can do a good job"). Over time, companies frequently increase the weight of the team measure, or link achievement of the team measure to payout for individual achievement.

In addition to, or as an alternative to, incentive pay, as we pointed out in Chapter 6, some companies use recognition programs to motivate and reward team success with customers. Increasingly, we observe that sales recognition programs are an important part of a company's customer leadership strategy. A recognition program for sales and other customer contact personnel is an incentive plan designed to encourage and reward outstanding achievement on a sustained basis. Top managers tell us that enhancing motivation and performance through recognition programs, particularly with sales teams and customer teams, contributes to increased customer loyalty and retention. The five most common objectives of these recognition programs are to:

1. Reward contributions
2. Retain good performers
3. Increase productivity, particularly as it pertains to customer retention
4. Increase morale
5. Communicate appreciation and respect to employees

We believe that recognition programs for teams—both sales- and customer-based—are an important element of a company's motivational system. Unlike cash, recognition awards are visible and therefore serve as a symbol or sign to peers and associates of the recipient's value and contribution to the company. Executives do not always realize that one dimension of a recognition program's value is that it, in effect, designates role models within the company for others to emulate. This is particularly important in companies that are just beginning to use teams in the sales and customer relationship management processes.

Consider this example: A well-known but old-line consumer brands company, competing in the health and beauty aids market, concluded that customer teams are here to stay. The company decided to "field" teams to serve its large customers. Top managers chartered the company's first team to work with Wal-Mart. Initially, it was difficult to recruit team members from functions outside the sales organization. People from the nonsales functions asked how this assignment would affect their careers in their functional areas of the business. If things didn't work out for them on the team, could they go back to their old job? Top managers did not anticipate this reaction, since several competitors in the industry were already using teams to work with big accounts like Wal-Mart, Kmart, Target, the price clubs, and others. In fact, Procter & Gamble had implemented its customer teams as long ago as 1988.

As part of the transition to teams, this company implemented a recognition program for team members. This Customer Effectiveness Awards program recognized both the most productive team and the most productive team members in all the teams. Each quarter, top managers and all members of teams nominate Team of the Quarter and Team Member of the Quarter. Customer survey results and business results are two of the primary factors they use to make nominations. They use multiple noncash awards to recognize winners. For example, at the end of the quarter, top managers host a picnic/barbecue event for the winning teams (weather permitting) or serve lunch for them in the company cafeteria. While it may sound hokey, we find that showing appreciation is a key ingredient to successful award programs. At this company, top managers agreed, and thus waiting on team employees at such an event conveys that caring.

At the end of the year, again through nominations and comparison of achievement to objectives—business goals and customer satisfaction standards—the Team of the Year and the Team Members of the Year are selected and recognized at an annual meeting. One of the significant awards the winners receive is time off with pay. In a time of high stress and compressed deadlines, team members said that one of the things they would most value would be time off. Thus, it became one of the top awards in the program.

The program is a visible centerpiece for the company's new sales culture. It communicates what constitutes sales excellence and shows appreciation to team members for their performance contributions. As a result, by the second year of the customer coverage program involving teams, the company did not have any difficulty recruiting team members and no one asked about going back to functional areas. The first team and the complementary recognition program provided the role model and assurance employees needed to go forward.

4. What Are Some of the Common Pitfalls to Avoid When Designing Incentives for Sales or Customer Teams?

Top managers are often sensitive to what could go wrong when the company changes the way it pays employees, particularly sales personnel. Because salespeople are in regular and frequent contact with customers, a miscue—signaled through a change in the compensation plan in terms of focus or direction—could have unintended negative consequences for the company. Sales could decline, customers become dissatisfied, and gross profits fall. Frequently, a company implements new sales roles at the same time it launches sales teams or customer teams. As a result, two significant life changes could be affecting salespeople at the same time: what they do (their jobs and careers) and how they are paid for it (their compensation plan). When this is the case, many of the questions we get express an interest in knowing what can go wrong, particularly when the incentive is cash delivered through a formal incentive pay plan. Here are the three most frequent pitfalls we tell top managers to watch out for:

Give Everyone the Same Dollar Incentive Pay Opportunity

In our opinion, this is not the right thing to do. When businesses bring individuals together on a team to contribute to the sales and customer relationship management processes, team membership does not alter the compensation value of their position. The incentive pay opportunity, in dollars, should vary by function and by job. Our research supports that view. In the summer of 1995, we surveyed private sector companies with revenues of at least $100 million. We asked the senior human resources or compensation professional (all members of the American Compensation Association) to report on reward practices covering sales and customer teams. Some 163 companies returned survey questionnaires. We asked respondents to report the incentive pay targets for the positions represented on their teams—sales teams, customer teams, or both. Respondents reported a wide range of incentive pay targets for each functional area included on teams—sales, marketing, customer service, distribution, information systems, finance, and technical support. The target incentive pay opportunity for sales positions was as high as 50 percent of salary, while functions such as technical support, finance, and information systems were eligible for much less incentive pay, an average of 20 percent of salary.

A more prevalent practice is to provide the same opportunity as a percent of salary to each team member. This practice, by its nature, provides a different dollar opportunity to all team members, and recognizes different skills and experiences (assuming that the company uses the base pay program to reward these factors).

Finally, the third practice we see companies use is to provide a different percent of salary as the incentive pay opportunity to each team member based on their role with the team. We believe that self-directed teams most commonly use this practice. The company prescribes the range of incentive pay opportunity available to team members. With the guidelines in hand, each team determines each member's target incentive pay opportunity at the beginning of the plan year.

Use of "financial" measures as the only indicators of success

Financial measures, including sales results, should continue to be a significant determinant of team incentive payouts. However, our research (the same study cited above) shows that companies use some qualitative performance measures to appraise the performance contributions of team members. You should introduce and give meaningful weight (15 to 25 percent) to nonfinancial measures in award determination.

Generally, businesses implement new sales roles to bridge a gap or resolve an issue they have identified in the customer coverage process. They frequently use teams in complex account environments, and they cannot measure the contribution of each member in financial terms. We have seen many teams use individual objectives (qualitative, but with milestones to judge success) that require the employee to acquire new skills. In fact, success of the team and of each team member in terms of contribution to company objectives frequently requires that each person, and the team as a whole, learn new behaviors and processes. Long-term success cannot always be measured with short-term financial gain.

Our research, cited above, does not support this practice. Other techniques are being used in combination with or as a replacement for the incentive formula. Many companies find that a formula does not provide the necessary flexibility for recognizing changes in the company's objectives or the team's goals. In our survey of American Compensation Association members, 30 percent of the respondents indicated that they use a process other than or in addition to a formula to calculate incentive pay awards for team members.

One popular, nonformula technique is a team decision-making process to arrive at incentive awards for each team member. In this process, other members, including the team leader, evaluate each team member's contribution to the team's results. While democratic in its approach, the principal challenge this process poses—and perhaps one reason it is not more widely used among the companies we survey—is ensuring that the process is related to individual contribution, team results, and reaching the company's objectives. Someone—either the team leader or the team leader with the top managers—must ultimately make that judgment. And, because such judgments are often viewed as subjective, we believe that a formulaic approach to incentive pay will never be completely abandoned.

5. I<small>N</small> C<small>OMPANIES</small> W<small>HERE THE</small> S<small>ALES</small> F<small>UNCTION</small> H<small>AS</small> N<small>OT</small> C<small>HANGED,</small> W<small>HAT</small> I<small>S THE</small> F<small>OCUS OF</small> T<small>HEIR</small> S<small>ALES</small> C<small>OMPENSATION</small> P<small>LAN</small>?

Actually, we come in contact with relatively few companies that are not changing. As top managers point out to us, the individual seller job is the appropriate way to go to market in some industries. In those situations, we find companies are altering the emphasis they place on performance measures. This is not the result of a new sales role; rather, it is a shift in business strategy. In rank order, the three most prevalent measures used today in those types of sales compensation plans are revenue growth, profitability, and customer loyalty. For example, the individual seller's personal persuasion skill is nowhere more prevalent than in a distribution business. One of the country's top distributors of maintenance, repair, and operating supplies relies heavily on a consultative sales approach to customers. Unlike other distributors, which use 100 percent commission plans to pay their sales representatives, this company uses an 80 percent salary/20 percent incentive pay plan. The plan strikes a balance between revenue growth and customer satisfaction in its incentive formula. It encourages sales representatives to know their customers and tailor solutions to their needs.

Taken in total, and relative to the big picture questions, we advise top managers that sales compensation plans do have a future and an important one when it comes to rewarding and recognizing employees in new sales roles. However, sales compensation plans as we know them today will be markedly different in the years to come because they will continue to evolve to meet the needs of companies that are changing their approach to doing business with customers. Increasingly, the companies we visit are using sales compensation plans that bear little resemblance to the traditional plans of years gone by. Yet the plans continue to be referred to as sales compensation. As we discovered recently at one company, the real need is to encourage top managers to change the name of their plan from sales compensation to "customer compensation" or some other more customer- and employee-inclusive name. At that company, all of the right pay elements and administrative processes were in place, but the company was turning off its employees—particularly those outside of the sales organization who were new to incentive pay—with the way it was marketing the plan to them.

SIX TOUGH DESIGN ISSUES THAT AFFECT COMPENSATION PLANS

Below the big picture issues is another level of sales compensation plan questions that are both more granular and often a good deal more complex. Typically, these involve a combination of business strategy topics—customer segments, new sales channels, new sales jobs and new forms of organization, performance metrics, and financial goals—and compensation policy issues. For example, what constitutes "on-plan performance," and how much could the company pay to plan participants at that level, below it, and above it? The challenges are often a source of noisy debate between plan designers and top managers. Our list of tough design issues is representative and not all-inclusive. It reflects what we hear from top managers and plan designers in meetings that involve new sales roles and how employees in those roles could be compensated. In fact, we know other issues exist; we believe, however, that the ones we discuss here address over 80 percent of the challenges you are likely to face when you design sales compensation plans for new sales roles at your company.

We discuss the issues in order of prevalence, the first being the most common. For each, we provide some perspective on why this is a tough issue to begin with, when or how you are likely to encounter it in your plan design efforts, and alternative solutions you could consider. The specific answer for your company, of course, depends on the particular objectives you had in mind when adopting new sales roles. There is no one-size-fits-all answer to these questions.

Tough Issue #1: Overloading the Sales Compensation Plan with Too Many Performance Measures

When it comes to performance measures, top managers need to think in terms of "sales compensation plan lite"! We see too many compensation plans that should be put on a diet when it comes to performance measures. Remember that in Chapter 6 we said that the ideal number is three. A plan loaded with too many measures tends to be ineffective and can cause a company to miss the business objective altogether. This is a tough issue—and the most common at that—because top managers and plan designers have a strong inclination to add measures to an existing plan rather than start with a clean slate.

You are most likely to encounter this tough issue when the sales strategy, job definition, or both lack clarity (if you are reading the book out of sequence, you may want to refer to Chapters 4 and 5 to understand how to avoid this situation). One way to clarify a job's definition, particularly after new sales roles are introduced, is to evaluate how salespeople spend their time. One company that has done a particularly good job at this is Browning-Ferris Industries (BFI), the waste services company based in Houston. Sandra Glatzau, senior vice president of marketing and sales, told us that, before she profiled how salespeople were spending their time, she suspected that they were not efficient enough. And sure enough, that's exactly what their time studies showed. The sales force was not spending enough time on selling. They were devoting as much as half their time to activities such as administrative tasks and travel. While the company has a goal to focus on large customers, salespeople were deployed by region instead of by size of account. As a result, BFI was not giving key customers the attention needed to win more of their business. To clarify job roles and ensure that salespeople were focused on high-value selling, BFI reorganized its sales force. The firm assigned each large customer to one sales representative who could handle all its needs and assigned smaller accounts to a telesales force. A change such as this offers the opportunity to align performance with the new sales roles. For example, instead of measuring sales by different sets of customers—large, midrange, and small—you can use a single measure—total sales—for one customer set because that defines the sales job's accountability.

To avoid overloading the sales compensation plan with too many measures, we suggest you use the Sales Strategy Matrix and the five W's described in Chapter 3. The principal benefit of using these tools is that they narrow the range of what to measure. Remember, your goal is to limit the number of measures to three or fewer.

TOUGH ISSUE #2: PAY THE JOB OR PAY THE INDIVIDUAL?

We see many companies experimenting with new approaches to employee pay at all levels of their organization. These initiatives reflect the realities of how business operates today, namely, with fewer organizational levels and therefore fewer jobs and people, a broader scope of work associated with jobs, and a greater degree of control and flexibility over the work one does. The issue of paying the job and the individual in it or paying the employee alone is part of a larger transformation that companies are undergoing. The issue, of course, is not specific to sales and other customer contact jobs. Given that context, the issue of paying the job versus paying the individual in the job is a challenge sales compensation plan designers will face if their company is experimenting with new pay programs, particularly with some type of "skill-based" pay.

The fundamental point of skill-based pay is to allow employees more latitude in the performance of work than would be the case in a job with set duties and responsibilities. Another difference between skill-based pay and job-based pay is that individuals paid on the basis of the job are assumed to be qualified when assigned the work. In a skill-based pay plan, on the other hand, one is paid more only when one obtains a skill specifically required by the company in one's work. A more in-depth discussion of skill-based pay is beyond the scope of this book. If you want to explore this subject further, our friends Jay Schuster and Pat Zingheim provide an excellent discussion in their book, *The New Pay: Linking Employee and Organizational Performance* (Lexington Books, 1992).

A company considering new sales roles faces a decision about tying pay to the job or to the individual in the job if the company is already using skill-based pay or some other competency-based pay system in other parts of the company. For example, we find that skill-based pay is quite common in manufacturing companies. It is also common in companies that have implemented teams throughout their organization, particularly self-directed teams. We have not seen many companies successfully use the concept of paying the individual (versus setting the pay opportunity based on labor market job pricing) when implementing new sales roles. This is because businesses use base pay to attract and retain individuals, particularly salespeople, who have the skills, abilities, and experience to perform successfully in the job assignment. If that were not true, individuals (particularly salespeople) would not be inclined to accept employment, since at the outset they are placing some portion of their pay at risk.

Some companies have tried to ensure that each individual is paid equitably through the sales compensation plan by using a percentage of salary as the basis for determining the incentive award opportunity; salary, reflecting the individual's skill level, is the multiplier in the incentive calculation. As discussed above, this approach ensures that each individual will have a different award opportunity, hopefully commensurate with her skills and level of contribution.

Here are some guidelines you should use when weighing the appropriateness of paying for the job rather than paying for the individual:

- Job roles and responsibilities are the key elements used to price the job in the market (both internally and externally).
- Mix is based on the total compensation for the job, concepts of effective incentive compensation, and competitive practice.
- Pay based on performance in a job is both equitable and practical, while paying each individual differently (i.e., different opportunities) within one job may be perceived as (or may actually be) inequitable and impractical.
- Base pay generally differentiates individual skills and experiences, and, thus, it is more appropriate to focus attention on it.

TOUGH ISSUE #3: "DELEVERAGING" THE INCENTIVE PLAN

You face the issue of "deleveraging" when the company makes a shift in the salary/incentive ratio from a low salary/high incentive pay opportunity to a higher salary/lower incentive pay opportunity. You are likely to face this issue when the company makes a fundamental change in the job's scope, in the people required to perform new or revised jobs, or both. To understand deleveraging, it's helpful to review the definition of leverage as it pertains to sales compensation. As Chapter 6 described, leverage represents the upside earnings opportunity associated with the portion of compensation placed at risk because of the nature and role of the sales job. The rationale behind the concept of leverage is that the business establishes target total cash compensation for a sales job (or any customer contact position, for that matter) based on what the company can afford to pay and the prevailing rates of pay for talented people in the labor market. The total pay level reflects the economic value associated with doing a fully effective job. When a salesperson signs on for the job, she opts for "betting on the come" relative to a portion of her total pay. The salesperson earns the portion placed at risk, as defined by the company's salary/incentive ratio for the job, when she achieves the assigned performance objective, for example, the sales volume quota. Placing a portion of total pay at risk should provide the opportunity to earn not just the at-risk amount, but more when the salesperson exceeds the performance objective(s). Essentially, salespeople bet on their belief that they can exceed company performance expectations and therefore leverage the at-risk pay by a multiple greater than one. How much greater is defined through the mechanics of leverage in a particular pay plan.

In practice, leverage can range from one time to as much as three times the at-risk pay. For example, a sales job with a target compensation of $60,000, a 70/30 mix, and triple leverage would have a base salary of $42,000 ($60,000 $\times$ .70) and a total incentive earnings potential of $54,000 ($18,000 $\times$ 3), for a total compensation opportunity of $96,000.

A change in the sales role of an account executive from a sales generalist to a new role as sales specialist typically requires a shift in the compensation mix—the salary/incentive ratio described in Chapter 6. The most prevalent examples of this type of shift in mix are (1) from 30/70 to 50/50, (2) from 40/60 to 60/40, or (3) from 50/50 to 70/30. When a company alters the mix in a manner that reduces the incentive and increases the base salary, the plan is deleveraged; the company is reducing the upside incentive earnings potential and, for that matter, the total potential compensation.

An illustration may be helpful to focus on how deleveraging actually works. The situation involves an account executive job with a target total compensation opportunity of $100,000. The sales role was changed as follows (see Table 11-1):

Traditional (historical) role: Only sales resource in the geographic area, responsible for all phases of the sales process; sold stock/commodity products to midlevel buyers; job viewed as requiring significant per-

Table 11-1.   Deleveraging an account executive position.

Compensation Element	From 30% Salary/ 70% Incentive ($)	To 50% Salary/ 50% Incentive ($)
Salary	30,000	50,000
Target incentive opportunity	70,000	50,000
Target total compensation	100,000	100,000
Upside incentive	140,000	100,000
Total potential compensation	240,000	200,000

suasion skills and, therefore, the salary/incentive ratio was set at 30/70; the plan provided for triple leverage.

New role: One of a team of resources in the geographic area to meet the account's end-to-end needs, from need identification to ongoing service; continues to focus on sales of same products to a team of buyers in accounts; and therefore salary/incentive ratio increases to 50/50 to provide account executive with more time to focus on the developmental needs of the account.

In this example, the company shifted additional risk to itself and reduced some of the risk that the account executive experienced in the past by increasing the base salary. The cost of doing so for the company was a $20,000 increase in base pay, along with an increase in the cost of benefits related to salary. For the employee, it was the loss of $40,000 in upside incentive opportunity.

TOUGH ISSUE #4: CONTROLLING SALES COMPENSATION COSTS

Top managers constantly struggle to control sales compensation costs. You are most likely to face this issue when margins are declining, when selling expenses are increasing at a rate greater than profitable volume, or both. Also, this is one of the tougher issues because, in large part, it is very difficult to separate it from some of the others. Margin decline is often a signal that suggests the business needs new sales roles. Customers do not present themselves to you as unprofitable business. In the main, companies themselves make some customers unprofitable to do business with because there was not a good fit to begin with between the customer's needs and the company's products and services or because the way the company sells to and services the customer is inappropriate. In the latter case, the company may be using too expensive sales resources to do business with those customers.

We find that one major factor contributing to a misalignment of selling costs with profit results is the approach a company uses to set the compensation opportunity for its sales and other customer contact jobs that are eligible to participate in the plan. Essentially, one can choose from two approaches when setting the pay opportunity: (1) cost of sales and (2) cost of labor.

Consider these examples: Company A needed to build market share quickly. To motivate sales growth, the company adopted a commission compensation plan. The more the sales reps sold, the more they made. This approach to sales compensation seemed to work; sales volume climbed and Company A captured more market share. After three years on this compensation program, sales growth flattened and Company A began to lose share. The sales representatives, however, continued to earn on average $80,000 in commission pay by retaining their current customers and by expanding business in a few accounts. At the same time, they were not opening any new accounts, and productivity studies showed that the sales force was not overworked. Moreover, market research revealed that significant untapped sales potential was available at accounts in many territories. What was happening?

Company B was an established company competing for business in markets that were growing at about 10 percent annually and where many competitors were vying for orders. The sales force was paid a salary plus a commission based on sales volume. Fifty percent of the target total pay was expected to be commission earnings. Sales rep Joe Jones worked in an established territory and consistently earned the target level of total pay. Sales rep Sue Smith faced an underpenetrated sales territory with low volume and established competitors. After one year on the job, with virtually no commission earnings and no market relief in sight, Smith, discouraged, resigned, like the last three sales representatives before her in that territory. The territory, and underpenetrated territories like it, would stay that way, and the best Company B could do was maintain current market share. What was happening?

When Company C first went into business, it needed to establish market share quickly. To accomplish this, management decided to pay the sales force on a 100 percent commission basis, with a relatively modest cash draw against future commission earnings. After two years, however, the company had a large base of business and customers began to complain that the salespeople were not spending enough time with them on service requirements and technical issues. The salespeople said they did not make any money on problem solving and they would rather spend their time finding and closing new accounts. What's more, salespeople spent little or no time selling the new products on which Company C was staking its future. Salespeople said they could sell the current, in-line products more quickly and earn more money both for themselves and for the company. What was happening?

Each case shares a common trait: The sales force was paid based on the philosophy "The more they make, the more the company makes." We refer to this as the "cost of sales" philosophy of sales compensation. In each case, however, the selling environment eventually changed while the prevailing pay philosophy—use of commission plan— remained unchanged. In fact, the commission plan got in the way of managing the business. Here is what was happening.

Company A was losing market share in part because its commissioned sales reps were comfortable with their $80,000 earnings. They had little motivation to increase sales over current levels or open new accounts. One result was that the cost of sales, particularly as a percent of gross margin, was going up, while income levels remained relatively high and attractive to the incumbents.

Company B lost sales representatives in low penetration territories because the commission pay plan did not provide sufficient earnings even to experienced sales reps in the short term. While the costs of sales have been reasonable, the hidden costs—turnover and lost business with potential customers—were really quite high.

Company C's commission plan did not differentiate between new and current products. Sales reps decided where and how they would earn their compensation, which turned out to be with the older, more established products they were comfortable selling. While selling cost overall may have been reasonable, when recast relative to gross margins on current products compared to new products, they were way too high.

All three of these companies missed the opportunity to manage their sales compensation costs because they relied solely on a cost of sales approach to pay calculation. A low base salary and high potential commission earnings frequently characterize this approach. In this approach to pay, the implicit assumption is that the sales rep will maximize his or her commission earnings and in doing so will also maximize the company's profitability. Generally speaking, this is true only in business environments characterized by high growth and without rapidly declining margins.

An alternative to the cost of sales pay philosophy is the "cost of labor" approach to setting the sales compensation opportunity. This approach requires management to define what the sales job is worth in the competitive labor market and pay that value to sales reps when they perform within established goals. This approach is a bit more complex because, as we explained in chapter 6, it requires determining the approach mix, leverage, performance goals (e.g., quota), and performance range (threshold, target, and excellence) for all of the organization's sales jobs (assuming there is more than one). The benefit is a much greater likelihood that selling expenses are more closely aligned with sales and profits and that sales force performance will be consistent with both. How could the cost of labor approach to sales pay help management better achieve company objectives in each of the three previous cases? Let's revisit each situation.

Company A, whose sales were leveling off, could have benefited from setting a labor market value for the sales job, paying a salary to recognize that certain competencies and skills were required to retain the base business, and offering an incentive opportunity (based on appropriate salary incentive ratio, e.g., 70/30) to penetrate the sales potential available in the territory. The incentive opportunity, tied to reaching sales goals, would link sales results to sales costs, thus giving management the opportunity to control selling expenses.

Company B, which turned over salespeople in low growth territories, would have been better served using both approaches. The cost of sales approach was getting the desired results in established territories, but underpenetrated territories required an investment where talented salespeople needed to earn a competitive salary while building the sales base. The cost of labor approach would reflect the value management placed on the job in a growth territory by paying target compensation at low sales levels until the territory was fully developed.

Company C was having trouble getting its sales force to focus on new products. A cost of labor approach, where management defines the job value according to the ability to sell both current, in-line products and new products and pays according to sales results with each, may work better here. For example, the company would pay the salary for selling current products, the incentive for selling new products.

Controlling sales compensation costs generally requires revisiting many decisions that were made prior to the development of a sales compensation plan, for example, buyer segmentation, account coverage strategies, and job definition. As we discuss in Chapter 13, the selling costs may be considered an investment in resources, and, like all investments, it should pay off within the time period defined for effectiveness.

TOUGH ISSUE #5: INTEGRATING SALES COMPENSATION PLANS ACROSS MULTIPLE BUSINESSES

You face this issue when a merger or acquisition involves two or more companies and the goal is to integrate the sales function into one national or global organization. Also, companies that combine two or more divisional sales forces into a single organization are likely to face this issue. This is a tough issue because there are usually widely different philosophies and approaches to compensation involved. We pointed out in Chapter 6 that sales compensation plans are situational. The characteristics of a particular sales environment, the business strategy, and the management philosophy of a company work in combination to influence the decisions that top managers make about the plan. Two companies operating in the same industry can arrive at quite different approaches to compensating their salespeople and customer support personnel as a result of how they decide to compete. Likewise, two divisions operating within the same company, selling to the same accounts but to different buyers, could use completely different compensation plans. The need to reconcile plans becomes an issue only when companies merge or divisions within an existing business are consolidated to achieve operating efficiencies. Because in recent years there has been so much merger activity and restructuring of corporations to gain cost efficiency, it is not surprising that this is a prevalent issue.

At the time of business integration, a company has to make a strategic choice about what type of sales compensation plan to use. Making that choice is the most difficult when two businesses are currently using plans that are at opposite ends of the continuum and both have been relatively successful with their plans (or at least neither is a clear disaster). For example, Company A is compensating its sales force, both field and inside sales staff, through a salary plus commission plan and the salary/incentive ratio is on average 50/50. Company B is compensating its sales staff through a salary plus bonus incentive pay arrangement and the salary/incentive ratios on average are 70/30. This situation is not that unusual. In fact, as we write this book we know of two; the first involves two companies in the medical products industry, and the other involves two companies in the electronics industry. Even though these are two different industries, the sales compensation issues are almost identical. Table 11-2 provides a reference guide we have found useful when helping top managers make a determination about which type of plan is best for their situation.

When we are asked to advise two or more companies (or internal

Table 11-2.   Sales commissions vs. bonuses.

Characteristics	Sales Commission Compensation	Sales Bonus Compensation
Plan definition	Variable pay—based on a rate that is either fixed or variable—paid as a percentage of sales measured in either dollars or units Commission rate can be applied to either total sales volume or segmented sales volume, to either selected customers or product(s)	Variable pay calculated as a percentage of salary, salary range midpoint, or a target dollar award value Bonus can be calculated based on either total sales or segmented sales for set of customers or product(s)

Selling environment
  Marketplace
  Purchase patterns
  Customer knowledge
  Selling persuasion
  Profit margins on products
	
	New or emerging
	No or unreliable forecast
	Evolving
	Determines selling success
	Relatively high and about the same
		
		Established
		Forecasted accurately
		Predictable
		One measure of success
		Vary widely

Pay philosophy	Cost of sales: "the more they make, the more we make"	Cost of labor: "sales pay levels should be managed in reference to affordability and labor market's compensation level"
Administrative requirements	Relatively equal territories Defined procedure for setting commission rates Capability to track and assign all sales	Procedures for determining the pay multiplier Procedure for determining sales performance range Capability to track and assign all sales
Advantages	Simple to understand Drives performance at a variable cost Provides maximum incentive Rewards/penalties are immediate	Offers opportunity to manage selling Stabilizes earnings Rewards/penalties are consistent with sales and business cycles

Table 11-2.   (Continued).

Characteristics	Sales Commission Compensation	Sales Bonus Compensation
Disadvantages	Limits control over selling efforts	Requires explicit and consistent communication about performance requirements
	Motivates self-directing behaviors	
	Treats all sales equally	Can be confusing to understand
	Creates wide swings in earnings	
	Makes territory realignments difficult	Rewards have potential to be too small when two or more bonuses are used
	Over time, has potential to become quite costly relative to net profits	

divisions of a larger corporation) that are merging their sales organizations into one entity and must decide which type of sales compensation plan to design, we facilitate a conversation around the three key characteristics of the business situation shown in the table: (1) selling environment, (2) pay philosophy, and (3) administrative requirements. We start the conversation by asking top managers to describe their selling environment in the context of five variables, as listed in the table. Next, we move to a discussion about the pay philosophy—cost of sales or cost of labor. (The previous section of this chapter is often useful as background to that conversation.) Finally, we inquire about the relative strength of the current administrative practices: How sophisticated are current sales management practices, procedures, and reporting systems? This information is helpful in determining the various elements of the plan that can be used with confidence. The result of that discussion reveals a predisposition to one type of sales incentive compensation plan, commission or bonus.

We have generally found it is wiser to develop a new-to-the-organization plan in this type of situation, since retaining one program while discarding the other generally leads to feelings of superiority among the people whose plan is retained or inferiority and decreased effectiveness among those whose plan is junked. While there is no magic formula to solve the dilemma faced by two organizations seeking to integrate apparently effective sales compensation programs, it is helpful for the team responsible for integration to ensure that:

- Design team members for this phase of the integration process have the knowledge and functional experience required to ensure that the decisions are consistent with business requirements.

- Any plan that the integrated organization will use is fully aligned with the job that it is being asked to do.
- A transition strategy has been developed that will allow movement from each old plan into any new plan.

TOUGH ISSUE #6: DETERMINING THE RIGHT PERFORMANCE RANGE FOR INCENTIVE COMPENSATION PAYMENT

This is a tough issue because it requires a decision, for most companies annually, about the performance expectations for the entire population of employees affected by the sales compensation plan. Defining what constitutes a good job (often referred to as "par" or "on-plan" performance) and the low and high associated with that good job is the challenge. This can be taxing because the incentive payment is associated with the low and high.

You are most likely to experience this issue in periods of significant change; for example, the company has introduced a new product or discontinued a significant line, the company is targeting a new segment, or a new competitor has entered the market. All changes that lessen the predictability of results will affect your ability to set performance ranges based on the past. In many companies, an interim period is used for the purposes of sales compensation to give management the time it needs to begin to establish (or reestablish) appropriate ranges. The interim period may use a very broad performance range, a new or different plan type (e.g., a commission for a short period of time), or a guarantee.

A CHECKLIST OF OTHER DESIGN ISSUES YOU ARE LIKELY TO FACE

While the tough issues listed and discussed throughout this chapter account for up to 80 percent of the issues and obstacles raised by sales managers, there are several others you are likely to face as the company develops a sales compensation plan for new sales roles. While the following list is not exhaustive, we have found that almost all design teams (or those who will administer the plan) have wrestled with these questions.

Terms and conditions. Although no one likes to see a plan document that is the weight of an unabridged dictionary, it is very important to address the plan's terms and conditions. The human resources department frequently must answer questions like, "How long do I have to be in the job before I'm eligible for the incentive plan?" "What happens to my payout if I quit (die, am disabled, am promoted)?" Even if the plan document does not spell out every possible term and condition, it is important to have discussed what they should be and to have decided on parameters *before* the questions are asked.

Nonexempts. As businesses invent and implement new sales roles, many teams now include both exempt and nonexempt team members. The Fair Labor Standards Act requirements for nonexempt employees are fairly straightforward; however, we have found that many companies either refuse to include nonexempt members in an incentive plan because they are afraid of complex requirements, or are not in compliance with the requirements because they have not researched the issue. We know of one company in the Midwest that has included nonexempt jobs in the sales compensation plan for many years. They devised a formula that is applied to payouts and takes into consideration the law's time-and-a-half requirements. While the firm found the plan difficult to implement in the first year, it also found that including these employees in the incentive plan was well worth the effort, as they are the front line with the company's customers.

Payout frequency. As companies move from a 100 percent commission plan (with or without a draw) to a salary-plus-incentive arrangement, the question of how often to pay incentives frequently comes up. Generally, the concern is that salespeople are used to receiving variable pay (the commission) weekly or monthly, and should continue to do so, even though they are now also receiving a regular salary. Several factors should be considered in determining payout frequency, as we discussed in Chapter 6. However, in summary, it's important to ensure that payouts are (1) frequent enough to motivate behavior, (2) consistent with the company's ability to track, measure, and pay, and (3) large enough to be visible and meaningful, since small weekly payouts may be much less meaningful than one large quarterly payout.

Legal requirements. No matter what the tough issue is, at least one other company has probably wrestled with it and arrived at a solution that is working. Design teams can learn a lot through industry meetings, networking, and reading industry publications. One thing all design teams must do, regardless of industry or new sales role, is to have any new compensation plan reviewed by competent legal counsel. Laws vary considerably across countries, and indeed within the United States. Something as simple as using a different word might make the difference between a plan that is effective (and in compliance with the law) and one that could cause the company significant financial harm.

SUMMING UP

Companies are changing the way they do business with customers, often redesigning sales and services processes to respond more quickly to customer requirements, and, as a consequence, the job of the individual seller is undergoing continuous change. Virtually no industry is immune, and new sales roles are emerging everywhere.

With these shifts are changes in sales compensation and the way companies use it to support and complement the role of sales. Virtually every sales executive we meet has concerns about their company's sales compensation plan, and incentive pay arrangements are a common thread.

Companies change their sales compensation plans more quickly than in the past because customers want different coverage, because markets are fragmenting, and because new distribution channels are evolving. Inappropriate sales compensation plans can be anticustomer, anticompany, or antiemployee (or all three), but in our experience the use of incentive pay is growing, not shrinking. More companies are rewarding more nonsales, team employees for success with customers, and therefore it is important to devise a fair and motivating formula to connect team performance to the incentive pay award.

Nevertheless, there are pitfalls to avoid: giving everyone on the team the same incentive pay opportunity, using financial measures (volume, margin) as the only indicators of success, and using incentive formulas as the only technique to determine an award. Even in companies where the sales function has not changed radically, management is changing emphasis, with more interest in measures like customer satisfaction.

Compensation plan designers have a number of tough issues they may have to deal with. These include overloading the sales compensation plan with too many performance measures; deciding whether to pay the job or pay the individual; deleveraging the incentive plan; controlling sales compensation costs; integrating sales compensation plans from different businesses; and determining the right performance range for incentive compensation payment. Even when the plan design team has resolved all these issues, it must still deal with the terms and conditions of the plan, nonexempt employees, payout frequency, and legal requirements.

And when the design team has developed a compensation plan for the salespeople, management must then turn its attention to a plan for sales managers and team leaders.

CHAPTER 2

HOW TO INTRODUCE COMPENSATION PLANS FOR NEW SALES ROLES

Picture this: Joe Bates, vice president of sales for an $800 million office equipment company, steps up to the podium in the main ballroom of the Walt Disney World Hotel in Orlando, Florida, to address his sales staff of over 700 people. This is the last day of the company's three-day national sales meeting. During the meeting, Bates and his associates have presented a number of new marketing and sales programs, many designed to help the sales organization achieve its rather aggressive, although realistic, 22 percent sales growth goal. This morning's presentation, however, is the one the entire sales organization has been waiting for. It's the presentation on the "mother of all programs"—the new sales compensation plan. As the applause greeting him dies down, Bates begins to speak.

> Thank you. Thank you very much. As we head into the home stretch of this year's national meeting, before presenting the new compensation plan, I'd like to compliment you on your enthusiasm and hard work during the many break-out sessions we've held these last two days. With the new programs and tools we've given you during this meeting, plus your continued commitment and dedication to our customers and our company, there's no way we can miss achieving this year's sales growth goal. Now, let's turn our attention to our new compensation plan.

Slide One: Business Is Increasingly Competitive

As you have heard throughout the last three days, the markets in which we do business are becoming increasingly more competitive. Also, our product line has grown substantially over the last couple of years, and it is no longer effective to cover our markets with just account executives.

Slide Two: A New Way to Cover Customers Effectively

We have had a sales effectiveness project underway for the past six months. That project examined our current sales and customer service processes. We were looking for ways to cover our best customers more effectively and to reduce our selling expenses, which have been increasing at a rate faster than the industry average.

Slide Three: Reassign Accounts to Less Expensive Sales Channels

We are going to make a number of changes in sales jobs; many of you will have new sales roles, and many of you will experience a change in your customer base as we reassign accounts to other less expensive sales channels, most notably telephone selling and sales management.

At this point, one can hear the hum of the slide projector's fan as the sales staff listen in expectation of a major change to the compensation plan.

Slide Four: Eliminate the Commission Plan and Replace It with a Salary Plus Bonus Plan

Consistent with the change in sales roles across our organization—both in the field and in our sales support staff in branches around the country—we are discontinuing last year's sales compensation plan. We are eliminating the commission plan and replacing it with a salary plus bonus plan. The benefits of this plan. . . .

This announcement is met with a great deal of shuffling around in seats and even a few faint boos from the audience. As Bates continues with his presentation, he senses this is not going as well as he had hoped. He can hear mutterings and an occasional hiss. He knows the changes are necessary, and he is confident that he and his management team have done a good job of designing the new plan. At the end of his presentation he asks the sales staff to keep open minds and sends them off to their break-out rooms to learn more about their new sales roles and the new compensation plan in meetings with their managers.

At the end of the morning, Bates meets with his management team, the five field sales vice presidents and the two directors of the company's telesales centers. The news is not good. The salespeople are not pleased with the new plan. The managers share with Bates a sampling of the staff comments, grouped by the major topics of concern.

New sales roles. Overall, the sales force understands and supports the change to new sales roles, which includes a redefinition of the account executive job to exclude small accounts and the increase in the role of the telecenter customer service staff to include the responsibility for selling to those accounts. Many of the experienced account executives, however, object to giving up some of their current customers to focus on only assigned customers. They feel this will limit their compensation opportunity in the new year.

The former commission plan. Many of the account executives and a handful of their managers say that they like the company's existing compensation plan. It pays them from the first dollar of gross profit, it's easy to understand, and it encourages them to sell as much as they can at prices as high as they can negotiate, something they thought the company wanted them to do.

The new compensation plan. The new plan sounds complicated to many of the account executives. There are now several different pieces of compensation to keep track of: a salary rather than a draw; a quota-attainment bonus; and specific product sales incentives. Some of the salespeople think that all of these different pieces are an attempt to confuse them about their pay opportunity, which they feel is going down and is not the same as the presentation indicated.

Quotas. There are mixed feelings about sales quotas. The account executives don't understand why they're needed—after all, the company never had them before and has been successful for years. Some of the frontline sales managers also expressed concern about their ability to assign realistic quotas. Notwithstanding all of the time spent on training these managers, some seem to lack confidence in their ability to make judgments about quota allocations.

As Bates listens to the feedback, he wonders how this situation developed. He had heard from fellow sales executives in other companies that when you change to a new sales compensation plan, the salespeople often feel that the best plan they ever had was the one you're replacing. But how can they think that about the company's new plan? Margins are declining, and if the company continues to pay the salespeople a percentage of declining margins, they will earn less and less. Clearly, this message has been lost somewhere along the line during the last three days. Bates wonders where he went wrong. What could have been done differently to prevent this reaction to the changes announced at the meeting? And, perhaps more importantly, how should he approach turning around this unhappy situation so he can be confident the sales organization will achieve its sales growth objective?

We will return to these questions at the end of this chapter. Using the guidelines and tools we described, we will suggest how Joe Bates could have approached the situation, which, although the executive's name is fictitious, is all too real. Too often, a top sales executive, his sales management team, or both significantly underestimate the time and effort required to plan and manage the transition to a new compensation plan designed to support new sales roles. Or worse, shocked by the reaction, they reverse the change they have announced and the company goes back to the former compensation plan, even though that plan does not support the new sales roles, which remain in effect. Consider this situation, which is also real but disguised.

The CEO of a major electronics company told us that a couple of years ago the company undertook an extensive study of its profitability. One conclusion was that the sales organization, both field and inside sales staff, was not selling the most profitable mix of business. So the management made changes. The firm developed new sales processes and defined new jobs. The company designed and announced new pay plans. Shortly thereafter, salespeople began leaving; in fact, they quit at such a rate that after three months top management had a crisis in confidence over the changes they had made. Finally, as the CEO portrayed it to us, "We caved. We announced we were going back to the old commission plan."

This CEO told us that he has always regretted that decision for two reasons. First, the company made the change back to the old plan after many excellent salespeople had left (the best are always the first to leave; they know what companies value their services), so the firm had already lost people who would have stayed under the former plan. Second, by the time management reversed course, some of the salespeople had begun to figure out what they had to do differently in their new sales roles and were actually beginning to turn in exactly the results the company had hoped they would. Those sales representatives were surprised, disappointed, and demoralized when the company shifted back to the old plan.

These situations are not unusual, and managers are likely to repeat them. To prevent such disasters, top managers must carefully consider the transition challenges associated with implementing new compensation plans to support new sales roles. The purpose of this chapter is to provide a blueprint for implementing a compensation plan so that you do not fall victim to situations similar to those we've just described.

THREE HURDLES TO IMPLEMENTING NEW SALES COMPENSATION PLANS

Our experience suggests that top managers must clear three hurdles when they implement a new sales compensation plan to support new sales roles:

- Resistance to the new sales roles
- Lack of frontline sales managers' support for change
- Objections to the new compensation strategy and plan

How to overcome these hurdles is best understood in the context of what is required for successful change management. Understanding those requirements makes it easier to anticipate the types of difficulties that often arise when you do something new or for the first time with the sales compensation plan.

Frontline managers usually understand that the company must cope with marketplace realities. Yet they and their top managers often miscalculate what it takes to bring about change. In general, managers make two assumptions about change. The first is a financial consideration: the notion that creating and implementing new programs will favorably alter the company's direction and thereby improve financial results. The second assumption is that employee behavior will be altered by changing a company's formal structure (including jobs and job definitions) and its management systems (including, of course, compensation programs). Research suggests that neither of these assumptions is fully valid. In fact, it has been reported that approximately 20 percent of the people in an organization will be change-friendly, 50 percent will be "fence sitters," and 30 percent will resist or deliberately try to make the change initiative fail.[1]

With that in mind, what does it take to successfully overcome the obstacles to implementing a new sales compensation plan? Let's look at the three hurdles.

Resistance to New Sales Roles

In our experience, employees resist assignment to jobs involving a new sales role for one or more of three main reasons: First, the sales role added to their job is not what they signed on for when they joined the company. A good example of this is a customer service job where the company adds up-selling or cross-selling to current responsibilities. The response from people in the job can be what many such employees have told us, "If I wanted to sell, I would have signed up for a sales representative job."

Second, employees may lack the skills, experience, or confidence to perform successfully in a job involving a new sales role. Service technicians whom the company has asked to be retention specialists in the selling process are a good example of this. Their skills and experience focus on keeping equipment up and running, not keeping and expanding business with the customers. These technicians are frequently very uncomfortable in anything that resembles a sales role.

Third, implied by any addition or subtraction of responsibility is a change in compensation, which many employees feel will have only negative consequences for them.

To overcome these obstacles, companies needs to do three things: First, provide advance orientation about the new roles and the implications for compensation to allay the very real and reasonable fears that people in new roles will have. Second, have a defined development plan ready to roll out to ensure that a formal process is in place for people to acquire the skills and experience they will need to be successful in their new role(s). Third, allow sufficient time for the change to be internalized and, therefore, reflected in the behavior of employees assigned to new sales roles. Employees in new roles need time to become comfortable with and effective in their new roles. Depending upon the magnitude of the change, a person may require three months to one full year to acquire competency in the work related to the new sales role. Thus, an attitude of "It's just like the last time we changed the plan" may not be true when new sales roles are involved.

Lack of Frontline Sales Managers' Support for Change

One reason frontline managers do not support change in either sales roles, the compensation plan, or both is because they were not invited into the change design process. It is human nature to resist something you do not understand or do not believe will benefit you. If you do not involve frontline managers in the compensation plan change process, it increases the likelihood that the salespeople who report to these managers will not view the plan favorably. After all, sales and other customer contact employees look to their immediate manager for guidance and counsel when doing their job. This relationship extends to the compensation plan. If a frontline manager tells his people he does not think the new plan is a good one (a not uncommon situation, unfortunately), our experience shows that the manager's attitude will have a significant and negative impact on the salespeople.

You can avoid this potential roadblock early in the process of designing and implementing new roles and new compensation plans. The most straightforward strategy is to involve respected frontline managers in the design process as ad hoc design team members. In most organizations, there's a "Joe," as in "If Joe says it's okay, it must be the right thing to do." As one executive told us, "It's better to have the Joe's of our organization in the tent so we can see each other." A note of caution: This approach works well if the new role and new plan are sales roles; it does not work well if a frontline manager is asked to help redesign the frontline management job and compensation program.

If the company does not include frontline management in the design process, the most important consideration for implementation is taking the time to train the trainers in the new plan, based on the new roles for which they will be responsible. Meeting with management far in advance of full roll-out is critical, since managers are likely to have questions and observations about the plan that need to be addressed before it is introduced to the salespeople.

OBJECTIONS TO THE NEW COMPENSATION PLAN

Changes in compensation are among the most difficult changes a company can make in its sales and customer contact operations. The longer the current plan has been in place, the more difficult it is to make substantive changes to it or to replace it with a completely new plan.

Recently, we worked with two large companies, both of which made the change from commission compensation plans to salary plus incentive (bonus) plans. In both corporations, the change took twice as long as top managers had expected. They thought the change could be planned and implemented within six months, at the beginning of a new fiscal year. In fact, the new plans were not fully implemented until, on average, fourteen months after the first meetings held to design the new plans. The reason: objections to paying the sales staff differently and to the implications of the changes all the way up the line for managers, both in the field and at the headquarters.

The most common objections to any new compensation plan generally fall into one or more of these categories:

Cash flow. Organizations that have had biweekly or monthly commission payments find that "base plus" does not generally meet the cash flow requirements of experienced salespeople. They are used to paying their bills one way and do not want to change.

"Compensation control." Any change in the way that people are paid frequently results in concerns about "compensation control and reduction." They assume that the company is making the change only to cut expenses by slashing employee earnings. This is certainly true of plans that are designed to support new sales roles. As one executive told us, "They honestly believed that this whole sales reinvention project was the company's ploy to reduce pay."

Performance measures. It is critical that salespeople believe in the company's approach to performance measurement. You must explain quotas or new success measures as clearly and in as much detail as the incentive formula requires to gain credibility with the sales organization. It is, perhaps, the company's most important internal marketing job.

Ultimately, however, experience with the new program overcomes the objections, and the results the new roles were designed to bring to the company begin to flow in. We have learned over the years that changing from a current to a new sales compensation plan is hard work. We believe that work can be attacked in a logical and orderly fashion and, at times, be made easier if you have a blueprint to follow for making the changes. What follows is a process we suggest companies use to successfully make that change.

THE CHANGE MANAGEMENT MODEL: A FOUR-STEP PROCESS

The thought of change in any aspect of sales compensation is daunting to most salespeople. It is a good idea, therefore, to use a change management model to guide your planning and decision-making tasks related to the change. There are many, many change management models available to top managers. A simple one and one we find relatively easy

Fig. 12-1. Change management model.

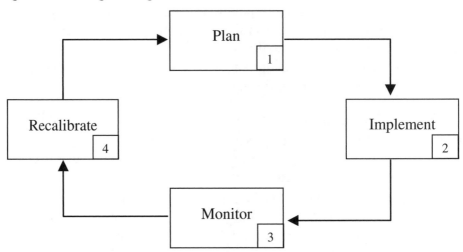

to use with sales organizations is the four-element model shown in Figure 12-1. Managing change is like assembling a jigsaw puzzle; the pieces must come together in the right way. The objectives of this basic change model, as it pertains to introducing a new sales compensation plan, are to help you:

- Define specific changes and accountabilities.
- Explain why change is important now.
- Provide a framework for guiding the change process.
- Determine whether desired benefits and improvements are being achieved.
- Provide feedback to work associates who need to remain "in the know" about change results.

A definition for each of the four elements in this model follows.

STEP 1: PLAN

A change from a current compensation plan to a new sales compensation plan requires a "plan" to guide that change. While this sounds obvious, over half the companies we come in contact with do not have a carefully mapped out plan for how the change is going to take place. The plan should include a clear vision and rationale for the change. For example, top managers ought to state clearly:

- What will change
- Why change is important

- How change will benefit the customers, the salespeople, and the company

The plan should also designate change leaders—people in the company dedicated to guiding and participating in the change to a new sales compensation plan. There must, of course, be enough change leaders and they must come from appropriate levels in the organization.

STEP 2: IMPLEMENT

To effectively introduce a new sales compensation plan, it is essential not only that the right people lead the change but also that other managers they work with have all the support materials they require for the change. This includes the leadership message from top management with the rationale for the change, the materials to teach frontline managers how to work with the new sales compensation plan, and the communications to announce the plan to the employees covered. The material must address not only the new plan, but also the new jobs that are driving the need for change. The message really brings all decisions full circle so that the audience understands the reasons for changes in jobs, what the new jobs look like, and how performance will be measured, as well as why and how the compensation plan has changed.

STEP 3: MONITOR

Too many companies do a terrible job of monitoring the results of change initiatives, and a change to a new sales compensation plan is no exception. The comment of one director of sales administration sums up how too many companies view this change. He told us, "I'm glad to be done with the redesign and implementation of the new sales compensation plan. I put all my files away, and I'm now on to the next project." When members of the headquarters sales staff view compensation as a project or an event and not a critical process of effective implementation and ongoing, effective management, companies miss the opportunity to sustain or enhance their competitive marketplace position.

In the context of the change process shown in Figure 12-1, you should do two things so that you do not fail to realize the benefits of monitoring a plan change in your company. First, establish clear measures of success and communicate them to the individuals responsible for managing the transition. To begin with, one purpose of a new sales compensation plan is to motivate, direct, and reward the results management expects from the new role. We often ask top managers, "What

behavior and results are you not now obtaining that you expect to realize with the new sales role after you launch the new compensation
plan?'' The answer to that question is a good place to start when thinking
about success measures for your company's new plan.

Second, once you are clear about the new compensation plan's success measures, you should set a specific time period over which results
will be tracked. Generally speaking, we observe that companies wait too
long to check on the results of a plan change. For example, the top sales
executive in a consumer products company told us that eight months
after the company had trained the salespeople in their new roles and
changed their compensation, management discovered that the sales
staff did not understand the new plan. Because it was an annual plan
with a midyear payout, and the first payment did not take place until
two months after the midyear close, salespeople did not appreciate how
much they were earning until the company distributed the first payment
checks.

Once they had their checks in hand, the salespeople were able to
see exactly how the company calculated their incentive pay. Up to that
point, many of them had adopted a wait-and-see attitude about how the
plan was going to pay out, which is what salespeople told us when we
interviewed them about the situation. That point alone startled us. A
major reason to change a compensation plan is to redirect behavior
based on the new role(s) and management expectations for business
results. If salespeople adopt a wait-and-see attitude about a new plan,
clearly the company has missed an opportunity for performance improvement.

STEP 4: RECALIBRATE

In the rush to implement change, companies often underestimate the
number of details that require attention. This is particularly true when
it comes to paying salespeople or paying others who for the first time
are being paid under a sales compensation plan. Because this is inevitable, it is essential that you quickly modify or correct any shortcomings
or omissions identified in step 3.

With this overview in mind, let's move to the more detailed aspects of
each step of the blueprint for introducing a new sales compensation
plan.

STEP 1: PREPARE TO LAUNCH THE NEW PLAN

Companies with successful sales compensation plans invest a significant amount of time and effort in implementation. Regardless of the size of the organization—10 or 10,000 salespeople—the launch of the new plan succeeds in direct proportion to the quality of planning and preparation of both the materials and the managers involved in the change. An effective implementation plan includes taking positive action on the following tasks:

APPOINTING A PROCESS LEADER FOR THE CHANGE

Change requires a leader, and implementing a new sales compensation plan to support new sales roles is no exception. Effectively implementing a sales compensation plan requires coordination, commitment, and competencies. Typically, the change involves many functions—sales, marketing, finance, human resources, MIS—and therefore close coordination of their activities must be assigned to a process leader. Commitment on the part of top managers is essential to new plan success. Commitment in this case means, "staying the course for the change." As we reported at the beginning of this chapter, at least one CEO found that reversing one's decision on the change is something one may regret. Finally, people often require new competencies (as we will explain later in this chapter) to successfully implement a new sales compensation plan. Someone must be charged with the responsibility for seeing that people develop those new competencies. For these and other reasons, the likelihood of successfully implementing a new sales compensation plan is materially increased by appointing a top manager to the temporary position of process leader for the change.

Typically, the process leader is not the top sales executive, but is either a trusted advisor to him (or her) or a member of his immediate management staff. Often, the process leader has been either the leader or a member of the design team for the new plan, as described in Chapter 4. The process leader is responsible for assuring the top sales executive that all aspects of the change blueprint have been thoroughly and effectively executed. An implementation team, not unlike the design team Chapter 4 outlined, often assists the process leader.

ASSESSING THE DEGREE OF COMPENSATION CHANGE THAT MUST BE PLANNED FOR

One of the process leader's first tasks is to determine the degree of change that must be planned for and managed relative to the new sales compensation plan. The degree of change in the sales compensation plan determines the amount of time and effort required to launch a new plan successfully. Table 12-1 provides a useful reference frame to help you understand the change continuum that pertains to a sales compensation plan. As the table illustrates, new sales roles generally require at least moderate tactical changes, and major strategic changes are typical.

DEFINING THE PAY CONVERSION METHOD USED

The next issue that the process leader and the implementation team must address is the method the company will use to convert employees from the former program to the new one. Here are some of the techniques they can evaluate:

"Cold cut." The company summarily "turns the switch" and changes to a new program—generally *not* the most useful approach during a time of significant change.

Parallel testing. Businesses frequently use parallel testing to illustrate to both internal and field employees that the new plan works and is a fair way to reward performance in the new role. It generally includes a "better of" guarantee of payout during the parallel test period (that is, people who had been paid under the old plan will be paid the "better of" the two payouts calculated under the old and the new plan for a short time). While employees generally perceive this approach positively, it will probably not result in new behaviors until the firm completes a full transition.

Phase in. This technique may be used to gradually make the transition to a new plan, and frequently includes some type of guarantee for the initial payout periods of the plan. It generally works well, as manag-

Table 12-1. Degree of change determines time and effort required.

	Degree of Change		
	Minor *"Tweak"*	*Moderate* *"Tactical"*	*Major* *"Strategic"*
Eligibility	No change	Add jobs	New rules
Target compensation	Increase	Realign	New structure
Mix	Small change	Realign	New concept
Performance measures	No change	Add/drop by job	New measurement system
Formula	Quota change	Modify payout rates	New method

ers encourage new behaviors and do not penalize the old, while they groom employees for success in their new roles.

PREPARING PERFORMANCE SCENARIO MODELS TO ESTIMATE PRODUCTIVITY AND COST OUTCOMES

You should prepare a computer model in either a spreadsheet or database application that provides senior management with potential costs and productivity expectations. The model may be the same one that you develop for cost modeling prior to plan approval, and it should have the flexibility to run multiple performance scenarios. These models are useful throughout the implementation of new plans, as they help set a benchmark for expectations of performance and what the company expects to pay for that performance.

DESCRIBING THE IMPLEMENTATION SCHEDULE

Based on the transition strategy the company has developed to introduce both the new sales roles and the new compensation program, you must develop a time line to ensure that meetings are planned and scheduled, materials can be prepared to support the implementation, and management is available throughout the process. Typically, implementation consists of at least the following steps:

- Implementation planning
- Materials design
- Meeting planning
- Materials production
- Rehearsals and systems validation
- Materials review
- Training the trainers
- Employee communications

Plan brochures, calculation sheets, and other materials can be used as supplements or as the key materials used to communicate the plan. However, terms and conditions, as well as definitions, should be assembled into one document. Therefore, formal plan documentation should be completed at this time. An example is included as Appendix B.

STEP 2: IMPLEMENT THE NEW SALES COMPENSATION PLAN

Once you have completed preparations for launching the new sales compensation plan, you are ready to proceed with the actual implementation, which has three important activities.

Deliver a Leadership Message to the Sales Organization about the Rationale for and Benefits of the New Plan

Communication is the most important aspect of the implementation of a new sales compensation plan. Too frequently, top managers jump right into a discussion of the new plan—its elements, how it works, and its benefits—assuming that the employees affected by the plan understand why a change is required. For most people, pay is a very emotional subject. Salespeople and other employees in new sales roles are no exception. Thus, the right place to start the communication process is with a leadership message built on a theme of why change is required and the benefits the company expects from the change, benefits for both customers and employees.

We observe that the top sales executive or the general manager of the business undergoing a change in sales compensation usually prepares the leadership message. There are many ways to approach this leadership message. Executives can formulate a leadership message by organizing their comments around the following four key topics:

Disconnect from the past. Provide your sales staff with information that shows that the old compensation program was not meeting customer needs, employee needs, or the business's needs, which is why there are new sales roles in the first place.

Provide a "statement of the future." Say to your sales team, "We require new compensation solutions for the future," solutions that are consistent with the new sales roles designed to stay ahead of competitive challenges.

Show appreciation. Congratulate your sales staff for past achievements; "Thank you for your efforts and your successes. . . ."

Issue a call for volunteers. Tell the sales team, "We have the best solutions for interacting with customers—now and in the future—reflected in our new roles; our new sales compensation plan supports that direction; we will continue to win. Can you meet the challenge of the new environment and thus benefit from the rewards available under the new plan?"

We have heard many sales executives adopt this approach to their leadership with positive results. Here is an example of one such message that was well received by the sales team of an industrial manufacturing equipment company:

> *Our past sales compensation plan:* We've had a great compensation program over the years. It has helped us attract and

retain talented people and grow the business profitably. Our commitment to our customers, our shareholders, and you requires frequent and regular examination of that plan to confirm that it continues to be appropriate for our business—to help us reach both financial and human resources goals.

Current business reality: You—our sales and customer contact people—know that the business is changing. You experience it every day. Competitors are more aggressive in going after our customers with promises of better services, better prices, and so forth. Our approach to meeting and exceeding our customers' expectations for doing business requires new processes for selling and interacting with them after the sale is closed. More and more people in our company are involved in those sales and customer relationship management processes. Our former compensation plan was designed at a time when these business realities were not as urgent as they are today. Our philosophy is to reward top performance; however, to do so, the techniques and mechanics we use must be consistent with business objectives, sales strategies, and the new sales roles we are implementing.

Your concerns: We have talked with a great many of you during the process of designing our new sales compensation plan. We know you have concerns about how this new plan will affect you: Will you be paid less? Can you affect the new performance measures we are including in this year's plan? Will your goals be reasonable? Will incentive checks come out on time? We considered these and many other questions when preparing the new plan for its rollout to you. Our goal is to continue to be an organization of winners; winning means that our people have the opportunity to be rewarded for their performance contributions. The new plan is not designed either to limit participation or to reduce the opportunity for incentive earnings. I think you will see that you will have to put forth a different level and type of performance in the new year; our goals are higher, and the mix of business required is much more specific. However, the opportunity to earn is comparable to last year's if you produce the results we expect and know you can attain.

Disconnecting from the past compensation plan, putting the business realities into the proper perspective, and addressing the concerns that salespeople are likely to be worrying over are the three most important things top managers can do in delivering a leadership message about plan change. In any change, people are likely to expect the worst. This is especially true of salespeople, many of whom have had unfavorable experiences with compensation plan changes over the years. The best approach, therefore, is to use the leadership message to address the hard issues—the ones you know are on their minds.

TRAIN FRONTLINE MANAGERS TO COMMUNICATE AND MANAGE EFFECTIVELY WITH THE NEW SALES COMPENSATION PLAN

We ask participants at our seminars the following question: "Does your company have a training course for frontline managers on how to manage with a sales incentive plan?" If the audience is predominantly sales and customer service managers (rather than human resources or compensation managers), we ask this follow-on question: "How many of you have been trained in how to manage with your company's sales compensation plan?" The percentage of positive responses to these two questions is alarmingly low. On average, about half of the companies have a program, and only about four of ten participants indicate they have had some formal training in how to manage effectively with the sales compensation plan.

Why is it surprising that these responses are so low? Two reasons: First, compensation cost as a percentage of total annual revenue ranges from a low of 2 percent to a high of 20 percent in some industries. At the high end, this can be a very significant cost for a company. Particularly during the first year in which the company implements new sales roles, the cost of sales may spike due to new processes and measurements. Rather than view compensation as simply a line item in the cost-of-sales calculation, it is more helpful to view the money spent as an investment in a critical resource. Many companies today treat the customer as an asset, as valuable as proprietary processes, patents, or brand equity. We can think of no better investment in the "customer asset" than compensation to the sales and service people who are in regular contact with those assets.

A financial services company told us that it was spending $50 million a year on sales incentives, both variable pay and recognition events. At the time, the company had no formal training for its frontline managers in how to manage with its programs. A year later, executives from the company attended one of our conferences. They told us they had taken our suggestion; they implemented a training program designed to educate frontline managers in the effective use of the sales compensation plan. The company had already realized two benefits from the training: (1) The pressure to change the plan when something was not going right with the business materially declined. This happened because managers and their people developed a better understanding of how the plan worked, recognizing that business shortfalls could not always be addressed by changing the compensation plan. (2) The performance distribution improved. A larger percentage of the sales staff actually achieved or exceeded their sales goals because as part of the training program managers were taught how to set those goals.

The second reason it is important to train frontline managers in how to manage with the sales compensation plan, particularly when new sales roles or jobs are involved, is that managers must be equipped to explain and defend how the plan works to their people. Managers, by the nature of the relationship, are role models for their people. Salespeople look to their manager for advice and counsel about how to be successful in their job and their career with the company. The frontline manager's attitudes and opinions about the company and its programs carry considerable weight with salespeople and other customer contact personnel. Our studies show a strong positive correlation between the managers' attitudes about role definition and a compensation plan, and the attitudes of the sales staff. Managers who support a new sales compensation plan and can show their people how to "win" under the plan generally have people who also favor the plan and have figured out how to perform to achieve high earnings. Conversely, managers who do not support the plan, cannot explain it to their people, and do not know how to sell to "win" under the plan have people working for them who underachieve the compensation opportunity available in the plan. Table 12-2 provides an outline of what to include in frontline manager training for how to manage with the new sales compensation plan.

COMMUNICATE THE NEW COMPENSATION PLAN TO EMPLOYEES

Talking with employees about a new sales compensation plan is, without doubt, the most challenging aspect of the implementation process. This is true because any change in an employee's pay goes to the very heart of the need for security. A change in how pay is earned and delivered will affect the employee's cash flow, and that concern is uppermost in salespeople's minds when they are listening to messages (speeches, company videos, small group meetings) about how the company plans to change their sales pay.

Table 12-2. Frontline manager training in "how to manage with a new sales compensation plan."

Topic	Time	Session Leader	Description
Introduction: Our Sales Strategy and Rationale for New Sales Roles	30–45 minutes	Vice president of sales	Philosophy Concepts Overview of the day
Description of New Roles, Responsibili- ties, and Organization Relationships	45–60 minutes	Sales management	Role definitions Performance expectations Processes for working to- gether
Company Compensation Philosophy	15 minutes	Human resources	Terminology Concepts
Incentive Compensation	30 minutes	Human resources	Terminology Concepts
New Sales Compensa- tion Plan: Overview	15 minutes	Sales management	Objectives Components Formula/mechanics
Performance Elements	45 minutes	Sales administra- tion	Formula and mechanics Reports and documenta- tion
Putting the Whole Pro- gram Together	45–60 minutes	Sales administra- tion and sales management	Illustrations
Skill Practices—Case Study, Working with New Roles, Using New Measures, Determin- ing Total Payout	60 minutes	Human resources, sales administra- tion, and sales management	
Implementation Over- view	30 minutes	Vice president of sales	Roles and responsibilities Time line

For this reason, we encourage top executives to go beyond the typi-cal communication brochure, plan description documents, memos, or other written communications such as announcements in the sales or-ganization newsletter to involve frontline managers in the communica-tion process.

Figure 12-2 is a simple checklist that all companies should be able to complete, based on providing employees with sufficient knowledge to understand, work with, and respond to the new plan positively.

STEP 3: MONITOR EMPLOYEE REACTION AND BUSINESS RESULTS

We pointed out earlier that companies often wait too long to gauge the success of a newly implemented sales compensation plan. While it is

Fig. 12-2.   Sales incentive plan communication and manager training.

Effectiveness Checklist: Successful companies prepare their managers to:

☐   Understand and communicate why the incentive plans are changing

☐   Deliver the leadership message: (1) need for change; (2) expected changes in behavior; and (3) commitment to change

☐   Support program implementation through an in-depth understanding of all changes

☐   Respond effectively to questions on the new plans

☐   Complete assignment of performance measures and quotas

☐   Use the incentive plan to communicate sales priorities through the collaborative development of strategic sales objectives

☐   Direct behavior in line with business objectives

Effectiveness Checklist: Successful companies prepare sales and support personnel to:

☐   Understand why the incentive plans are changing

☐   Understand how their pay will be structured under the new incentive plan

☐   Direct their time and sales initiatives in accordance with business priorities

☐   Understand where team sales initiatives are appropriate and how their performance will be measured

---

true that it requires at least one full calendar (or fiscal) quarter before you can assess a new plan's financial impact, you can gauge the plan's motivational and behavioral impact much sooner. Within the first month after the company introduces a new plan, you should gather answers to the following questions:

- Do affected employees understand the new plan?
- Is the plan working; that is, is it directing the types of behavior that it was designed to motivate and direct?
- What continued or new actions are required to ensure that the plan helps frontline management accomplish the business objectives the plan was designed to reward?

To answer these questions, a formal approach to assessment is important. Implementation planning includes developing a tool to assess the effectiveness of implementation, as well as assessing the results that the new plan has produced. While we will discuss this in more detail in chapter 13, the critical elements are:

- An employee assessment tool, for example, an e-mail or postcard survey of employee understanding of the plan
- An analytical framework for reviewing financial results
- Ongoing review and discussion with frontline management

STEP 4: RECALIBRATE—RESOLVE ANY GLITCHES QUICKLY

No matter how well prepared managers are for launching a new sales compensation plan, some glitches always arise. The larger the sales organization or the change, the more likely it is that you will run into some unanticipated issues. It is important to respond quickly to these issues when they surface. With that in mind, we suggest to top managers that they first understand what type of glitch they are dealing with. This is helpful in determining both the resources required to resolve the problem and the time it is likely to take to fix it.

Two types of issues can come up unexpectedly during the implementation process and require a recalibration. The two broad categories of implementation issues you should be on the lookout for are plan design changes and communication and plan administration modifications. Plan design changes include exactly what is implied: The plan is being rolled out, and you discover a flaw in a key feature. Most common in our experience is a flaw in some aspect of the sales incentive compensation formula. Examples include (1) too much weight assigned to a performance measure that salespeople do not affect in their new sales role (e.g., gross profit for a sales job with no pricing authority); (2) too much weight assigned to qualitative performance measures, with the consequence that salespeople perceive that incentive pay determination is highly subjective; or (3) the incentive formula proves to be too complicated and the firm cannot determine incentive payouts.

It is unusual that a company does not discover design flaws of this magnitude until the plan is being rolled out. Sometimes a company's inexperience with either a new sales role or a particular performance measure that it is using for the first time is the reason why it missed the flaw during the design process. An example: A semiconductor manufacturer believed that a critical success factor for a new inside sales role was on-time product delivery. The measure was designed into the plan for the new role, because the company insisted, "There is nothing we can't measure." As implementation time approached, however, a sales analyst brought the design team's attention to a serious flaw in the measure: The inside salesperson could change the promised delivery date at will.

While hypothetically this was critical to reliable knowledge of schedule changes, it created a tool that could be too easily manipulated by the employee whose pay would be based on the results. The manufacturer delayed introducing the measure until the "promised delivery date" entry field could be programmed to accept only management changes.

Issues related to communication and plan administration are much more common, and we advise top managers that rarely can they expect every aspect of change in these areas to go smoothly. Some of the most common problems that arise include:

Things that aren't clear. For example, new performance measures were implemented, but sales crediting related to these measures has not been defined. The salespeople misunderstand the incentive formula mechanics; the most common problem when calculation involves multiple steps. Quotas appear too high, which means salespeople either misunderstood or are challenging the process by which they were set. Salespeople have many questions about the plan but they cannot get straight answers; no "hot line" is available for their inquiries.

Systems that aren't working. For example, sales results are late, incomplete, or inaccurate, and therefore salespeople and their frontline managers spend a great deal of time trying to sort out results and the implication for incentive payment under the new plan. Incentive payouts are delayed either because sufficient time was not allowed to reprogram systems to make incentive payments or because there are problems in tracking and crediting sales results.

SUMMING UP

Top managers must clear three hurdles when they implement a new sales compensation plan to support new sales roles: the resistance to the new sales roles, lack of frontline sales managers' support for change, and salespeople's objections to the new compensation strategy and plan. Unfortunately, executives often assume that creating and implementing new programs will favorably alter the company's direction and improve financial results. They also assume that changing jobs and job definitions and management systems—including compensation programs—will alter employee behavior. While this may be true for some people, it is not generally the case.

Joe Bates could have avoided the situation described at the beginning of this chapter if he had focused on the change management activities well in advance of the national meeting. For example, at the outset of the sales effectiveness project that ultimately led to new sales roles and the need for a new compensation plan, Bates should have challenged his sales management team with this question: "What needs to be done to prepare our people—at all levels—for change in how we do business?"

Even though Bates and his sales staff at that point may not have known the specific details of the change, they could have begun to lay the groundwork for receptivity to change. For example, with frontline sales managers, Bates and his sales staff could have focused on the importance of improving "top-to-bottom" sales planning and, as a critical step in that process, begun work with field managers on how to improve sales quota allocations to salespeople. Next, long before a new sales compensation plan was completed, Bates and his staff could have talked with managers about possible changes.

He had at least two choices of how to prepare the entire organization for that change. One approach could have been to communicate that a change was coming and provide an overall description of the change. Managers are naturally afraid that when employees learn of this, they will begin making their plans to leave the organization. Our experience is quite the contrary. Employees, particularly sales and other customer contact personnel, leave for green pastures when change is sprung on them and there appears to be little or no opportunity to "win," not when the company openly and honestly shares as much as it can about what will affect the employees.

Another approach Bates could have taken was to implement a "pilot project" involving all dimensions of new sales roles and the compensation in one area of the business. This provides the opportunity to fine-tune details associated with the change. It also communicates to the rest of the organization what the future could look like in terms of new sales roles and the compensation plan.

The point is this: Bates and his sales management staff should never have arrived at the national sales meeting to learn what the frontline managers and sales personnel told them. That information should have come out well in advance of the meeting so that Bates and his top managers could deal with the more positive aspects of the change, namely, how the changes in sales roles and compensation would complement efforts to compete and win in the market. Although Bates now finds himself in a difficult situation, it can be turned around. The way to do so is to use the change management model and tools we have described in this chapter. Specifically, Bates could follow the advice that we provide to top managers.

To overcome employee resistance to change, therefore, the company should provide advance orientation about the new roles and the implications for compensation to allay the very real and reasonable fears that people in new roles will have. It should have a defined development plan ready to roll out to ensure that a formal process is in place for people to acquire the skills and experience they will need to be successful in their new role(s). And it must make enough time for the change to take hold.

To obtain frontline manager support, involve respected managers in the design process as ad hoc design team members. If your company does not use frontline management during the design process, it must take the time to train the trainers in the new roles for which they will be responsible.

To overcome entirely natural employee fears that a new compensation plan will slash their pay, top management must define specific changes and accountabilities, explain why change is important now, provide a framework for guiding the change process, determine whether desired benefits and improvements are being achieved, and provide feedback to associates who need to remain "in the know" about change results. The company requires a process leader who, ideally, is a senior executive appointed to the temporary position to lead the change.

It is critical to monitor the results of change initiatives, something that most companies do not do well. They wait too long and small oversights become large problems. Without monitoring the change process and promptly adjusting for unforeseen flaws and unintended consequences, any success is more a matter of luck than managerial ability.

Once you have designed and instituted a new sales compensation plan, the next step is to evaluate the results.

EVALUATING RESULTS UNDER A NEW SALES COMPENSATION PLAN

A large, well-known telecommunications company designed and implemented a new sales compensation plan to support its new customer-oriented field organization. As top managers described their experience with compensation plan design to us, it appeared that they had been very particular at every step in the process they used. It sounded like a model for a best-practices initiative. After two fiscal quarters of operating under the plan, however, the company was not reaching its business objectives. Concerned that it might have missed something in plan design or implementation, management ordered up a complete evaluation of the new plan. Virtually everything was analyzed over a period of about four weeks; no stone was left unturned as the sales staff and their counterparts in the finance department graphed results and correlated numerous variables. When the staffs had exhausted the time allotted for this examination, they still were not sure they actually knew why the new compensation plan was not "working" or if, in fact, it was even the problem. That was because they were not exactly sure what they were looking for. Was it right to compare current results to past business performance and compensation payouts? Or were other comparisons more appropriate?

   This situation—in particular, the question of what to evaluate and how to make comparisons between current and past results—is the final stage of the journey toward putting in place a successful sales compensation plan to support new sales roles. No sales compensation plan can be judged a success until you have evaluated whether it is truly achieving the goals you've set for it. The results you want from a new sales compensation plan depend on the objectives you intend to achieve with the new sales roles implemented at your company. Those objectives are, of course, unique to each business. Our experience shows, however, that across industries, senior executives focus on three areas when they evaluate results. This chapter explores those three areas and provides suggestions of what results to assess and how to interpret information related to them.

THREE KEY AREAS TO EXAMINE FOR RESULTS

When evaluating results under a new compensation plan, top managers focus on customers, internal financial results (costs, productivity, and profitability), and employees. At the outset of this chapter, although the areas may seem self-evident, we believe it is helpful to describe exactly why these are important topics to examine after the business has implemented a new sales compensation plan.

CUSTOMERS

Successful companies know how to retain valuable customers, increase sales to existing customers, convert competitor accounts, and sell into new markets. To sustain and enhance their competencies in doing this, these companies create and implement new sales roles. As we have described in previous chapters, the compensation plan must be aligned with the new sales roles so that a company can benefit from the change. Since in many situations customers are the motivating factor for doing business differently or more effectively, it is not surprising that most senior executives are quite interested in the compensation plan's contribution to improved results with customers.

Generally speaking, executives ask about two areas involving customers when they review a new compensation plan's effectiveness. Those are (1) revenue growth and (2) product placement. Top managers expect the sales compensation plan will help them generate revenue growth by realizing more volume from existing customers and new volume from new customers. We have never seen a sales compensation plan, particularly one designed for new sales roles, that does not emphasize the importance of volume growth. Even when companies introduce new sales roles to help enhance sales profitability overall or on an individual account basis, most strive for growth. This is because many companies look to volume growth as an indication of their capability to make the market bigger, gain market share, or both. Also, top managers currently have a great deal of interest in revenue growth. Demonstrating that the company knows how to grow indicates that the firm is contemporary, keeping in step with what investors are looking for. Thus, plan designers can be reasonably confident that top management will be asking how the new sales compensation plan contributes to that goal.

Product placement means two things in the context of a new sales compensation plan. First, the plan motivates and rewards the sales or customer contact person for retaining and growing the company's core business. The core business typically includes current or in-line products and services. As we pointed out in Chapter 5, it is very difficult for a company to achieve double-digit growth—the expectation in many investor circles—if it does not retain and expand its business with current customers. The influence of the new sales compensation plan in contributing to that goal must therefore be clear.

Second, the plan should motivate and reward salespeople for successfully selling new products or services—often the most difficult and challenging type of selling. The successful sale of new products fuels growth. Many companies have a stated objective to achieve 20 to 40 percent of their long-term revenue growth from successfully developing and introducing new products. In fact, we believe that the best way a company can retain its current customers is by continually offering new products and services. A senior officer at one of our clients, one of *Fortune*'s ten best-managed companies, tells his people, "The way we retain and grow our business is by selling more to our customers, because, when they buy more, that's the ultimate indicator of loyalty and satisfaction." Thus, programs designed to motivate and reward employees, particularly a new sales compensation plan, are essential to realizing growth objectives through new product sales.

COSTS, PRODUCTIVITY, AND PROFITABILITY

Managers frequently perceive implementing new sales roles as costly in the short run, and their companies must offset this cost with improved productivity. Successful companies know how to manage costs and improve productivity so they continuously increase their profitability. A new sales compensation plan should play a critical role in helping a company do all three.

Some companies' goal is to achieve a lower cost per order dollar in their sales transactions with customers. Paper distributors are a good example. They operate in a mature market with average gross margins in the range of 17 to 21 percent. Compensation costs average 20 percent of gross profit. One distributor client found itself plagued with declining profit; the gross profit had grown while net profit mysteriously dropped. When we were called in to examine the situation, we found that the sales representatives had been concentrating on small orders. It is easier to sell small orders, often to smaller accounts, than to sell to larger accounts where the sales cycle is longer. Larger accounts, however, have lower service and processing costs relative to the sale total. The growth in small orders drives up a distributor's overhead faster than the increase in gross profit, thus depressing the net profit margin. Redefining the sales and service process so that outside sales representatives focus only on large accounts—a new sales role for many distributors—and replacing commission-based compensation that the distributor paid solely on gross revenue with a salary plus bonus plan that linked gross profit and order size helped this distributor achieve a lower cost per order.

Improving sales productivity is another way to increase profits. Essentially, this means achieving a better sales return on your compensation and other selling expenses. Three years ago, a major computer company expected an $80,000-a-year salesperson to book $1.5 million in business. Today, for that same earnings level (which is the company average), to be price competitive and to maintain an acceptable profit level, the company expects account executives to book twice as much business as they did three years ago. While these account executives have a new sales role—they only focus on large, named accounts—top managers in the company determined that to achieve its profit goals it was absolutely essential to sell more with the current base of resources. They had no choice but to systematically increase productivity.

EMPLOYEES

Finally, successful companies know how to attract, retain, and motivate sales and customer contact personnel so that they meet or exceed customer expectations. Many factors affect the company's ability to do so, including labor market pay practices, job requirements, and the support programs the company has put in place to support management's objectives. A key management tool is the sales compensation plan; it both motivates customer contact people to stretch and rewards the ones who do so successfully. Thus, it is important to take a careful reading among all employees affected by a new sales compensation plan to understand how they feel about its influence on them.

A new sales compensation plan is the visible sign from the company that it is serious about its programs to support new sales roles. In a competitive job market, the compensation plan frequently signals to candidates that working for the company in a new role is a desirable career move. Companies that have implemented new roles often find that there is some "bidding up" going on in the market for talented people who are equipped to balance the new job requirements with customer expectations. Senior management's demand that the company develop a compensation program to attract and retain talented personnel is never truer than when the firm is implementing new sales roles.

We find that the sales compensation program, by its nature—and especially when the incentive portion is at-risk pay—serves as a tool for companies to sort out the employees who will thrive in a new sales role from those who will not. Most people successful in selling have the ability to take acceptable risks; they have enough self-confidence to take on new challenges.

In traditional sales compensation programs, the plan served as a guide for salespeople relative to management expectations. New sales roles generally require new skills and behaviors for success, and the sales compensation program by itself cannot and should not be used as the "guide to successful behavior." The sales compensation plan should, however, directly reward those employees who have acquired new skills to accomplish the results required.

To evaluate the effectiveness of a sales compensation program designed for new sales roles, it is therefore necessary to obtain information and complete analyses to assess the degree to which the plan has supported and rewarded achievement in these three areas: customers; costs, productivity, and profitability; and employees.

WHAT NOT TO EVALUATE

When you evaluate the effectiveness of a new sales compensation plan, it is wise to focus your evaluation on the factors that reflect the plan's objectives and the factors that the employees covered by the new plan can influence. Figure 13-1 lists eight relatively common sales effectiveness expectations that top managers have of salespeople.

We find that different support programs and practices affect to varying degrees how well sales personnel meet these expectations. Some sales management programs and practices—supervision, appraisals, training, base pay, or cash incentives—are more effective than others in

Fig. 13-1. Relative influence of support programs on sales management issues: How can incentive compensation be used?

Typical Sales Effectiveness Expectations	Influence Factors or Programs				
	Supervision	Appraisal	Training	Base Pay	Cash Incentives
Maintain or increase profitability	P				S
Provide or ensure superior customer service	P	S	S		
Work with other team resources effectively	P			S	S
Work with other company resources effectively	P	S		S	
Sell optimal product mix	P				S
Manage time and territory effectively	P	S		S	
Optimize available opportunity in defined market segments	P		S		
Develop the skills and abilities required in each position	P		P	S	

influencing the salesperson's ability to achieve specific expectations as indicated by the "P" (primary) versus "S" (secondary) in the figure. As the company develops new sales roles and prepares compensation plans to support them, it is helpful to keep a proper perspective on the likely impact that compensation will have on the other tools managers have available. Among the issues that frequently interest management are:

Skill levels of the personnel in the new sales role. Are the sales and customer service people gaining the new skills required for effectiveness? Unless the plan has been designed specifically to address this question (one example is a plan that links gaining individual objectives to specific competencies), this is not a factor that you can or should evaluate as an outcome of effective sales compensation.

Time and territory management. Are the salespeople using their time efficiently and managing their territories effectively? A new sales compensation plan could complement effectiveness in these two areas; however, as we reported on BFI's experience in Chapter 11, job definition and the proper assignment of salespeople to customers is the first step in increasing time and territory management effectiveness. Thus, time studies and appraisal rating of sales rep performance in territory coverage should not be used as primary indicators of sales compensation plan effectiveness.

Working across all functions. Are salespeople working across functional boundaries as congenial members of the corporate family? Although companies frequently use sales compensation to motivate and reward effectiveness as a team or contributing team member, the program probably has not been designed to include salespeople in a corporate network. Unless other functional resources are involved directly or indirectly with the customer, it is unlikely that a review of internal communications would be a valid indication of sales compensation effectiveness.

As Figure 13-1 shows, the single most important factor that influences positive and effective management of sales and customer contact personnel, particularly in new sales roles, is supervision. Nevertheless, sales compensation clearly plays a part in many of the key issues that management wrestled with as the new sales role was developed. Therefore, although it is important to evaluate other critical programs to develop a complete picture of both the role's and the program's effectiveness, sales compensation is both a key driver and a key management tool.

PREPARING FOR THE EVALUATION PROCESS

Evaluating the effectiveness of the sales compensation plan is an ongoing process. The team or individuals charged with implementing the evaluation procedures should prepare an interim analysis and a complete evaluation at the end of each performance period. For example, if the company has implemented an annual quota-based bonus with quarterly payouts, the team should complete an evaluation annually with interim (quarterly) analyses.

The first task, of course, is to confirm what, exactly, the evaluation process should accomplish. Typically, an evaluation includes examining the plan's alignment in three areas:

Business objectives: the extent to which the plan performance measures and mechanics support corporate culture, motivate the achievement of company business objectives, and are consistent with the requirement to attract and retain talented salespeople, service people, or both

Job requirements: the extent to which the plan is aligned with the expectations for the new sales role, as well as other roles with which this job interacts

Competitive practice: the extent to which current practice is consistent with competitive practice and generally accepted principles of effective incentive compensation design

Once the team has confirmed the evaluation process's objectives with management, it should make final a plan for completing the evaluation. Since this ongoing assessment is crucial for recognizing warning signs (or clear signals that things are going well), plan designers should have been thinking about critical indicators throughout the design process. Before the company has implemented the plan, designers have ensured that the systems are in place to measure the factors included in the incentive plan. They should take the same care to ensure that systems are in place to check plan effectiveness.

Before they can do the evaluation, those responsible for completing the work should develop and confirm a checklist of evaluation criteria (i.e., what they will be checking), the work plan (who will do the work), milestone dates (when), and information requirements (what the information is and where it can be obtained). These elements provide a solid foundation for systematically evaluating the plan throughout the plan period. An example of a detailed sales compensation audit checklist appears in Appendix C.

HOW TO CONDUCT AN ACCURATE EVALUATION IN FIVE STEPS

Once you have a well-defined plan of attack, the most important tools you will need are accurate, valid information and adequate time to complete the analysis. The five-step process outlined below explains the activities you will need to complete before you can write an evaluation report. These steps, however, can be both frustrating and time-consuming unless the team has done a good job of both ensuring the availability of systems for tracking and measurement and communicating the plan throughout the organization. Here is the process that should serve as an outline for the work plan for conducting an evaluation.

STEP 1: REQUEST DATA

As part of organizing the evaluation, you have already determined what information you will need. Many times, obtaining detailed data through a company's systems is the longest step in the process, and therefore it is useful to submit a request for the data you will need as the first step. Depending on the sales compensation plan, its key objectives, and the evaluation, you are likely to need detailed sales and profit information by product, individual compensation information by plan element by payout period, and employee information such as tenure. Figure 13-2 illustrates the format of a data request you can submit to the appropriate departments in your company (sales administration, MIS, human resources/compensation, and finance). It is helpful to obtain the data in

Fig. 13-2. Illustrative data format for spreadsheet data retrieval.

1. Columns on spreadsheet for all possible components. Data provider to complete only those applicable for each job.

2. Name columns appropriately, based on products or other compensation elements.

3. Complete a sheet in the workbook for each job.

Column	Data	Column	Data
A	Company or auto numbering	O	Commission: Achievement Element 3
B	Position name	P	Payout
C	Region/territory identifier	Q	Commission: Achievement Element 4
D	Date of hire	R	Payout
E	1999 actual salary	S	Total Commission Payout (L+N+P+R)
F	1999 salary grade midpoint	T	Bonus Element 1 Achievement
G	2000 actual salary	U	Payout
H	2000 salary grade midpoint	V	Bonus Element 2 Achievement
I	Salary grade	W	Payout
J	Most recent performance appraisal rating	X	Total Bonus Payout (U + W)
K	Commission: Achievement Element 1	Y	Guarantee or Draw
L	Payout	Z	Other
M	Commission: Achievement Element 2	AA	Total Paid Cash Compensation (G+S+X+Z)
N	Payout		

the spreadsheet or database program the company already uses so you can complete analyses easily.

Step 2: Develop Evaluation Tools

While the data request is being processed, you will need to develop or confirm the tools you will require to complete the evaluation. The three primary tools are:

- Results analysis, based on financial, compensation, and perform-ance data
- Surveys of the employees
- Interviews with key managers and focus groups with salespeople

Perhaps the key indicator of success for executive management will be the degree to which the sales compensation program has supported the delivery of the financial results that the new job intended. Therefore, you should develop a rigorous analysis plan that fully utilizes all avail-able data. Table 13-1 suggests the analyses you could undertake to pre-pare a profile of results under the new sales compensation plan. Table 13-1 also describes how the data should be "cleaned" by MIS and sales administration so you can use them in the analyses. You may find it helpful to provide the plan and a data layout template to the data pro-vider; they can facilitate efficient data delivery and use of the data as they are provided.

Since in most cases the financial results are not the only indicators of plan effectiveness, you will require tools to gather more qualitative information. We describe survey tools and interview and focus group guides later in the chapter.

Step 3: Analyze External Data

To assess the plan's competitiveness, and the extent to which your com-pany is achieving results as good as your competitors', or better, you should obtain external survey data and industry analyses. If these sources are available, here is an overview of the process used to assess competi-tiveness of the sales compensation payouts and achievement levels:

Select data sources. Many companies participate in salary surveys to be sure they have competitive data available for analysis. When no published surveys are available, many companies conduct formal sur-veys among competitors through a third party. This type of benchmark-

Table 13-1. "Pay for performance": database and suggested analyses.

Date	Analysis
"Clean" data	Consistent data across jobs
	Incumbents in the particular job role for one year or more
	Full-year data for each incumbent, and each cash compensation component (salary and each element of incentive compensation)
	Any guarantee, corporate award, or signing bonus would not be included
	Both objectives (in units or dollars) and achievement levels should be available
	Achievement levels should be available for each level of measurement if possible, particularly those levels of measurement used to calculate incentive pay
	Collection and analysis tools should be flexible, to enable input of updated information as it becomes available
Financial analyses	Sales by product or product category by salesperson
	Distribution of product mix by sales job, by geography
	Sales by market or customer segment
	Distribution of profitability versus goal by job role, by individual
	Distribution of ratio of selling cost to sales (average, historical, distributed by sales job, by individual)
	Distribution of individual quota achievement versus goal: by job role, individual
Other performance analyses	Turnover over last three years
	Relationship between pay and appraisal rating, between pay and tenure
	Relationship between achievement of quantitative and qualitative measures: by job role, by management area, by individual
Compensation analyses	Relationship between individual incentive payout and achievement of objectives: by performance measure, by management area, by job role, by individual
	Distribution and range of incentive payouts (minimum, median, maximum)
	Distribution and range of total cash compensation: by job role, individual

ing is generally fairly reliable, and is as up-to-the-minute as possible. In some smaller industry segments, however, competitors are unwilling to share even the most "high level" conceptual information about pay and jobs. If that is the case, you may talk with executive recruiters to get a feel for current market practice.

Complete job-matching process. To ensure that the data being used are aligned with the job being done, you should complete a summary of the new sales role based on defined parameters. You can then compare this summary to the benchmark job description used in the survey source or sources. Jobs that are noticeably less than or more than the benchmark description may need to be adjusted in value. For example, if your new sales role has essentially all the same characteristics as a job defined in a survey for which the total pay is $50,000, you would use $50,000 as the competitive pay benchmark. If, however, your new sales role has demonstrably more responsibilities and is more complex than the $50,000 job, and there are no closer matches, you might decide your job is worth more than the survey position.

Complete data analysis. Once you have the external survey or market data, you can use them to estimate the job's market value. A couple of words of warning: Survey data are always retrospective, so the levels need to be "aged" forward from the year the data were current to the year for which you are doing the estimate. This aging factor is generally based on average market movement. Also, market data generally tell you what *has* been paid, not what companies *intended* to pay at target. Therefore, you should always view pay levels from the perspective of actual achievement. This type of analysis is generally completed to show the percentiles of pay from the twenty-fifth percentile (the lowest paying companies) to the seventy-fifth or ninetieth percentile (the highest paying companies). The comparison is especially critical if your company has defined the market level that it will use as its floor, that is, the level of market pay at which it wants to compete.

Record results. A written report with graphics gives executives and others information about the degree to which the company's compensation is competitive. Figure 13-3 provides an illustrative summary of a competitive analysis. Remember that the levels the survey reported may need to be adjusted based on the match of the company job to the survey job.

STEP 4: ANALYZE INTERNAL DATA

As Figure 13-3 illustrated, the first step is to be sure the internal data are clean, that is, valid, accurate, and complete. This set of analyses focuses on pay for performance compared to the measures used in the compensation plan, as the most typical "first cut" at analyses to assess plan effectiveness. The key objectives of the analysis are to assess (1) the degree to which the plan paid what it should have paid for the results

Fig. 13-3.   Illustrative competitive analysis (field sales position).

Field Sales Position: Reports directly to the Regional Sales Director. Responsible for the promotion of Company products and achievement of assigned sales goals. Incumbents will be selling and promoting Company products to specialists, other professionals, and institutions. Attainment of sales objectives will require familiarity with, or a background in, science/ medicine, strong familiarity with customer environments and the drug selection process, and strong communication, business, selling and interpersonal skills, and abilities. Effective promotion of Company products will require extensive efforts in customer education, relationship building, effective communications, and analytical problem solving, as well as knowledge of reimbursement issues and solutions.

		Survey Average	
		Hospital Rep	**Sales Rep Intermediate**
Compensation Element	**Entry "Package"**	**Industry Survey** (Aged 2 years)	**Special Survey** (Aged 1 years)
Target Cash Compensation	$76,500	$64,205	$72,111
75th Percentile Target Cash	N/A	$81,365	$81,841
Base Salary	$55,000 - $64,000 (max.)	$50,891	$47,708
Target Incentive Opportunity	$21,500	$13,314	$23,985
Target Mix	72/28	74/26	67/33

- Survey data aged 5%/year

achieved; (2) the competitiveness of the pay levels (in conjunction with the analysis of external competitive data); and (3) the degree to which the new role reached company financial objectives. Once you do this type of basic analysis, you can turn to more specialized analyses. Some examples of these include:

Conversion-penetration-retention. Many companies have implemented new sales roles specifically to convert competitors' customers, to attract new business, to retain more of the business than it currently retains with its customers, or to gain more business from current customers. As discussed in Chapter 5, a CPR Analysis is crucial to understanding where growth has come from in the past and where it will come from in the future. Many companies implement a system that provides frequent CPR reports that enable management to determine quickly the extent to which the strategic intent of a new role is being achieved. As illustrated in Table 13-2, a CPR Analysis can quickly indicate the areas of

Table 13-2. Sample CPR Analysis.

	2000	*Total*	*As % of 2000 Company*
Company goal: Total units	624,868		
Company goal: Total sales	$61,465,750		
Western conversion units		6,200	.99
Western conversion dollars		$468,800	.76
Western penetration units		8,189	1.31
Western penetration dollars		$844,711	1.37
Western retention units		303,002	48.5
Western retention dollars		$29,867,063	48.6

- Western division goal: $36,879,450
- Percent of company goal: 60%
- Western division achievement: $31,180,574
- Achievement percent: 85% of division goal

opportunity for a new sales role. In this example, the division is falling far short of its revenue and units goals, perhaps due to a lack of new customers (conversion is very low), and an apparent difficulty in selling additional lines to current customers (penetration is also very low). This type of analysis is particularly useful in determining the extent to which the company's customer objectives are being achieved.

Return on investment. Most companies consider compensation a cost. The sales compensation program, however, is really the company's investment in sales resources, the way a new factory is an investment in production. As with any investment, an analysis that clearly defines the return the company is receiving on the funds invested is critical. Once you have defined objectives, or key measures of success, for a job, the return on the compensation dollar is related to how close the company comes to reaching those objectives. If revenue is the key driver of success, the "cost of sales" figure many companies use is really a return on investment analysis. Figure 13-4 provides an example of a year-over-year cost of sales analysis. In this example, the company anticipated that the cost of sales would increase in direct proportion to the revenues achieved (COS 1). However, as new sales roles were implemented, the cost of sales skyrocketed in 1995 (COS 2) and then leveled off as employees in the new role became more productive. This result is typical of a company that invests in its sales organization; although the cost of sales may spike, increased productivity decreases the cost of sales within a defined period of time.

Fig. 13-4.   Cost of sales.

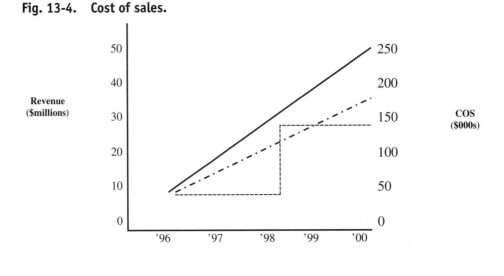

_____   Revenue
–·–·–·–·–·–·–·–·–   COS 1: Incremental cost to organization each year (anticipated COS)
- - - - - - - - - -   COS 2: Periodic investment in sales (actual COS)

STEP 5: COMPILE EMPLOYEE INFORMATION

Competitive labor market data are not the only tool you should use to
determine the degree to which a sales compensation program is achieving employee objectives. Many companies develop employee surveys
and conduct interviews and focus groups to obtain key information on
the extent to which the plan is both meeting employee expectations and
supporting the requirements for new skills and behaviors. (Remember,
the sales compensation plan cannot *teach* new behaviors, but it can reward employees who acquire the new skills they need to achieve the
plan objectives.)

Figure 13-5 illustrates an employee opinion survey that the firm
could circulate several times after it institutes a new sales compensation
plan. Ideally, the survey should be conducted within thirty days after the
company announces a new plan and then at the end of every business
quarter for at least three quarters. The survey results provide management with information on how well the plan was introduced and employee perceptions of it.

Table 13-3 is the agenda and discussion topics one company uses
twice each year with groups of salespeople after it has implemented a

Fig. 13-5.   Sales compensation opinion survey.

This year we introduced a new sales compensation plan. We are conducting this brief survey each quarter to see how it is progressing. Please answer the questions below and return the questionnaire to us by (date). Thank you.

1.   Position/Title _____   Region _____

2.   I have a good understanding of the plan mechanics

☐ Yes   ☐ No

3.   What I like best about the plan:

☐ Performance measures   ☐ Performance range   ☐ Other_____

☐ Frequency of payout   ☐ Size of incentive opportunity   ☐ Other_____

4.   What I like least about the plan:

☐ Performance measures   ☐ Performance range   ☐ Other_____

☐ Frequency of payout   ☐ Size of incentive opportunity   ☐ Other_____

5.   My behavior will change as a result of the new plan.

☐ Agree   ☐ Disagree   ☐ Uncertain

Please explain your response: _____
_____
_____

new role in its customer coverage process. The firm records the focus group results and compares them to prior results to determine the extent to which a new sales role has been implemented successfully from the perspective of the focus group participants.

Some companies supplement the focus group approach with interviews of key employees. Figure 13-6 is a sample interview guide for these interviews, in which the interviewee remains anonymous. The open-ended questions provide an opportunity to obtain information on perspectives related to both the performance measures used and the incentive plan mechanics.

These approaches to obtaining information are perhaps the only way that a company can determine the specific factors that have contributed to, or detracted from, plan effectiveness. For example, a plan that has been poorly communicated may be well designed, with appropriate performance measures. A lack of understanding and buy-in, how-

Table 13-3.   Focus group discussion guidelines.

Topic	Time Allocation	Discussion Questions
Job definition	30 minutes	What are the primary roles and responsibilities of your/the new job in the sales process? In what ways do field and headquarters resources work together?
Customers	30 minutes	How do you prioritize your customers? What competition do you see for your customers?
Buying/sales process	30 minutes	Describe the sales process and your recent experiences: new account; maintenance selling. What decision-making processes do your customers use? What are your product priorities?
Performance measurement and incentive compensation	60 minutes	What are the measures of success for your job? What types of goals do you have? Describe the incentive plan. What observations do you have about performance measures and the incentive plan?

Fig. 13-6.   Field interview guide.

- Performance measurement
  - How is performance measured: yours and (if appropriate) that of those who report to you?
  - How are goals set?
  - Observations/comments

- Compensation
  - How the program works
  - Key strengths and potential drawbacks
  - What the program tells you to do
  - Impact on your day-to-day activities and planning
  - Observations and comments

- Sales performance tracking, measurement, crediting, and reporting processes: describe; comments ever, may significantly decrease plan effectiveness. On the other hand, a well-communicated plan may have used performance measures that are outside the influence of the salesperson, and due to this flaw the employee was not able to reach the performance measure objectives.

A blending of the survey and interview approaches is illustrated in figure 13-7. This company asked for input in three key areas through an e-mail survey. Executive management followed up with interviews conducted with frontline managers. The results provided the company with significant information about areas for enhancement in the following year.

How to Report the Results of an Evaluation

As you are developing a report on results, it is important to determine the message's audience. Implementing new sales roles requires ongoing assessment of effectiveness, and both executive management and employees will have a vital interest in the extent to which the new sales roles are producing the intended results. Therefore, while the analyses and other fact-finding initiatives that go into the evaluation process are frequently time-consuming and detailed, a report on the results should be structured to provide both information and recommendations. An ideal report includes:

- An overview of the job and the results expected
- Analyses conducted
- An executive summary of results
- Detailed results
- Recommendations

Because the report has potentially two audiences, those developing it should consider a "consumer" and a "decision-maker" version. The consumer version would include results of the evaluation keyed to employees and results. This version would not include information that could be considered executive-level only (e.g., company financials). The decision-maker version includes recommendations based on results.

Many companies have found that the design team that developed the sales compensation plan, together with technical resources such as sales administration or information systems, are best suited to provide recommendations to executive management. This can be done in a formal presentation, or informally in a roundtable discussion of strengths

Fig. 13-7.   Field input and recommendations.

Survey Questions

- How did the plan work for your position, and the positions that report to you?
- What did associates like and dislike about the plan?
- What suggestions do you have?

Summary of Identified Issues: Key Interview Topics

- Performance measures: volume vs. profit
- Span of measurement
- Level of measurement: team vs. individual
- Budgeting process
- Payout: uneven quarters

Topic	Recommendations
Payout	• Provide payout for "stand-alone" quarters • Provide even payout opportunities per quarter
Reports Used	• Use only one report tool
Budgeting	• The budget-setting process should be reviewed and objectives set equitably • For cash contribution, managers should submit the target for which they will be accountable; the target should be reviewed and adjusted if necessary • If territory-level budgets cannot be set equitably for reps, this position should be measured only at a region level
Measures	• Sales positions should be measured primarily on the volume of the product line that is their primary focus • Company-owned outlets' results should be included in the measurement system for sales positions • The rep position should have a more significant weight on a measure focused on team (e.g., region) results to encourage a team focus

and opportunities for enhancement. Such a presentation focuses on both the effectiveness of the sales compensation program as a management tool and the degree to which employees and customers have embraced the new role. Once the evaluation has been completed, and the report has been delivered to management, the logical next step is planning for the future.

Recalibrating Again: Updating Your Plan for a New Year

The results of the evaluation, and the report to decision makers, should provide a firm basis for determining the extent to which the sales compensation plan needs to be recalibrated for the new year. If the plan as designed has the flexibility for tweaking, the change should involve a seamless transition. Some examples include a change in performance weights, linking previously unlinked measures, and changes in payout rates.

Because a new sales role develops history as it evolves, some companies may find that the plan needs to change more significantly. If this is the case, the company should develop a transition strategy to ensure that plan changes support company objectives, while also ensuring that employees continue to focus on their roles' key responsibilities. The transition strategy to an all new plan may include a pilot test of the new plan, extensive communication, and an interim plan that lays the groundwork for the new plan for eligible employees.

Of course, the company should communicate *any* change in the plan based on the evaluation's results to employees as early as possible, so that each person has an opportunity to begin to adjust behaviors and expectations. Generally speaking, salespeople are accustomed to plan changes based on business objectives; however, newly eligible participants in a sales compensation plan may require additional information in order to ensure ongoing focus and effort.

Design team members should also keep up to date on new and innovative approaches to compensating new sales roles. Ongoing communication with industry contacts and review of current articles and new publications are ways in which managers can learn about approaches that other companies are trying, and the strengths and drawbacks of those approaches. Appendix D contains a list of articles related to the topic, with a brief synopsis of each article.

SUMMING UP

No sales compensation plan is complete until the company evaluates it. Is it doing what you want it to do? If not, what should be changed? When evaluating a new compensation plan's results, senior executives focus on customers (are they buying more, are they buying our new products), internal financial results (costs, productivity, and profitability), and employees (are we able to attract, retain, and motivate sales and customer contact personnel). To evaluate a sales compensation program, therefore, it is necessary to assess the degree to which the plan has supported and rewarded achievement in all three areas.

At the same time, it is not necessary to evaluate every factor affecting the sales organization. While managers may want to know whether the salespeople are gaining the skills required to be effective in their new roles, it is generally not a factor you should evaluate as an outcome of effective sales compensation. Similarly, you should not use salesperson time studies or willingness to work across functional boundaries as measures of sales compensation effectiveness.

Rather, the evaluation process should consider business objectives, job requirements, and competitive practice. The process has five steps: (1) obtain financial and other data from sales administration, MIS, human resources/compensation, and finance; (2) assemble the proper tools (results analysis based on financial, compensation, and performance data; surveys of the employees; and interviews with key managers and focus groups with salespeople); (3) analyze external data; (4) analyze internal financial data; and (5) analyze employee information.

The final report may be tailored for two audiences, the salespeople and senior management. The point of such a report is to highlight the strengths of the new compensation plan and to suggest opportunities for enhancement. Because the world does not stop turning, however, the evaluation leads back to the beginning of the process. Because a new sales role develops history as it evolves, because customers' demands change, because new competitors appear, and because company growth by itself changes the environment, it will be necessary to develop new sales roles and modify existing roles.

CHAPTER 4

FUTURE CHALLENGES

"The hardest work is figuring out what to do in a world of infinite choice."[1] This quote, from Bill Jensen's book *Simplicity*, accurately describes the challenge we faced as we wrote this chapter. To increase a company's return on its investment in sales compensation, it often appears that there is a never-ending list of things that one could work on. Our objective was to narrow that list to a limited number of topics. The three topics we selected to focus on are the ones that we believe top managers should anticipate and address when working on compensation plans to support new sales roles.

For most companies, the essence of business success is the ability to attract, retain, and expand business with customers. Because a company's sales resources—regardless of the sales channel—are a vital link between the company and its customers, they hold the key to revenue growth and profitability. Properly directed, motivated, rewarded, and recognized sales resources will make a significant contribution to the achievement of these business measures. We believe that the sales compensation plan is one of the more powerful tools available to management to achieve optimal employee motivation and performance, and that, therefore, it will continue to be an important focus among top managers.

Successful sales compensation plans are situational. This is because at any given point in time, a company's sales strategy reflects a combination of two or more of the following goals: revenue growth, profit improvement, expense control (or reduction), and sales productivity improvement. Thus, sales compensation is the caboose, not the engine. By itself, the sales compensation plan cannot create a successful business—although we have observed companies that persist in their efforts to use compensation to do so, only to fall short of their business objectives. Rather, the plan must align with a company's strategy so that it encourages the type of behavior and performance required to achieve the desired business results. We believe that in the future, top management will continue to ask for increased sales performance and profitability—regardless of whether the business is part of the new economy (i.e., dot.coms) or the old economy (traditional businesses).

A sales compensation plan designer needs to be responsive to top management's direction to align plans with business goals. To do so, the designer will have three challenges:

- *The "talent" challenge.* The demand for talented people—particularly individuals who are qualified to work effectively in new sales roles—and, therefore, the importance of compensation in attracting and retaining those people.
- *The "sales crediting" challenge.* The pressure to devise compensation plans that foster channel harmony in a world where channels are proliferating and thus make it almost impossible to determine who or how to credit for sales success. Our experience shows that it is often a company's sales crediting policies (or, more correctly, the lack of such policies) that undermine a compensation plan for new sales roles.
- *The "frontline manager effectiveness" challenge.* The need to equip sales leaders and managers—particularly frontline supervisors—with the skills they need to successfully manage employees in new sales roles with a new compensation plan is pervasive in most companies. Our research shows that less than 10 percent of frontline sales managers are formally trained in how to manage with sales incentive compensation.

The purpose of this chapter is to provide you with information and advice on how to address these challenges so that your company can gain the maximum motivational mileage from its compensation plans for new sales roles. We will have succeeded in that objective if this chapter clarifies for you how to go about taking action when one of more of these forces stands in the way of compensating new sales roles.

THREE GUIDING PRINCIPLES TO HELP YOU ADDRESS FUTURE CHALLENGES

In the quest for growth, more and more companies will continue to expand their business through organic growth, mergers and acquisition, or both. As a result, the sales organization—and, for that matter, all jobs involving customer contact—in these companies will experience frequent and continuous change. Mergers that have taken place in the pharmaceutical, software, and telecommunication industries, to mention a few, have fundamentally altered the way the sales organization does business with customers. After a merger, the sales organization is often characterized by a mix of globally and locally deployed resources focused on meeting the shifting needs of increasingly complex customers. Products, channels, or both increase in size and complexity and, therefore, must be carefully considered as the new company considers its future go-to-market and sales strategies. Additionally, as companies are merged or acquired, sales organizations, often with widely different sales cultures and value systems, must be brought together successfully to realize the benefits of consolidation.

The key to successful design of sales compensation plans in this ever-changing business environment is to consider three guiding principles: "focus, flexibility, and simplicity."[2]

1. *Focus* means knowing what to concentrate on. One of the most effective ways to establish focus for a sales organization is through the measurement system, especially as a key factor in a company's reward system. Whether a company is expanding globally or integrating sales organizations, a common set of metrics—usually no more than three—increases the likelihood of success.

2. *Flexibility* is required in the design of sales compensation plans, since selling situations vary widely, not only in local markets within the United States, but also on a global basis. The challenge faced by the plan designer is how much flexibility to provide in the elements of the compensation plan. We find that the creation of design templates is an effective approach to help guide the customization of plans.

3. *Simplicity* in plan design is required so that sales personnel not only understand how they are paid but also can easily make professional moves through the company's national or global sales organization. Typically, simplicity is most important in constructing the payout formula. Our research shows that if participants in a sales compensation plan cannot readily calculate their actual earnings under the plan, a significant amount of motivational value is lost.

We believe that as plan designers consider the more specific challenges of talent, multichannel sales credit, and frontline manager training, it's important that they use these three guiding principles—focus, flexibility, and simplicity—when faced with the constantly changing business environment in which the plans must operate.

THE TALENT CHALLENGE

In most companies, top managers look to compensation to help the company attract and retain the caliber of people it needs if it is to successfully sell to and interact with customers. Attracting and retaining top-notch talent is one of the most serious challenges faced by companies today, according to a recent McKinsey & Company research study.[3]

The study indicates that the number of 35- to 44-year-olds in the United States will decline by 15 percent between 2000 and 2015. Our own experience shows that this age group provides approximately 60 percent of the typical sales force. Another study, which focuses on the subject of sales talent, puts this challenge into sharper focus. The Corporate Advisory Board's study reports that CEOs view labor shortages as the number one key growth barrier. They believe that the shortage of marketing and sales staff is one of their three most critical employee shortages.[4]

Top managers will be challenged to develop processes and programs to win the talent war and, as the McKinsey study also points out, to use "differentiated compensation" more effectively, because it is among the top five factors that motivate talented people to select and remain with a particular employer. We acknowledge that pay, while very important, is not the complete answer to the challenge companies face in attracting and retaining top talent in the sales force. Because a more comprehensive solution to this challenge is beyond the scope of our book, to gain a more thorough perspective on the alternatives, there are other references that you may want to investigate.[5]

A strong sales force is a major advantage, especially in highly competitive markets—markets characterized by high product parity, markets in which all the major players offer virtually equal high levels of product quality and customer service. In such situations, a company's advantage is the relationship between the customer and the salesperson. As one executive told us, his company's objective in this type of competitive environment was to "shrink-wrap" the salesperson around the product offering so that a company employee became the source of differentiation. The sales compensation plan plays a pivotal role in attracting and retaining talented salespeople. Thus, a question that top managers must ask and that plan designers must answer is, What should we do to keep top talent in our company?

We believe that companies will have an easier job ahead of them in retaining top talent if they act on two or more of the following four imperatives:

- Create and implement new sales roles, thereby providing an environment in which many employees—sales and all other customer contact personnel—can work in jobs that contribute to business success with customers.
- Expand participation in sales incentive compensation to all employees who contribute to sales success with customers, particularly sales support staff.
- Increase participation in stock ownership plans among sales and customer contact personnel to actively engage these employees in the requirements to achieve company-wide success.
- Broaden the use of nonmonetary rewards—e.g., formal recognition plans, promotional opportunities, other valued rewards—particularly for customer and sales support staff, to recognize employees for their contributions to business success with customers.

We realize that what is suggested here is tough work, and we do not underestimate the difficulty a company faces when acting upon these imperatives. However, we believe that great companies will do just that—they will act because not doing so further increases the likelihood of losing their talented people.

THE SALES CREDIT CHALLENGE

As the channels available for selling to and servicing customers proliferate, the ability to track and measure results becomes a significant issue. Our associate David Fritz has defined sales credit as "rules guiding the allocation of sales results amongst resources who have participated in the selling process."[6] For the purpose of sales compensation, that definition is frequently broadened to include resources that participated in the end-to-end customer management process. As more and more companies implement new channels and new sales roles, sales crediting is becoming an important feature in the design of the sales incentive plan. The plan is motivational, and thus a good investment of compensation dollars, only if it directly influences behavior and rewards for results that the individual can affect. Based on our work with companies that have wrestled with sales crediting issues, we have found that the following questions must be addressed during the process of designing a new sales compensation plan:

- Are the roles and responsibilities for each job well defined?
- Is success in each job defined primarily in terms of quantifiable results?
- Can sales results be tracked (attributed) directly to an individual who expended the selling effort that created the sale?
- Is only one job responsible for getting and keeping business with customers?

If the answer to any of these questions is no, then there is a high potential for sales crediting problems when the incentive mechanics are implemented. Also, our experience suggests that the potential for pay problems increases exponentially with every no answer. We provided some "rules of the road" for sales crediting in Chapter 6 (Figure 6-5). Based on those types of guidelines, we find that companies frequently try to anticipate and answer every sales crediting question with a different policy. The result of that exercise is a long document that is considered "the bible" for every decision a sales resource makes when participating in any sales process. These types of sales crediting policy documents must therefore be well designed to address how the company wants eligible resources to behave in order to achieve results, the actual measurement and reporting ability of the company, and the financial implications of the policies.

With that background in mind, we believe that a company can increase the effectiveness of a sales compensation plan covering current and new sales roles by paying careful attention to the following three sales crediting topics:

1. A sales compensation design team must answer two questions: What results are we looking for from a specific role, and what behaviors must be put forth by employees in the role to achieve those results? If the answer is, "We want our sales and service roles to be customer-centered, working to achieve our company's objectives in a process that benefits the customer as well," then sales crediting becomes a key con-

sideration. If sales success is measured principally in terms of volume (either dollars or units), then sales crediting policies must be thoroughly and correctly designed and communicated. The type of sales crediting policies used must align the customer contact resource with the type of behavior expected. For example, splitting sales credit generally results in independent selling behaviors, whereas double crediting is more conducive to teamed selling behaviors. As a general rule, that is why split crediting is used with commission plans and double crediting is used with quota attainment bonus plans.

2: The information technology capabilities of a company should not prohibit management's thinking about the right approach to sales measurement and the sales crediting policies required to support sales success. However, those capabilities are a key determinant of successful implementation, and must therefore be carefully reviewed to ensure that what the design team thinks can be measured is practical. Consider this example: In the software industry, "referral" or "influence" revenue is a measure of a successful partnership relationship between the software developer and the third-party partner who recommends the use of the software to an end user. While this is the right measure to use, crediting sales success is difficult at best, since it requires that the software company's system "talk to" the alliance partner's system to crosscheck referrals and actual sales. Also, it requires the sales resources involved in "deals" with end users to communicate with one another during the actual sales process.

Similar issues are involved if multiple company resources are involved in the sales process. For example, in a large-scale integrated solution sale (as we described in Chapter 9), "sales success" may be spread over many years and should be attributed to multiple resources. Crediting must be done on a deal-by-deal, resource-by-resource basis over multiple years. This type of crediting frequently is not systematized and is the responsibility of someone in finance.

3. The types of credit assignments that a company can apply to particular sales processes must be well understood and carefully weighed by the design team. As we explained in Chapter 6, the options include double credit (more than 100 percent of the sales value is credited, and the credit is spread across more than one party), split credit (100 percent of the sales value is credited, but the value is divided among two or more parties), and partial credit (less than 100 percent of the sales value is credited to one or more parties). To determine the sales crediting alternative that is best suited to a company's objective, we be-

lieve, the finance department must be involved in the decision process. The role of the CFO or chief accounting officer is to assess the financial impact of the crediting options on revenue goals, product goals, and selling expense. For example, if double crediting is selected because multiple resources are involved in the sale or because sales success is measured at an aggregate level, the company must forecast the financial implications of incentive payout under this crediting option prior to announcing it to the sales organization.

In companies that have historically rewarded all sales resources through a commission scheme, sales credit is frequently split to ensure that each sale remains profitable after the cost of the commission is taken into account. Split crediting may result in autonomous or "maverick" sales behavior, since few resources want to have their credit subtracted or divided. When these companies implement new roles such as teleweb sales or channel managers, they may need to consider other sales compensation plans that give double credit to ensure teamwork and customer focus.

For companies that have implemented a complex sales process for integrated solutions and those that use many channels to access, persuade, and fulfill a customer or set of customers, partial crediting may be the answer. Both the financial acceptability of this alternative and the role of each resource should be addressed when companies consider this type of crediting for specific sales.

Many companies use multiple approaches to sales crediting, based on the type of sale that has occurred and the resources involved. "One size fits all" is seldom the case in companies that sell products or services today. An example of one company's policy is illustrated in Figure 14-1. As you can see, the type of crediting rule applied is situational, based on the types of deals or transactions that make up the majority of the company's business.

In summary, a company's sales crediting policies must be addressed in complex selling situations, particularly in sales processes that use new or expanded sales roles. A company's ability to design an incentive plan may not rest exclusively with its ability to accurately track and credit results to an individual, but, in the end, the ability to reward resources appropriately for the results they affect may be the result of solid sales credit definitions and policies. Often, the ability to operate the business with appropriate sales crediting policies requires additional investment in IT. Our experience suggests that such investments, while expensive and time consuming to implement, pay off in the long run

Fig. 14-1. Sales crediting policy for complex deals.

Situation	Crediting Policy
The customer is referred by a partner, and buys directly from us.	Full credit to the direct sales representative
The customer is a telemarketing customer, and has no field sales coverage. Telemarketing asks for help from our direct sales force to close additional business with that customer	Multiple credit: full credit to all of the following: channel and direct sales representatives, field sales management
Our Integrated Solutions team closes a multiyear contract with one of our customers. The process has included sales, service, finance, legal, and technology resources.	Partial credit: initial sales team receives credit for 75% of the net present value of the contract
The product offering requires both a Named Account Sales Rep and a Product Specialist to successfully sell the product	Split credit: 75% credit the Named Account resource, 25% to Product Specialist

because selling expense is reduced and the motivational behaviors of salespeople contribute to the "right" sales.

THE EFFECTIVE FRONTLINE MANAGER CHALLENGE

Our experience suggests that a sales employee's feelings about the compensation plan are largely shaped by his or her immediate supervisor or team leader. Therefore, one would expect companies to spend a great deal of time and money on equipping frontline managers with the skills needed to manage effectively with the compensation plan, particularly when new sales roles are introduced into the business. However, our research and that of others shows that most companies are poor at developing their frontline managers in how to manage effectively with a sales compensation plan.

A recent Conference Board study reported that there is little or no emphasis on understanding leadership fundamentals—individual motivation and development was one prominent example—in the management training practices in the *Fortune* 1,000 companies studied. Further, that same study indicated that when executives were asked to rate the effectiveness of their own managers on a key list of leadership behaviors, a significant percentage reported that their own managers were lacking in these behaviors. Three of the top five areas of ineffectiveness were

providing clear objectives, achieving unit goals, and enhancing performance.[7] We believe that all three of these leadership skills are critical to
managing effectively with sales compensation.

In a recent survey we conducted among first- and second-level sales
managers for a leading software company, on a scale of 1 to 5, with 5
being the highest rating, the respondents indicated their needs as follows:

- Performance planning (4.15), i.e., how to set objectives
- Fundamentals of how to manage with incentive pay (4.02)
- Performance assessment (4.02), i.e., how to hold an effective con-
  versation with sales employees about their performance
- Communications (3.95), i.e., what to say/what not to say about
  the plan
- How to explain the use of performance measures (3.67)

These ratings are consistent with the findings in other surveys we
have conducted. These surveys and our experience in working with
companies supports our view that top managers have a great deal of
work to do to build the skills and confidence of their frontline managers
so that they can manage with incentive pay effectively.

Why is it that companies do not focus attention and resources on
equipping their frontline managers with the skills they need in order
to manage with a new or changed sales compensation plan? We have
discussed this question with top managers in many companies. Based
on those conversations, we reached two conclusions: First, many companies believe that they do equip their managers with the information
they need to implement the new sales compensation plan and that, with
that information in hand, it is the job of the frontline managers to carry
the message forward to their people. To support this belief, top managers point to elaborate (and often expensive) communication materials—
including a web site devoted exclusively to the sales compensation
plan—and costly rollout meetings, often held in a resort destination like
Hawaii, the Caribbean, and the like.

Second, some companies do not believe that there is anything particularly unique about managing with the sales compensation plan that
frontline sales managers don't already know or have not already learned.
When confronted with this attitude, we find it difficult to convince a
company to take action. However, in the former case, when we have
shown top managers that they are actually operating under some mis-
conceptions about what their company has been doing, we have been

successful in gaining top management's agreement about an appropriate plan of action.

What should companies do to equip their frontline managers with the skills and confidence that they need in order to manage effectively with a new sales compensation plan? Regardless of the type of sales compensation used, companies should take action on three fronts to help their managers gain maximum motivational mileage and performance from the plan.

1. Make learning about how to manage with sales incentive pay a fundamental part of your frontline managers' training program. The foremost influence on a frontline manager's approach to working with the sales incentive plan is the way in which that manager was treated by his or her boss when he or she was paid under the compensation plan. Thus, many companies are constrained by the inconsistencies under which their managers learned how to manage with incentive pay. To overcome this limitation, we suggest that companies design frontline manager training to achieve four learning objectives:

- Impart thorough knowledge about how a company's compensation plan works.
- Equip participants with the skills required to manage with the plan.
- Help participants formulate a plan of action for managing with incentive pay.
- Practice the use of skills and action planning techniques.

To accomplish these objectives, our research shows that companies must focus on three important skills:

- *Communication*: how to discuss the plan with employees
- *Performance planning and feedback on results*: how to assign goals or objectives; how to set expectations and assess results
- *Problem resolution*: how to answer objectives or solve problems that are typically associated with the launch of a new compensation plan

If you are not convinced that these objectives are right for your company's training initiative, then you may want to survey your frontline managers to either confirm these needs or identify additional needs. To help you with that effort, Figure 14-2 provides a relatively short sur-

Fig. 14-2.   Managers' skill needs survey.

Next year we will introduce a new sales compensation plan. Prior to implementing the new plan, we will conduct a manager training seminar to help you develop your skills and increase your confidence to manage with the new plan. We would like to have your input on topics that should be covered during the training seminar. Please answer the questions below and return the questionnaire to us by (date). Thank you.

1.   Areas Where You Would Like Additional Help or Information
(Rate each statement, where 5 is the highest and 1 is the lowest, by placing an "X" in one box)

Statement	5	4	3	2	1
The labor market(s) information our company uses to set incentive pay rates					
How the incentive pay opportunity **is determined** by job					
Why incentive opportunity **varies** by job, e.g., why doesn't everyone have the same opportunity					
The "fundamentals" of managing with incentive pay, e.g., definition of terms, how to talk with employees about the plan, how to answer questions					
Communications, e.g., what to say/what not to say					
How to explain **why** various performance measures were selected for the plans					
Our company's rationale for introducing changes to incentive plan(s) this year					
Performance **planning**, e.g., how to set objectives					
Performance **assessment**, e.g., how to have an effective conversation about the payout related to a certain level of performance					
Career planning and incentive opportunities, i.e., how to talk about what your people can look forward to in higher level position(s)					

2.   Additional Comments

Please share with us any additional comments that you have about managing with the incentive plan(s) that you believe will be helpful to us in planning for the training seminar.

vey questionnaire that can be distributed to frontline managers who have responsibility for managing with the sales compensation plan. The tabulated results of this survey will either confirm that your managers need training in the skills identified above or highlight other areas of need.

Training your managers in how to manage effectively with the sales compensation plan should not be a one-time event. Initially, all current managers should be trained, and as new managers are appointed, they too should learn how to manage with the sales compensation plan. After the initial training effort to bring everyone up to speed, your company should deliver a "refresher" training session on an annual basis. This session should accomplish three objectives in the upcoming business year:

- Build managers' confidence in working with the plan with their people
- Improve managers' skills in the critical areas related to managing with a plan
- Help managers help their people win under the plan

2. Encourage frequent and regular manager-to-manager conversations about how the compensation plan contributes to the achievement of business objectives. An effective sales compensation plan emphasizes two or three important business goals and rewards for success when those goals are achieved. The best plans also complement the management process. While training is an important starting point in the process of improving frontline managers' skills, it will not be fully effective by itself. In companies where the sales compensation plan is judged by top management to be effective, we observe that the top sales executive and his or her next level of management regularly talk with frontline managers about how the compensation plan is or is not helping them achieve desired business results.

3. Create forums where frontline managers can share experiences and therefore learn from one another about how to manage effectively with the sales compensation plan. Not surprisingly, learning how to manage effectively with a company's sales compensation plan is a continuous process and one that should always be improved. We have observed that one of the most effective and timely ways for managers to learn the do's and don'ts of managing with the sales compensation plan is to share their "real-life" experiences with one another.

To create a framework for frontline managers to have productive conversations about their experiences and thus learn from one another, we have used a team exercise technique called "What to Do When. . . ." The premise behind this technique is that frontline managers are faced with a wide variety of different questions and challenges from their people when it comes to their compensation plan. A "What to Do When . . ." exercise selects one particular question or topic—for example, "What to do when one of your sales reps challenges a sales credit decision"—and provides the managers with the opportunity to comment on their experiences and discuss how to address the issue. Equally important, the exercise provides the facilitator with the opportunity to indicate how the company suggests that the question be addressed.

SUMMING UP

The purpose of this chapter is to identify the three challenges—talent, sales crediting, and frontline manager training in plan management— that we believe will continue to stifle the effectiveness of sales compensation plans in the future if they are not properly addressed. Our experience suggests that one or more of these challenges, when not addressed correctly, can derail the success of even the most technically elegant sales compensation plan. Thus, unless top managers are willing to address these challenges when they are present in their own company, the benefits of a new sales compensation plan will fall short of the potential.

CLOSING COMMENTS

Overall, our experience suggests that sales roles in companies are constantly changing to meet and exceed the requirements of the competitive environment. Sometimes those changes are relatively minor and/or informal; for example, customer service or technical support personnel are asked to step in to play a role in addressing certain types of issues or problems faced with customers. More likely, however, are the situations we have described in the book—fundamental change is taking place in the sales and customer relationship management processes. An important response to that change is defining and implementing new sales roles and designing compensation plans to support them.

We wrote this book to help you sense and respond to the need for those changes before it is too late. In this context, "too late" means after business opportunities are missed—opportunities for revenue growth, enhanced profitability, increased customer loyalty and satisfaction—or employee morale is diminished because of ineffective leadership in addressing new customer requirements. The real benefit we hope readers gain from this book is the confidence to act in situations where it appears that new sales roles are needed. Frequently, we find that top managers have the inclination to act, but they are often uncertain what to do first, second, third, and so forth. Nor do they know, if change does not appear to be unfolding as planned, what course corrections they should make. We believe that when top managers have a road map for change and the tools to effect the change that we have presented in this book, the opportunity for success increases materially.

You will know that this book has benefited you and your company when the concepts, processes, and tools we have described become part of the way you lead and manage the sales function, and the vocabulary in the book becomes embedded in conversations about sales leadership in your company. Like any set of concepts and tools, what we suggest is neither a panacea nor a "silver bullet." Not all sales issues and problems will be resolved with new sales roles and the implementation of compensation plans to support those roles. If your situation matches those described in other companies throughout the book, however, and if you aptly apply the suggestions we offer, you can expect visible sales performance improvement.

We sincerely hope that the second edition of this book proves to be a valuable guide and reference source to you and your company in change management initiatives related to compensating new sales roles!

GLOSSARY OF TERMS

award: form of payment that is given within the context of a recognition event or program; may be in the form of money, prizes, plaques, or public commendation

base salary: fixed payment; adjusted to reflect cost of labor, negotiated settlement, seniority, and performance

bonus: a percent of base pay, or fixed dollar amount, for accomplishing objectives; may be capped or uncapped

cap: the total incentive opportunity a salesperson can earn in a given period

commission: compensation paid as a percentage of sales measured in either dollars or units

competitive assessment: analysis conducted to determine a company's relative position to its defined labor market in terms of total compensation, salary, or opportunity for variable compensation

costing: analysis conducted to estimate the cost of a plan; typically uses current plan mechanics and past sales performance

cost of labor: a comparative measure of external pay practices; data on labor market costs (total compensation amounts) are obtained from labor market competitors and used as a reference when establishing target total compensation opportunity.

cost of sales: a relative measure of internal costs; the cost of sales, expressed as a percent, is calculated by dividing the total sales dollar volume sold by the sales force into the total compensation costs of the sales forces.

cumulative: a type of performance cycle; a performance cycle is cumulative when the performance of the incumbent is measured over subsequent performance periods, e.g., "While payouts are made each month, performance is cumulative because it is measured from the start of quarter to date."

discrete: a type of performance cycle; a performance cycle is discrete when the performance of the incumbent is limited to a defined performance period without any connection to past or future performance periods, e.g., "Each month is discrete, because performance is measured for that month and payout is made for that month independent of past or future performance."

draw: a compensation payment paid in advance of performance. There are two types of draws: recoverable and nonrecoverable. In both cases, if performance produces incentive earnings in excess of the draw, then the sales representative receives the additional monies beyond the draw amount. If the sales representative's incentive earnings are less than a recoverable draw, then the sales representative must return the amount of the draw that was not earned, or the unearned amount is carried forward to the next performance period. However, with a nonrecoverable draw, if the incentive earnings do not exceed the draw, draw monies are not returned or carried forward; the sales representative gets to keep the draw.

excellence: individual sales performance that is in the 90th percentile (top 10 percent) of all individuals whose performance is being measured

gross margin: a performance measure calculated by subtracting the cost of goods from the sale price

guarantee: a compensation payment paid regardless of performance. Paid separately from the base salary, it acts as a nonrecoverable draw. Guarantees may be temporary (e.g., for new hires) or permanent.

incentive: any form of variable compensation

leverage: the amount of "upside" opportunity beyond total target compensation that outstanding performers are expected to earn

payout frequency: the timing of incentive payouts: can be made weekly, monthly, quarterly, or annually

performance period: the time span over which performance is measured for incentive purposes

performance standards (range): levels of achievement relative to defined objectives that are used to determine the point at which payout begins, and the payout rate between defined points of achievement (i.e., payout line)

progressive incentive: an incentive that features an increasing incentive rate as performance exceeds predetermined levels of performance

recognition program: program with focus on long-term objectives, continuity; emphasis on intangible reward; uses objective and subjective performance measurement

regressive incentive: an incentive that features a declining incentive rate as performance exceeds preestablished levels

salary/incentive ratio: also called incentive mix or salary/incentive mix; ratio of base salary to incentive opportunity as percentages of the total target compensation; expressed as two portions of 100 percent

target performance: expected level of sales results or individual performance

target total compensation: total cash compensation (including base salary and variable incentive compensation) available for achieving expected results

threshold: minimum level of performance that must be achieved before an incentive can be paid

upside potential: see *leverage*

variable compensation: includes any compensation component linked to performance: commission, bonus, nonmonetary reward

B

ILLUSTRATIVE FORMAL SALES COMPENSATION PLAN DOCUMENT

Company Name
Executive Approval:
Fiscal Year 2001 Incentive Compensation Plan

Position Titles

Business Unit Controller   Date   Vice President, Sales   Date

---

Legal   Date   Vice President,   Date
                                           Human Resources

Company Name
Executive Summary:
Fiscal Year 2001 Incentive Compensation Plan

Position Titles

Plan Overview: Designed to attract, retain, and motivate high incumbents in these positions employed by the Company, payouts under this incentive plan are closely matched to both sales performance and individual contribution.

Plan Objectives: The objectives of this plan are to reward achievement of defined objectives, both financial and nonfinancial, with specified accounts, and to support the development of the skills required for success in these positions.

Plan Framework:

Performance Hurdle: Must Be Met for Any Payout

Company Performance: 90%

Account(s) Goal Achievement (60% of Opportunity at Target)

Weighted Avg. % to Goal		Payout
Excellence	110%	42% of salary
Target	100%	18% of salary
Threshold	90%	3% of salary
<Threshold	<90%	-0-

+

Individual Contribution (20% of Opportunity at Target)

Average Rating	Payout
3.0	9% of salary
1.5–2.9	6% of salary
<1.5	-0-

+

Account Objectives (20% of Opportunity at Target)

Achievement	Payout
All Obj. Achieved for Key Acct	9% of salary
1 Obj. Achieved for Key Acct	6% of salary
No Acct Obj. Achieved	-0-

Participant Compensation:

Compensation Elements	Position A	Position B
Target incentive payout	$106,720 * 0.3 = $32,016	$98,329 * 0.3 = $29,499
Forecasted total incentives paid at target	$32,016 * 5 = $160,080	$29,499 * 12 = $353,984
Average participant's base salary	$106,720	$98,329
Average participant's total compensation at target	$138,736	$127,828
Salary/incentive ratio	77/23	

Company Name
Fiscal Year 2001 Incentive Compensation Plan

Position Title

Purpose	This document presents the Fiscal Year 2001 Incentive Plan for the above named positions within the Company. This incentive plan is not intended to, nor may be construed to provide any guarantees of employment to any plan participant for any period of time.
Incentive Plan Document Sections	The Fiscal Year 2001 Incentive Plan document is presented in the following sections:

Section	Description
1.	Eligibility
2.	Incentive Plan Objectives
3.	Incentive Determination
4.	Payment: Calculation and Frequency
5.	Incentive Plan Terms and Conditions
6.	Plan Modifications
	Appendices

Section 1. Eligibility	All position incumbents who are assigned to specified accounts January 1, 2001, or after, shall participate in the Incentive Plan unless otherwise stipulated by the Business Unit Vice President/General Manager. Incentive under the plan is in addition to, and not a part of, base salary.
Section 2. Incentive Plan Objectives	This plan is designed to support the objectives of the Company, including: • Profitable sales revenue growth in specified accounts • Account loyalty • Development of personal skills and competencies

Section 3. Incentive Determination

- **Definition.** Incentive is the variable cash compensation opportunity that is paid for achievement of defined objectives related to sales growth, account development, and individual development.

- **Incentive opportunity.** Target incentive will be calculated annually as 30% of the base salary for each individual, providing a salary/incentive mix of 77/23.

- **Incentive payout.** Incentive payout will be determined based on the following components:

Plan Component	Weight/Opportunity at Target
Corporate performance	No weight; used as a hurdle or requirement for any payout
Account growth versus goal	60%
Individual contribution	20%
Account objectives	20%

(Insert specific procedures for calculation, e.g., definition of a sale, sales quotas and thresholds. Refer to appropriate appendix for specific illustrations of mechanics.)

Section 4. Payment: Calculation and Frequency

Incentive is calculated and paid quarterly based on cumulative year-to-date results. Based on receipt of data, calculations for payout are anticipated to be completed within four weeks of the close of the quarter.

Section 5. Incentive Plan Terms and Conditions

1. All Position incumbents will be eligible to participate in the Incentive Plan the date they are assigned to a region.

2. All Position incumbents assigned to a region are eligible for incentive for the number of full months assigned to the region.

3. Position incumbents terminating during the year may receive a prorated incentive for the number of months eligible. The amount of such incentive and date of payment will be at the discretion of the President, and will consider draws paid to the employee.

4. Position incumbents who have been assigned to a region, but whose performance has not yet been appraised by their Region Director, will be nonprobationary for bonus calculation purposes until the first performance appraisal is completed.

5. When a Position incumbent is transferred from one region to another, the bonus for the full year will be based on a pro rata calculation using the performance of the former region to which they were assigned and the performance of the current region to which they are assigned.

6. Position incumbents terminating during the year may receive a prorated bonus for the number of months eligible. The amount of such bonus and date of payment will be at the discretion of the President. This condition also applies to Position incumbents transferring to other positions in the Company not covered by the Field Sales Bonus Plan. They will receive their bonus during the first quarter of the following year.

7. Newly assigned Position incumbents terminating with less than six full months on region will not receive a bonus payment.

8. The annual bonus payment to a Position incumbent will be limited to 175% of the incentive opportunity for the plan year.

9. No bonus will be paid to any Position incumbent on probationary status with the Company.

Section 6. Plan Modifications

The President of the Company or his delegate reserves the right to change, suspend, or discontinue the Incentive Plan at any time without prior notice. Nothing in this Plan shall be construed as a guarantee of employment for any participant for any fixed period of time.

The Company reserves the right to alter sales objectives at any time during the year to reflect its evaluation of windfall gain or shortfall loss, based on market adjustment, epidemic or unusual cause, price changes, product obsolescence, new products, account realignment, etc.

Plan Appendices:

- Exhibit 1: Illustration of Account Growth Bonus
- Exhibit 2: Illustration of Individual Contribution Bonus and Rating Worksheet
- Exhibit 3: Illustration of Account Objectives Bonus and Worksheet
- Exhibit 4: Illustration of Annual Payout, with Calculations for Each Component

Exhibit 1: Illustration of Account Growth Bonus

Performance Hurdle: Must Be Met for Any Payout

Company Performance: 90%

Account(s) Growth Goal Achievement (60% of Opportunity at Target)

Weighted Avg. % to Goal		Payout
Excellence	101%–110%	18% plus 2.4% of salary per percent
Target	100%	18% of salary
Threshold	90%–99%	3% plus 1.5% of salary per percent above 90%
<Threshold	<90%	-0-

Calculation Tool

Achievement of Product Growth Goals in Assigned Account(s)

Product Category	Weight	% Goal Achieved in Account(s)	Weighted Achievement
A	40%	98%	39.2%
B	40%	106%	42.4%
C	20%	100%	20.0%
		Achievement	101.6%

Exhibit 2: Illustration of Individual Contribution Bonus

Performance Hurdle: Must Be Met for Any Payout

Company Performance: 90%

Individual Contribution (20% of Opportunity at Target)

Average Rating	Payout
3.0	9% of salary
1.5–2.9	6% of salary
<1.5	-0-

Calculation Tool

Achievement of Individual Objectives

Competency	Score
1. Customer focus	2
2. Business skills	2
3. Implementation/achievement orientation	3
Rating (simple average)	**2.33**

Individual Contribution Rating Worksheet

Employee: _____   Position: _____

Manager: _____   Date: _____

Competency	Score	Comments
1.		
2.		
3.		
Rating (simple average)		

Exhibit 3: Illustration of Account Objectives Bonus

Performance Hurdle: Must Be Met for Any Payout

Company Performance: 90%

Account Objectives (20% of Opportunity at Target)

Achievement	Payout
All obj. achieved for key acct	9% of salary
1 obj. achieved for key acct	6% of salary
No acct obj. achieved	-0-

Calculation Tool

Achievement of Account Objectives

Account/Objective	Status
Account: Growth	Achieved
Account: Compliance	Not Achieved
One Objective Achieved with Account	

Account Objectives Worksheet

Employee: _____   Position: _____

Manager: _____   Date: _____

Account: _____   Account Contact: _____

Account	Objective	Status and Comments
		Mid-Year
		Year-End
		Mid-Year
		Year-End
		Mid-Year
		Year-End

Approved: (Vice President)   _____

Reviewed/Agreement: (Account Contact)   _____

Exhibit 4: Illustration of Annual Payout

Step	Description	Payout
Step 1: Determine corporate achievement	If 90% or greater, proceed to step 2	If less than 90%, no payout will occur
Step 2: Determine account performance to goal	• Calculate achievement of each product category • Apply weights • Calculate weighted achievement	Achieved 101.6%, round to 102% 18% of salary at 100% + 2.4% × 2 (4.8%) = **22.8% of salary**
Step 3: Review and evaluate achievement of individual objectives	• One objective achieved and competency demonstrated • Two objectives were not achieved based on external factors; competencies demonstrated	Rating of 2.33 is within target range **6% of salary**
Step 4: Review and assess achievement of account objectives	One of account's objectives achieved	Target achieved **6% of salary**
Step 5: Calculate total payout		**22.8% + 6% + 6% = 34.8% of salary**

C

SALES COMPENSATION AUDIT CHECKLIST

Sales Compensation Audit Checklist

Evaluation						Sales Management Programs/Processes and Evaluation Points
Poor 1	2	Avg. 3	4	Excel. 5	n/a	**Sales Compensation Plans** **First through Fourth Quarters**
❑	❑	❑	❑	❑	❑	• Has the company correctly applied the compensation plan to each job?
❑	❑	❑	❑	❑	❑	• Has the compensation plan been matched and calculated correctly for each job incumbent?
❑	❑	❑	❑	❑	❑	• Do all sales personnel fully understand the structure of their compensation plan and their expected performance on the plan?
❑	❑	❑	❑	❑	❑	• Is the organization performing as expected on the compensation plan?
❑	❑	❑	❑	❑	❑	• Are average performers earning target incentive or above?
❑	❑	❑	❑	❑	❑	• Are excellent performers earning the anticipated upside potential?
❑	❑	❑	❑	❑	❑	• Are marginal performers earning threshold-level incentive?
❑	❑	❑	❑	❑	❑	• Are all components of the plan (i.e., revenue, profit, new accounts bonus, and expense bonus) operating as expected?
❑	❑	❑	❑	❑	❑	• Are total pay levels and incentive pay levels positively correlated with revenue and profit performance?
❑	❑	❑	❑	❑	❑	• Is the turnover rate appropriate?
❑	❑	❑	❑	❑	❑	• Has the company successfully recruited talent?
						Sales Goals **First through Fourth Quarters**
❑	❑	❑	❑	❑	❑	• Has the company established individual sales goals that sum to the company's total sales goal?
❑	❑	❑	❑	❑	❑	• Has the company used a potential-based method for establishing and allocating these goals to sales personnel?
❑	❑	❑	❑	❑	❑	• Do all sales personnel fully understand their performance expectations? Do they understand how these expectations relate to their compensation plan and to the company's total goal?
❑	❑	❑	❑	❑	❑	• Is the company performing as expected to its sales goals? Is performance distributed as expected across the organization?
❑	❑	❑	❑	❑	❑	• Does goal attainment significantly differentiate top performers from average and marginal performers? Does this differentiation carry through to the compensation plan?
❑	❑	❑	❑	❑	❑	• Are the top performers to goal actually the company's most competent personnel, or are performance levels indicative of inaccurate goal allocation?
❑	❑	❑	❑	❑	❑	• Has the company evaluated its goal setting and goal allocation regularly (e.g., monthly and quarterly) to continuously improve its accuracy?

Evaluation						Sales Management Programs/Processes and Evaluation Points
Poor		Avg.		Excel.		
1	2	3	4	5	n/a	**Sales Goals** **Fourth Quarter**
❑	❑	❑	❑	❑	❑	• Has the company evaluated its goal accuracy for the first year and developed individual goals for 2001 based on the company's sales plan?
❑	❑	❑	❑	❑	❑	• Has the company provided accurate monthly performance data on each measure to corporate?
						Performance Evaluation Processes **First through Fourth Quarters**
❑	❑	❑	❑	❑	❑	• Has the company performed as expected on the customer results metrics?
❑	❑	❑	❑	❑	❑	—Market and Customer Penetration?
❑	❑	❑	❑	❑	❑	—New Customer Conversion, Customer Penetration, Customer Revenue Retention?
❑	❑	❑	❑	❑	❑	• Has the company performed as expected on the financial metrics?
❑	❑	❑	❑	❑	❑	—Revenue Growth?
❑	❑	❑	❑	❑	❑	—Gross Profit Dollars?
❑	❑	❑	❑	❑	❑	—Gross Profit Margin?
❑	❑	❑	❑	❑	❑	—Sales Expenses?
❑	❑	❑	❑	❑	❑	—Sales Compensation Expenses?
❑	❑	❑	❑	❑	❑	• Has the company performed as expected on the results-driven metrics?
❑	❑	❑	❑	❑	❑	—Sales Productivity?
❑	❑	❑	❑	❑	❑	—Close Rates?
❑	❑	❑	❑	❑	❑	—Sales Workload (sales time per account)?
❑	❑	❑	❑	❑	❑	—Sales Time Allocation?
❑	❑	❑	❑	❑	❑	• Has the company used information collected with these performance measures as input to make course corrections and performance improvements in the Sales Management System areas above?

ARTICLES OF INTEREST ON SALES COMPENSATION

COMPENSATION FOR MANAGERS AND FOR TEAMS

Title: Are You Making Enough Money?
Publication: *Sales and Marketing Management,* 10/96
Synopsis: Review of compensation levels for sales management
               positions. Discussion of the various structures of man-
               ager compensation plans.

Title: Rewards Practices for Customer Teams
Publication: *ACA Journal: Perspectives in Compensation and Benefits,*
               Autumn 1996
Synopsis: Summarizes key findings of a survey of ACA members
               about reward practices for customer teams. Covers data
               from many different types of companies.

Title: Pay Dirt: What Teamwork Costs
Publication: *Motivation Strategies,* September 1999
Synopsis: Q&A about tips and techniques for designing plans that
               motivate and reward team members.

SALES COMPENSATION DESIGN

Title: Is It Time to Revise Your Sales Compensation Plan?
Publication: *Supervision,* 8/96
Synopsis: Basic-level article about changing a compensation program. Includes a checklist to determine if a compensation plan needs change.

Title: Developing Incentive Compensation Strategies in a Global Sales Environment
Publication: *ACA Journal: Perspectives in Compensation and Benefits,* Autumn 1996
Synopsis: Details techniques and reviews several case studies related to developing sales compensation plans for global companies. The challenges of developing a consistent plan across diverse business climates are discussed.

Title: Developing a Competitive Pay Plan
Publication: *Sales and Marketing Management,* 4/97
Synopsis: Benchmarking your plan against other industries.

Title: Effective Variable Compensation Plans
Publication: *ACA Journal,* Spring 1997
Synopsis: Concepts in designing a variable compensation plan. Examples of documentation and communication pieces for a sales plan are included.

Title: Talking Money
Publication: *Sales and Marketing Management,* 12/97
Synopsis: Roundtable discussion with a leading compensation consultant and executives from IBM and Quick International Carriers.

Title: Adding Up Sales Incentive Pay
Publication: *National Business Employment Weekly,* March 15–21, 1998
Synopsis: Comparing the value of different compensation plans— a sales representative's perspective.

Title: Navigating the Potholes of Incentive Compensation to Improve the Bottom Line

Publication: *Solutions Magazine*, September 1999
Synopsis: Milestones of success from strategy to implementation
                in designing and installing a sales compensation plan.

Title: What Are You Worth?
Publication: *Selling Power*, January/February 2001
Synopsis: How to simplify sales compensation plans and still keep
                them focused on achievement of business objectives.

Title: Dollars & Sense Salary Surveys from A–Z
Publication: *Workspan*, February 2001
Synopsis: Summary of several sources of data for field and corpo-
                rate jobs.

Title: Optimizing Your Sales Compensation Plan
Publication: *SalesDoctors Magazine*, May 2000
Synopsis: Steps to designing a sales compensation plan that
                meets your company's and sales employees' objec-
                tives—and is easy to track and manage.

Performance Measures

Title: Dead Solid Perfect: Achieving Sales Compensation
                Alignment
Publication: *Compensation and Benefits Review*, 4/96
Synopsis: Describes development of performance measures and
                design of a compensation plan to meet company top-
                line and bottom-line objectives.

Title: Multiple Perspectives: Essays on Implementing Per-
                formance Measures
Publication: *ACA Journal: Perspectives in Compensation and Benefits*,
                Spring 1996
Synopsis: An in-depth look at performance measures centering
                on selection of appropriate performance measures for
                the various stages of the selling life cycle.

Title: How Do You Get 'Em to Do What You Want 'Em to Do?
Publication: *American Salesman*, 3/97

Synopsis:	How to influence representative behavior through performance measures and management.

Title:	Multiple Sales Compensation Plans Based on Predetermined Profits Work Best
Publication:	*Real Estate Broker's Insider,* May 1999
Synopsis:	How to develop plans that are based on desirable profit levels, not merely sales.

Title:	Elimination of Quotas: A Salesperson's Dream?
Publication:	*ACA News,* May 1999
Synopsis:	New findings about the effectiveness of territory quota-type plans.

IMPLEMENTATION, JOB DEFINITION

Title:	Change Management Initiatives: Moving Sales Organizations from Obsolescence to High Performance
Publication:	*Journal of Personal Selling & Sales Management,* Spring 1997
Synopsis:	Discusses change management initiatives undertaken by companies for the purpose of sustaining competitive advantage with customers and preventing sales force obsolescence.

Title:	Predicting the Long-Run Impact of a Contemplated Sales Force Compensation Plan
Publication:	*Journal of Operational Research Society,* 12/97
Synopsis:	Methods for predicting the effect of compensation change. Very technical, includes Markovian model for predicting results of change.

Title:	More Than Sizzle
Publication:	*LAN,* April 1999
Synopsis:	Pluses and minuses of a sales force that's selling challenging products successfully.

Title:	Growing Pains
Publication:	*Sales & Marketing Management,* November 1999

Synopsis: How to change pay packages when your company is growing quickly without losing your best salespeople.

LEGAL ISSUES

Title: Many Companies Should Undergo an FLSA Compliance Checkup
Publication: *ACA News,* 7/95
Synopsis: Outlines guidelines and requirements for ensuring that incentive plans meet FLSA requirements.

Title: Inside Sales Reform Pitched to Congress
Publication: *Industrial Distribution,* 7/97
Synopsis: Reports on legislation concerning payment of overtime compensation to inside sales positions.

Title: Classification of Workers: Independent Contractor vs. Employee
Publication: *ACA Journal,* Summer 1998
Synopsis: Comprehensive review of classification criteria for determining independent contractor status. Covers recent pronouncements.

AUTOMATION

Title: Why Compensation Doesn't Compute
Publication: *Sales and Marketing Management,* 3/97
Synopsis: Short article regarding problems with software that computes sales compensation.

Title: Working Smart: Amdahl's Sales Compensation System
Publication: *CIO,* 4/1/97, vol. 10, no. 12
Synopsis: Study of Amdahl Corporation's implementation of a sophisticated compensation system. Based on Antares Alliance Group's ObjectStar software.

Title: Bringing Sales Home
Publication: *InfoWorld,* 9/8/97

Synopsis: Report on Oracle's introduction of its newly rejuvenated sales force automation application package.

Title: Show Me the Money—Compensation Tracking Made Fast and Easy
Publication: *Selling Power*, March 2000
Synopsis: The impact of implementing sales compensation automation on the Cabletron sales reps and sales managers.

Title: Bean Counters and Salespeople Can Get Along
Publication: *Wired Executive*, June 2000
Synopsis: How a sales force automation tool can facilitate positive relationships between financial and sales management.

REWARDS/RECOGNITION, TEAM INCENTIVES, TELEMARKETING

Title: Non-Financial Rewards to Motivate and Drive Performance
Publication: *IIE Solutions*, 3/96
Synopsis: Sibson surveys of manufacturing companies showing that the traditional methods of recognition are no longer effective. Includes incentives for nonsales positions.

Title: World Class Telemarketing Quality Assurance through Call Monitoring
Publication: *Direct Marketing*, 9/96
Synopsis: How to monitor calls and use results to develop performance measures to use in recognition programs.

Title: Tying It All Together
Publication: *Incentive*, 10/96
Synopsis: How to combine different recognition programs into one. Case study of AirTouch Cellular using BI Performance Services OneSystem program.

Title: When Is Compensation Not Enough? Rethinking How to Reward the Workforce
Publication: *Compensation and Benefits Review*, 2/97

Synopsis: Basics on how to design and select reward programs based on solid motivation principles.

Title: When Their Ship Comes In
Publication: *Sales and Marketing Management*, 4/97
Synopsis: Compares open-ended to closed incentive programs.

Title: Cash Isn't King
Publication: *Sales and Marketing Management*, 7/97
Synopsis: Discusses examples where noncash incentives are more motivational than equal-value cash incentives.

Title: This Is Not an Incentive
Publication: *Sales and Marketing Management*, 10/97
Synopsis: Explains how to plan a successful incentive trip.

Title: Sales Contests: A Research Agenda
Publication: *Journal of Personal Selling*, Winter 1998
Synopsis: Stresses fundamentals of sales contest design.

GENERAL INDUSTRY/COMPANY SPECIFIC

Title: Sales Compensation Strategies: Time for Change
Publication: *LIMRA's MarketFacts*, 4/96
Synopsis: Financial services/insurance industry compensation models.

Title: Global Gamble
Publication: *Sales and Marketing Management*, 7/97
Synopsis: IBM's overhaul of its compensation plan to reward teamwork and support global operations.

Title: Five Classic Sales Compensation Flaws
Publication: *Beverage World*, 8/96
Synopsis: Beverage industry—five most common flaws found in pay plans.

Title: Trust Sales Compensation: Designing the Perfect Plan
Publication: *Trusts and Estates*, 10/96

Synopsis: Trust sales—designing a sales compensation plan that recognizes full economic value of each trust sale.

Title: More Than a Paradigm
Publication: *American Printer,* 11/96
Synopsis: Printing industry—compensation for digital short-run work.

Title: Walt Disney Company
Publication: *Sales and Marketing Management,* 11/96
Synopsis: Walt Disney Resort's sales force strategy and compensation strategies.

Title: Not So Easy to Digest
Publication: *Sales and Marketing Management,* 2/97
Synopsis: *Reader's Digest* switches from a 90/10 to a 65/35 incentive plan.

Title: What's behind the Cost of Career?
Publication: *LIMRA's MarketFacts,* May/June 1997
Synopsis: Career insurance companies' cost-cutting actions. Includes controlling compensation costs and sales productivity.

Title: Putting Sales Theory into Practice
Publication: *US Banker,* 9/97
Synopsis: Banks' movement away from traditional compensation plans to ones that are incentive-based tied closely to individual performance.

E

REWARD AND RECOGNITION QUESTIONNAIRE

I. Definition of Reward and Recognition Programs

Reward and recognition programs are designed to encourage and reward outstanding achievement. This questionnaire is designed to gain your perspectives on forms of recognition outside bonus, merit increase, or career development practices.

Typically, reward and recognition programs are designed to encourage and reward individual and/or team achievement. They can be either "spot award" programs or programs that focus on long-term objectives and continuity. For the purposes of this survey, teams include account teams, departments, and teams organized for short-term project objectives.

II. Directions for Completing the Questionnaire

The following pages of the questionnaire ask for your response to a series of statements. You will be asked to circle a response for "Individual" and for "Team." Please rate your responses from 1 to 7, using the following scale:

1 = Strongly Disagree/Highly Undesirable
2 = Disagree/Undesirable

3 = Slightly Disagree/Somewhat Undesirable
4 = Neither Agree nor Disagree/Neither Desirable or Undesirable
5 = Slightly Agree/Somewhat Desirable
6 = Agree/Desirable
7 = Strongly Agree/Highly Desirable

The term "Desirable" pertains to Section III; the term "Agree" pertains to Sections IV and V.

III. Types of Rewards

In this section of the questionnaire, you are asked for a response to a series of statements about different types of rewards as each reward could be used to motivate you as an individual contributor or as a member of a team. For each statement, you should circle one response under the heading "Individual" and one under the heading "Team." Responses will indicate the degree to which you view each statement as desirable.

INDIVIDUAL	STATEMENT	TEAM
1 2 3 4 5 6 7	Reward with special cash bonuses for "long-term" recognition (sustained outstanding performance over a long period of time) (e.g., one-time bonus of $1,000 or more)	1 2 3 4 5 6 7
1 2 3 4 5 6 7	Reward with special cash bonuses for "on the spot" recognition (e.g., one-time bonus of $500 or less)	1 2 3 4 5 6 7
1 2 3 4 5 6 7	Reward with trips to resort locations for "winners" with spouses	1 2 3 4 5 6 7
1 2 3 4 5 6 7	Reward with special recognition by top management at national meetings	1 2 3 4 5 6 7

INDIVIDUAL	STATEMENT	TEAM
1 2 3 4 5 6 7	Reward with special recognition by team management at team meetings	1 2 3 4 5 6 7
1 2 3 4 5 6 7	Reward with certificate for "dinner for two" or evening out	1 2 3 4 5 6 7
1 2 3 4 5 6 7	Reward with plaques/certificates/trophies	1 2 3 4 5 6 7
1 2 3 4 5 6 7	Reward with tangible gift	1 2 3 4 5 6 7
1 2 3 4 5 6 7	Reward with time off with pay	1 2 3 4 5 6 7
1 2 3 4 5 6 7	Reward with letter of appreciation	1 2 3 4 5 6 7

IV. Types of Recognition

In this section of the questionnaire, you are asked for a response to a series of statements about different types of recognition as each statement regarding recognition could pertain to you as an individual contributor or as a member of a team. For each statement, you should circle one response under the heading "Individual" and one under the heading "Team." Responses will indicate the degree to which you agree with each statement.

INDIVIDUAL	STATEMENT	TEAM
1 2 3 4 5 6 7	Recognition should be given for outstanding customer service	1 2 3 4 5 6 7
1 2 3 4 5 6 7	Recognition should be given for outstanding sales results	1 2 3 4 5 6 7
1 2 3 4 5 6 7	Recognition should be given for creative suggestions that improve performance	1 2 3 4 5 6 7
1 2 3 4 5 6 7	Recognition should be given for significant achievement "on the spot"	1 2 3 4 5 6 7
1 2 3 4 5 6 7	Recognition should be given only for sustained outstanding performance over a long period of time	1 2 3 4 5 6 7

INDIVIDUAL	STATEMENT	TEAM
1 2 3 4 5 6 7	The primary value of recognition is acknowledgment of performance by management	1 2 3 4 5 6 7
1 2 3 4 5 6 7	The primary value of recognition is acknowledgment of performance by us to our customers	1 2 3 4 5 6 7
1 2 3 4 5 6 7	The primary value of recognition is tangible reward, e.g., cash or merchandise	1 2 3 4 5 6 7
1 2 3 4 5 6 7	The primary value of recognition is clearer definition of expectations	1 2 3 4 5 6 7

V. Reward and Recognition Administration

In this section of the questionnaire, you are asked for a response to a series of statements about administrative practices of reward and recognition programs as each statement could pertain to individual contributor or team reward and recognition practices. For each statement, you should circle one response under the heading "Individual" and one under the heading "Team." Responses will indicate the degree to which you agree with each statement.

INDIVIDUAL	STATEMENT	TEAM
1 2 3 4 5 6 7	Senior management should determine who receives an award	1 2 3 4 5 6 7
1 2 3 4 5 6 7	Team members should be able to nominate the team or peers for an award	1 2 3 4 5 6 7
1 2 3 4 5 6 7	Team members should be able to nominate other teams or peers outside of their team for an award	1 2 3 4 5 6 7
1 2 3 4 5 6 7	Formal recognition events increase the motivational value of a recognition program	1 2 3 4 5 6 7

INDIVIDUAL	STATEMENT	TEAM
1 2 3 4 5 6 7	Informal recognition is of equal importance as formal recognition events	1 2 3 4 5 6 7
1 2 3 4 5 6 7	Broad recognition at a national event increases the motivational value of a recognition program	1 2 3 4 5 6 7
1 2 3 4 5 6 7	Local recognition events are important in a recognition program	1 2 3 4 5 6 7

Rewards may be tangible, e.g., cash or prize, or intangible, e.g., praise. In your opinion, what percentage of *tangible* rewards should be cash versus noncash?

a) Cash	
b) Noncash	
	100%

Recognition can be national, local (e.g., business unit), or regional. In your opinion, what percentage of a reward and recognition events budget should be spent for each?

a) National	
b) Local (Team)	
c) Regional	
Total	100%

NOTES

Chapter 1 Notes

1. Geoffrey Colvin, "Old Consultants Never Die; They Just Go 'E,'" *Fortune*, June 12, 2000, 130–142.
2. Brian C. Mashburn and Robert D. Obray, "Tough Questions at Stockholders' Meetings in 2000," *Director's Monthly*, National Association of Corporate Directors, Washington, DC, vol. 24, no. 4, April 2000, 7–8.
3. Alan S. Horowitz, "The Cisco Sales Machine," *Selling Power*, May 2000, 74–78.
4. "E-Business or Bust," *Sales & Marketing Management*, June 2000, 63–65.

Chapter 2 Notes

1. Curtis Hartman, "Sales Force," *Fast Company*, June/July 1997, 134–46.
2. "Sales Compensation: Are You Getting What You're Paying For?" *Sales Manager's Bulletin* (Bureau of Business Practice, 30 December 1995), 6–7.
3. Jerome A. Colletti and Lawrence B. Chonko, "Change Management Initiatives: Moving Sales Organizations from Obsolescence to High Performance," *Journal of Personal Selling and Sales Management* 17 (2 November 1997): 1–30.
4. Sandra O'Neal, "Compensation Programs Are Becoming More Strategic," *ACA News*, November/December 1996, 19.

Chapter 3 Notes

1. Christen P. Heide, *Dartnell's 29th Sales Force Compensation Survey* (Chicago: The Dartnell Press, 1996), 222–25.

CHAPTER 4 NOTES

1. Michelle Marchetti, "Global Gamble," *Sales & Marketing Management,* July 1996, 69.

CHAPTER 5 NOTES

1. Louise B. Yarnoff, "Razor Sharp," *Customer Relationship Management,* April 2000, 14.

CHAPTER 7 NOTES

1. Malcolm Campbell, "The New Sales Force: Swimming Against the Tide Is Out, Channels Are In," *Selling Power,* July/August 1999, pp. 48–55.
2. Frederick Newell, *Loyalty.Com: Customer Relationship Management in the New Era of Internet Marketing* (New York, McGraw-Hill, 2000), p. 115.
3. R. Brian Dixon, *The Federal Wage and Hour Laws* (San Francisco: SHRM Foundation, 1994).
4. Jerome A. Colletti and Mary S. Fiss, *Designing Incentive Plans for Customer Teams* (American Compensation Association, Scottsdale, AZ, 1995).
5. Bob Nelson, *1001 Ways to Reward Employees* (Workman Publishing, New York, 1994).
6. Valerie Sloan, with Theresa Arvizo Jackson, *Telephone Sales Management and Motivation Made Easy* (Business by Phone, Inc., Omaha, NE, 1996).

CHAPTER 9 NOTES

1. EDS news release posted on June 12, 2000, at EDS's Web site, www.eds.com.
2. Sarah Lorge, "Enron: #1 on the SM&M List of the Top 25 Sales Forces," *Sales & Marketing Management,* July 1999, pp. 48–52.
3. Honeywell 1999 Annual Report, "Management Discussion and Analysis," as posted on Honeywell's Web site, www.honeywell.com.
4. Louise B. Yarmoff, "Straight to the Top," *Customer Relationship Management,* April 2000, p. 16.

5. Honeywell International Web site (www.honeywell.com).
6. Honeywell International Web site.

CHAPTER 10 NOTES

1. Adapted from Jerome A. Colletti, "Maximize Growth by 'Segmenting' Your Customers," *Strategic Edge* (The Economic Press, Inc.), no. 101 (June 1996): 4.

CHAPTER 12 NOTES

1. Jerome A. Colletti and Lawrence B. Chyonko, "Change Management Initiatives: Moving Sales Organizations from Obsolescence to High Performance," *Journal of Personal Selling & Sales Management* 17, no. 2 (spring 1997): 1–30.

CHAPTER 14 NOTES

1. Bill Jensen, Simplicity: *The New Competitive Advantage in a World of More, Better, Faster* (Cambridge, MA, Perseus Books, 2000).
2. Elizabeth G. Chambers, Mark Fouler, Helen Handfield-Jones, Steven M. Harkin, and Edward G. Michaels, III, "The War for Talent," *The McKinsey Quarterly*, no. 3, 1998, 44–57.
3. David G. Schick, "Developing Incentive Compensation Strategies in a Global Sales Environment," *ACA Journal*, Autumn 1996, 54–67.
4. Working Council for Sales Executives, "Retaining Top Sales Talent," The Corporate Advisory Board, Washington, DC, 1998, p. 5.
5. Helen Axel, "Strategies for Retaining Critical Talent," *HR Executive Review*, Vol. 6, No. 2, The Conference Board, Inc., 1998; Ed Gubman, "Finding the Talent Solution," *ACA News*, November–December 1998, 14–17; and Patricia Zingheim and Jay R. Schuster, *Pay People Right: Breakthrough Reward Strategies to Create Great Companies* (San Francisco, Jossey-Bass, 2000).
6. David J. Fritz, "Sales Crediting: Issues and Ideas," *Connections*, Profitable Growth Solutions, Naperville, IL, 2000.
7. Louis S. Csoka, "Bridging the Leadership Gap," Report Number 1190-97-ES, The Conference Board, New York, 1997, pp. 6–7.

INDEX